HISTORY IN THE MAKING
Series Editor: John Jones

6 World Conflict in the Twentieth Century

HISTORY IN THE MAKING

S. M. Harrison

Humanities Adviser,
London Borough of Havering

6 World Conflict in the Twentieth Century

Macmillan Education

To Hilary

Text © S.M. Harrison 1987
Maps and artwork © Macmillan Education 1987

First published 1987

Published by
MACMILLAN EDUCATION LTD
Houndmills, Basingstoke, Hampshire RG21 2XS
and London
Companies and representatives
throughout the world

Designed by Wendi Watson

Photoset in Plantin by
CAS Typesetters, Southampton

Printed in Great Britain by
R. J. Acford, Chichester

British Library Cataloguing in Publication Data
Harrison, Scott Michael
World conflict in the twentieth century.
———(History in the making)
1. History, Modern———20th century
I. Title   II. Series
909.82   D421
ISBN 0–333–39814–9

Series Preface

Changes in the teaching of history over the last decade have raised many problems to which there are no easy solutions. The classification of objectives, the presentation of material in varied and appropriate language, the use and abuse of evidence and the reconsideration of assessment techniques are four of the most important. Many teachers are now encouraging their pupils individually or in groups to participate in the processes and skills of the professional historian. These developments have led naturally to the National Criteria for History for the General Certificate of Secondary Education, which seek to stimulate interest in the past through the acquisition of knowledge and the development of appropriate skills and concepts.

History in the Making seeks to develop these skills and concepts within a secure framework of historical knowledge from the first years of secondary school onwards. The first five volumes form a firm foundation for the GCSE approach. Now two new volumes have been written specifically for GCSE syllabuses in **Modern World** and **British Social and Economic** history.

Each chapter in all the volumes has four major components.

1 **The text** This provides the basic framework of the chapters, and although the approach is essentially factual, it is intended to arouse and sustain the interest of the reader of average ability. It recognises, and seeks to convey, the fascination of the good tale and the drama of human life, individual and collective. The text of the two new volumes has been written specifically to cover the information required for GCSE syllabuses in British Social and Economic History and Modern World History.

2 **The illustrations** These have been carefully selected to stand beside the written pieces of evidence in the chapter, and to provide (so far as is possible) an authentic visual image of the period/topic. Photographs, artwork and maps are all used to clarify and support the text, and to develop the pupil's powers of observation.

3 **Using the evidence** This is a detailed study of the evidence on one particular aspect of the chapter. Did the walls of Jericho really come tumbling down? Was the death of William Rufus in the New Forest really an accident? What was the background of the torpedoing of the *Lusitania*? These are the sort of questions which are asked, to give the pupil the opportunity to consider not only the problems facing the historian, but also those facing the characters of history. Different forms of documentary evidence are considered, as well as archaeological, architectural, statistical, and other kinds of source material; the intention is to give the pupil a genuine, if modest, insight into the making of history. The pupil's ability to empathise with people in the past is particularly valued.

4 **Questions and further work** These are intended to test and develop the pupil's reading of the chapter, and in particular the **Using the evidence** section. Particular attention is paid to the development of historical skills, through examination and interpretation of evidence.

The differences between primary and secondary sources, for example, are explored, and concepts such as bias in evidence and its limitations. By applying the skills which they have developed, pupils may then be able to formulate, at a suitable level and in appropriate language, ideas and hypotheses of their own.

History in the Making is a complete course in seven volumes, to meet the needs of pupils between the ages of 11 and 16 (in other words up to and including the first public examination). However, each volume stands by itself and may be used independently of the others; given the variety of syllabuses in use in schools today this flexibility is likely to be welcomed by many teachers. *The Ancient World* and *The Medieval World* are intended primarily for 11–13-year-old pupils, *The Early Modern World 1450–1700*, for 12–14-year-old pupils, *Britain, Europe and Beyond 1700–1900* and *The Twentieth Century* for 13–14-year-olds, and *British Social and Economic History* and *World Conflict in the Twentieth Century* for GCSE examination candidates.

It is our hope that pupils will be encouraged, within the main topics and themes of British, European and World History, to experience for themselves the stimulus and challenge, the pleasure and frustration, the vitality and humanity that form an essential part of History in the Making.

John Jones

Contents

List of maps

The First
World War

1 The First World War 1914–18

The nineteenth century had witnessed several European wars. These were seen as swift, glorious struggles between the fighting men of both sides as champions of their nations. The First World War, which began in August 1914, was very different. It swept away the cobwebs of the nineteenth century and wrenched the world into the twentieth. Millions died in this dreadful war. It lasted four and a half years. Civilians were exposed to the brutality of war as never before. Fighting was no longer confined to artillery and guns: war was now fought with new weapons such as tanks and gas; it was fought in new theatres of war – in the air and beneath the sea. Few corners of the earth remained untouched in some way by the war. Finally at its end, it was to cause as many problems as it solved.

International rivalry and the outbreak of the First World War

Germany before 1870 consisted of 25 states dominated by Prussia. Under the leadership of Bismarck they united in the new German Empire, 1871.

In 1870 Germany, a newly formed nation, had decisively defeated France in a short, sharp war. From that point on, Germany became a major power in Europe – with efficient industry, strong armed forces, and great ambition, as expressed by Hans Delbruck, a German politician of the time (1899):

We want to be a World Power and pursue colonial policy in the grand manner. There can be no step backward. The entire future of our people among the great nations depends on it.

Delbruck expressed the feelings of many Germans when he said that a German empire would be gained peacefully if possible, but if not, then by war.

France, too, was willing to go to war. Not only was France humiliated by the defeat of 1870, it had also lost the provinces of Alsace-Lorraine. France wanted these provinces back, but also wanted revenge. Even so, French politicians were aware of the dangers of war. To make France more secure, in 1894 they negotiated a treaty with Russia, which had itself been isolated by an alliance between Germany and Austria of 1879. Europe was dividing into armed camps.

Dual Alliance – a secret treaty between Austria and Germany. In 1882 they were joined by Italy, making the Triple Alliance.

At first Britain stood aloof. However, Britain more than any other country was threatened by Germany's desire for an empire and a navy to guard it. Britain expanded its own navy, building the first of the great Dreadnoughts in 1905. Even so, Britain feared isolation and in 1907 joined France and Russia in the Triple Entente.

The Anglo-French entente was signed in 1904, and extended to include Russia in the Triple Entente as a direct rival to the Triple Alliance.

All of these powers were willing to fight for what they thought to be important principles: national pride; empire; territorial gains within Europe; trade and commerce; industrial superiority; control of the oceans. In this atmosphere any crisis made war more likely, and both sides began their planning very early. Germany had to face the possibility of war on two fronts, against France in the west, and Russia in the east. As the Schlieffen plan of 1905 established:

Count von Schlieffen – Chief of German General Staff 1891–1906.

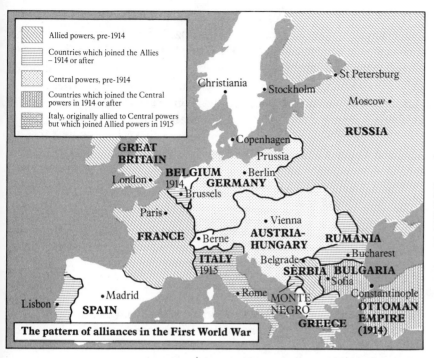

Legend:
- Allied powers, pre-1914
- Countries which joined the Allies – 1914 or after
- Central powers, pre-1914
- Countries which joined the Central powers in 1914 or after
- Italy, originally allied to Central powers but which joined Allied powers in 1915

Christiania
St Petersburg
Stockholm
Moscow
RUSSIA
Copenhagen
GREAT BRITAIN
Prussia
London
BELGIUM
1914
Berlin
GERMANY
Brussels
Paris
FRANCE
Berne
Vienna
AUSTRIA-HUNGARY
RUMANIA
Bucharest
ITALY
1915
Belgrade
SERBIA
BULGARIA
Sofia
Rome
MONTE NEGRO
Constantinople
Lisbon
Madrid
SPAIN
GREECE
OTTOMAN EMPIRE (1914)

The pattern of alliances in the First World War

THE BOILING POINT.

Trouble in the Balkans. Austria, Russia, Germany, France and Britain are featured here. Can you identify them? What is the cartoonist suggesting?

The whole of Germany must hurl itself against one opponent, the one who is the strongest, most powerful, most dangerous; this cannot but be France.

France too made early preparations for a rapid offensive against Germany. Both sides knew that, given a crisis, they could not wait in hope of a peaceful settlement before mobilising their armies. Mobilisation for a massive offensive took time to prepare, so any decision to act had to be taken as early as possible. The problem was that once the decision was taken, it would be very hard to reverse.

A number of crises did bring Europe close to war. The early years of the century saw mounting tension between France and Germany, and between Russia and Austria. In 1905 Germany flexed her muscles by trying to gain influence in North Africa at the expense of France. This, the first Moroccan crisis, was resolved by an international conference in which Britain stood firmly behind France. A second Moroccan crisis occurred in 1911 when the Kaiser sent the gunboat *Panther* to counter French influence there. Again the problem was solved by diplomacy, and Britain and France grew closer together.

North Africa was important to Britain and France, and the new Germany sought to extend her influence there.

Meanwhile France and Germany's respective allies were fighting for influence in the Balkans, and it was here that the final crisis which led to war came. In 1908 Austria had increased her power in the region by taking control of the states of Bosnia and Herzegovina. Russia was hostile to this but did not intervene. After further Balkan wars in 1912–13 Serbia emerged as the most powerful Balkan state, hostile to Austria and friendly to Russia. A clash between Austria and Serbia seemed inevitable, and Russia was ready to support Serbia when that moment came.

The Balkans – a key in the struggle for power between Russia and Austria.

BRAVO, BELGIUM!

How does the cartoonist express his view of the two countries?

Britain had been pledged to defend Belgium since the Treaty of London, 1839.

RED CROSS or IRON CROSS?

WOUNDED AND A PRISONER
OUR SOLDIER CRIES FOR WATER.
THE GERMAN "SISTER"
POURS IT ON THE GROUND BEFORE HIS EYES.
THERE IS NO WOMAN IN BRITAIN
WHO WOULD DO IT.
THERE IS NO WOMAN IN BRITAIN
WHO WILL FORGET IT.

This cartoon is typical of the propaganda used by both sides

Dum dum bullets – bullets with soft heads to inflict maximum damage.

On 28 June 1914 the Austrian heir, the Archduke Franz Ferdinand, was assassinated by a Serbian. Austria, backed by Germany, issued an unacceptable ultimatum to Serbia. When Serbia asked for more time to consider the ultimatum, it was refused, and Austria declared war on 28 July. Russia mobilised, and when a German demand that it demobilise was refused, Germany declared war on Russia. According to the Schlieffen plan France had to be attacked first, even in a war against Russia. The invasion began through Belgium on 3 August, and Britain declared war on Germany on the next day. The affair in the Balkans had escalated to world war.

Official statements on both sides were solemn, but unbending. According to the Kaiser:

This is a dark day and a dark hour . . . The sword is being forced into my hand. . . This war will demand of us enormous sacrifice in life and money, but we will show our foes what it is to provoke Germany.

According to the British foreign secretary, Sir Edward Grey:

There is but one way . . . of keeping outside this war and that would be . . . a proclamation of unconditional neutrality. We cannot do that. We have made the commitment to France. The Belgian treaty obligations, the possible position in the Mediterranean with damage to British interests – . . . if we were to say that all these things mattered nothing . . . we should, I believe, sacrifice our respect and good name and reputation before the world, and should not escape the most serious economic consequences. If . . . we are forced to take our stand upon these issues, then I believe we shall be supported throughout not only by the House of Commons, but by the determination, the resolution, the courage and the endurance of the whole country.

Politicians' speeches were met with enthusiasm by most people in all the countries involved. In Germany Princess Blucher watched

a never ending procession of troop-filled trains hurrying their way to the west; shouts of enthusiasm, fluttering of handkerchiefs, bursts of song, flushed eager faces of soldiers, field grey uniforms, white-robed girls and women with the Red Cross on their arms. And all this which might be some great national festival, means but the entry of death and foul disaster.

Rivalry between nations soon turned to mutual hatred. No sooner were the first shots fired than the atrocity stories began to appear.

No matter that most were false – like the notorious story appearing in the Scottish paper of the young Belgian nurse who had both breasts cut off by the Germans and was left to die while the hospital burned down; all were eagerly reported in the national presses and widely believed. In France and Britain such tales had a basic formula, involving the raping of nuns, impaling of babies on bayonets, mutilation of Belgian girls. German stories were similar – the use of dum dum bullets by British soldiers, and amongst the most gruesome – the systematic gouging out of captured German soldiers' eyes.

In this tense and patriotic climate, young men by the hundred thousand flocked to join up, to train, and to go as quickly as possible to the front.

Questions

1 Explain how an apparently distant event like the assassination of the Archduke was sufficient to trigger a world war.
2 Use a base-map of Europe to show
   (a) the pattern of alliances.
   (b) the sequence of events which led to the outbreak of war.

The western front

The theory of the Schlieffen plan depended on a knock-out blow against France. The German army began by attacking Belgium, a poorly defended neutral country. This gave access to France, while avoiding French defences. At first the plan seemed to be working as Brussels fell on 20 August and the German army rolled on into France. By the end of the month the Germans were only fifty miles from Paris, but there the plan went wrong. This was partly because of stubborn Belgian

The retreat from Mons. A nineteenth-century army defeated in a twentieth-century war.

Gone to the dogs. The French army retreats to Antwerp.

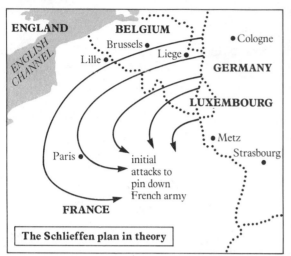

The Schlieffen plan in theory

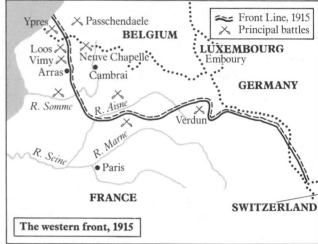

The western front, 1915

A small force of British regular soldiers left for France soon after the outbreak of war.

resistance, and unexpected opposition from the British expeditionary force at Mons. In addition, the German generals made strategic errors including the dispatch of German troops to the eastern front, and a change of plan by General von Kluck which led to the battle of the Marne (see map). Both sides consolidated along a line from Switzerland to the English Channel, and by the end of the year were digging in. Each had already lost half a million men. The worst was yet to come.

The following three years on the western front were characterised by massive offensives and counter-offensives against enemy trenches by artillery and infantry. Some gained a few miles of land, some a few yards. The advantage lay increasingly with the defenders as the trench systems grew more complex.

Trench warfare. An Australian artillery brigade takes a rest at Ypres, 1917

Even without the fighting the trenches were terrible places. A Frenchman remembered:

The trenches are no more than cesspools filled with a mixture of water and urine. The trench is nothing more than a strip of water. The sides cave in beside you as you pass with a soft slither. We ourselves are transformed into statues of clay, with mud even in one's very mouth.

Siegfried Sassoon, an English officer and poet, described the trenches in his own way:

Siegfried Sassoon (1886–1967), awarded MC, books included *Counterattack* and *Memoirs of an Infantry Officer.*

The place was rotten with dead; green clumsy legs,
High booted, sprawled and grovelled along the saps,
And trunks face downward in the sucking mud,
Wallowed like trodden sandbags loosely filled;
And naked sodden buttocks, mats of hair,
Bulged, clotted heads slept in the plastering slime.

Lieutenant J. A. Raws of Melbourne, trying to dig a trench under artillery fire and buried twice, wrote

We are lousy, stinking, ragged unshaven, sleepless. I have one puttee, a dead man's helmet, another dead man's gas protector, a dead man's bayonet. My tunic is rotten with other men's blood and partly spattered with comrades' brains.

puttee – a strip of cloth wound round the leg from ankle to knee.

Raws was critical of the 'incompetence, callousness and personal vanity of those in high authority'. He would not have been impressed by this order from the British commander, General Haig:

I had occasion to call the attention of corps commanders to the lack of smartness, and slackness of some of its battalions in the matter of saluting when I was motoring through the village where I was billeted.

Trench warfare. Better to give than to receive

The tactics of trench warfare

The generals believed that, in order to capture enemy trenches, there must be a co-ordinated attack between artillery and infantry:

Co-operation of Artillery with Infantry
The ideal is for the artillery to keep their fire immediately in front of the infantry as the latter advances, battering down all opposition with a hurricane of projectiles. The difficulties of observation and communication renders this idea very hard to obtain.

Lifts – increases in range.

Experience has shown that the only safe method of artillery support during an advance is a fixed timetable of lifts to which both the infantry and artillery must rigidly conform. This timetable must be regulated by the rate at which it is calculated the infantry can reach their successive objectives.

Tactical Notes, 4th Army HQ, 1916

Once high explosive had done its work, the generals relied on the bayonet:

The bayonet is essentially an offensive weapon. In a bayonet attack all ranks go forward to kill or be killed, and only those who have developed skill and strength by constant training will be able to kill. The spirit of the bayonet must be impressed on all ranks, so that they will go forward with aggressive determination and confidence.

The theory was all very well. In practice soldiers found that it often did not work. Here is an account of what happened to the 8th Corps attacking the German lines during the Battle of the Somme (see map, page 14):

When the bombardment had ceased across the whole length of the 8th Corps Front it was the last signal of confirmation the Germans had needed to warn them that the assault was under way. That had happened not at Zero, but ten minutes before the troops were to go 'over the top'. The Germans had ample time to rush up from shelters and dug-outs, ample time to garrison their line, ample time to set up machine guns, to man hidden posts, to train their guns on gaps in the wire, accurately sighted on the arrow lanes through which the Tommies would have to pass into No Man's Land.

L. Macdonald, *The Somme*, 1984

A German machine-gunner at the Battle of Loos (see map, page 14) in September 1915, remembered:

Never had the machine-gunners such straightforward work to do. They traversed to and fro along the enemy's ranks unceasingly. The men stood on the fire steps, some even on the parapets, and fired triumphantly into the mass of men advancing across the open grassland. As the entire field of fire was covered with the enemy's infantry the effect was devastating and they could be seen falling literally in hundreds.

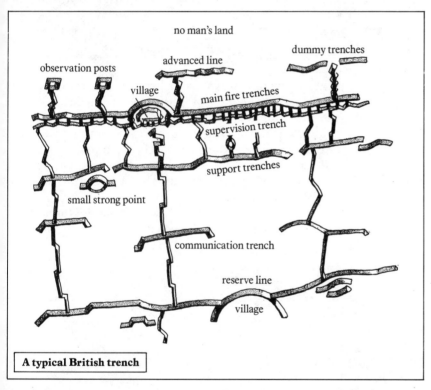

A typical British trench

Private Ernest Deighton remembered what it was like being on the receiving end:

As soon as they started across, the machine-guns opened up. These bullets are flying all over the place. It were Maxims they were firing, and shooting across each other with this hissing noise as they went past.

I were in the first row and the first one I saw were my chum Clem Cunnington. I don't think we'd gone twenty yards when he got hit straight through the chest. Machine-gun bullets. He went down. I went down. We got it in the same burst. I got it through the shoulder. I hardly noticed it, at the time. I were so wild when I saw that Clem were finished.

Trench warfare. French troops on the receiving end at Verdun

I got up and picked up my rifle and got through the wire into the trench and straight in front there was a dug-out full of Jerries, and one big fellow was on the steps facing me. I had this Mills bomb. Couldn't use my arm. I pulled the pin with my teeth and flung it down and I were shouting at them, I were that wild. There you are! Bugger yourselves! Share that between you! Then I were off! It was hand to hand. I went round one traverse and there was one – face to face. I couldn't fire one-handed, but I could use the bayonet. It were him or me – and I went first! Jab! Just like that, It were my job.

We were climbing out of the trench when they got me again, through the fingers then . . . and another one straight through the foot. Well, that finished it.

Trench warfare. 'Delville wood'

In the rare event of victory, the prize was the capture of a few hundred yards of enemy land:

A little further on we passed a crater big enough to take a good-sized house below ground level – an exploded underground dump perhaps. It was full of water, green from gas and putrefaction. Most of our dead had been buried, but here and there from the churned up ground there stuck out the arms and legs of submerged bodies. Stakes, wire, sandbags, concrete blocks, Boche helmets and boots (quite a number still occupied) discarded rifles and equipment, trench mortars, boxes of bombs, all in the most fantastic jumble and confusion.

H. Gordon, *The Unreturning Army*

One of the developments which came close to breaking the deadlock was the tank. Lance Corporal Lovell remembered the tank's first appearance at the Somme in 1916:

It was marvellous. That tank went on, rolling and bobbing and swaying in and out of shell-holes, climbing over trees as easy as kiss your hand! We were awed! We were delighted that it was ours. Up to now Jerry had supplied all the surprises. Now, it was his turn to be surprised.

The tank waddled on with its guns blazing, and we could see Jerry popping up and down, not knowing what to do, whether to stay or to run. We were sheltering behind the tank. The Jerries waited until our tank was only a few yards away and then fled or hoped to. The tank just shot them down and the machine gun post, the gun itself, the dead and wounded just disappeared. The tank went right over them.

At the Somme, and later in other tank engagements, early successes were not followed up. New enemy tactics and mud stopped the tank from turning this into a mobile war. At the end of 1917 the deadlock on the western front was unbroken, and no end to the war was in sight.

New weapons of war. French tanks near Juvigny, 1918

New weapons of war. Russian troops during a gas attack at Baranovichi, 1917

Questions

1 There are many accounts of trench warfare, in the form of memoirs, letters, poems and other forms of writing. Use the sources given to describe life and action in the trenches in one of these forms from the viewpoint of one who fought there. Your description should include fact and feeling — fact about the trenches and the fighting, feelings about conditions, food, leadership, the enemy and so on.

2 Use the map on page 14 and the table below to show the main offensives of the war and the losses incurred.

Note: Try to visit the Imperial War Museum, London, where you can see exhibitions which recreate war in the trenches, and other aspects of the Great War.

THE WESTERN FRONT 1915–17

Date	Offensive	Army	Significance
Jan 1915	Champagne	French	Five miles gained, 90 000 French casualties.
March	Neuve Chapelle	British	One mile gained, 12 000 men fell.
April	Ypres	German	Gas was used for the first time. It devastated the French troops, but then blew back on the advancing Germans.
May Sept	Vimy Ridge Vimy Ridge	French	100 000 casualties, no success on either occasion.
Sept	Loos	British	50 000 casualties.
Feb 1916	Verdun	German	The German generals decided to wear the French out by attacking their strongpoint at Verdun. The fortress was not captured. There were 315 000 French and 282 000 German casualties.
Summer/Autumn	Somme	British/French	A concerted attempt to make a breakthrough which failed; 60 000 British died on the first day, July 1st. Total casualties included 418 000 British, 194 000 French, 650 000 German.
April 1917	Arras	British	84 000 British casualties, 75 000 German.
April	Aisne	French	120 000 casualties.
Summer	Ypres/Passchendaele	British	360 000 British, 245 000 German casualties.
Nov	Cambrai	British	Although tanks had appeared before, here they were used effectively for the first time.

Comrades at arms – but not for long. Officers during the Christmas truce, 1914

Air warfare

While millions of soldiers battled out the war in the trenches, a small number of men were involved in a completely new style of war – the war in the air.

Before the war there was little faith in the potential of aircraft, even for observation. An Allied commander said at the start of the war,

I hope none of you gentlemen is so foolish as to think that aeroplanes will be able to be usefully employed for reconnaissance in the air. There is only one way for a commander to get information by reconnaissance and that is by use of cavalry.

And as for fighting:

There was little thought of arming such aeroplanes. RFC officer Sykes said at the start of the war, that 'There should be no attempt at aerial conflict', and the Germans agreed with him. In 1913 their general staff had pronounced that seeing, not fighting, was the role of aircraft.

New weapons of war. A De Havilland bomber and a Nieuport fighter, 1918

The few aircraft in action in 1914 were only used for spotting, and relationships between enemy pilots were gentlemanly. However, the pilots could not ignore the butchery taking place beneath them, and soon aerial combat began. The number of fighter squadrons grew as the importance of air warfare was realised:

British squadrons

1915	0
1916	3
1917	13
1918	30

In 1918 the Royal Flying Corps merged with the Royal Naval Air Service to become the RAF.

Pilots ceased to be regarded as observers:

Official order, May 1916
As the number of combats in the air is constantly increasing, it has been decided that pilots under instruction should be trained as far as possible in fighting in the air.

Gradually, aircraft were developed into sophisticated killing machines, and the role of the pilots changed accordingly:

So the pilots stopped saluting. Instead they began taking pot shots at one another with pistols, carbines and rifles. Then the French produced the idea of dropping bags of bricks or showers of steel arrows on enemy aircraft. The British preferred hurling grenades and petrol bombs of canned gasoline at the hun machines. The Germans countered with shoulder arms and small bombs. . .

The aircraft as a lethal weapon of war really came into its own when Roland Garros fastened a Hotchkiss machine gun to the cowling of his small Morane-Saulnier plane.

Garros was forced to land behind enemy lines. His plane was forwarded immediately to Berlin where it was inspected by the Dutch plane designer, Anthony Fokker. Within forty-eight hours Fokker improved Garros' invention by an arrangement of cam and rods attached to the engine of his Fokker Eindecker. His invention synchronised the firing of a machine gun to permit the bullets to pass through the spinning prop without striking it.

P. J.Carisella and J. Ryan, *Who killed the Red Baron?*, 1974

Air-aces – one of the best known figures of the First World War was Baron von Richthofen, who shot down over 80 Allied aircraft before his own death in 1918.

Soon pilots gained reputations as air-aces, although the average life span of pilots at the height of the war was only three weeks. Survival depended on the capability of the aircraft and skill of the pilot. This is the official report of an action in which William Barker was shot down but survived:

On 27 October 1918 – William Barker observed an enemy two-seater at 21 000 feet N.E. of the Forêt du Normal. Enemy aeroplane climbed east and Major Barker followed, firing one short burst from underneath at point blank range. Target broke up in the air and one of the occupants went out with a parachute. Barker then observed a Fokker biplane 1000 feet below shooting up at him, one of the bullets wounding him in the right thigh. He fell into a spin, from which he pulled out in the middle of a formation of about fifteen Fokkers. He turned and getting on the tail of one which was attacking him, shot it down in flames from within ten yards range. At that moment he was again wounded in the left thigh by others of the formation who were diving at him. He fainted and fell out of control again. On recovering he pulled his machine out and was immediately attacked by another large formation between twelve and fifteen aircraft. He at this moment received a third wound. The bullet shattered his left elbow. He then noticed heavy smoke coming from under his machine, and under the impression he was on fire, tried to ram a Fokker just ahead of him. He opened fire from two or three yards and the enemy aircraft fell in flames. He dived down and returned to our lines a few feet above the ground, finally crashing close to one of our balloons.

The war saw rapid development of the aircraft, and more and more ideas about how it could be used. Fighters such as the Sopwith Camel and the German Albatross D1 were killing machines feared by other pilots and enemy troops on the ground below. By 1918 bombing was more sophisticated and the aircraft carrier was used for the first time.

Questions

1 'War accelerates the pace of change'. Show how the war produced changes in aviation.
2 Why do you think aircraft became important to men in the trenches? Answer this question carefully – there are several possible reasons.

The war at sea

Although naval rivalry had an important part in the build-up to the war, the expected clash between the two great fleets did not come until May 1916.

The war at sea was carefully planned. Britain controlled the English Channel and the North Sea, and was able to establish a blockade on Germany. Occasionally German raiders such as the *Emden* stole out of port, but they proved little threat to Britain's dominance.

The *Emden* sank 70 000 tons of Allied shipping before she was forced to run aground following a battle with the Australian cruiser, *Sydney*.

Thus it was not the Dreadnoughts which made the headlines, but another new weapon of war – the submarine. Germany, aware of its weakness in surface vessels, concentrated on building *untersee*, or 'U' boats. in 1915 Germany retaliated against the Allied blockade by an unrestricted U boat campaign against Allied shipping. The Allies were unprepared, and lone merchant vessels were easy targets. One of the most notorious events of the war was an attack by the submarine U20. On 7 May 1915 Kapitän Lieutnant Schweiger of U20 reported:

Starboard ahead four funnels and two masts of a steamer with course at right angles to us . . . the ship is made out to be a large passenger steamer.

U20 submerged and converged on the steamer. Schweiger's report continued with the firing of a torpedo on target:

An unusually heavy explosion took place with a very strong explosion cloud. The explosion of the torpedo must have been followed by a second one. The superstructure right above the point of impact and the bridge were torn asunder. The ship stopped immediately and heeled over to starboard very quickly, immersing stimultaneously at the bow. It appeared as if the ship were going to capsize very shortly. Great confusion ensued on board; the boats were made clear and some of them were lowered to the water. In doing so great confusion reigned; some boats, full to capacity, were lowered, rushed from above; and foundered immediately. On the bow the name *Lusitania* became visible in golden letters. the funnels were painted black, no flag set astern. Since it seemed as if the steamer would keep above the water only a short time, we dived to a depth of 24 metres and ran out to sea.

The death of over one thousand people was greeted with uproar. In particular, the people of the USA were furious that 120 of their citizens had died. Schweiger was received coldly by officials in Berlin because of this, but the German press justified his actions:

Every human life is, of course, valuable and its loss deplorable, but measured by the methods of this world war, by the methods introduced by our enemies, forcing us to retaliatory measures in self-defence, the death of non-combatants is a matter of no consequence.

Frankfurter Zeitung, 8 May 1915

Indeed it would seem from the circumstances that the *Lusitania* destruction was deliberately courted by the British Admiralty as a means of embroiling America in the war.

The Fatherland, 30 June 1915

Even so, the German High Command saw fit to restrict the operations of submarines until January 1915.

One way of stopping the U boats – Royal Marines blockade the U boat base at Zeebrugge, April 1918

In May 1916 the two great fleets finally met. The German High Seas Fleet, in an attempt to trap a small part of the British fleet, was itself trapped by the British Grand Fleet near Jutland. The battle was indecisive – both sides claimed victory. However, Britain's loss of the Queen Mary and thirteen other ships against eleven German ships, and a poor showing from both gunnery and armour proved that the Royal Navy was not invincible. Even so, the High Seas Fleet retreated to port and failed to come out in force again during the war.

The German fleet was taken to Scapa Flow and scuttled in 1918.

In 1917 unrestricted submarine warfare was resumed. Over two million tons of British and Allied shipping was sunk in the first four months of the year. Britain responded with mines, depth-charges, and convoys. America responded by entering the war against Germany. By the end of the year losses had fallen considerably. At the same time the continued blockade against Germany was having terrible consequences. This, as much as the fighting in the trenches, was to bring victory to Britain and its allies.

Other factors which influenced the USA to join the war included the execution by Germany of the nurse Edith Cavell and the exposure of treaty negotiations between Germany and Mexico.

Questions

1 According to his report, did Kapitän Lieutnant Schweiger know that he was attacking the *Lusitania*?
2 Why were the German officials unhappy about Schweiger's action?
3 Why do you think that this event so shocked Britain and the USA?
4 For what reasons was the war at sea important in its contribution to Allied victory?

Other war fronts

Fighting on the western front was matched by developments on the eastern front. In August 1914 the Russians attacked Prussia with some success, but a German counter-attack drove the Russian army back with heavy casualties. A new offensive in 1915 gained the Germans two hundred miles along the whole front, and Russian dead, wounded and captured numbered over two million. There the fighting became bogged down until, in 1917, the Russians made advances against Austria. However, the cost in lives and resources had been too great for Russia to bear and the war was a major cause of the Russian revolution (see page 121).

Italy entered the war against Germany and Austria in 1915 and opened a new front. The fighting there was indecisive until 1917, when, in October, Ludendorff, the German commander-in-chief, decided to create a new offensive. The Austrians had been unable to break through difficult alpine territory, but Ludendorff sent German troops to assist them in an attempt to knock Italy out of the war before concentrating on the western front. The offensive was launched at Caporetto. When

Trench warfare – Russian version

Massive casualties on the eastern front

Gallipoli – Anzac Cove, 1915

Turkey was involved in bitter fighting against Russia in 1914–15. During this time 1.5 million Armenians were massacred by the Turks who feared that these border people would help the Russians.

Caporetto fell, the Italian armies began a retreat which turned into a rout. Not until the Italians reached the river Piave did they make a stand to defend their new line and the city of Venice.

The entry of Turkey into the war on the side of Germany in October 1914 created new fronts in the Middle East. The Turkish Empire was attacked from Egypt, and with the help of an Arab revolt the British advanced into Arabia and Palestine in 1917 (see page 251). Possibly the most controversial of these new fronts was Gallipoli. The British plan was to attack Turkey at its heart – Constantinople. The attack was to be launched in the Dardanelles with the capture of the strategically vital Gallipoli peninsular.

In March 1915 the British fleet shelled the Turkish fortresses, but then withdrew. Some weeks later in April an Allied force of British, French, Indian, Australian and New Zealand troops landed on the Gallipoli beaches. However, after the March bombardment the Turks had sent massive reinforcements to Gallipoli. Ignorant of this, the

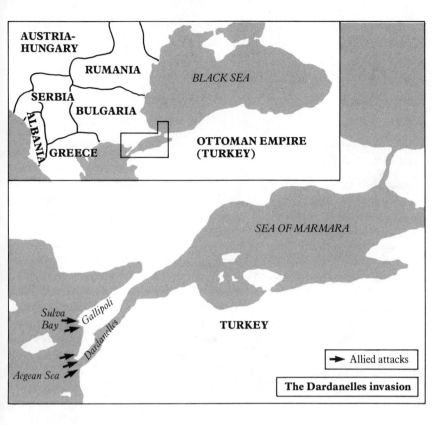

The Dardanelles invasion

Allied force was being sent to a slaughter. An Australian folk song describes the landing:

How well I remember that terrible day,
How our blood stained the sand and the water;
And how in that hell that they called Sulva Bay,
We were butchered like lambs at the slaughter.
Johnny Turk he was waiting, he'd primed himself well,
He showered us with bullets, and rained us with shell,
And in five minutes flat, he'd blown us to hell:
Nearly blew us right back to Australia.
And the band played Waltzing Matilda,
As we stopped to bury the slain.
We buried ours and the Turks buried theirs,
Then we started all over again.

Eric Bogle

An Australian force was told to charge the enemy stronghold and fight with bayonets as loading and firing would slow them down:

Go! ordered Lieutenant Colonel White, and he led the first wave of 150 Light Horsemen as they leapt over the parapet. They were hit by sheets of bullets fired at no more than sixty yards range. Hardly a man got more than ten paces; in thirty seconds the line was annihilated.

Padre Creighton of the 88th Brigade saw the same scene repeated over and over again:

Only about 1300 of the brigade came back, the brigadier and two colonels killed and some 1700 men knocked out, practically nothing gained, and a whole brigade put out of action. These things seem to happen in every battle. The amount of unnecessary lives simply thrown away is appalling.

Private Charles Watkins of the Lancashire Fusiliers had another word for it:

What an amateurish, do-it-yourself cock-up the whole conduct of this campaign must have been.

Censorship of the press was used to stop the news of disaster leaking out. Ellis-Ashmead Bartlett of the *Daily Telegraph* wrote this account in criticism of the censors:

It is almost impossible to know what to write but I could put together an official bulletin which would apply to all these attacks out here! After a concentrated bombardment our infantry advanced against the demoralised enemy and captured four lines of trenches. We were on the verge of taking Achi Baba when unfortunately something (generally the French) gave way on our right, leaving us with an exposed flank. Our centre then had to retire, suffering heavy casualties. We are now back on the same line from which we started this morning. The enemy's counter-attacks were most gallantly repulsed with enormous losses. Our troops are much elated by their success, and declare themselves ready to attack again any time. We have made a distinct advance of five yards in some places.

In January 1916 the army of the Dardanelles was secretly evacuated. Private Watkins remembered;

I found myself wracked with unmanly sobbing. It was all the thousands of blokes who'd never breathe the air again, but most it was the dreadful feeling of the shame of it all – the British army having to evacuate the Peninsula like this, and after all this gigantic wasted effort.

The Australian folk song continues:

They collected the crippled, the wounded and maimed
And they shipped us back home to Australia,
The armless, the legless, the blind and insane,
All the brave wounded heroes of Sulva.
And when our ship pulled into Circular Quay,
I looked at the place where my legs used to be,
And thanked Christ there was nobody waiting for me –
To grieve, to mourn and to pity.
And the band played Waltzing Matilda,
As they carried us down the gangway,
But nobody cheered, they just stood there and stared –
And they turned all their faces away.

John Laffin, author of *Damn the Dardanelles*, (1980), blames people at three levels of command. First he blames the commanders in the field. However, greater blame is set at the door of Field-Marshal Lord Kitchener, minister of war.

Kitchener's guilt is fundamental. He delayed in sending an attacking force to the Mediterranean; he chose the wrong generals. Having chosen them he kept them short of reinforcements, artillery, and shells until too late. He was guilty of criminal negligence in not knowing what he was asking of his generals and his troops.

At the top level he blames First Lord of the Admiralty Winston Churchill:

Winston Spencer Churchill was a victim of his own imagination and a puppet of his self-confidence. He had a brilliant scheme, and because it was so appealing Churchill leapt to the conclusion that successful accomplishment must follow. He did not carefully consider what forces were necessary to gain victory – and he did not weigh the consequences of failure.

The other front of war was in the colonies across the world. South Africa defeated the Germans in South West Africa. British and Japanese forces took control of German possessions in the Pacific including, in September 1914, the fort at Kiao-Chow in China. The colonial war was quickly won.

Japan had joined its allies by declaring war on Germany in 1914.

However, the continued contribution to the war effort by British Empire countries, and from 1917 by the USA, maintained the conflict on a world scale.

Questions

1 Look at Bartlett's account of the effects of censorship. How does he use this passage to ridicule
   (a) the campaign?
   (b) the censors?
2 Bartlett would have liked to tell the truth about Gallipoli. Write the newspaper article that he would have liked to write.

The home fronts

Many soldiers returning to Britain from the trenches were disillusioned to find that life at home seemed little affected by the war. For example the writer, Robert Graves, found Londoners 'generally indifferent to, and ignorant of the war, and more interested in "business as usual".' In fact this war had a greater effect on the masses behind the lines than soldiers could have realised.

Robert Graves – his war poetry included 'Over the Brazier', 1916, and he later wrote books including a wartime autobiography *Goodbye to All That*, and *I, Claudius*.

The enthusiastic response of certain groups to the war effort continued right through the war. Young men out of uniform were targets for those, mainly women, who felt that they should join up. An example of the call to arms was written by Baroness Orczy:

Women and Girls of England.
Your hour has come. Together we have laughed and cried over that dauntless

Baroness Orczy – authoress of *The Scarlet Pimpernel*, the story of a daring English gentleman in the French Revolution.

There's no mistaking who he means

'Conchies' usually refused conscription on religious or political grounds. The public had little sympathy with Christians, let alone socialists who refused to kill fellow workers.

But if anyone remains unpersuaded by Kitchener . . .

Englishman, the Scarlet Pimpernel and thrilled with enthusiasm over the brave doings of his League.

Now we shall form ourselves into an Active Service League, its sole object: influencing sweethearts, brothers, sons and friends to recruit. Pledge: I hereby pledge myself most solemnly in the name of my King and Country to persuade every man I know to offer his services to his country, and I also pledge myself never to be seen in public with any man who has refused to respond to his country's call.

Daily Mail, 1914

In July 1915 a notice in *The Times* read:

Jack F. G. – If you are not in khaki by the 20th I shall cut you dead.

Despite the pressure to join up, and despite the introduction, in May 1916, of conscription for all males aged 18 – 41, some said no. These were conscientious objectors, who refused to fight mainly on religious grounds. They joined non-combatant corps at the front or at home, or faced imprisonment.

Of those who went to fight, millions never returned. Throughout the countries involved there was hardly a community which did not suffer the loss of its young men. At least two million Germans, one and a half million Frenchmen, one million British and Empire, three million Russians, and more millions from other combatant nations were mourned.

Civilians suffered in other ways too. Of course those people who lived near the front lines found their lives devastated by the war. As far away from the front as Paris there was heavy shelling which drove people into the underground system for shelter. New weapons of war were used against civilians in Britain too. German raiders attacked Yarmouth, Scarborough and Whitby in 1914. If inland communities thought they were safe, they were wrong. On the night of 8 September 1915, a sinister cigar-shaped craft crossed the channel and headed for London. It was Zeppelin L13, 530 feet long, commanded by Commander Mathey:

Mathey picked out St. Paul's and laid a course which he thought would take him over the Bank of England. Although they had been fired on with great inaccuracy from all points, they had not yet dropped a bomb on London proper. Mathey ordered 'fire slowly'. A mixture of incendiaries and high explosives left the racks in widely spaced bunches.

K. Poolman, *Zeppelins over England*, 1974

The first bombs fell in the neighbourhood of Euston Station. Mathey takes up the account:

Maneouvering and arriving directly over Liverpool Street Station I shouted 'rapid fire' through the tube and bombs rained down. There was a succession of detonations and bursts of fire and I could see that I had done great damage.

At first London was shocked. The significance of the attack quickly became apparent to the American journalist, W. G. Shepherd:

Seven million people of the biggest city in the world stand gazing into the sky from the darkened streets. Here is the climax to the twentieth century.

Suddenly you realise that the biggest city in the world has become the night battlefield in which seven million harmless men, women, and children live. Here is war at the very heart of civilisation, threatening all the millions of things that human hearts and human minds have created in past centuries.

Few people died in that or later raids, and by 1917 fighter pilots, such as Second-Lieutenant Sowrey who destroyed the L32, and anti-aircraft gunners had found the tactics to shoot Zeppelins down. However, by that time Germany had developed a bomber with five hours flying time – enough to reach Britain and return home. The trend for the future was clearly set.

Civilian life also changed dramatically because of the shortage of manpower. All warring nations came to realise the usefulness and importance of womanpower.

In Britain there was established a 'Register of Women for War Service' in March 1915. Women took work which would not have been considered suitable before the war, either because of class or occupation. Soon women were found working for the Post Office, in agriculture, in transport, milk delivery, as drivers, and many other ordinary jobs. Other women worked in munitions factories. This was dangerous work – an explosion in a factory in 1917 killed 69 and injured nearly 400 others. Women also joined the forces, as WAACs, WAAFs or WRENs for example. Amongst their important jobs in this capacity were communications and ciphering.

There was a significant political outcome of this war service. The

TAKE UP THE SWORD OF JUSTICE

And in case there is anyone left . . .

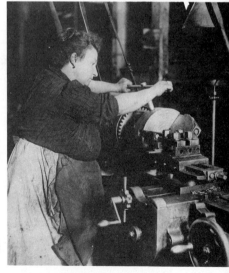

Dangerous work on the home front – in the armaments factory

Land girls at work

The vote was given to women in 1918, and for the first time they could stand for parliament.

House of Commons, for so long hostile to the idea of votes for women, approved the idea overwhelmingly in March 1917.

Food shortages

Despite submarine warfare and heavy losses of shipping, Britain had a relatively plentiful supply of food until late 1916. By early 1917 potatoes were in short supply, as was sugar, and increasingly wheat. The government was loath to introduce rationing, but a campaign was launched to persuade people to eat less and waste nothing. By April 1918 rationing was used – for meat, bacon and fat. France too found

Right royal rations

shortages of food. However, Germany suffered throughout the war. From the outset bread was made from substitutes, such as rye and potato flour, and from 1915 was rationed. No fresh meat was available, and by 1916 the most astonishing attempts were made to find substitutes for fat – from rats, mice, hamsters, crows, cockroaches, snails and earthworms, even hairclippings and old leather boots.

None of them succeeded. By 1917 the shortage was even affecting the wealthier classes – Princess Blucher wrote:

If we are lucky, we are doled out one egg every three weeks. Our bread is being stretched in every way possible, and is now mixed with some of those subterranean vegetables coming under the common name 'turnip' of whose existence we never dreamed before.

Black crows were the only meat to be found in the butchers' shops, and most basic commodities were in short supply.

In Britain, France and Russia, 1917 and 1918 saw growing disillusionment with the war, and protest took various forms. In England there were wage strikes in engineering works in the midlands and amongst London's transport workers. There was also talk of a general strike.

In France the Renault workers walked out in protest at their government's rejection of Germany's 1917 peace offer, and also at further conscription. However, this was insignificant in comparison to events in Russia where an accumulation of grievances led to revolution. (see page 121).

The German people, too, were unhappy. In a protest against food shortages a quarter of a million engineering workers in Berlin went on strike. This unrest, and possibly a threat of revolution in Germany too, made the German government determined to win the war quickly in the spring of 1918.

The defeat of Germany, 1918

By 1918 Germany was starving. In addition its government realised that a spring offensive might be the last chance of victory. Russia was out of the war, but US troops had not yet begun to arrive in great numbers. In March 1918 the great German offensive began, first at Amiens and the Somme, and later at Ypres. The Amiens offensive began with success. A massive artillery barrage was followed by a push which carried the German army forward for fourteen miles on parts of the line. The Allies, at first disorganised, then appointed Marshal Foch as the overall co-ordinator, and the advance was halted. In May a second German offensive took their army to the Marne, only 56 miles away from Paris. In June, and again in July, the German army attempted to cross the Marne, but each time they failed and were left the weaker.

Britain and France had sustained heavy casualties in these attacks, but in July 29 US divisions arrived, and a fight back began. A new, more mobile strategy recaptured the lost ground and the German army was pushed back to the Hindenburg line. On one day, 8 August, there were over 40 000 German casualties.

The German generals had gambled on victory and lost. Even though they were still fighting on foreign soil they realised that the war was over. Staring defeat in the face, they advised their politicians to negotiate a surrender.

Questions

1 In what ways were civilians affected by the war?
2 How did the civilian attitude towards the war change? Do you think you can make an answer to this question which represents all feelings?
3 How did the First World War affect the place where you live? Consult a local history book to find the answer.
4 Explain the defeat of Germany and her allies in the First World War.

2 The peace settlement of Versailles

Peace at last. A street party to celebrate

Wilson had high ideals that were rejected by both his allies and the people of the USA. Disillusioned, he retired from politics in 1920.

National self-determination – the principle that a people should be allowed to choose their own leaders and policies.

11/11 – this is still remembered every armistice day, but includes a memorial for those who fell in later wars.

In January 1918 the President of the USA, Woodrow Wilson, laid down the Fourteen Points on which he hoped a peace settlement could be based. These were the main ones:
 – Open diplomacy in talks to bring about peace.
 – Free navigation of the sea in peace and war.
 – Free trade.
 – Disarmament.
 – Government of colonies to be carried out on the basis of an agreement between the inhabitants and the governing power.
 – The boundaries of specific named states to be redrawn according to the principle of national self-determination.
 – An association of nations to be formed.

By October 1918 Germany was in a state of collapse. The generals advised the new government, now led by Prince Maximilian of Baden, that the army was about to collapse, and that he should negotiate for a peace. Baden wrote to Wilson declaring that Germany was willing to talk on the basis of the Fourteen Points. However, the Allies demanded an unconditional surrender before any negotiations could take place. With Germany exhausted, the Kaiser abdicated on 9 November, and fled to the Netherlands. The surrender was given at 11 a.m. on 11 November, 1918.

In December 1918 and January 1919 the leaders of the victorious powers met at Versailles in France to consider how they should deal with Germany, and other problems. There was no thought of negotiation, and Germany was not represented. This was to be a dictated peace. The main problem they discussed was the terms to be dictated.

The aims of the victors

France

Of the five victorious powers France had suffered most, was most embittered, and feared most for the future. The French leader, 'Tiger' Clemenceau, went to Versailles determined to punish Germany, and never to allow the German nation to become strong again. French newspaper headlines during these months reveal how Clemenceau was in line with popular opinion.

Clemenceau was well-known for his determination to win both the war and the peace.

GERMANY REMAINS MENACING
Take Care. We must expect to be faced before long with a Germany reconstituted politically, if not indeed militarily. Hun Democracy is becoming daily more aggressive.

Homme Libre, 27 and 30 January

GERMANY WILL NOT ACCEPT DEFEAT
Figaro, 7 February

GERMANY, BY THE NEW ARMISTICE, OUGHT TO BE RENDERED INCAPABLE OF DOING HARM.
Parisien, 11 February

Clemenceau's hardline attitude can be seen in his response to a plea for food to help the starving in Germany, where as many as 500 000 people may have died of hunger in the months after the war:

France 'had been ruined and ravaged . . . over two million men had lost their lives . . . and yet what guarantees had France that anything would be received in payment for all this destruction? . . . She merely possessed a few securities which it was now proposed to take away in order to pay those who would supply food to Germany. . . .' In a word he was being asked to betray his country.

Noble, *Policies and Opinions at Paris*, 1919

Britain

There were many people in Britain who agreed with the French view – like Sir Auckland Geddes who said 'we would squeeze the German lemon until the pips squeak'. Lloyd George, the British prime minister, had also made anti-German remarks during his campaign for re-election. However, by the time he reached Versailles his view was that a moderate settlement should be made:

Lloyd George – took over as prime minister when the war was going badly in 1916 and gained a great reputation as a war leader. He agreed with the ideas of Wilson but had to pay attention to cries for revenge from the British public.

The maintenance of peace will depend on there being no causes of exasperation constantly stirring up either the spirit of patriotism, of justice, or of fair play to achieve redress. Our Peace ought to be dictated by men who act in the spirit of judges . . . and not in a spirit of vendetta, which is not satisfied without mutilation and the infliction of pain and humiliation.

Lloyd George was mainly referring here to the treatment of German-speaking peoples in Europe and not to German territories outside

Europe. Britain wanted to maintain her power throughout the world, and this could best be achieved by gaining Germany's colonies, and those of her allies.

Italy

Italy had come into the war in 1915, and by the Treaty of London had been promised not only an extension of her borders at the expense of Austro-Hungary, but also colonies in Africa. Italy had suffered significant defeats in the war, but even so Italian representatives went to Versailles as victors to claim their spoils.

Japan

Like Italy, Japan was more concerned with territorial gain than with the fate of Germany. Japan wanted the settlement to include the authorisation of the 'Twenty-one demands' of 1915, which had given Japan widespread powers in China. Japan particularly wanted confirmation of her own possession of Shantung and some German islands in the Pacific, which were already under informal Japanese control.

The settlement of 1919 was the product of these conflicting demands. Wilson, despite the fact that he was losing support from voters in the USA, kept to the principles of the Fourteen Points. The other victorious powers sought to argue their own case, and inevitably the outcome was a compromise.

Russia was not represented at Versailles. Indeed, the war was still going on there.

The terms of the Treaty of Versailles

1 War guilt

The Allied Governments affirm and Gemany accepts the responsibility of Germany for causing all the loss and damage to which the Allies have been subjected as a consequence of the war imposed upon them by the aggression of Germany.

Article 231, *Treaty of Versailles*

For this aggression, it was demanded that Germany pay to the victors the sum of £240 billion in reparations. In addition, Article 160 of the Treaty stated:

After the war of 1870 Germany had demanded reparations from France. Now the idea was used against Germany.

The German Army must not comprise more than seven divisions of infantry and three divisions of cavalry.
The total number in the Army . . . must not exceed one hundred thousand men. . . . The Army shall be devoted exclusively to the maintenance of order within the territory and to the control of frontiers.

Furthermore, fortresses on the German border were dismantled. The navy was restricted to six battleships, six cruisers, twelve destroyers, and twelve torpedo boats. No submarines were allowed. The rest of the fleet, including ships under construction, were destroyed.

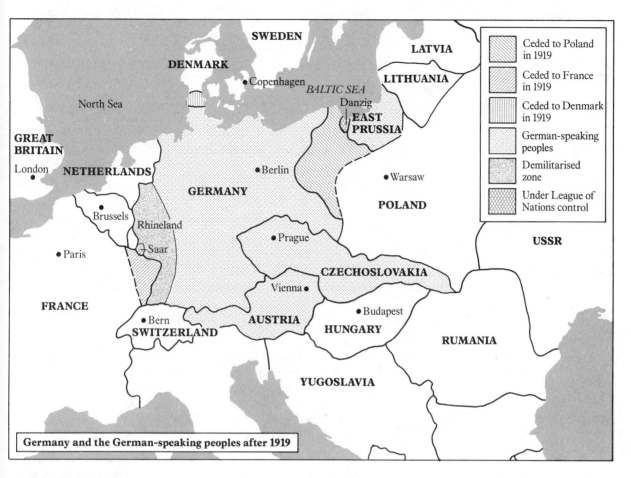

Germany and the German-speaking peoples after 1919

Legend:
- Ceded to Poland in 1919
- Ceded to France in 1919
- Ceded to Denmark in 1919
- German-speaking peoples
- Demilitarised zone
- Under League of Nations control

2 European frontiers

The map shows European frontiers after the Treaty of Versailles. The main changes were, in summary:

From Germany

Alsace-Lorraine to France.
Schleswig to Denmark.
Part of Prussia to Poland.
Danzig to become an international city.
The Rhineland to remain German, but to be demilitarised.

From Austro-Hungary

Poland recreated as an independent state.
Czechoslovakia created in areas dominated by Czech and Slovak peoples.
Rumania enlarged.
Yugoslavia created as a state for South Slavs.
Southern Tyrol to Italy.
Hungary recreated as a separate Magyar state.
Austria forbidden to make any future union with Germany.

From Russia

Poland recreated as an independent state.

Lithuania, Latvia, Estonia and Finland created as independent states.

3 The Ottoman Empire

Mandated powers were given
control of mandated states with
the purpose of guiding them
towards self-government.

Turkey was another of the defeated powers. Iraq, Transjordan, Saudi Arabia, and Yemen were at first mandated to Britain (see page 251), but soon became separate states. Palestine was also mandated to Britain and Cyprus became a British possession. Turkey and Syria were mandated to France.

4 Colonies

German colonies were also mandated as follows:

To Britain: Tanganyika

To Britain and France: Cameroons and Togoland

To the Union of South Africa: South West Africa

To Belgium: Ruanda Urundi

To Australia: New Guinea

To New Zealand: Samoa

To Japan: The Caroline Islands, The Marianas, The Marshall Islands, and Shantung and Kiaochow

5 The League of Nations

President Wilson's last Point had been to set up an association of nations. In accordance with this, the League of Nations was established with two main aims: to prevent any repetition of this horrifying war; and to settle disputes peacefully as they arose.

Article 8, for example, stated:

The maintenance of peace requires the reduction of national armaments to the lowest point consistent with national safety and the enforcement by common action of international obligations.

Furthermore, all treaties were to be made public and registered with the League.

Under Article 11 the League could take any action which seemed advisable to maintain or restore peace. Disputes between members were to be solved by arbitration. In the event of a member disregarding the League, financial and economic boycotts were allowed for, and even the use of armed intervention.

In addition to these two principal aims, the League was to encourage social and economic progress through international co-operation.

With regard to membership and organisation, the League was to be dominated by the five victorious powers. The USA, Britain, France, Italy and Japan were each to have a permanent seat on the Council of the League, plus four representatives from other states elected on a temporary basis. All members were to have a vote in the Assembly. In

THE GAP IN THE BRIDGE.

The keystone is missing!

both cases decisions were to be arrived at democratically.

At first the members of the League were the victors and neutrals. The defeated powers were placed on probation, with the promise of membership as a reward for good behaviour. One of the great weaknesses of the League was revealed at the outset. Wilson, the architect of the League, could not persuade the people of the USA to keep up their new commitment to international affairs. The American senate would not allow Wilson to join the League, and so the USA was the one major victorious state not to ratify the Treaty of Versailles. This was to prove a serious weakness in the years to come, severely undermining the strength of the League of Nations.

Wilson was a Democrat. In 1918 his rivals, the Republicans, gained control of the senate and refused to co-operate with his policies.

Germany's attitude towards the Treaty

Throughout the negotiations the German delegation had not been consulted. Finally they were invited to appear. This was a cruelly symbolic moment. In 1871 the German Empire had been proclaimed after victory in the Franco-Prussian war – in the Hall of Mirrors at Versailles. Now, in that same Hall of Mirrors, the Germans faced humiliation. When their leader, Count Ulrich Brockdorff-Rantzau, was asked for observations, he replied,

We have heard the victors' passionate demand that as vanquished we shall be made to pay and as the guilty we shall be punished. The demand is made that we shall acknowledge that we alone are guilty of having caused the war. Such a confession in my mouth would be a lie.

The Germans were given fifteen days to respond, and in the light of those responses some small concessions were made, including more

Can you explain the ghosts of Versailles?

GHOSTS AT VERSAILLES.

talks on the total sum of the reparations debt. However, no changes were made on the other points outlined above, and for a time it seemed that Germay might refuse to sign. Finally, with its people starving, and the nation too weak to return to war, Germany signed.

Questions

1 In the light of their hopes for a peace settlement, why were the Germans so angry at the final terms of the treaty?
2 Why do you think the French were the most bitter about the war? In what ways did the treaty answer the fears expressed in the French newspaper headlines?
3 Complete the following table to show the hopes of the victorious parties and what they actually achieved.

Country	Hopes/expectations	Actual outcome

4 The most controversial clause of the treaty was the 'War Guilt' clause. What information would you wish to see to help you judge whether Germany was indeed guilty?
5 Describe the purposes and organisation of the League of Nations.

Inter-war Europe and the Second World War

3 The survival of democracy in Britain

Problems facing the democratic states

In 1919 all of the major European states had democratic governments. There are many types of democracy, but the following features are common to all:

1 People are allowed different opinions about how governments should be run.
2 Parties, or groups of parties, put themselves forward for election on the basis of agreed policies.
3 Disagreements are resolved by discussion.
4 The elected party serves for a fixed term, and then submits itself for re-election.
5 The governments operates according to a constitution, a set of fundamental laws which limits its power, and which can only be waived in exceptional circumstances.

During the years after 1919 European democratic governments faced major problems. They were blamed for the failings of the Treaty of Versailles, and for the economic problems which hit most countries between the wars. People turned towards extremist groups such as the growing fascist or communist parties. In Britain and France democracy survived. In Italy, Spain and Germany fascism took control.

Fascism, like democracy, can take a number of forms, but it has the following features:

1 It does not allow criticism, or contrary opinions.
2 Once fascism controls the state, there is only one party.
3 Fascism supports a strong leader figure.
4 Fascism is highly nationalistic.
5 Fascism is anti-communist.
6 Fascism is aggressive and glories in militarism.

The case of Britain

Britain shared the economic difficulties of the rest of Europe, and was hit badly by the decay of older industries such as shipbuilding and steel. Unemployment rose quickly, and was over two million by 1921. Prices rose steadily, but wages fell behind and there were strikes by many groups of workers including the police in 1918 and 1919, and railwaymen in 1920. It was at this time that the government passed an Emergency Powers Act.

In this atmosphere, many people saw the rise of the Labour Party as a threat. After the First World War Lloyd George's Liberal government became divided and discredited, and Labour became the alternative government to the Conservatives, taking office for the first time in 1924. This frightened those people who saw Labour's socialism as one short step away from communism, so recently successful in the Russian revolution of 1917. Such fears were made greater just before the general

Emergency powers – exceptional powers taken by a government to cope with an emergency, and sometimes overriding the Constitution.

After 1918 the Liberal Party declined as Labour rose to become the main opposition.

CIVIL WAR PLOT

MOSCOW ORDERS TO OUR REDS.

GREAT PLOT DISCLOSED YESTERDAY.

"PARALYSE THE ARMY AND NAVY."

AND MR. MACDONALD WOULD LEND RUSSIA OUR MONEY!

DOCUMENT ISSUED BY FOREIGN OFFICE

AFTER "DAILY MAIL" HAD SPREAD THE NEWS.

A "very secret" letter of instruction from Moscow, which we publish below, discloses a great Bolshevik plot to paralyse the British Army and Navy and to plunge the country into civil war.

The letter is addressed by the Bolsheviks of Moscow to the Soviet Government's servants in Great Britain, the Communist Party, who in turn are the masters of Mr. Ramsay MacDonald's Government, which has signed a treaty with Moscow whereby the Soviet is to be guaranteed a "loan" of millions of British money.

The letter is signed by Zinoviev, the Dictator of Petrograd, President of the Third (Moscow) International, and is addressed

Zinoviev, whose real name is Apfelbaum.

...paign of disclosure of the foreign policy of MacDonald.

ARMED INSURRECTION.

The IKKI [Executive Committee, third (Communist) International] will willingly place at your disposal the wide material in its possession regarding the activities of British imperialism in the Middle and Far East. In the meanwhile, however, strain every nerve, in the struggle for the ratification of the Treaty, in favour of a continuation of negotiations regarding the regulation of relations between the S.S.S.R. and England. A settlement of relations between the two countries will assist in the revolutionising of the international and British proletariat not less than a successful rising in any of the working districts of England, as the establishment of close contact between the British and Russian proletariat, the exchange of delegations and workers, etc., will make it possible for us to extend and develop the propaganda of ideas of Leninism in England and the Colonies. Armed warfare must be preceded by a struggle against the inclinations to compromise which are embedded among the majority of British workmen, against the ideas of evolution and peaceful extermination of capitalism. Only then will it be possible to count upon complete success of an armed

The Daily Mail *makes its view of the Labour Party quite clear*

election of 1923. The *Daily Mail* published the 'Zinoviev letter' which linked the British Labour Party with the Communist Party in Russia. Part of the letter read:

There are so many communists today in the so-called 'Labour Party', and so strong are they, that even our socialist government must do their bidding.

The letter played an important part in Labour's defeat in the election.

The General Strike of 1926 was also seen by many as a move towards revolution. The causes of the strike can be traced back to the decay of the coal industry, and a fall in coal prices and profits. Employers wanted to cut their own costs by cutting wages. When this was first threatened in 1925 the government stepped in, realising that the miners could call upon the support of fellow trades unionists whereas they were unprepared to deal with a general strike. For the time being the government agreed to subsidise the miners' wages, and a Royal Commission was set up to recommend a longer-term solution. However, the subsidy only lasted until 1926, and the miners' unions then asked the Trades Union Congress to support them in a general strike against wage cuts.

Punch *doesn't take the Zinoviev letter quite so seriously*

Using the evidence: the General Strike

A from the *Daily Mail*, 3 May 1926:

The miners, after weeks of negotiation, have declined the proposals made to them, and the coal mines of Britain are idle.

The Council of the Trades Union Congress . . . has determined to support the miners by going to the extreme of ordering a general strike. We do not wish to say anything hard about the miners themselves. As to their leaders, all we need to say at this moment is that some of them are (and have openly declared themselves) under the influence of people who mean no good in this country.

The general strike is not an industrial dispute; it is a revolutionary movement, intended to inflict suffering on the great mass of innocent persons in the community and thereby put pressure on the government.

This being the case it cannot be tolerated by any civilised government and it must be dealt with by every resource at the disposal of the community. A state of emergency and national danger has been proclaimed to resist attack.

B from the *British Worker*, 10 May 1926:

The quiet determination of the men on strike has impressed the outside public. The strikers' confidence and enthusiasm are contagious. They have spread to other sections of the nation . . . a procession of transport workers, bemedalled and in Sunday attire, marched in fours to Brockwell Park. The immense crowd in the park gave a clear indication of where the sympathies of the British nation lie in this dispute. Many of the crowd were Trade Unionists, including strikers and their families, but at least a third of them were of the class which the press loves to call 'the general public' – bank and insurance clerks, small shopkeepers, holders of season tickets, dwellers in suburban villas.

A convoy of essential foodstuffs, 1926

One way of getting to work during the General Strike

C *British Worker*, 10 May 1926:

In a two hours wait (at Kings Cross) no engine stirred with carriages behind it, and no train went out. . . . I mounted my motor cycle and looked in at Euston and St Pancras. But locomotives were even more scarce here than at Kings Cross.

I circled round past several of the big dock gates. All were closed and guarded by police and pickets. . . . Inside the docks not a man was visible . . . no rattle of winch or hauling gear broke the silence.

D *Daily Express*, 11 May 1926:

Greater improvements in the main line train services continue to be made throughout the country.

Approximately 1000 trains ran yesterday on the LMS railway system. Daily trains from Euston . . . came into operation this morning. The company has doubled their service since last Wednesday.

E *Manchester Guardian*, 5 May 1926:

5000 STRIKERS CONFLICT WITH POLICE

Ugly scenes were witnessed in chief thoroughfare of Leeds about noon today. The trouble began when several thousand strikers attacked the emergency tram-cars with lumps of coal taken from a striking lorry. . . . The strikers rushed towards another tram-car a moment later, but were held back for a time by a strong body of police.

Amid loud cries of 'down with the Police' the strikers rushed on to them. The police . . . defended themselves with their batons.

Getting to work made difficult!

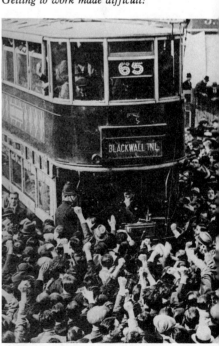

F *Manchester Guardian*, 7 May 1926:

In Camberwell this morning some women laid their babies on the road in front of commercial vehicles and when the cars stopped, men jumped on them, turned out the driver, and smashed the machine of the car.

G from the *Diary of King George V*, 12 May, 1926:

At 1 p. m. I got the good news that the TUC had been to the Prime Minister and informed him that the General Strike was forthwith called off. . . . Our old country can well be proud of itself, as, during the last nine days, there has been a strike in which four million men have been affected; not a shot has been fired and no one killed. It shows what wonderful people we are.

1 The Zinoviev letter was a fake. Why do you think many people were willing to believe that there was a threat from communism?
2 (a) Read document A. Which sentences show that the fears aroused by the Zinoviev letter still existed?
  (b) What is implied in document A about the view of the strike held by the general public?
  (c) How does document B disagree with document A?
3 Read documents C and D. How do these sources differ about the effectiveness of the strike?
  Can you suggest why they differ?
4 Read documents E, F, and G. Why do you think that the incidents in E and F took place?
  In the light of these incidents could the king justify his remarks in document G?
5 An event like the General Strike poses particular problems for the historian trying to write a balanced view of the past.
  (a) What other sources might a historian wish to consult?
  (b) Write your own balanced view of the Gerneral Strike, focussing both on events and their importance.

Britain after the General Strike

After nine days all workers except the miners returned to work. The General Strike did not undermine the government. Indeed, it strengthened it, because people realised that it was better to take the battle into parliament than try to fight it outside. Certainly it was not the end of the Labour Party, which took power again in 1929 with Ramsay Macdonald as prime minister. Almost immediately they were faced with the Wall Street Crash of 1929 and the trade slump which followed. With the economy in a seriously weakened condition, high unemployment, and mounting foreign debt, Ramsay Macdonald formed a National government by making a coalition with the Conservatives. The crisis was so severe that they asked for special powers known as 'The Doctor's mandate'. However these powers never presented any threat to

Coalition – where two or more political parties unite to form a government. In Britain this has only happened in time of crisis.

Oswald Mosley with Italian fellow fascists, 1923

1936 – Unemployed miners from Jarrow in County Durham march to London to publicise the conditions of those hardest hit by the Depression

democracy. During the thirties, with the economic slump at its worst, only small numbers of people drifted toward extremist movements such as Oswald Mosley's British Union of Fascists, which was formed in 1932. Its membership never rose above 20 000 and most people disliked the violence and anti-semitism advocated by the BUF.

With a long parliamentary tradition, a solid two-party structure, and on the basis of government by consent, democracy in Britain remained intact. In moments of crisis politicians did not divide and fight each other, but found enough common ground to unite them until the trouble was passed. Emergency powers were used on a very limited scale, and there was never the serious threat of dictatorship which occurred in other countries.

A BUF rally at Olympia in June 1934 saw 'blackshirt' brutalities which shocked the nation.

Hatred of Jews has been seen in many countries throughout history. Being 'different' has caused the Jews to be blamed for all sorts of problems, such as plague in the Middle Ages.

4 The rise of fascism in Italy

Mussolini's followers celebrate outside the palace while their leader confers with the king within, 1922

Italian government was terribly corrupt and out of touch with the people. Elections were a farce and in the 75 years to 1922 there were 67 governments.

Fiume was supposed to be under international control. D'Annunzio held the port for over a year and was regarded as a hero by Italians, and especially by fascists.

Italy in 1919 was a country beset with problems. Italians hoped that peace would bring stability, glory, prosperity, and empire, but they were wrong. There was little stability. The Italian government was weak and corrupt, and could not control the post-war problems. There was little glory. Although victors, Italians could not forget the humiliating defeat at the battle of Caporetto (see page 25). There was prosperity for a few, but the majority of Italians lived in poverty. As for empire, Italy was grudgingly given the border territories of Trentino, South Tyrol, Trieste and Istria, but was denied the port of Fiume, and gained no empire in Africa (see page 38). Individuals and groups reacted quickly to these disappointments – for example: communists went on strike to achieve higher wages; in September 1919 the poet D'Annunzio seized the port of Fiume against the wishes of the government; and most significant of all, Mussolini created the fascist movement. In this atmosphere the democratic government was quickly overwhelmed.

Benito Mussolini

Mussolini had an unusual background. After a wild childhood he became in turn a teacher, a labourer, a vagrant, a soldier, and a newspaper writer. During these years his ideas formed, and they were extreme and often contradictory. For example, he was at first a socialist leader, a republican and anti-church, all of which were to change. During the First World War he had a chance to show his nationalism, and his description of the wounds he received in a mortar explosion in 1917 tells us something of his character – but was he brave, or just a boastful braggart?

I am proud to have reddened the road to Trieste with my own blood in the fulfilment of a dangerous duty. . . . I faced atrocious pain, my suffering was indescribable. I underwent practically all my operations without the aid of an anaesthetic. I had twenty-seven operations in one month; all except two were without anaesthetics.

After the war Mussolini gathered around him a group of ex-soldiers who formed the *fascio di combattimento*, or fascist squads. The origin of the term fascism is disputed, but one version is that the men in these squads were bound together by ties as close as the *fascinae*, the bundle of rods and axe which were a symbol of authority in ancient Rome.

These squads soon gained a reputation for violence. Their main target was the communists; communist officials, strikers, and anti-fascists were beaten up with truncheons or shot. Despite this violence, support for the fascists grew. People admired their strength, and Mussolini won much support by giving up some of his extreme ideas – for example his republicanism and anti-clericalism. Whereas in the elections of 1919 he had won only 5000 votes, his Partita Nazionale Fascista gained 314 seats in the parliament of 1921.

Republicanism – support of a state with no monarch.

Mussolini creates an image in the Chamber of Deputies

Mussolini now wanted unlimited control of Italy. He said to his followers in October 1922. 'I assure you in all solemnity that the hour has struck. Either they give us government or we shall take it by falling on Rome!' Fascist squads gathered in three great colums on the roads into Rome ready to march for power. In fact the 'March on Rome' was not necessary. The previous government under Giolitti had already fallen. The weak-willed King Victor Emmanuel was unwilling to risk confrontation with the fascists and summoned Mussolini by telegram. On 30 October 1922 he became the new prime minister. Consider the

Although there was no need for the March on Rome to go ahead, it did take place for propaganda purposes.

fascist programme, issued at the time of the 'March on Rome':

Fascists, Italians! The hour of the decisive battle has struck. Today Leaders and Legionaries have been put into force. The army, the last reserve and safeguard of the nation, must not take part in the struggle . . . nor does Fascism march against the members of the public administration, but against a class of imbecile and weak minded politicians, who for four long years have not known how to give a government to the nation.

The . . . productive bourgeoisie know that fascism wishes to give aid to all those forces which advance its economic expansion and well being.

The working classes, those in the fields and factories, the transport workers and the clerks, have nothing to fear from Fascism. Their just rights will be loyally preserved.

Fascism draws its sword to cut the many Gordian Knots which enmesh and strangle Italian life. We call upon Almighty God and on the spirit of the five hundred thousand dead to witness that only one impulse moves us, only one desire unites us: to contribute to the salvation and to the greatness of our country.

Having gained power, Mussolini wished to make himself secure. His tactics, both inside and outside government, were ruthless. On the streets of Italian towns, anti-fascists were beaten up or murdered. The most famous victim was Giocomo Matteotti, the secretary of the Socialist Party and an outspoken critic of the fascists. He was murdered in June 1924. Although it was quite clear who was responsible, neither the police, the courts, nor even the king would interfere. When challenged, Mussolini said

I now declare . . . that I assume full political moral and historical responsibility for all that has happened. . . . Gentlemen, Italy wants peace, tranquillity, calm in which to work. We will give her this tranquillity and calm, by means of love if possible, but by force if necessary.

Inside government, Mussolini bypassed the traditional governing body, the Cabinet, by setting up his own Grand Council. He gained control of parliament by passing the Acerbo law in 1923 which gave two thirds of seats to the party which gained most votes in the election. There was intimidation at the polls, and the fascists swept to victory. Other parties were in no position to stop Mussolini, and when in 1925 opposition deputies walked out in protest (an act known as the Aventine Secession) the fascists had just what they wanted. Finally by the terms of the Italian Decree Law of 1925, parliamentary government was ended, and Mussolini was now answerable only to the king.

Questions

1 What factors explain the rapid success of fascism in Italy?
2 Look carefully at the fascist programme quoted above. List the groups of people to whom it appeals, and say what fascism offers them.
3 Draw up a timeline to show Mussolini's progress to total power.

Mussolini – the image

Mussolini wished above all to create a magnificent image, both for himself and for fascism. His concern for the effect of his own appearance was constant. He wanted to be seen as an athlete, a sportsman, a musician, a thinker, a worker. These photographs show the image which he put forward to the public. To spread the idea that he worked hard, his staff were told to leave a light on in his office until late at night. In fact he did take many tasks upon himself, doing the work that a prime minister and seven cabinet ministers would normally be expected to do. Whether he did it well is another question. He ignored important matters of business while issuing orders about the number of buttons on uniforms or inspecting lists of minor civil servants who had reported for work after nine o'clock. What did people think of his image? One writer has said,

Mussolini the man was being replaced by the ludicrous legend. Press photos showed him in every garb imaginable, in riding kit, in yachting rig, in uniform and top boots, or bare-chested in the wheatfield, and at every possible activity – driving a sports car, haranguing a crowd, training wild animals, playing his violin. His portrait appeared on women's swimsuits and in babyfood advertisements, while entrepreneurs did a brisk trade in perfumed Mussolini soap at 2 lira a cake.

R. H. Collier, *Duce. The Rise and Fall of Benito Mussolini*, 1971

Another image of Mussolini

Mussolini did not realise that, for many, his image was ridiculous. He once confessed 'often I would like to be wrong, but so far it has never happened and events have always turned out just as I foresaw'.

Fascist propaganda

Mussolini wanted Italians to be good fascists throughout their lifetime. For this reason his first target was the young. Schools were little more than branches of the party, the curriculum being dominated by fascist ideas and the fascist version of history. Outside school, children aged from eight to fourteen were expected to join the Ballila, named after an Italian boy who, by an act of courage, had started a rising against the Austrian conquerors of Italy in 1746. At fourteen, boys would move on to the Avangardisti. On joining they were told

The Ballila on parade

Fascists, young Blackshirts! Today you have the great fortune and supreme privilege of taking the oath to the cause of the Fascist Revolution of the Fatherland. Remember also that fascism does not promise you honours, or jobs, or rewards, but only duty and fighting!

Throughout their time in these organisations young people were taught obedience, military discipline and physical training, and fascist culture; at eighteen, men joined the Fascist Party itself. Adult life, too, was organised for the state. Leisure facilities were controlled by the Dopolavaro, the National Institute for After Work Activities. This controlled such things as theatres, libraries, orchestras and sport. Achievement in the arts or the world of sport was boasted as the achievement of fascism. Victors were greeted with the sort of reception given to the emperors of ancient Rome. Marching displays, pageant, noise, were the characteristics of fascist activity.

Again, the question arises, how much were people convinced by all of this? Undoubtedly many were. Others tolerated Mussolini for reasons of self-preservation. As long as it seemed that they supported him, all was well for them. When Mussolini made his speeches from the balcony of his palace, government offices were closed and attendance at the speeches was compulsory. For many it may have been best not to resist, or to enjoy the benefits of being a party member, such as gurantees of the best jobs.

Mussolini also used the Church as an instrument of fascist propaganda. In his early years he had hated the Church and all it stood for – he even wrote a book called *God Does Not Exist*. However, once in power he saw that he had much to gain if he appeared to be a loyal churchman. Also, the fascists and the Church did have some common ground:
– Both were anti-communist.
– Both wanted to keep to ancient traditions.
– Both were against birth control.
– Both were against divorce.
– Both called for high morals of a kind – for example, the fascists punished people for adultery and swearing, and campaigned against such things as modern dancing, night life, and alcohol.

The conquest of Rome in 1870 was the last stage of the unification of Italy. The Pope, who thus lost his independence, opposed the Italian governments from that time onward.

Before Mussolini could call the Church his ally he needed to solve two problems. Firstly, there had been a quarrel between the Italian government and Church since 1870, when Italian troops had conquered Rome. Mussolini solved this in the Lateran Agreement of 1929 when the Pope was given the Vatican and £30 million in compensation. Secondly there was the problem of Catholic organisations and schooling which conflicted with fascist organisations. Children could only join the Ballila, and Catholic teaching in schools had declined. Adult organisations such as Catholic Action were also under attack in an attempt to make people loyal to fascism alone. This was solved by a compromise. Catholic action and youth organisations were allowed to continue, but were to keep to strictly religious affairs.

Many Catholics undoubtedly despised Mussolini – but he appeared to have the Pope's blessing, and this had tremendous propaganda value.

Mussolini liked to be referred to as 'the man sent by God to Italy' or 'our spiritual father', By order of the party, pronouns referring to him had to be capitalised like those referring to God.

Denis Mack-Smith, *Mussolini*, 1981

The police state in Italy

Totalitarian – where a government takes upon itself the right to control every aspect of life.

Many Italians were not convinced by Mussolini's propaganda and showed it, and for them the Fascist Party had an answer. Since gaining control of Italy, Mussolini had established totalitarian government. In

1926, after the fourth assassination attempt against him, the Defence of the State Act was passed which abolished other political parties and independent newspapers, established a political police force, and set up a new type of court – the Tribunal of State. Unlike the normal courts this was secret, swift, and intimidating. Its success lay not so much in what it actually achieved, but in the terror which it inspired. It could impose the death penalty, or send convicted anti-fascists to penal settlements such as the one on the island of Lipari.

As Mussolini's government increased its hold, so the police state intensified. Eventually there were separate police forces, and vast sums of money were spent on surveillance of foreigners and suspected persons. Anti-fascists could not rely on justice. Some, such as the writers of the newspaper *Italia Libera* were assassinated, while others were beaten up by fascist gangs, the *squadristi*. The fascist guards also meted out summary justice. After the fourth attempt on Mussolini's life,

Squadristi – the fascist squads notorious for their brutality.

the presumed marksman, a boy of sixteen was lynched on the spot by fascist guards and his body was torn to pieces in a horrifyingly macabre ceremony. The boy was almost certainly an innocent bystander, and there were no very convincing eye-witnesses except Mussolini himself, who gave two contradictory descriptions of his assailant, neither of which fitted the youth.

Denis Mack-Smith, *Mussolini*, 1981

Even so, two of the boy's relatives were subsequently imprisoned as accomplices.

Mussolini's rule, so often amusing in a farcical way, had much that was in common with its Nazi counterpart in Germany.

Mussolini flexes his muscles to join the harvesting – the land has been reclaimed from the Pontine marshes

Questions

1 Use the documents and photographs to explain why Collier describes Mussolini as 'the ludicrous legend'.
2 Describe the ways in which fascism won or forced the support of the Italian people.

Mussolini and the economy

Certain features of the Italian economy in the 1920s and 1930s might have convinced the casual observer that it was in good shape. For example, four thousand miles of new roads were built, with four hundred new bridges. The railways were modernised, and six hundred new telephone exchanges further improved communications. New aquaducts were built, and a major rebuilding plan was begun in Rome. Mussolini was particularly proud of the draining of the Pontine marshes. In 1932 he inaugurated Littoria, the first town to be built there, with these words:

Once, in order to find work, it was necessary to go beyond the alps or across the ocean. Today the land is here. It is here that we have conquered a new province. It is here that we have waged and shall wage true war operations. This is the war we prefer.

Mussolini liked to speak of his plans for the economy in terms of battles. Some of the battles, such as the battle for land reclamation, he won. Others he lost, and were severely damaging to the Italian economy.

The birth rate battle was Mussolini's drive for a larger population. Of course, his main motive here was to breed a great army of fascists for the future, but the economic impact of such a campaign was important. 'What,' said Mussolini, 'are 40 million Italians compared to 90 million Germans and 200 million Slavs.' To bridge the gap, he urged parents to bear as many children as possible. Bachelors were taxed heavily, while fathers received better jobs and concessions on bus and train and fuel prices. Women were given awards for child-bearing. Mussolini considered twelve children to be ideal, and on Christmas Eve 1933 he gave a reception for 93 women who, between them, had over 1300 children. Army officers had to salute pregnant women as they went by.

What Mussolini didn't take into account was the effect of such a policy. Italy already had high unemployment and inflation, both of which would be made worse by a population explosion. However, the impact was not too great as, despite his policy, the birth rate continued to fall!

The battle for the lira also had severe repercussions for the economy. As a matter of pride Mussolini wanted to maintain a rate of 100 lira to the pound. However, this made Italian exports very expensive, and some companies closed because they were unable to compete.

The battle for wheat was another disaster. True, Mussolini's target of higher wheat production was achieved, but it would have been better for Italy to import cheap foreign wheat and concentrate on what Italy could best produce – oil, grapes, and fruit.

Perhaps Mussolini's most ambitious scheme for the economy was the corporative system. The idea here was that all industry would be regulated by a corporation consisting of employers and employees. This would be for the good of all classes and the state, as it would involve high production, no strikes, and good working conditions. In practice the system didn't work. Some powerful employers had influence within the Fascist Party, and they used the corporations to control their workforce in their own interests. Worse, the corporations were run by large bureaucratic offices which duplicated each others' work and were yet another heavy burden on the economy.

Question

Divide your page into two columns. Draw up a 'balance sheet' of the achievements and failures of Mussolini's economic policy. Weighing them against each other, was he 'in credit' or not?

Mussolini's foreign policy

Mussolini's greatest ambition was to found an empire. He looked back with horror at the time when the Italian army was defeated at the battle of Adowa, Abyssinia (now Ethiopia), in 1896:

> That day I was ill. At about 10.00 a. m. one of my school friends . . . ran into the dormitory with an open newspaper shouting 'Read! Read!' I grabbed the paper . . . from the first page to the last it talked of nothing but the disastrous battle – ten thousand dead and 72 cannons lost. Those figures are still hammering in my skull.

Mussolini's fascist state was first of all a military state, and he wanted to build up armed forces to rival the greatest in the world. Vast sums of money were spent on armaments. However corruption in Italy was rife, and much of this money went into private pockets rather than on planes and guns. The chief of police, Carmine Senise, remembered:

> His gullibility encouraged everybody to let him believe one thing for another. Once, for instance, he was taken to see aviation field on which over a thousand planes were lined up to be shown off. Proudly Mussolini admired that superb display of force, and never knew that only a few of those planes could rise from the ground and fly.

Italy had taken the colony of Eritrea in 1890, but it proved difficult to govern and Ethiopian tribesmen defeated an Italian army at Adowa in 1896.

Mussolini's air force. But would it get off the ground?

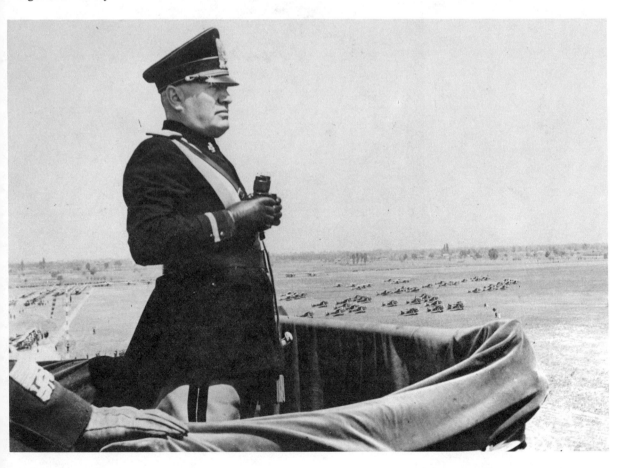

Galeazzo Ciano, Mussolini's son-in-law, wrote in his diary:

The military makes a big ado with a lot of names. They multiply the number of divisions, but in reality they are so small that they scarcely have more than the strength of regiments. The ammunition depots are lacking. Artillery is outmoded. General Valle [undersecretary of aviation] made the statement that there were 3006 first class planes, while the information service of the navy says they amount to only 982.

But what is the Duce doing? His attention seems to be spent mostly on matters of form. There is hell to pay if the 'present arms' is not done right, or if an officer does not know how to lift his legs in the Roman step. . . . In spite of my formal charges in connection with the efficiency of our aviation he has done nothing, absolutely nothing. . . . Does he fear the truth so much that he is unwilling to listen?

Italy's forces were not put to a true test in the early years, and these deficiencies did not show. Mussolini's first foreign policy venture was the reconquest of Abyssinia, and revenge of Adowa. He built up a large force including ten divisions of Italians and two native divisions, with aircraft support. On 3 October 1935, they crossed into Abyssinia. Haile Selassie, Emperor of Abyssinia, appealed to the League of Nations, but

Abyssinia's finest – the White Horse troop of the imperial cavalry

while international action was indecisive, the Italian forces moved forward. And Mussolini interfered as much as he was able:

Giving orders excited him, gave him a feeling of participation in the war; as if he smelled the gunpowder and saw the streaming blood, he became war crazed and was seized by the frenzy revealed in his innumerable letters and telegrams to military commanders. . . . 'I authorise you to use gas as a last resort to overcome the enemy's resistance. . . . I authorise the summary shooting of subjects. . .'

Laura Fermi, *Mussolini*, 1961

On 9 May Mussolini addressed a crowd at the Palazzo Venezia:

A great event is accomplished: today, 9th May of the fourteenth year of the Fascist era, the fate of Abyssinia is sealed . . . The African victory stands in the history of our Fatherland whole and pure as the fallen legionnaires and those who survived dreamed it and wanted it. At last Italy has an Empire!

Mussolini intended to keep this empire. He went on to conquer Somalia, and then appointed Cesare de Vecchi as governor.

To show his disrespect for local customs de Vecchi used to ride into mosques on horseback. True to his habit as a *squadrista* he ordered the burning and sacking of rebellious villages, and to increase fascist prestige, the shooting of captured prisoners, hundreds at a time.

Denis Mack-Smith, *Mussolini*, 1981

Questions

1 Why was Abyssinia so important to Mussolini?
2 (a) How much credit do you think Mussolini deserved for the victory in Abyssinia?
  (b) Does he seem to have been a success as the head of the armed forces?

Italian foreign policy and the Spanish civil war

In 1931 the Spanish king, Alfonso XIII, abdicated and was replaced by a republic run by elected governments. There were many parties with opposing views on the future of Spain, and the only way to get a majority to rule was for a number of them to join together in coalitions. Until 1933 Spain was ruled by a coalition of right-wing groups. From 1933 to 1936 left-wing groups took over. Neither of these satisfied Spanish extremists. On one side there were communists and anarchists who plotted to overthrow the government. On the other extreme were the Falangists. This right-wing group wanted to replace the elected government with a fascist regime modelled on Italy. From 1934 these Falangists, including generals in the army, had been plotting with Mussolini, who was delighted to support them. Not only was he flattered, but also he saw his own chances:

'Right' tends towards conservatism and capitalism, 'Left' tends towards socialism or communism.

As a maximum goal, Mussolini must have set his sights on gaining control of the West Mediterranean by establishing naval bases in the Balearic Islands and obtaining the active support of a friendly Spain.

J. F. Coverdale, *Italian Intervention in the Spanish War*, 1975

This could well involve the expulsion of the British from Gibraltar, which would effectively turn the Mediterranean into an 'Italian lake'. The civil war began on 18 July 1936, when General Francisco Franco, leader of the Falangists, was flown from exile in the Canary Islands into Spain. Immediately Spain divided into armed camps, fighting for

Thumbs up from Franco, celebrating the capture of Bilbao

different causes. Fascists were fighting communists over political ideals. Downtrodden peasants were fighting the rich, and especially wealthy churchmen. Basques in northern Spain and Catalonians in the north-east were fighting for their independence. Thus the rising was welcomed by some and bitterly opposed by others. At the outset the north and west fell to the fascists or nationalists, while the south, east and north-east remained loyal to the government. Within these regions, anyone who supported the other side was likely to die.

Personal, class and ideological fury ran riot. More than half the total deaths occurred behind the fronts, for in both Nationalist and Republican camps spontaneous terrorism was followed by scientific terror.

David Mitchell, *The Spanish Civil War*, 1982

The spontaneous terrorism tended to occur on the republican side, and was particularly directed at the wealthy, and churchmen. An American journalist, H. E. Knoblauch, wrote,

Singly and in clusters they lay along the roadway, riddled with bullets . . . some of the bodies were horribly mutilated. Some were left with pieces of cardboard on their chests on which were scrawled the alleged offences for which they had been killed. In the first days . . . there were many bodies of priests and nuns amongst the victims. We could generally identify them by the rosaries and bits of religious clothing jammed into their mouths by the executioners. Some of the victims were lined up against the wall in firing squad style. Others were told to run and were shot down like rabbits as they zigzagged away.

Nationalist terror was organised. In the face of resistance, the fascist general, Quiepo de Llano, announced over the radio:

In various villages of which I have heard, right-wing people are being held prisoner and threatened with barbarous fates. I want to make known my system with regard to this. For every person killed I shall kill ten and perhaps even exceed that number.

The leader of these village movements may believe they can flee; they are wrong. Even if they hide beneath the earth, I shall dig them out; even if they're already dead I shall kill them again.

In the face of strikes he said,

. . . anyone caught inciting others to strike or striking himself shall be shot, immediately. Don't be frightened. If someone tries to force you to strike I authorise you to kill him like a dog and you will be free of all responsibility.

Much famous literature came out of this war including Orwell's *Homage to Catalonia* and Hemingway's *For Whom the Bell Tolls*.

In the face of massive aid from the fascist states for the nationalists, the work of the non-intervention committee was to some a sentence of death on the republic.

The Spanish civil war quickly became the focus of world opinion. Many individuals who believed strongly in the cause of right or left went to fight there. Most famous of these were the left-wing 'international brigades'. George Orwell, the writer, joined one of these. The republic hoped for official support from Britain and France. Britain, however, led the way to the forming of a farcical non-interventionist committee, which refused help, despite knowledge of the fascist alliance. Only Russia sent aid to help the left.

No quarter given – civilian casualties of the war

Bitter street fighting amongst the ruins of Alcazar, defended by the rebels

Mussolini poured in arms and men. Here is a summary of Italian war material sent to Spain, during the period July 1936 to March 1939:

Cannon 1801	Fighter aircraft 414
Mortars 1426	Bombers 213
Machine guns 3436	Other aircraft 132
Tanks 197	
Vehicles 6791	
	Officers 5037
	Men 67 738
Ammunition 320m rounds	Air Force 5 699
Artillery shells 7.7m	

J. F. Coverdale, *Italian Intervention in the Spanish Civil War*, 1975

An alliance made firmer by the Spanish civil war – Mussolini and Hitler

Junkers – German bombers.

Undoubtedly these forces had an important effect on the war. In particular the nationalists had few pilots, and the Italians filled the gap. Italian submarines compensated for the lack of nationalist seapower, and even sunk Russian shipping.

Steadily the war went the nationalists' way. At the same time, on the international front, the fascist alliance was formally sealed. Italy, isolated after Abyssinia, now forgot differences with Germany over Austria and the two countries drew together. Mussolini said 'This Berlin-Rome line is an axis around which can revolve all those European states with a will to collaboration and peace'. Thereafter the fascist countries were known as the Axis powers. However, it soon became obvious which was the dominant partner. Italy, the first fascist state, was eclipsed by Hitler's Germany. In September 1937 Mussolini went to Munich and met Hitler. He was deeply impressed, and on his return to Italy introduced goose-stepping into the army and anti-semitism into the country, in imitation of Hitler's fascism.

In Spain, too, it was German involvement which stole the headlines. Whereas Mussolini wanted a triumph for fascism, Hitler's motives were more sinister. As Göring said, this was an opportunity to 'test my young Luftwaffe in this or that technical respect'. If the Spanish civil war is remembered for one thing, it is for the bombing of Guernica, in 1937. Father Alberto de Onaindai remembered:

Late in the afternoon of April 26th I was going by car to rescue my mother and my sisters . . . we reached the outskirts of Guernica just before six o'clock. The streets were busy with the traffic of market day. Suddenly we heard the siren, and trembled.

Soon an aeroplane appeared over Guernica [followed by] a squadron of seven planes followed a little later by six more, and this in turn by a squadron of five more. All of them were Junkers. Meanwhile Guernica was seized by a terrible panic. . . .

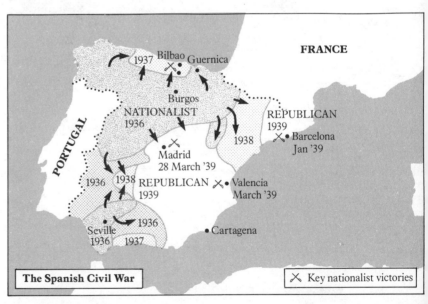

The Spanish Civil War

✕ Key nationalist victories

For more than an hour these eighteen planes dropped bomb after bomb on Guernica. The sound of the explosions and of the crumbling houses cannot be imagined. . . . Bombs fell by thousands. Later we saw the bomb craters. Some were sixteen metres in diameter and eight metres deep.

The aeroplanes left around seven o'clock and then there came another wave of them this time flying at immense altitude. They were dropping incendiary bombs on our martyred city. The new bombardment lasted thirty-five minutes, sufficient to transform the town into an enormous furnace. Even then I realised the terrible purpose of this new act of vandalism. They were dropping incendiary bombs to try to convince the world that the Basques fired their own city.

When it grew dark the flames of Guernica were reaching to the sky, and the clouds took on the colour of blood, and our faces too shone with the colour of blood.

Guernica symbolises two things: the destruction of the Basques and Spanish republicanism, and the coming of Nazism.

Picasso's La Guernica – *an alternative view of the horrors of war*

Questions

1 Why, and with what effect, was Mussolini involved in the Spanish civil war?
2 Why do you think that this war was so bitterly fought?
3 What explains the nationalist victory?
4 Why do you think the bombing of Guernica has been seen as such a significant event?
5 'Mussolini succeeded in creating a successful image. In reality he was a failure.' Use all of the evidence from this chapter to decide whether you agree with all or part of this statement.

The rise of fascism in Germany

Adolf Hitler

In 1909 Reinhold Hanisch, a tramp, found a bed for a night in a dosshouse filled with the down-and-outs of Vienna. Later Hanisch was to remember that night, and his first meeting with a man who was to be his partner for a year in a degrading search for a meagre living:

There sat next to . . . me a man who had nothing on except an old torn pair of trousers – Hitler. His clothes were being cleaned of lice, since for days he had been wandering about without a roof and in a terribly neglected condition.

It was the experiences of these years which shaped the thinking of Adolf Hitler. For him, these were bitter times. He had little success at school, and had failed to get a place at art college. He was unemployed and spent much of his time in lazy brooding. It was at this time that he first blamed the Jews for his plight, and possibly they were a scapegoat for his own inferiority. With the First World War came moments of triumph. He joined the army, and received the Iron Cross for bravery. According to a German school textbook, published in 1942, he was on dispatch duty in the trenches, crawling along under heavy fire:

But nothing could stop a man as brave as Hitler. He leapt from one shell crater to another, fleet as a deer, brave as a lion, doing his sacred duty. Suddenly he was confronted by a detachment of Frenchmen.

What to do? Capitulate? Not Hitler. Not our Führer. Never would he do that! He raised his gun to his shoulder. 'Surrender' he commanded 'Behind me is a whole company of soldiers. Anyone who makes a false move will be shot'

The Frenchmen threw away their weapons and raised their hands in surrender. Single-handed, Adolf Hitler took them prisoner.

Heil Unserem Führer, (Official biography for school use)

The defeat of Germany in November 1918 came as a terrible shock to Hitler. He was in hospital when the news came to him:

Everything went black before my eyes as I staggered back to my ward and buried my aching head between the blankets and the pillow . . . the following days were terrible to bear, and the nights still worse. . . . During these nights my hatred increased, hatred for the originators of this dastardly crime.

A. Hitler, *Mein Kampf*

The idea that Germany had been betrayed occurs throughout Hitler's later writing and speeches:

We want to call to account the November Criminals of 1918. It cannot be that two million Germans should have fallen in vain and that afterwards one should sit down at the same table with traitors. No, we do not pardon, we demand vengeance! The dishonouring of the nation must cease. For betrayers of the Fatherland, and informers, the gallows is the proper place.

Adolf Hitler and seven friends

With this thought in mind, Hitler decided to enter politics.

After the abdication of the Kaiser a new democratic government, the Weimar Republic, had been established. The early days of the republic in Germany had not been easy, and Hitler was one of many extremists ready to plot its overthrow. In 1919 the Spartacist rising attempted to set up communism in Berlin. In 1920 the Kapp *Putsch* (coup) tried to set up a right-wing government. Neither succeeded, but it was in these unsettled conditions that Hitler first attended a meeting of another extreme party, the German Workers' Party. When Hitler first visited the beer cellar where meetings were held, the party had about forty members. At a committee which he attended a few days later party funds stood at 7.50 German marks. Even so, Hitler found much in common with this small group, and by 1920 he was working full time on party propaganda. Public interest in the party was growing. In particular, there were many ex-servicemen who approved of party policy – but there were also contacts with the army, the police, and business. By 1923 Hitler felt ready to act. In November, backed by a force of brown-shirted storm troopers, he arrested some Bavarian

This was to become the National Socialist Party, or NSDAP, commonly abbreviated as Nazi.

Fascism attracted ex-soldiers – the NSDAP in 1924

Adolf Hitler's powerful friend, General Ludendorff (centre), and a future rival, Ernst Röhm (foreground). Before the coup of 1923

This event, the Munich *Putsch*, was regarded by Nazis as one of the most significant moments in their history.

Mein Kampf, (My Struggle) – one of the worst books ever written, and which few people outside Germany took seriously.

politicians at Munich and announced that he was setting up a national government. Hitler hoped that there were enough important people on his side to carry the rebellion through. In fact, politicians, police and the army wavered and finally stood against him. His supporters were dispersed by gunfire and Hitler arrested. There were two main outcomes: Hitler was now well known, and was regarded by many as a hero; and he was sent to jail, where he served only one year of a five-year sentence, and wrote his book, *Mein Kampf*.

By the time of his release he had decided on his policy for the future. The national socialist German Workers' Party was not a force to be reckoned with – but Hitler was confident of success by legal means.

When I resume work it will be necessary to pursue a new policy. Instead of working to achieve power by armed conspiracy, we shall have to hold our noses and enter the Reichstag against the Catholic and Marxist deputies. If outvoting them takes longer than out-shooting them, at least the results will be guaranteed by their own constitution.

The policy of national socialism

National socialism, or Nazism, had much in common with fascism in Italy. One notable feature is the lack of a firm philosophy or programme. Hitler said 'all programmes are vain; the decisive thing is human will, sound vision, manly courage, sincerity of faith.'

Even so, some basic principles behind Nazism can be identified.

Nazism is *nationalistic*. Nazis believed that:

The German people, the Aryans, are a superior race. They are the culture creators.

It is natural that the Aryans should win an empire with more living space [*Lebensraum*] in the lands to the east of Germany.

The lesser races, such as the Slavs, are only culture-borrowing races. They should become servants of the master race.

The inferior race, the Jews, is a culture-destroying race. This race should be cast out.

Nazism is *socialistic*:

Socialism [to the Nazis] means all classes working together in the national interest.

Nazism is *totalitarian*:

The Nazi government must have total control over every aspect of life. Government will be in the hands of one person, a genius, a hero, with total responsibility for ruling on behalf of the pure race in the national interest.

Such policies as these, which underlie Nazi beliefs, hardly seem to be vote-catchers. In many ways early Nazism can be recognised by what it stood against rather than what it stood for.

Nazism is *against democracy*:

The invention of democracy is most intimately related to a quality which in recent times here grows to be a real disgrace, to wit, the cowardice of a great part of our so called leadership. What luck to be able to hide behind the skirts of a so-called majority in all decisions of any real importance.

The parliament arrives at some decision whose consequences may be ever so ruinous – nobody bears any responsibility for this, no one can be taken to account.

A. Hitler *Mein Kampf*

Nazism is *against communism*:

The Jewish doctrine of Marxism rejects the aristocratic principle of nature and replaces the eternal privelege of power and strength by the mass of number and their dead weight. Thus it denies the value of personality in man . . . the result of such a law could only be chaos, on earth it could only be destruction for the inhabitants of this planet.

A. Hitler, *Mein Kampf*

Nazism is *anti-semitic*:

Was there any shady undertaking, any form of foulness, especially in cultural life, in which at least one Jew did not participate? On putting the probing knife carefully to that kind of abscess one immediately discovered, like a maggot in a putrescent body, a little Jew who was often blinded by the sudden light.

A. Hitler, *Mein Kampf*

Nazism *is against international capitalism*. An example of this can be seen from the text of a Nazi leaflet of the time:

Attention! Gravedigger at work!
Middle Class Citizens! Retailers! Craftsmen! Tradesmen! A new blow aimed at your ruin is being carried out in Hanover. The present system enables the gigantic concern
WOOLWORTH (AMERICA)
supported by finance capital to build a new vampire business in the centre of the city.

Questions

1 Consider this official army account of Hitler's medal-winning action, written soon after the event:

On one of Hitler's trips out front in June he got a glimpse of something in a trench that looked like a French helmet. He crept forward and saw four poilus (infantryman). Hitler pulled out his pistol . . . and began shouting orders in German as though he had a company of soldiers. He delivered his four prisoners to Colonel Von Tubeuf personally and was commended. 'There was no circumstance or situation' recalled Tubeuf 'that would have prevented him from volunteering for the most difficult, arduous, and dangerous tasks and he was always ready to sacrifice his life and tranquillity for his Fatherland and for others.'

(a) In what ways does this account agree with the textbook account?
(b) In what ways does it differ, and how would you explain the differences?

2 Use the swastika as the basis of a diagram to show what Nazism stands for and against. Briefly define each term.

3 Examine the extracts which show what Nazism stands against. Four of them are from Hitler's writings, the last from a handbill.
(a) Select words or phrases in the sources which display forcefully the hatred inspired by Nazism.
(b) How much fact is offered in support of these arguments and how much is opinion?

Factors which helped Nazism to grow

Thirteen years after his first visit to the German Workers' Party, Hitler was able to look back on an astonishing success story:

I cast my eyes back to the time when with six other unknown men, I founded this association, when I spoke before eleven . . . twenty, thirty, fifty persons. When I recall how after a year I had won sixty-four members for the movement. I must confess that that which has today been created, when a stream of millions is flowing into our movement, is something unique in German history.

To most people today there is little in Nazi policy to show why the movement attracted millions. The reasons for their support owe much to the background of the 1920s in Germany, and to the way in which Hitler persuaded the people to accept Nazism.

1 The humiliation of Germany

When Germany had signed the Treaty of Versailles, optimists had hoped that it would keep to the spirit of Wilson's Fourteen Points – but not so. The treaty showed that the Allied powers wanted revenge – to punish Germany for the 1914–18 war, and make sure it would never again threaten peace. The final cost of reparations was to be the sum of 132 billion gold marks, to be paid by annual instalments of two billion marks and a tax of 26 per cent on exports.

The humiliation did not end there, and three times during the 1920s salt was rubbed into the wound. In December 1922, because of a technical non-payment of reparations, French and Belgian troops were moved into the Ruhr, Germany's industrial heartland – 80 per cent of German pig iron was produced there, and more than 80 per cent of its coal.

The response of one young man who lived in the Ruhr is typical:

There has never been such a brutal act of violence without any justification whatsoever. . . .

It should not have surprised the French that they were met with a wave of rage and hatred – not a raging fire, but an icy, grim silence of the deepest contempt. Shops closed down, the railroads stopped running, and telephone connections were cut off. Passive resistance started.

The brutal conduct of the French invaders soon brought me around to the desire to join an organisation which would turn the passive into active resistance.

P. H. Merkl, Political Violence under the Swastika, 1975

French troops occupy the Ruhr, 1923

In 1924, and again in 1929, the reparations paid by Germany were renegotiated – the Dawes plan, and the Young plan. Payments were fixed to a scale which would rise until 1965, and then decrease steadily until 1988. Hitler was quick to criticise the 'surrender of the human dignity of the German and the pacifist cowardice' of the negotiators. His propagandists called the agreement

the death penalty passed on the unborn. The German people have been forced to tread between Versailles . . . and London, the tragic path . . . into commercial serfdom. With the Dawes Plan the last remnants of our sovereignty were mortaged . . . a development that converted a people of heroes into an army of Helots (slaves). . . .

Versailles was a bleeding wound. The Dawes–Young Plan is a people with a wasting disease. Credits and loans are only shots of morphine.

2 The economy in ruin

The Germany economy, broken by war, was further damaged by reparations and the economic slump which characterised Europe between the wars. The first great economic problem was inflation, which reached its height at a time when the government was printing money to pay strikers who were resisting the French occupation of the Ruhr.

The kite, worth more than the paper money it is made from

Date	Dollar quotation for the Mark
July	4.2
January 1919	8.9
July	14.0
January 1920	64.8
July	39.5
January 1921	64.9
July	76.7
January 1922	191.8
July	493.2
January 1923	17 972.0
July	353 412.0
August	4 620 455.0
September	98 860 00.0
October	25 260 208 00.0
November	4 200 000 000 000.0

Inflation was a catastrophe to almost everyone. One story recalls:

I was the advertising chief of a rubber factory. That was during the inflation. I had a monthly salary of two billion marks. We were paid twice a day, and then everybody had a half hour's leave so that he could rush out to the stores and buy something before the next quotation on the dollar came out, at which time the money would lose half its value.

Craig, *Germany 1886–1945*, 1981

Inflation hurt the middle classes, whose savings were wiped out and who had to sell treasured possessions at ridiculous prices. Those who suffered most were the young, the old, and the sick. A survey in Berlin in 1923 showed that 31 per cent of children were unable to work because of diseases related to malnutrition; 8.2 per cent of schoolchildren had rickets, as against 0.8 per cent in 1913. Discontented people flocked to Nazism, and it was in this disturbed atmosphere that Hitler felt confident enough to launch the Munich *Putsch*. However, between 1924 and 1929 the economy recovered, and the democratic government of Stresemann won back much of the ground at the expense of extreme parties. Then, in 1929 a worse slump occurred with the Wall Street Crash (see page 164) and dreadful economic depression in Europe. This time unemployment was the greatest problem, and numbers unemployed rose steeply.

(see page 164)

Gustav Stresemann was highly respected for his efforts to regain the friendship of other powers. This policy was despised by Hitler.

September 1929	1 320 000
September 1930	3 000 000
September 1931	4 350 000
September 1932	5 102 000
January 1933	6 000 000

Again, the Nazi star began to rise. Hitler did not offer any magic cure for economic problems – but his very effective attacks on the government won much support.

3 The weaknesses of the Weimar Republic

Hitler's attacks on the Weimar government were all the more effective because the government did not appear to be working. Strong government was needed, yet no party could get a majority in the Reichstag. Weimar democracy, for most people, meant weakness, and compared badly with the traditional autocratic rule to which Germany was accustomed. The reasons for this were largely the fault of the system, which in a way was too democratic.

Reichstag – the German parliament.

The voting system was proportional representation, and it gave a number of seats in the Reichstag according to each party's proportion of the total votes. This meant that there were a large number of parties, extreme groups were able to survive, and no single party gained a majority. This resulted in what one historian has described as 'a game of musical chairs as coalitions were made and unmade and ministries formed and reformed'.

Even so, while conditions were not too bad, government muddled through. From 1930, when government was in a permanent state of crisis, it didn't. The Weimar constitution did allow for such a state of emergency by giving special powers to the president. In normal times the president had substantial power – to appoint the chancellor, to command the armed forces, and to order elections. In time of emergency, Article 48 of the constitution could be applied:

President – head of state, directly elected. He appointed the chancellor, usually leader of the largest party in the Reichstag.

Should public order and safety be seriously disturbed or threatened, the President may take the necessary measures to restore public order and safety; in case of need he may use armed force and he may for the time being, declare the fundamental rights of the citizen to be wholly or partly in abeyance.

From 1930 a succession of governments – under Chancellors Müller, Bruning, von Papen, and Schleicher – governed by presidential decree. Hitler wanted to have this total power in his own hands – by securing enough support to become chancellor, and then, by changing the constitution, to free himself from the control of the president. The table of election results below shows the rise of Nazi support until they became a major force in German politics:

Date	Nazi vote	Seats won	Rank order
1928	810 000	12	9th
1930	6 410 000	107	2nd
1932 (July)	13 745 000	230 (37%)	1st
1932 (Nov)	11 745 000	196 (33%)	1st

Nazi tactics

The conditions were right for the growth of Nazism, but even so Hitler had to win popular support if he was to take power 'legally'. Some people may have been attracted to Nazi policies, but probably the majority were carried along on a wave of unthinking fervour, whipped up by Nazi fanatics.

Youth drummers beat out the Nazi message

Hitler and his propagandists realised the power of radio

1 The power of oratory

A Nazi later remembered:

I don't know how to describe the emotions that swept over me as I heard Adolf Hitler. His words were like a scourge. When he spoke of the disgrace of Germany, I felt ready to spring on any enemy. His appeal to German manhood was like a call to arms; the gospel he preached, a sacred truth . . . I forgot everything but the man. Then, glancing around I saw that his magnetism was holding these thousands as one. Of course I was ripe for this experience. I was a man of thirty-two, weary with disgust and disillusionment, a wanderer seeking a cause, a patriot without a channel for his patriotism, a yearner after the heroic without a hero. The intense will of the man, the passion of his sincerity seemed to flow from him into me. I experienced an exultation that could be likened only to religious conversion.

2 The power of intimidation

The Nazis had, from the outset, a military wing known as the SA. The oath of the SA began:

SA – stormtroopers or brownshirts. Hitler's muscle created in the early days of the German Workers' Party.

As a member of the storm troop of the NSDAP I pledge myself its storm flag: to be always ready to stake life and limb in the struggle for the aims of the movement, to give absolute military obedience to my military superiors and leaders . . .

Here is one account of the SA in action at a meeting of their opponents, the Bavarian League, whose leader Ballerstedt was due to speak.

NS youths had early on taken seats near the speakers platform and . . . were distributed as well through the hall. When Hitler . . . appeared in the hall he was greeted by his followers with applause. His arrival gave the cue for the violence that followed. . . . Ballerstedt pushed his way through to the platform, but could not speak because the National Socialists were all the time shouting 'Hitler'. . . . Ballerstedt declared that anybody who tried to disturb the meeting would be charged with disturbing the peace. . . . After this the young people on the platform surrounded him, beat him up, and pushed him down the platform steps. Ballerstedt received a head injury which bled badly. . . . A fairly strong group of state police then cleared the hall.

Münchner Neueste Nachrichten, September, 1921

Right: What makes this such a fine example of Nazi propaganda?

Far right: Hitler appealed to many sentiments

The Nazi poster promises work and bread

3 Electioneering and propaganda

Hitler was a brilliant electioneer with tremendous energy:

Once more eternally on the move, work has to be done standing, walking, driving, flying. The most urgent conferences are held on the stairs, in the hall, at the door, on the way to the station . . . one is carried by train, motor car, and aeroplanes criss-cross through Germany.

Mass rallies, the use of radio, and rapid travel by plane (an innovation in those days) enabled Hitler to get to the people to convey his ideas in the way he like best – the spoken word. However, the effectiveness of Nazi propaganda can also be seen in these pictures.

Questions

1 Use the documents and text in the section 'The humiliation of Germany' to show what the Nazi propagandist meant when he said
   (a) The death penalty passed on the unborn.
   (b) Commercial serfdom.
   (c) Versailles was a bleeding wound
2 It is quite easy (and worthwhile) to put unemployment figures on to a bar – or line graph. But how can you graphically show inflation figures? Is there a better way to show the extent of inflation?
3 What was the effect of the German proportional voting system on the success of minority or extreme parties in winning seats? Use the election figures on page 70 to illustrate your answer.

4 In essay form, describe the various ways in which the Nazis
  campaigned for votes.

Note: The next section (pages 73–79) deals with Hitler's seizure of
power. You may find it helpful to answer question 1 (page 79), as you
work through the section.

*The Social Democrats provide a
different view of the swastika*

Hitler's seizure of power in Germany, 1933

Hitler's success was a grave concern to other parties. For a time the SA
and SS were banned, but they continued their activities out of uniform.
Some people in government said that the whole party should be
abolished, because it threatened the constitution. Yet Nazism was
allowed to grow further. Some feared revolution if the Nazis were
banned. Others thought the movement would fizzle out. Others still
hoped that Nazism could be used to further their own aims.

The turning point for Hitler came in 1933. The five elections of 1932
had produced a succession of chancellors who failed to rule effectively,
and government had passed from the Reichstag to the president. In
their jockeying for power, men such as Papen and Schleicher needed
Hitler's support – but Hitler was only interested in power for himself.
However, the election results of 1932 had shown that he could wait no
longer. In the January election the Nazis had won 39.6 per cent of the
the vote. By November Hitler's vote had fallen by two million. He
could not risk further loss of popularity, or the possibility that the SA
would take power into their own hands, and start a revolution.

The answer came from Papen, a friend of President Hindenburg, and
a man who had himself failed as chancellor. He proposed that Hitler be
made chancellor, himself vice-chancellor and that the cabinet be rigged
– with only two other Nazis – so that Hitler could be controlled.
Reluctantly, Hitler agreed. His next target was to obtain a sufficient
majority in the Reichstag to be voted emergency powers.

The Nazis stepped up their election campaign, encouraging their
supporters and intimidating their opposition. The campaign was in full
swing when, on 27 February 1933, the Reichstag building was set on
fire, and this proved to be a key to Nazi success.

Hindenburg – German general of
the First World War who
emerged with a high reputation
and became president in 1925.

Using the evidence: the Reichstag fire

A The report of Rudolph Diels, head of Prussian political police, on
arriving at the Reichstag:

A few officers of my department were already interrogating Marinus Van der
Lubbe. Naked from the waist upward, smeared with dirt and sweating, he sat
in front of them, breathing heavily. He panted as if he had completed a
tremendous task. There was a wild, triumphant gleam in the burning eyes of

The Reichstag in flames

DEM DEUTSCHEN VOLKE

Reichsmarshal Hermann Göring, First World War air-ace, an early Nazi, and creator of the Luftwaffe. He was hated by many but held the confidence of Hitler to the very end.

his pale, haggard young face. I read the communist pamphlets he carried in his trouser pockets.

B Report of Martin Sommerfeldt, Göring's press officer, on his account of the fire and how it was received, made after the Second World War:

I learned that the fire was discovered at 9 p.m. by a civilian who notified the nearest policeman. The latter alerted a police patrol, the police alerted the fire brigade. The policeman saw a man tugging wildly at a curtain over one of the large panes in the lobby and fired a shot at him. When the people entered the building they found burning firelighters everywhere, which suggested arson. They managed to collect about a hundredweight of this material and arrested a man who seemed to be running beserk in the corridors.

Göring looked at it. 'That's sheer rubbish! [he said] It may be a good police report, but its not at all the kind of communique I have in mind. One hundredweight of incendiary material? No, ten or even a hundred.' And he added two noughts to my modest one.

'That is quite impossible minister! No one can possibly believe that a single man can have carried that load!'

'Nothing is impossible! Why mention a single man? There were ten or even twenty men! Don't you understand what's been happening? The whole thing was a signal for a Communist uprising! . . . They must have come through the tunnel.'

C Report of Rudolph Diels, head of Prussian political police, who joined Göring and Hitler on the balcony overlooking the fire:

Hitler turned to the assembled company. Now I saw that his face was purple with agitation and with the heat gathering in the dome. He shouted uncontrollably, as I had never seen him do before, as if he was going to burst. 'There will be no mercy now! Anyone who stands in our way will be cut down. The German people will not tolerate leniency. Every communist official will be shot where he is found, the communist deputies must be hanged this very night. Everybody in league with the communists must be arrested. There will no longer be any leniency for the Social Democrats either!'

D Statement of Dr Zirpin, detective inspector, 3 March 1933:

The scene of the crime and his activities there were described by Van der Lubbe in such detail – seats of fire, damage caused, trails left and paths taken – as only the incendiary himself could have supplied. Had he not been there himself he could not possibly have described and later demonstrated on the spot, all these facts. . . .

The strong suspicion that Van der Lubbe acted on the orders of Communist leaders is confirmed by these unequivocal facts – contact with workmen in welfare offices, at meetings etc., where he started discussion with them . . . on his arrest he was found to carry . . . communist leaflets in his pockets.

E Report of the Committee for Victims of German Fascism, 1933:

(1) Van der Lubbe is not a member, but an opponent of the Communist Party; no connection whatsoever can be traced between the Communist Party and the burning of the Reichstag.
(2) Van der Lubbe cannot have committed the crime alone.
(3) The incendiaries made use of the subterranean passage leading from the Reichstag to the house of the President of the Republic; that the happening of such a fire at the period in question was of great advantage to the National Socialists; that for these reasons grave grounds exist for suspecting that the Reichstag was set on fire by, or on behalf of, leading personalities of the Nazi party.

F Testimony of Karl van Ernst, SA Gruppenführer. He was killed in a purge in 1934. His testimony turned up in Paris soon afterwards:

I suggested to Göring that we use the subterranean passage . . . because that would minimise the risk of discovery. Goebbels insisted on postponing the fire from 25 February to 27 February because 26th was a Sunday, a day on which no evening papers appeared so that the fire could not be played up sufficiently for propaganda purposes. Göring and Goebbels agreed to throw suspicion on the communists. . . . The Dutchman had to climb in the Reichstag after we had left and the fire was already started . . . Van der Lubbe was to be left in the belief that he was working by himself.

Joseph Goebbels was an early Nazi and companion of Hitler who came to control the Nazi propaganda ministry.

G Van der Lubbe's testimony, made at his trial:

I started the fire as a protest. . . . As to the question whether I acted alone, I declare emphatically that this was the case. No one at all helped me, nor did I meet a single person in the Reichstag.

On your own, or as a class, use the evidence and the following guidelines to simulate a trial:

1 Read all the evidence carefully.
2 Identify the following characters. If this is a class exercise, allocate parts.

Marinus Van der Lubbe   Dr Zirpin
Rudolph Diels   Karl Van Ernst
Martin Sommerfeldt
Spokesperson for the committee for victims of German Fascism
Counsels for prosecution and defence (2–3 each)
The jury, and its spokesperson.

SCENE: THE COURT OF HISTORICAL TRUTH

Purpose: To try Adolf Hitler for burning down the Reichstag.

Procedure: in advance of the trial, the counsel must prepare questions – on the basis of the evidence provided only. The court is timeless, and can call the dead, and it is beyond reach of revenge. Witnesses must be familiar with their evidence, can only use given information, and must tell the truth as they see it. The trial will work best if the script is well prepared. It could then be taped or filmed.

Hints for the counsel for the prosecution:

(a) Your first questions should be asked to reveal the basic facts of the case – place, time, etc. (A and B).

(b) You must slant your questions to show that the Nazis were responsible, with or without Van der Lubbe's knowledge, for the fire. (E. F, and if well used, B).

(c) You must show what Hitler stood to gain from the fire. (B and C).

(d) You must cast doubt on the evidence of witnesses who may undermine your case. (A, D, G, and if well used, B)

Hints for counsel for the defence:

(a) Ask questions which show that Van der Lubbe was working for the communists. (A and D).

(b) Find a way of explaining Göring's statement in B so that it cannot be used against you.

(c) Show that Hitler was surprised and furious. (C)

(d) Discredit the witnesses against you. (E, F and G)

When you have prepared and delivered your questions the jury should consider its verdict. Was Hitler guilty? If not, who was?

The enabling law

In fact the truth is hardly relevant. The fire was just the excuse Hitler needed to attack the Communist Party, and immediately Hindenburg signed a decree 'for the protection of the people and the state' which allowed Hitler the freedom to do so. With this advantage, the election campaign continued. It is estimated that fifty-one people were killed, mainly by the brutality of the SA and SS. One such death occurred on 3 March during an SA raid on the Social Democratic party newspaper office:

The Nazis broke the big display windows and pushed into the building through the holes. They opened fire inside the building with a number of rifles and revolvers . . . the advertising manager was killed with a shot in the stomach. Richard Neuenfeldt was beaten on his head and face with cudgels, steel pipes, revolver butts and metal tools until he was unconscious. The Nazis looted the building. Anything that was moveable they dragged out into the yard. . . . The fire burned for three days and nights.

In a massive climax to the campaign, Hitler called on the people to 'hold your heads high and proudly once more' and vote for him. Despite all his advantages and the brutality of his methods, he gained only 43.9 per cent of the votes and the opposition parties held firm. Even so, with the communists banned, and with the votes of other right-wing parties in the Reichstag, he had a majority of votes.

Hitler's next target was to pass the Enabling Act to give him emergency powers. To make this change in the constitution, he needed a two thirds majority in the Reichstag. By a mixture of promises, threats and appeals to patriotism, he gained the support of enough of the smaller parties to make him confident of success.

On 23 March 1933 the Reichstag met. The story of what happened is told by a representative of the Social Democratic Party:

The assembly hall was decorated with swastikas and similar ornaments . . . the SA and SS men lined up at the exits and along the walls behind us.

Hitler read out his government declaration in a surprisingly calm voice. Only in a few places did he raise it to a fanatical frenzy when he demanded the public execution of Van der Lubbe and when, at the end of his speech, he uttered dark threats of what would happen if the Reichstag did not vote for the Enabling Act he was demanding. . . . Otto Wels read out our reply to the government declaration. It was a masterpiece in form and content, a farewell to the fading epoch of human rights and humanity. In concluding, Otto Wels,

SS or blackshirts, originally Hitler's bodyguard. An elite force feared by all for their brutality.

A mass rally to hear Hitler

77

with his voice half choking, gave our good wishes to the persecuted and oppressed in the country who, though innocent, were already filling the prisons and concentration camps simply on account of their political creed.

Hitler jumped up furiously and launched into a passionate reply . . . we tried to dam the flood of Hitler's unjust accusations with interruptions of 'No', 'An error', 'False'. But that did us no good. The SA and SS people who surrounded us in a semi-circle along the walls of the hall hissed loudly and murmured 'Shut up', 'Traitors', 'You'll be strung up today'.

The vote was 441 for the Enabling Act, 94 against. Hitler had been voted absolute power for four years.

The consolidation of power

Any hopes that Hitler could be controlled were now proved to be baseless. Hitler ignored Papen, and immediately struck at the organisations which still had the power to oppose him. The German trade union movement, thought to be very powerful, was made illegal. The states, which had considerable powers of self-government, were quickly taken over. The most powerful of them, Prussia, was already controlled by Göring. For the rest, the right of free elections and independent states' parliaments were abolished. Nazi Reich governors were appointed to control each state. Another threat to Hitler came from the continued existence of the other parties. In May 1934 the SDP buildings and funds were confiscated, and the party was banned as an enemy of the people. Leaders of other parties were arrested, and subsequently they closed themselves down. Even Hitler's right-wing allies ceased to exist. Finally on 14 July a law was passed declaring that 'The National Socialist German Workers' Party constitutes the only political party in Germany.'

Hitler had now come very close to the moment when the struggle inside Germany could cease, and he could concentrate on rebuilding the German nation in his own way. However, in order to begin a programme of rebuilding, he needed the support of some important groups of people such as the army, and businessmen, who had been threatened by Nazi policy. The problem for Hitler was that the powerful SA, which had helped Hitler gain total power, now wanted him to use it against those groups. This was a dangerous split within the party. Hitler tried to win over Röhm, the SA leader, by giving him a more important post in government. Röhm responded by increasing his demands, especially that the SA should now become the foundation of the new German army and that he should become its leader.

Röhm had few friends in Germany, and even his lieutenants such as Himmler, head of the Gestapo and SS, disliked him intensely. Hitler and Röhm had worked together for many years, but now Hitler realised that Röhm would have to be removed, and that the SS should be his weapon.

In June 1934 Hitler either believed, or was persuaded to believe that the SA were planning a coup. Hitler unexpectedly flew to Munich;

Prussia came under Nazi controls when Göring became minister-president there. He created the Gestapo to enforce his policies in Prussia.

Ernst Röhm was a leader of the SA, from the early days when it was an illegal organisation surviving in disguise as a sports club.

Heinrich Himmler was Nazi police chief, and under his control the Gestapo became a terrifying secret police force.

drove to the Bavarian ministry, and immediately ordered the arrest of SA leaders. He then drove to the hotel where Röhm was staying, burst into his room, and arrested him. Soon the cells were filled with SA leaders. Hitler did not intend to try them. He marked a list of SA leaders and sent SS men to carry out the executions. Thus began 'the night of the long knives'. When the Bavarian minister protested, Hitler shouted down the phone, 'You refuse to carry out an order from me? Are you in sympathy with that criminal scum?'

The executions began. Röhm had not been on the list. However, on 1 July, Hitler finally and reluctantly gave the order, but he stressed that Röhm should first be given a chance to commit suicide. Three SS men went to Röhm's cell, and according to the prison governor:

There they handed over a Browning to Röhm, who asked to speak to Hitler. They ordered him to shoot himself. If he did not comply, they would come back in ten minutes and kill him. When the time was up, the two SS men re-entered the cell, and found Röhm with his chest bared. Immediately one of them from the door shot him in the throat, and Röhm collapsed on the floor. Since he was still alive, he was killed with a shot point-blank through the temple.

Over one hundred, and possibly as many as four hundred died, including some who were not linked with the SA – these included General von Schleicher, who was said to have been involved in Röhm's plot, and also a famous cellist, who was mistaken for an SA namesake. At the end, Hitler justified the entire affair to President Hindenburg, who was able to sign a telegram congratulating Hitler on his 'determined action and gallant personal intervention . . . You have saved the German nation from serious danger'. The SA was defeated and ceased to be of importance. Its place was taken by the SS, which never threatened Hitler's power.

Within weeks President Hindenburg died. Hitler could now make his power complete. Immediately, on 2 August 1934, came the government announcement of a new law:

The office of Reich President will be combined with that of Reich Chancellor. The existing authority of the Reich President will consequently be transferred to the Führer and Reich Chancellor, Adolf Hitler.

Questions

1 Explain the circumstances by which Hitler became
  (a) Chancellor.
  (b) Chancellor with a Reichstag majority.
  (c) Chancellor with emergency powers.
  (d) Chancellor and leader of the only political party.
  (e) Chancellor and leader of an undivided Nazi party.
  (f) Chancellor and President.

2 Trades unions, state governments, and political parties were all very powerful organisations. How did Hitler manage to get rid of all of them so easily?

3 Complete this summary diagram, *Hitler's rise to power*:

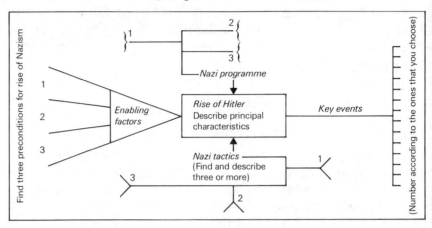

National socialism at work

Hitler wished to rebuild Germany as a totalitarian state. So far he had won support with promises. Now he had to produce results, and prepare the German people for the next, and even more ambitious, aims of national socialism.

Results came quickly through sweeping economic reform. Hitler launched a programme of work to create wealth by boosting both industry and agriculture. To create work in industries such as building, repairs and supply, the government issued Labour Exchange Bonds. The government itself employed large numbers of people in arms manufacture and the building of motorways. New industries, such as motor vehicle production, also thrived. Women were encouraged to stay at home and work on domestic tasks, and bear children. As a result, unemployment figures fell as follows:

The motor car which became common in Germany at this time was, of course, the Volkswagen.

1933 (January)	6 013 612
1934	3 772 792
1935	2 973 544
1936	2 520 499
1937	1 853 460
1938	1 051 700
1939	301 900

National socialism not only provided work. It also used work to advance its own movement. When the trade unions were abolished, they were replaced with the German Labour Front. The purpose of the GLF was to

educate all Germans who are at work to support the National Socialist state and to indoctrinate them in the National Socialist mentality.

It was stressed to all workers that they laboured not only for money, but for Germany. Manual work was seen as glorious, and groups who in the past may have looked down on it – such as students – now had to take their share of hard physical labour. The importance of leisure was also stressed, and the 'strength through joy' campaign gave opportunities for sport and travel, and encouraged community spirit.

All of this was, of course, a form of propaganda. Nazi propaganda can be seen at its most efficient in education. A decree issued by the Ministry of the Interior defined the purpose of education:

The principle task of the school is the education of youth in the service of nationhood and state in the National Socialist spirit.

At the beginning of every lesson the teacher goes to the front of the class, which is standing, and greets it by raising his right arm, and with the words 'Heil Hitler'; the class returns his salute.

Children were also encouraged to achieve such excellence in their school work that, by the age of twelve, they could attend special 'Adolf Hitler' schools. All children were encouraged to join the Hitler Youth until, 1936, a law was passed making membership compulsory. Its purpose was:

All German young people will be educated in the Hitler Youth physically, intellectually and morally in the spirit of National Socialism to serve the nation and community.

Education reform even affected universities. New subjects were added, such as Military and Racial Science, but anyone who opposed national socialism was expelled. The great physicist Albert Einstein emigrated to escape Nazism, and the Nazis described his world-shattering theory of relativity as 'Jewish speculation'.

They salute with both hands now.

The image of Nazism

The Nazis also got rid of ideas they did not like. Massive 'book burnings' were held by supporters to destroy works disliked by Hitler. Hitler's success, and the influence of propaganda, may have won over many who did not originally support him, but apart from the many who fled from Germany during these years, others remained who were opposed to him. These groups and individuals had no protection, and even the law was turned against them. Judges were appointed only if they favoured Nazism and enforced a law which said:

Any person who commits an act which is deserving of punishment according to healthy popular feeling shall be punished under that law the basic idea of which fits best.

Even then, Hitler reserved the right to override judgements, as shown by this letter:

The Führer has been shown the enclosed press cutting concerning the sentencing of the Jew, Markus Luftgas, to 2½ years imprisonment.
The Führer desires that Luftgas should be sentenced to death. I would be obliged if you would make the necessary arrangements as soon as possible.

Arrest and punishment of political prisoners was in the hands of the SS. Their powers went far beyond the law, as shown by Göring's orders of 1933:

Police officers who make use of fire-arms in the execution of their duties will, without regard for the consequences of such use, benefit from my protection; those who, out of a misplaced regard for such consequences, fail in their duty will be punished in accordance with the regulations. Every official must bear in mind that failure to act will be regarded more seriously than an error due to taking action.

Once arrested, people were sent to concentration camps, such as

Dachau. Between October 1935 and May 1936, 7266 people were arrested solely because they were alleged to be communists or socialists. Punishment at Dachau was harsh, and included drilling, beatings, and periods tied to stakes. Anyone guilty of 'ironical remarks to a member of the SS, deliberately omitting the prescribed marks of respect' received solitary confinement for eight days, and 25 strokes, both before and afterwards. In addition, 'anyone who, for the purpose of agitating, discusses politics, carries on controversial talks, or loiters with others', was hanged.

Nazi persecution of the Jews

The most tragic story of life in Nazi Germany is that of the the Jews. Action against Jews had been encouraged from the moment that the Nazis assumed power. The American consul reported an attack by members of the SA in 1933:

In Dresden several uniformed Nazis raided the Jewish prayer house, arrested twenty-five worshippers and tore the emblems from their head-covering worn while praying.

Eighteen Jewish shops had their windows broken by rioters led by uniformed Nazis.

Five Polish Jews arrested in Dresden were each compelled to drink one half litre of castor oil. Some of the Jewish men assaulted had to submit to the shearing of their heads. One Polish Jew had his hair torn out by the roots.

There followed growing official penalties against Jews. They were excluded from the civil service, as doctors, as judges. Schoolchildren were ridiculed in front of their classmates. In September 1935 a Law for the Protection of German Blood and German Honour forbade either

One aspect of the Nazi humiliation of Jews

marriage or sex between Germans and Jews. Unofficially, shops were boycotted and Jews constantly harassed.

The policy at this stage was only to drive Jews out of Germany. Certain Jews such as veterans of the First World War, were protected. Those who wished to go to Palestine were encouraged, and were allowed to go with their money. Furthermore, Hitler still needed the important business and export connections of Jews, and had to be careful in his relations with other countries. By 1936, the year of the Olympic Games, policies against Jews were relaxed, and many must have stayed in Germany because they thought the worst was over.

Then, in November 1938 a German official in Paris was shot by a young Polish Jew. In retaliation Goebbels let it be known that the government would not discourage anti-semitic riots. There followed 'The night of broken glass' or *Kristallnacht*, reported here by the US consul in Leipzig:

These games were of immense importance to Hitler, who was furious when German sprinters were beaten by the black US athlete Jesse Owens.

Jewish buildings were smashed into and the contents demolished or looted. In one of the Jewish sections an eighteen-year-old boy was hurled from a third storey window to land with both legs broken.

Jewish shop windows by the hundred were systematically smashed throughout the entire city. . . . Three synagogues were fired by incendiary bombs. No attempts whatever were made to quench the fires, the activity of the fire brigade being confined to playing water on adjoining buildings.

Having demolished dwellings and hurled most of the moveable effects on the streets, they threw many of the trembling inmates into a small stream, commanding horrified spectators to spit at them, defile them with mud, and jeer at their plight. There is much evidence of physical violence, including several deaths. The most hideous phase of the so called 'spontaneous' action has been the wholesale arrest and transportation to concentration camps of all male German Jews between the ages 16–60.

All of the local crowds observed were obviously benumbed over what had happened and aghast over the unprecedented fury of the Nazis.

The Jewish community was charged a fine of one billion marks for the events of *Kristallnacht*, as well as having to pay for all damage. Further, they were now excluded from school, from owning shops, from parks and restaurants.

Not until 1941 did the Nazis organise the 'final solution' to the Jewish problem. By October, mass deportations were taking place to the extermination camps. Having been packed into cattle-wagons, unable to move and sometimes with others lying on top, Jews were taken to the camps. On arrival the healthiest were chosen for work. The elderly and the children were picked out first and sent to the death chambers. The mentality of the criminals who did this can be seen from the evidence of Rudolph Hess, given at the Nuremberg trials after the war.

Belsen, Auschwitz and other camps have been preserved as reminders of these terrible atrocities.

I visited Treblinka to find out how they carried out their extermination. The commandant told me that he had liquidated 80 000 in the course of six months. He used monoxide gas, and I did not think that his methods were very efficient. So when I set up the extermination building at Auschwitz, I used

This Polish boy is about to be arrested for the greatest crime against Nazism – being born a Jew

Cyclon B, crystallised prussic acid which we dropped into the death chamber through a small opening. It took from three to fifteen minutes to kill the people in the death chamber, depending on the climatic conditions. We knew when the people were dead because their screaming stopped.

These stories are hard to believe in what is thought to be a civilised society. When the camps were liberated, well within the lifetime of many people living today, the liberators could not believe what they heard. The proof lay in the remaining bodies, dead and living dead; in the teeth, rings, and other valuables taken from those already destroyed; and in the terrible exhibits of heads, brains, organs, and skin, the latter of which was made into lampshades by the Nazi guards. The fullest horror of the 'final solution' was there, staring these liberators in the face.

Questions

1 By what means did Hitler try to win the support of the whole German people?
2 Examine the possible fates of any individuals, who spoke out against him.
3 Put Göring's order of 1933 into as few words as possible.
4 Describe the likely fate of
  (a) Jews in Germany, 1933/4.
  (b) Jews who remained and were living there in 1936.
  (c) Jews in Germany on and after *Kristallnacht*.
5 Why do you think Hitler wished to acquire power by legal means, while his followers on the street had so little regard for the law?

6 The causes of the Second World War

Hitler's foreign policy was spelled out in *Mein Kampf*. First and foremost, he was against every article of the Treaty of Versailles. The treaty, which intended to keep Germany weak, had given Hitler plenty of vote-winning ammunition, and played an important part in his rise to power. Now that he had won power he demanded that:

1 Germany should re-arm.
2 Germany should reoccupy the Rhineland.
3 Germany should regain those lands which lay within her borders before 1914 (see map, page 37).
4 Germany should go beyond past borders, and should consist of all German-speaking peoples, including those in Austria, Czechoslovakia, and Poland.
5 Germany should expand into Eastern Europe. The land there should provide resources for Germany, and the 'inferior' peoples who lived there should become slave labour for the 'superior' German *Herrenvolk*.

Questions

1 Draw the base map and use different colours to shade and label
   (a) Countries which contained German-speaking peoples which would be absorbed into the greater Germany.
   (b) Areas which Hitler wished to restore to Germany.
   (c) Areas to the east which would provide resources and labour.
   (d) Countries threatened by Germany's rearmament.
2 The next section deals with the phases of Hitler's policy. As you read it through, construct a timeline of Hitler's foreign policy.
3 At the same time, draw up a table of Hitler's foreign policy tactics under the following headings. Examples have been provided in the columns.

Hitlers objective (policy, area, state)	Hitler's tactics (eg, Germany wronged, bluff, lies, threats, dividing opposition)	Response (from other powers)	Outcome (what happened)

Diplomacy in the 1920s and the rise of Hitler

During the 1920s several attempts were made by European statesmen to stop any future war. From 1925 to 1928 the situation was promising. The German foreign minister, Gustav Stresemann, brought Germany back into international diplomacy as a major power. In 1925 Germany signed the treaty of Locarno, which guaranteed Germany's western borders, and an agreement to go to arbitration if a dispute arose over its eastern borders. In 1926 Germany became a member of the League of Nations, and in 1928, with 64 other countries, signed the Pact of Paris.

This sought to solve all quarrels between countries by peaceful means.

This international goodwill ended in 1929–30 with the death of Stresemann, the collapse of prosperity in Europe, and the rise of Hitler. France, in particular, felt threatened by Hitler, and looked for alliances and mutual guarantees to protect itself. This was the idea of 'collective security'. If Germany broke a treaty, or threatened another country, she would have to face the combined forces of the other powers.

Hitler knew that every step he took was a risk. He had to judge how far and how fast he could go – and although he saw that war was inevitable, the later it came, the better, as far as he was concerned.

1 The rearmament of Germany

In 1933 Hitler was involved in a European conference on disarmament. His demands can be seen in this speech of 17 May:

It is in the interests of all present that problems should be resolved in a reasonable manner. Germany, in demanding equality of rights such as can only be achieved by the disarmament of other nations, has herself carried out the provisions of the treaties.

When his demands were refused, Hitler withdrew Germany from the League of Nations and the disarmament conference. On 16 March 1935 Hitler issued this proclamation:

Germany is the one power which has disarmed; now that the other powers, far from disarming themselves, are actually beginning to increase their armaments, Germany has no option but to follow.

In fact Hitler had already trebled the size of the German army to twenty-one divisions and a panzer brigade. Now, in 1935, he announced his intention to build a new army of thirty-six divisions and three Panzer brigades, and an air force with one hundred aircraft. In addition an Anglo-German pact of June 1935 recognised his right to build a new navy. Although there were limits on the numbers of surface vessels, submarine strength was allowed to rise to equal that of Britain and the Commonwealth.

Lord Allen of Hurstwood spoke for many people when he said,

We are compelled to admit that we have not handed out to Germany that full measure of wise and fair play which the country merited.

2 Reoccupation of the Rhineland

The Rhineland was demilitarised by the Treaty of Versailles. Hitler wanted to repossess this area, but knew that France would object strongly. However, in February 1936 French opinion was already bitterly divided over a newly signed treaty with the USSR.

On 7 March 1936 Hitler announced,

France has replied to Germany's repeated friendly offer and assurances of peace by infringing the Rhine Pact through a military alliance with the Soviet Union directed exclusively against Germany. In this matter the Locarno-

THE GOOSE-STEP.
"GOOSEY GOOSEY GANDER.
WHITHER DOST THOU WANDER?"
"ONLY THROUGH THE RHINELAND—
PRAY EXCUSE MY BLUNDER!"

The goose-step, Nazi style

Rhine pact has lost its inner meaning and ceased in practice to exist. Consequently Germany regards herself for her part as no longer bound by this dissolved treaty . . . and the German Government have today restored the full and unrestricted sovereignty of Germany in the demilitarised zone of the Rhineland.

At 11 a.m. German troops started to march over the Hohenzollern bridge on the Rhine. An historian has described the feelings of the German people at the moment:

Here, eighteen years earlier, dejected German soldiers had retreated from France, leaving their guns behind. Suddenly the crowd could hear the tramp of feet, the rumble of ironclad whels and the clop of horses' hooves. There was fervent cheering as the first soldiers moved onto the bridge. Other units were crossing at least five other bridges as a handful of fighter planes flew cover overhead.

J. Toland, *Adolf Hitler*, 1954

Meanwhile Hitler addressed the Reichstag with the words 'At this moment the German troops are marching!' However, his generals had secret orders to stage a fighting withdrawal if they met with resistance. In Britain, Lord Lothian defended the action 'The Germans, after all, are only going into their own back yard.' The French chief-of-staff was less charitable, but declined to take action, saying 'A war operation, however limited, entailed unpredictable risks and could not be undertaken without decreeing a general mobilisation.' Thus no resistance was given. Hitler later remembered:

The forty-eight hours after the march into the Rhineland were the most nerve-racking in my life. If the French had then marched into the Rhineland we would have had to withdraw with out tail between our legs.

3 Anschluss with Austria

Hitler was born on the Austrian-German border, and the union or *Anschluss* of the two countries was of great personal importance to him. The power most likely to oppose the *Anschluss* was Italy, but Mussolini was isolated after the attack on Abyssinia and was allied with Germany in the Spanish civil war. Hitler correctly assumed that he could now count on Italy's support.

Austria itself was divided. Some Austrians wished to be free and independent, but there was also a strong Nazi party. In July 1934 the Austrian Nazis had assassinated Chancellor Dollfuss and attempted to take over government. They failed, and Hitler denied all knowledge of the plot. However, by February 1938 Hitler felt strong enough to ask the Austrian Chancellor Schuschnigg to a meeting. To Schuschnigg's surprise, Hitler began to make demands, such as the release from prison of Dollfuss' assassins and the appointment of a prominent Nazi to head the army and police.

Schuschnigg refused to give way on these issues, and Hitler blazed at him:

Austrians welcome the Nazi troops as they enter Salzburg

The whole history of Austria is just one uninterrupted act of high treason. I can tell you, Herr Schuschnigg, that I am absolutely determined to make an end of all this. The German Reich is one of the great powers, and nobody will raise his voice if it settles its border problems. I have achieved everything I set out to do, and have thus become perhaps the greatest German in history. You don't seriously believe that you can stop me, or even delay me for half an hour, do you? After the army, my SA and the Austrian Legion will move in, and nobody can stop their just revenge, not even I. Do you want to make another Spain of Austria? I would like to avoid that if possible.

Hitler gave Schuschnigg three days to give in to his demands. Schuschnigg tried to escape by planning to put the issue to a vote by the Austrian people in a plebiscite (referendum). Hitler then sent a final ultimatum and prepared to mobilise his troops. Schuschnigg appealed to the British prime minister, Chamberlain, for help. The reply read:

His Majesty's government cannot take responsibility of advising the Chancellor to take any course of action which might expose his country to dangers against which His Majesty's Government are unable to guarantee protection.

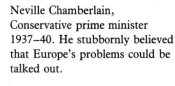

Neville Chamberlain, Conservative prime minister 1937–40. He stubbornly believed that Europe's problems could be talked out.

Draw your own version, and fill in the question marks

Schuschnigg then resigned, the plebiscite was cancelled, and President Miklas appointed a Nazi chancellor. On 12 March German troops moved into Austria. The two countries were now one.

4 Czechoslovakia

Czechoslovakia contained a minority group, the Sudeten Germans, who occupied an area of great strategic and industrial importance. The surrender of this area to Germany would mean the end of Czechoslovakia.

The leader of the Sudeten Germans, Henlein, was advised by Hitler to demand increased right for his people from the Czech government. Britain and France urged the Czech government to respond favourably, but Henlein made negotiations difficult by stepping up his demands. Chamberlain became directly involved in negotiations. He flew to meet Hitler on 15 September and again a week later. Hitler assured him that Sudetenland was the last territorial claim he had to make in Europe.

As negotiations dragged on, Hitler mobilised forces on the Czech border. War seemed inevitable until, on 29 September 1938, Chamberlain, Daladier, Mussolini and Hitler met at Munich. No Czech representative was present, yet the Sudetenland was handed over to Hitler.

Edward Daladier, French prime minister 1933, 1934, 1938–40. French governments were short-lived in these troubled years.

Hearing the news, Winston Churchill said, 'We are in the presence of a disaster of the first magnitude.'

Chamberlain's view was expressed rather differently:

On my side, in spite of the hardness and ruthlessness I thought I saw in his face, I got the impression that he was a man who could be relied upon when he had given his word.

This view was proven wrong when, in March 1939, Hitler occupied all of Czechoslavakia. He justified this action by saying that German minorities were being ill-treated. The Czech president, Hacha, offered no resistance, well believing Hitler's threat that Prague would be destroyed by bombing in the event of any trouble.

The outbreak of the Second World War

At the beginning of 1938, most English people sympathised with German grievances. The Sudeten Germans had a good case. By September the bottom had been knocked out of this case. Hitler ceased to be an idealistic liberator of fellow nationals; he appeared instead as an unscrupulous conqueror, bent on war and domination.

A. J. P. Taylor, *The Origins of the Second World War*, 1961

Two events of 1939 persuaded Britain and her allies that a stand must now be taken. First, Germany's position was strengthened by the surprise signing of the Nazi–Soviet pact (see page 149). Second, when Hitler made demands concerning Poland, the critics of appeasement

The faces of these Czechs reveal their attitude to the Munich settlement

were proven correct in their fears, and Britain and France came out with a treaty in support of Poland. Hitler did not anticipate this:

Whereas before he had displayed a sense of timing amounting to extra-sensory perception – the recovery of the Ruhr, the Czechoslovakian bluff, the rape of Austria – in September 1939 he acted more like a brainless hussar than a great captain. . . . Hitler should have understood that Chamberlain's spring guarantee to Poland was different to anything that Britain had so far undertaken. It was public . . . here at last was a promise on which even the British would find it difficult to rat.

He had launched the wrong war. And he had done so at the wrong time.
Ronald Lewin, *Hitler's Mistakes*, 1984

On 1 September German troops moved into Poland. Their tanks were met by cavalrymen, charging with lances. The British response was immediate:

This morning the British ambassador in Berlin handed the German Government a final note saying that unless we heard from them by 11 o'clock that they were prepared at once to withdraw their troops from Poland, a state of war would exist between us.

I have to tell you now that no such undertaking has been received, and consequently this country is at war with Germany.

You can imagine what a bitter blow it is to me that all my long struggle to win peace has failed. Yet I cannot believe that there is anything more or anything different that I could have done and that would have been more successful'
The Times, 1 September 1939

Chamberlain's decision received the following comment from the editor of *The Times*:

Certainly this nation has never in its history been so unanimous in support of any decision taken by its leader as it is now, on the eve of entering upon the war that must be waged. In coming to the help of Poland we have no material interest of our own to maintain. Nonetheless we shall be fighting for that which is vital to our life, and the life of all civilised peoples.
The Times, 2 September 1939

AN OLD STORY RETOLD
Herr Hitler. "It's all right; you know the proverb—'Barking dogs don't bite'?"
Signor Mussolini. "Oh, yes, *I* know it, and *you* know it; but does the dog know it?"

7

The Second World War in Western Europe

Using the evidence: Blitzkrieg, 1939–40

The German invasion of Poland on 3 September signalled the outbreak of the Second World War. The Soviet Union also attacked Poland, and by the end of the month it had fallen and was divided between the invaders. The western powers now braced themselves against German attack, but from September 1939 to April 1940 (the 'phoney war') all was quiet. Then in April 1940 the German army invaded Norway, and in May they mounted Blitzkrieg (literally, 'lightning war') attack on the western Allies. Consider the following documents:

A Mr Daladier, the French prime minister, led France into war with calmness and dignity. France is quite confident of victory. For twenty years the present struggle has been prepared for. Everything has been done in the army, the navy and the air force. After the French government the name most often mentioned by the man in the street is that of Andre Maginot, creator of the great line of fortifications which bears his name.

The Times, 5 September 1939

B The Poles had no armoured or motorised divisions. Poland's leadership still pinned their trust to the value of a large mass of horsed cavalry, and cherished a pathetic belief in the possibility of carrying out cavalry charges.

Liddel Hart, *The Second World War*, 1970

C The Belgian government have addressed all governments, recalling that Belgium intends to remain absolutely neutral in the present conflict.

The Times, 5 September 1939

Blitzkrieg – Stukas begin the attack

D For the first time, tanks shattered an enemy front by shock action. No effort was wasted capturing Allied army headquarters. Instead Guderian swept westward, simply severing communications and frightening the whole population to such an extent that all resistance to him was undermined.

L. Deighton, Blitzkrieg, 1979

E Dive bombers, stukas with wing sirens, attacked. The chaps were absolutely shattered. I think afterwards that the officers and a few sergeants got up and tried to get things moving, but the chaps just sat about in a complete daze. The effect was truly fantastic.

Major I. R. English, an eye-witness, quoted in Blitzkrieg

F The surprise attack on the key Belgian fort Eben Emael was carried out by 78 parachute engineers on 10 May. Of these, only six men were killed. This small detachment made a completely unexpected landing on the roof of the fort, overcame the anti-aircraft personnel there, and blew up the guns with a new highly intensive explosive previously kept secret, and transported by another new weapon, the freight-carrying glider.

Liddel Hart, The Second World War, 1970

G Crediting our enemies with our own procedure, we had imagined that they would not attempt the passage of the Meuse until they had brought up ample artillery: the five or six days necessary for that would have given us time to reinforce our own dispositions.

The crossing of the Meuse on 14 May was perhaps the first time that a decisive battle was won without having to engage the bulk of the enemy forces.

General Doumenc

1 Study documents A-C. In what ways were France, Poland or Belgium unprepared for war?
2 Look at documents D-F. What are the weapons of war which help to explain the success of the Blitzkrieg?
3 What aspects of the command and organisation of the Blitzkrieg help to make it so successful?
4 In your own words answer the question: Why was the German advance so rapid?

Using the evidence: Dunkirk, May 1940

The invasion of Belgium and France began on 10 May 1940, the same day that Winston Churchill became prime minister in Britain. Belgium surrendered on 18 May. A force of British, French and Belgian troops was pushed back towards the coast, trapped in the area of Dunkirk.

A The Panzers were pushing on to Dunkirk to cut off the British retreat so that not a single British soldier would get away. That was the situation when von Brauchitsch received an amazing order which even the most ignorant private soldier would have recognised as a mistake. Hitler instructed him to halt the Panzer attack on Dunkirk.

Colonel von Lossing

B In the meantime a tight column of men was moving on to the battered quay where a small ship was tied up. I don't know how many men managed to pack aboard, but as she swung out from her moorings, decks as crowded as a rush hour tube train compartment, another attack came in from the west. The quay was hit repeatedly, but luck was with the little ship. We watched her reach the open sea untouched.

An eye-witness at Dunkirk

British troops retreat through Dunkirk

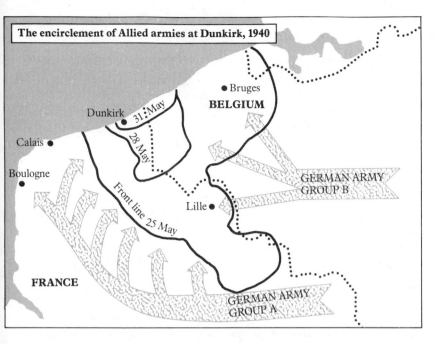

The encirclement of Allied armies at Dunkirk, 1940

Bruges
BELGIUM
Dunkirk
31 May
28 May
Calais
Boulogne
GERMAN ARMY
GROUP B
Front line 25 May
Lille
FRANCE
GERMAN ARMY
GROUP A

C Our barge moved toward the beach at 8.20 a. m. Soldiers were running down the beach to meet her when an air raid siren began to blow ashore and the soldiers took what cover they could find. Two destroyers outside us began to open fire as fifteen enemy planes began to bomb them and the destroyers were twisting and turning at high speed to dodge the bombs.

Captain A. J. Barker

D Dunkirk, completely in ruins, was burning from one end to the other. On the sea floated ships of all sizes, sometimes being taken by storm by the waiting soldiers, while the German bombers swooped overhead. The boats moved off dangerously overloaded weaving between high watery columns flung up by the bombs, guns thundered without rest.

An eye-witness at Dunkirk

The Allies hoped to bring away 45 000 men. In the nine days during which the evacuation took place 233 000 British and 112 000 French were taken to England.

E All night and all day men of the undefeated British army have been coming home. From the many reports of their arrival and of interviews with the men, it is clear that if they have not come back in triumph, they have come back in glory; that their spirits are as high as ever; that they know they did not meet their masters; and that they are anxious only to be back again soon – as they put it – 'to have a real crack at Jerry'.

BBC news bulletin, 31 May 1940

F The full extent of our victory in Holland, in Belgium and in the north of France can be measured by enemy losses in men and material. The English, French, Dutch and Belgians have lost 1 200 000 as prisoners, plus dead and wounded. The arms and equipment of the whole Allied army including tanks and vehicles of every type have also been destroyed or captured.

Official German bulletin, 4 June 1940

At times the evacuation was chaotic. Here, a moment of calm

1 Read document A on page 94. What gave the Allied armies the time they needed to escape from Dunkirk?
2 Describe the type of boats used in the Dunkirk operation, and the methods by which troops reached them.
3 Use the documents and illustrations to write or tape a (friendly) argument between a soldier and a sailor: who faced the greater danger at Dunkirk?
4 Would Colonel von Lossing have agreed with the German bulletin of 4 June?
5 Do you think that evacuated soldiers would have agreed with the BBC?
6 How do you explain that both sides claimed victory at Dunkirk?

Using the evidence: Summer 1940 – The Battle of Britain

Hitler's plan after the fall of France was the execution of 'operation Sealion': the invasion of Britain. First, however, the RAF had to be destroyed, for they controlled the skies over England and the Channel and could tear an invasion fleet apart. The Luftwaffe set out to destroy the RAF in the air, and its bases in the south-east England. This was operation *Alderangriff*, or the Battle of Britain. It began on 8 August 1940 and built up to a crisis by 15 September. The failure of the operation was the first great setback for Hitler.

Consider the following documents:

A The ME 109 was superior to the Hurricane, and above about 6000 metres superior to the Spitfire also. I believe that our armament was better . . . on the other hand, the British fighters could turn tighter than we could. Also I felt that the ME 109 was not so strong as the British fighters and could not take so much punishment.

Oberleutnant Gerhard Schoepfl

The ME 109F

The Spitfire

Scramble. Aircraft receive last moment attention as the pilots answer another call

Examples of combat losses, 18 August 1940. Compare the fates of other examples from RAF 32 Squadron and Bomber Geschwader 53

32 Squadron	Hurricane V 7363	Destroyed	Flt Lt H. Russell *wounded*	Shot down by Messerschmitt 110 of Destroyer Geschwader 26 near Edenbridge at about 1.45 pm. Pilot baled out
32 Squadron	Hurricane V 6536	Damaged	Sgt B. Henson *wounded*	Aircraft hit by return fire, while attacking a Dornier 17 of Bomber Geschwader 76 at about 1.45 pm. Forced-landed near Sevenoaks
32 Squadron	Hurricane N 2461	Destroyed	Sdn Ldr M. Crossley	Shot down by Messerschmitt 109 of Fighter Geschwader 26 near Gillingham at about 5.40 pm. Pilot baled out
32 Squadron	Hurricane V 6535	Destroyed	Plt Off R. De Grunne *wounded*	Shot down by Messerschmitt 109 of Fighter Geschwader 26 near Canterbury at about 5.40 pm. Pilot baled out
32 Squadron	Hurricane R 4106	Destroyed	Sgt L. Pearce *wounded*	Shot down by Messerschmitt 109 of Fighter Geschwader 26 near Canterbury at about 5.40 pm. Pilot baled out

Bomber Geschwader 53

II Gruppe		He 111	Destroyed	Major R. Tamm *killed*	Shot down by Fg Off R. Milne of No 151 Squadron, over Essex at about 5.45 pm. Wreckage fell in the sea. All six men on board killed
II Gruppe		He 111	Damaged		Damaged in action, two crewmen wounded
III Gruppe		He 111	Destroyed	Uffz W. Grasser *prisoner*	Shot down off the Essex coast at about 5.50 pm, probably by Flt Lt H. Hamilton of No 85 Squadron. Aircraft ditched. Crew spent 26 hours in the water before rescue and capture
III Gruppe		He 111	Destroyed	Ltn W. Leber *prisoner*	Damaged during attack by Fg Off P. Weaver of No 56 Squadron, finished off by Plt Off W. Hopkins of No 54 Squadron at about 5.35 pm. Crash-landed at Smallgains on Foulness Island. One crewman killed, rest taken prisoner
III Gruppe		He 111	Destroyed	Uffz G. Gropp *killed*	Shot down off the Essex coast at about 5.55 pm. Probably aircraft attacked by Flt Lt H. Beresford and Sgt A. Girdwood of No 257 Squadron; or by Plt Off J. Marshall of No 85 Squadron. All five men on board killed

B German pilots suffered from *Kanalkrankheit*, Channel sickness. 'Either the water or the Spitfires, one was enough', commented Oberleutant Julius Neumann, 'but both together was a bit too much'.

Shortly after 2 p. m. on 15 September a new wave of enemy aircraft returned in about the same strength as before. Twenty-one squadron attacked them. The sky was full of criss-crosses of condensation trails. Every now and then the blue was stained by the black plume of a dying aeroplane, German or British.

Winston Churchill, absorbed in the operations room, asked what fighter reserves were available. Park replied 'There are none'. Ten minutes later the action ended. The Germans had cracked. By tea time the tide of the enemy offensive had turned.

D. Bader, *Fight for the Sky*, 1975

C The gratitude of every home in our island, in our Empire, and indeed throughout the world, except in the abodes of the guilty, goes out to the British airmen who, undaunted by odds, wearied in their constant challenge and mortal danger, are turning the tide of the world war by their prowess and by their devotion. Never in the field of human conflict was so much owed by so many to so few.

Speech by Winston Churchill

1 Use documents A-C to explain the victory of the RAF over the Luftwaffe in the Battle of Britain.
2 What does document C reveal about the leadership of Winston Churchill during these difficult times?

Using the evidence: 1940 – the blitz; 1940–44 – counter-attack

From the outbreak of war people prepared themselves to face the bombing of their cities. Children were sent from their homes in the inner city areas to the relative safety of the countryside. They were billeted with strangers and there were sometimes difficulties on both sides:

A An evacuated girl presented such a dirty unkempt appearance that the woman refused her. Nobody would take her in. At the end of the day a woman took compassion on her and gave her shelter. The child was nervous, dirty and badly clad. She wet the bed the first night and was terrified of the consequences.

One boy, 13, refused to eat cereal and milk, saying, 'I want some beer and some bloody chips!'

Having failed to destroy the RAF, the Luftwaffe turned its attention to the bombing of British cities. The first raid on London began on 15 November, 1940. Thereafter raids on London and other cities were continuous. The height of the blitz was 29 November when a massive raid hit London. On 10 March 1941 another major attack caused

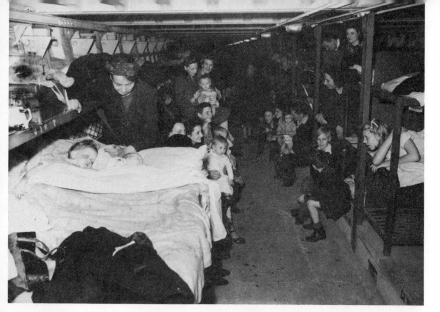

Deep shelter. Life under London during the blitz

Evacuees look unhappy about their immediate future

widespread damage, including the House of Commons. Eye-witness reports described the scene:

B Of course the press version of life going on as normal in the East End on Monday are grotesque. There was no bread, no electricity, no gas, no milk, no telephones. . . .

The tidal wave of refugees spread all over the country after the first hideous weekend. Nobody saw that the rest centres would be overflowing, that people would flock to the tubes and unofficial deep shelters rather than use the official surface shelters which they regarded as death traps.

C We could see the docks blazing from here, or rather the terrific red glow in the sky. We have a refugee family from Wapping in an empty house in our road, they arrived about 7 p. m. with bedding but practically nothing else. But the woman was amazingly brave, and she certainly proved that what the papers say about the morale of east-enders is quite true. . . .

Saved from a ruin in Buckingham Gate, London

On the Sunday night a large public shelter in Beaufort Street had received a direct hit. There were no survivors and as soon as it got light on Monday the rescue and demolition squad were sent to remove the human remains. They had to put what they could into blue waterproof bags and take them to the mortuary.

In the summer of 1940 the RAF began a major campaign of bombing raids against Germany. After initial strikes against the French channel ports, Munich was bombed in November and Berlin in March 1941. As the war swung in favour of the Allies, mass bombing of German cities was stepped up. One of the biggest and most controversial raids of the war was against Dresden in 1944. A pilot remembered:

D There was a sea of fire covering in my estimation some 40 square miles. The heat striking up from the furnace below could be felt in my cockpit. The sky was vivid in hues of scarlet and white, and the light inside the aircraft was that of an eerie autumn sunset. We were so aghast at the awesome blaze that although alone over the city, we flew around in a standoff position for many minutes before turning for home, quite subdued by our imagination of the horror that must be below. We could still see the glare of the holocaust thirty minutes after leaving.

The miracle of St. Paul's – hardly damaged during the blitz

1 Study documents A and B. What do they show about the groups of people concerned?
2 What are the points of argument between B and C? Where do they disagree and how do you explain that disagreement?

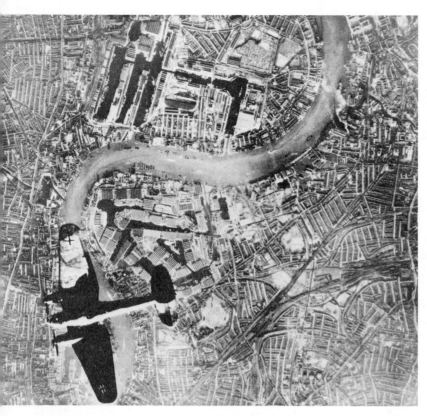

Gravesend Home Guard – a defiant
dad's army

Silvertown from a Heinkel bomber

Bomb damage in Bromley – but
spirits remain high

3 Use the photographs and documents to write an account of London life during the blitz.
4 What were the effects of the war on the area where you live? In particular was it bombed, or did it receive evacuees? What local stories can you find about these events?
5 According to Anthony Eden, targets were not chosen according to the 'military or economic importance of a target; they are determined solely by the amount of destruction and dislocation caused.' Dresden was not a military or economic target, but 300 000 died there.
  (a) What might Eden have thought about that?
  (b) What is the attitude of the pilot towards the scene at Dresden?
  (c) In your opinion, were such raids justified?

The Battle of the Atlantic, 1939–45

On the first day of the war the British liner *Athenia* was sunk by a German submarine. From that moment the Atlantic became a major theatre of war. The German navy, with its submarines and powerful surface raiders, hoped to gain mastery of the ocean. This would starve Britain out, and stop supplies reaching British and Allied armies.

Allied merchant shipping sunk, 1942–3

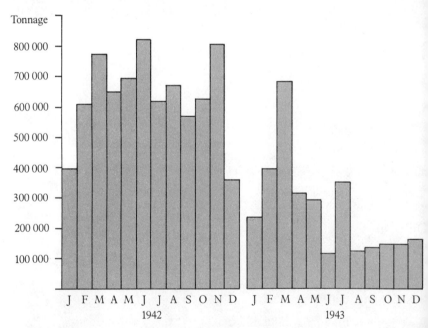

The Royal Navy too had its successes – for example the scuttling of the *Graf Spee* at the River Plate in 1939, and the sinking of the *Bismarck* in 1941.

Much depended on the ability of convoy escorts to defend merchant vessels in their care. Here is the story of one failure and one success.

In June 1942, convoy PQ17 was taking supplies to Russia. It consisted of 36 ships with an escort of destroyers and cruisers. On 1 July

The sinister shape of a U boat on patrol

the convoy was attacked by aircraft and submarines, but little damage was done and only one ship lost. On 4 July intelligence reports suggested that the battleship *Tirpitz* had left port. The following signals were sent:

SECRET MOST IMMEDIATE. CRUISER FORCE WITHDRAW WESTWARD AT HIGH SPEED OWING TO THREAT OF SURFACE SHIPS CONVOY IS TO DISPERSE AND PROCEED TO RUSSIAN PORTS

An officer on one of the escort ships, *Offa*, remembered his feelings:

We all dashed off westward as the convoy scattered in all directions. The submarines and aircraft moved in to the kill. The *Tirpitz*, with her objective achieved without firing a shot, turned for home.

On *Offa*'s bridge we argued and discussed. 'We can't do this' we said, 'we must go back'. But we always came back to the belief that we must be doing what we were for a purpose.

I hate 4 July, the Navy's day of shame and mine.

Only eleven of the 36 ships arrived. Lost war material included 3350 vehicles, 430 tanks, and 210 aircraft for the Russian front.

In December 1943, convoy JW55B was heading for Russia with nineteen freighters, and an escort of destroyers and cruisers backed by the battleship *Duke of York*.

Wind and sea conditions made the task of the destroyers extremely difficult, huge breaking seas from astern caused the slim ships to yaw and threaten to broach, calling for high seamanship as the force continued at 19 knots eastward.

G. C. Connell, Arctic Destroyers: The 17th Flotilla, 1972

At 8.40 a.m. *HMS Belfast*, the flagship of Admiral Burnett, sighted the *Scharnhorst* at 25 000 yards distant, thirty miles from the convoy. Belfast fired a star shell and *HMS Norfolk* opened fire, hitting the

HMS Belfast *here pictured in 1950 with an enclosed bridge*

Convoy lookout, eyes peeled for enemy aircraft

Scharnhorst three times. Other British ships closed in as the *Belfast* with two other cruisers and four destroyers pursued the pocket battleship.

At 7.01 p. m. both the *Duke of York* and *Jamaica* opened fire at a range of five miles, scoring repeated hits on the stricken ship which caused fires and explosions and reduced her to a shambles. Nevertheless even when her main armament was put out of action the *Scharnhorst* bravely continued to fight back. At 7.19 Admiral Fraser ordered the *Belfast* and *Jamaica* to sink her with torpedoes. At 7.42 the *Scharnhorst* went down by the bows, rolled over to starboard, and disappeared. Of her crew of 2000, only 36 were saved.

B. B. Schofield, *The Russian Convoys*, 1964

The Atlantic convoys experienced terrible losses at the hands of submarines and surface raiders in 1941 and 1942. By early in 1943 new specially equipped destroyers and frigates were ready to escort convoys, and to hunt the submarine wolf-packs. Furthermore, long-range bombers were used to provide cover. These were turning points in the Battle of the Atlantic.

The Graf Spee *in flames off Montevideo*

HMS Belfast is now a museum on the River Thames. It contains many more details of the war at sea. Best of all, however, is the opportunity to go and see what life on a cruiser was really like.

Questions

1 Why do you think that the escort of PQ17 was withdrawn, and why was the officer on *Offa* so ashamed?
2 Why do you think that the same order was not repeated for JW55B?
3 Describe the particular difficulties of the Atlantic war.
4 In your own words, describe the sinking of the *Scharnhorst*.
5 Describe and explain the trend shown on the graph at the beginning of this section.
6 As a research project, investigate another aspect of the war at sea: for example, the sinking of the *Bismarck* or the *Graf Spee*.

The Mediterranean and North Africa, 1940–43

Yugoslavia, Greece and Crete were overwhelmed by German and Italian forces in the spring of 1941. The Axis attack then focussed on Malta, which fought such a brave defence with the help of the RAF that it was named the George Cross Island. The Axis powers also failed to gain control of the Mediterranean itself. The Italian fleet was defeated in a skirmish by British battleships and thereafter remained in port. Spain remained neutral throughout the war.

The main battlefield in this area was North Africa. Conditions in this theatre of war were terrible for both sides:

The troops were suffering from fly swarms so multitudinous that it was often impossible to raise food to the lips before it became black with intruders. Only the strictest sanitary discipline could stave off an epidemic: any carelessness bred disease. 'Gippy tummy' or jaundice were the consequences, and just as frequently men were troubled with the desert sore. Very rapidly the slightest scratch would extend into a wide suppurating circle which would take months to heal.

Ronald Lewin, *The War Lords*, 1979

The SAS, a key section of the desert army

In September 1940 Italian forces had advanced towards Egypt as far as Sidi Barani, but were then driven back. In Spring 1941 the German Afrika corps reinforced the Italians, and this time they advanced as far as Tobruk. After a prolonged battle Tobruk fell in May 1942, and the 8th Army retreated to El Alamein. At this time General Montgomery was made commander of the 8th Army.

Within an astonishing short space Montgomery imposed his will on his officer corps and his personality on his troops. It was a feat of generalship that half won his battles before a shot was fired – to inject a new sense of purpose into a puzzled, uneasy, jaded army of such diverse origins, Australia, New Zealand, South Africa, India, and Great Britain.

Ronald Lewin, *The Life and Death of the Afrika Corps*, 1972

British Valentine tank being piped into Tripoli, 1943

As well as raising the morale of his men, Montgomery consolidated a large force. He also benefited from the secret war:

ULTRA (the British decoding machine) picked up German signals disclosing that Rommel had quit the desert to be treated for nasal diphtheria, chronic stomach ailments, and poor circulation. All were reported to Roosevelt. The President commented that Rommel must have suffered a demoralisation more severe because he had been used to a diet of victories 'based on intelligence from inside the British camp which, thank God, we have now terminated'.

W. Stevenson, *A Man Called Intrepid*, 1976

With the two sides confronting each other at El Alamein, it was Montgomery's plan to break through one weak spot in the enemy line.

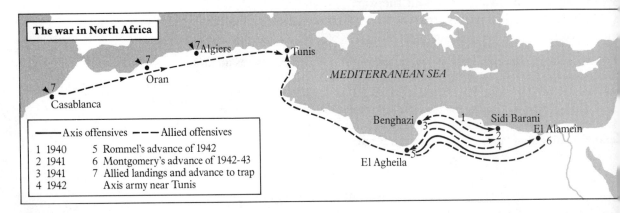

The war in North Africa

—— Axis offensives	--- Allied offensives
1 1940	5 Rommel's advance of 1942
2 1941	6 Montgomery's advance of 1942-43
3 1941	7 Allied landings and advance to trap
4 1942	Axis army near Tunis

The attack was launched on the night of 22 October. One of the men who led the attack was Major Samwell, M C:

About 9 p. m. we moved forward and took up our positions on the start line. It was deathly still and a full moon lighted the bleak sand as if it were day. Suddenly the silence was broken by the crash of a single gun, and the next moment a mighty roar rent the air and the ground shook under us as salvo after salvo crashed out from hundreds of guns. Shells whined over our heads in a continuous stream, and soon we saw the enemy line lit up by bright flashes

The barrage prepared the way for an infantry advance to remove mines and anti-tank guns before the main Allied tank offensive. A five-day battle followed. The German commander, Rommel, describes one counter-attack by a combined German and Italian force:

Unfortunately the attack gained ground very slowly. The British resisted desperately. Rivers of blood were poured out over miserable strips of land which, in normal times, not even the poorest Arab would have bothered his head about.

After five days it appeared that the two sides had reached stalemate. In fact Rommel was close to defeat:

It seemed doubtful whether we would be able to stand up much longer to attacks of the weight the British were now making, and which they were in any case able to increase. It was obvious to me that I dared not await the decisive breakthrough but would have to pull out to the west before it came.

Hitler ordered Rommel not to yield one yard. His instruction were, 'To your troops you can offer no other path than leading to victory or death,' But on 2 November a new Allied offensive began which broke through two days later. Withdrawing rapidly, Rommel reported the defeat:

On the right of the Afrika corps, powerful enemy armoured forces had destroyed the XX Italian motorised corps and thus burst a twelve mile hole in our front through which strong bodies of tanks were moving to the west.
    So now it had come, the thing we had done everything in our power to avoid - our front broken, and the enemy streaming into our rear. We had to save what there was to be saved. I issued orders for the retreat to start immediately.

At the same time as the Axis armies were retreating westwards, the Allies' 'operation Torch' had landed a combined British and American force at Casablanca. In May 1943 the two sides closed in and forced the surrender of 250 000 German and Italian troops. The desert war was over.

Questions

1 Use the accounts and the map to draw your own diagram to show the ebb and flow of the North African campaigns. Colour coding will help.
2 The documents give several reasons which help to explain the victory of the 8th Army. Write an account of the Battle of El Alamein, emphasising the reasons for the Allied victory.

Allied victory in Italy, 1943–45

Churchill had wanted to complete the conquest of North Africa before attacking Italy, 'the belly of Hitler's Europe'. In July 1943 the first stage in that attack was launched with 'operation Husky'. The target was Sicily. A surprise assault involving paratroops and a seaborne force

The Allied invasion of Italy

Milan •

Jan–May 1945

Florence •

GOTHIC LINE

US Army

8th Army

August/ September 1944

Rome •
Cassino •

GUSTAV LINE

May 1944

Naples •
Salerno •

ITALY

Taranto

• Palermo

SICILY September 1943

Monte Cassino under fire – a bombardment that lasted for six months

gained the advantage, and after hard fighting won Sicily on 17 August.

While this was happening, Mussolini had been overthrown by the fascist Grand Council, which had met for the first time in twenty years. He was arrested, and Marshal Pietro Badoglio became prime minister. On 3 September he signed an armistice with the Allies. Rather than lose Italy, Germans took hold of Italian weapons and strongholds. However, they failed to get the Italian fleet which was handed over to the Royal Navy.

On 3 September the Allied invasion of Italy began. By the end of the month southern Italy was secured, but the German army made its stand in the mountainous central area of the Gustav line, south of Rome. Part of this line was the hill topped by the monastery of Cassino.

Any thoughts that conditions in Italy would be better than in North Africa were soon lost. An American soldier remembered:

Our troops were living in almost inconceivable misery. The fertile black valleys were knee deep in mud. Thousands of men had not been dry for weeks. Trench foot comes from a man's being wet and cold for long periods and not taking off his shoes often enough. In extreme cases gangrene occurs.

The fighting on the mountaintop almost reached the cavemen stage sometimes. Americans and Germans were frequently so close that they actually threw rocks at each other. Many more grenades were used than in any other phase of the Mediterranean war. And you have to be pretty close when you throw hand grenades.

Defences on the Gustav line, and especially at Cassino, were formidable. The monastery was destroyed, but after three major assaults the defenders were unmoved. British war correspondent, Christopher Buckley, himself an eye-witness, describes an early assault:

Just before 2 p. m. a formation of Mitchell bombers passed over. They dipped slightly. A moment later a bright flame, such as a giant might have produced by striking titanic matches on the mountainside, sparked quickly upwards at half a dozen popints. Then a pillar of smoke five hundred feet high broke upwards into the blue. Then the column paled and melted. The abbey became visible again. Its whole outlined had changed. The west wall had totally collapsed.

The diary of a German soldier records his feelings:

15 March Today hell let loose at Cassino. Almost 1000 aircraft bomb our positions at Cassino and in the hills. We can see nothing but dust and smoke. In addition the artillery puts down a concentration of fire throughout the whole day. The ground is shaking as if there was an earthquake.
25 March There has been a heavy fall of snow. It is whirling into our post. You would think you were in Russia. Just when you think you are going to get a few hours rest to get a sleep, the fleas and bugs torment you. Rats and mice are our companions too.

Eventually, on 18 May 1944, a Polish force walked into Cassino. The last defenders had left during the night. The German army retreated northwards, giving up Rome to the Allied armies. The winter of 1944/5 saw another stalemate, this time on the Gothic line. By 1 May 1945 a new offensive had secured most of Italy, and partisans had captured and executed Mussolini. A British gunner, J. M. Lee Harvey, reached Milan soon after this event:

Mussolini and his mistress had been shot by communist partisans, and their bodies brought into Milan on a truck. They were dumped in the Piazzale Loreto. Allowing for typical theatrical Italian exaggerations, what we were told was reasonably true.

The next day the crowd surveyed the bodies for a time with nothing more than idle curiosity. And then it happened. A man rushed up and kicked Mussolini in the head and the people began to dance round the bodies, singing in exaltation. Many women urinated on his upturned face and others ripped off his shirt and set light to it. Another woman fired shots into his body, one for each son she had lost in the war. Then the final indignity was performed when their bodies were strung up by their feet to the girders of a bombed out petrol station. Meanwhile the bells from all churches in Milan rang out their peals of freedom to the whole city.

Questions

1 J. M. Lee Harvey's book is called *D Day Dodgers*, a sarcastic reference to accusations made against the 8th Army for having missed the major Allied assault against occupied France. Imagine that you were labelled a 'D Day Dodger'. Furious, you write a letter to the press telling of the achievements of the 8th Army. If you wish, include the Africa campaign.
2 Why do you think that Mussolini was treated in this way by ordinary people? Reference back to Chapter 4 may help you.

6 June 1944: D Day

By Spring 1944 the Allies were prepared to launch 'operation Overlord', the invasion of France. Hitler was expecting this, and boasted an 'Atlantic wall' supported by sixty divisions which would thrust the invaders back into the sea. Under the directions of Generals Eisenhower and Montgomery preparations went ahead. The best day was considered to be 5 June, but bad weather forced a postponement. On 6 June Allied troops began their landing on the Normandy beaches. A German soldier remembered 6 June:

Aren't we having any breakfast today?' Frerking called out through the open bunker door. Severloh pulled an army loaf out of his haversack. There was a strange silence. The curtain of haze which had covered the sea lifted. Frerking came out of the bunker. He wanted his breakfast. But first he picked up the binoculars. He leant against the bunker wall. 'Holy smoke!' was all he said. 'Holy smoke! Here they are'.

Ships as far as the eye could see. Big ships, and little ships, with turrets, superstructures, funnels, aerials, and grotesque barrage balloons. Like some mysterious city in the first light of day.

The enemy did mistake the Glimmer convoy for a genuine threat and believed that the ABC patrol was cover for operations in the Somme area. As well as sending a number of E boats to investigate the Glimmer convoy they opened up with artillery searchlights and guns. The night fighter force was sent into the ABC area.

Official Report

An essential element of each force was its bombarding group. One hundred and thirty seven ships had mustered for drenching bombardment of the German defences. . . . the Royal Navy provided battleships *Nelson*, *Warspite* and *Ramilles* with *Rodney* in reverse, whilst the *USS Texas*, *Nevada*, and *Arkansas* were supplied by the United States navy.

W. Tute, D Day, 1974

A report from the *USS Texas* on the landings at Omaha beach:

All boats came under criss-cross machine gun fire. As the first men jumped, they crumpled and flopped into the water. Then order was lost. Some were were hit in the water and wounded. Some drowned there and then. But some moved safely through the bullet fire to the sand, and then, finding that they could not hold there, went back into the water and used it as cover, only their heads sticking out. Within ten minutes of the ramps being lowered a company had became almost incapable of action. Every officer and sergeant had been killed or wounded.

General Bradley reported receiving word that the Germans were using a church tower as an observation post. The Admiral ordered the ship to open fire and the first salvo scored a direct hit.

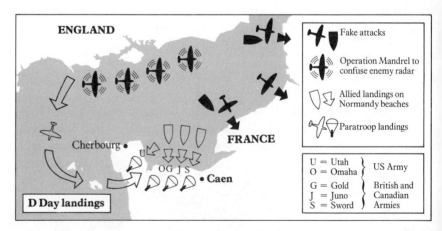

The following report from Utah Beach was radioed back to Allied headquarters:

HEAVY SHELLING OF THE BEACH HAS COST INCREASING CASUALTIES IN PERSONNEL AND EQUIPMENT X ALTHOUGH THREE ROADS ARE OPEN AND MOVING INLAND PROGRESS IS SLOW X CONTINUED BOMBARDMENT WITH ADEQUATE AIRSPOT OF ENEMY IS ESSENTIAL IF BEACHES ARE TO BE PROTECTED AND EARLY ADVANTAGES MAINTAINED NAVISTREP 5

*D Day – The coast of France,
6 June 1944*

Although records are uncertain, over 130 000 men were landed from the sea (75 000 on the British beaches and 57 500 at Utah and Omaha). In addition 7000 British and 15 500 American airborne troops were in action. In view of the strength of the 'Atlantic wall' and the high risks of the invasion, the casualty rate was far lighter than many experienced soldiers expected. Fears of another Gallipoli were mercifully proved false. Some 3000 British and Canadians were killed or wounded, as well as 600 men of the 6th Airborne. On the American side, over 6000 were wounded or lost their lives, including airborne casualties.

Much of the success could be attributed to the Allied air forces, which from the night of 5 June to the end of D Day flew 14 000 sorties and lost 127 aircraft.

Another Allied parachute landing on both sides of the Orne, together with a sharp attack by English tanks, forced me to give up my hold on the coast. I retired to take up a line just north of Caen. By the end of the first day my division had lost almost 25 per cent of its tanks.

General Feuchtinger

The *Times* correspondent describes the liberation of the first French city:

Crowds of young and old people stood today in the cobbled streets of this town from which the Allied troops had just driven the Germans. Some of the French people had tears streaming down their faces; all were shouting 'Vive l'Angleterre', 'Vive l'Amérique', 'Vive la France' and raising their fingers in the Victory-V sign.

Once the bridgehead was established Allied troops poured into France. The US army moved east, while the British moved north towards Belgium. Paris was liberated by French troops on 25 August. The German army attempted a counter-attack in the Ardennes but the Allies continued their advance towards Germany itself. The fall of Germany is described in Chapter 9.

Questions

1 Allied High Command has agreed that the time has come to prepare for the invasion of occupied France. Prepare a Top Secret File with suggestions for preparations and strategy, with accompanying maps and lists. You must think of every possible requirement to give this operation the maximum chance of success.
2 What part was played on D Day by (a) secret operations, (b) aircraft, and (c) ships?
3 Describe the action as seen by a soldier landing on Omaha beach.
4 How did the Allies secure their bridgehead?

The recovery of Western Europe

Twice within thirty years Europe had been devastated by war. In 1945 European countries emerged from war with a new desire for unity. One reason for this was the 'cold war', which united the independent western states against what they saw as a threat from the east. Another reason was the idea that unity would aid economic recovery.

Belgium, the Netherlands and Luxembourg led the way towards economic union in 1944. In 1947 the ideas of a European customs union was put forward, and in 1949 a further idea of a European defence community was proposed. The latter failed, but steps were taken towards economic co-operation in 1952 with the European Coal and Steel Community (ECSC) and 1958 (the European Economic Community). It was the success of the ECSC, which raised steel output of member nations by 40 per cent between 1953 and 1958, which paved the way towards complete economic union, including a community government at Brussels. This government now includes a council of ministers, a commision, a parliament, and a court of justice.

One problem facing the EEC from the outset has been the position of Great Britain. At first Britain was relucant to join at all. Britain had a special relationship with Commonwealth countries, and was unwilling to 'betray' them by joining Europe. Also the British were more isolated and had a traditional mistrust of 'continentals'. Even so, many politicians were impressed by the early performance of the EEC. In 1961, and again in 1967, Britain applied for membership – on both occasions the application was vetoed by France. Finally in 1973 Britain, Eire, and Denmark were admitted to the EEC. The admission of Spain, Portugal, and Greece now adds a further dimension.

The membership of the EEC has brought problems: the struggle between nationalism and internationalism; quarrels over budget quotas; the creation of 'mountains' of surplus commodities at a time when millions in the world are starving; and apathy in the election of members of the European parliament.

Even so, European states are working together and the barriers which caused such friction before 1914 and 1939 are being broken down.

8

Russia, 1905–39

Russia in 1905: the extremes

Life at court

A distinguished visitor to Russia in the years before the First World War must have been impressed by the wealth and style of court life in the capital, St Petersburg.

A Of all the St Petersburg parties none was more brilliant than that given by the Countess Kleinmikhel to present the three daughters of her sister-in-law to St Petersburg society. It was a costume ball, and everyone wanted an invitation, which proved a little embarassing to the Countess, whose house could only accommodate three hundred guests. She arranged an elaborate programme of dances. Petersburg dances were long affairs. Dancing started at five in the afternoon and went on to five in the morning with an interlude for supper – a glittering affair served on plates of gold and silver, gleaming with candelabra and centerpieces of ice or pastry in the shape of the Kremlin Towers or Peter the Great on a rearing stallion.

When the First World War was two years old, and after millions of Russians had died on the front, the high society of St Petersburg

St Petersburg – in 1914 was changed to Petrograd because it sounded 'too German'. Later changed again to Leningrad.

Tsar Nicholas II with King George V of Britain

continued to display its great wealth. The revolutionary, Leon Trotsky, described the social scene of 1916:

B Enormous fortunes arose out of the bloody foam. The lack of bread and fuel in the capital did not prevent the court jeweller, Fabergé, from boasting that he had never done such flourishing business. Lady-in-waiting Vyrubova says that in no other season were such gowns to be seen as in the winter of 1915–16, and never were so many diamonds purchased.

Leon Trotsky – a prominent revolutionary, he spent many of his early years in exile or Siberia. He was to have an important part in all three revolutions.

At the heart of this high society was the ruler of all Russia, the Tsar. Tsars were autocrats, having total power over their people. In his 'fundamental law' of 1905–6 Tsar Nicholas II said,

Tsar of all the Russias – more than kings, being also the head of the Orthodox Church, the Tsars were very powerful and extremely wealthy.

The Emperor of all Russia has supreme autocratic power. It is ordained by God himself that this authority should be submitted to, not only out of fear, but of a genuine sense of duty.

The peasantry

The great mass of Russian people had no share in this wealth or power. Most of them were peasants. Before 1861 many of the peasants had been serfs (or slaves) but in that year they were 'freed' and given some land. For many reasons this allocation of land was inadequate. In 1861 each peasant family was given, on average, five *desyatins*. Often, however, this had to be shared amongst a growing family so that by 1900 many peasants had only 1.5. *desyatins*. In total, in 1905, ten million peasant families owned 73 million *desyatins*. Yet the 18 000 greatest landowners had between them 63 million *desyatins*.

Desyatin – 109 acres (approximately).

Furthermore, the peasants did not really control their own land. They were answerable to the local commune or *mir*, which in turn was controlled by the regional council or *zemstvo*. The *zemstvo* was in turn told what to do by a land captain appointed by the government.

Far from improving, the life of the peasants was getting worse. A report of 1905 noted:

Very often peasants do not have enough allotment land, and cannot during the year feed themselves, clothe themselves, heat their homes, maintain their tools and livestock, secure seed for sowing, and pay their taxes.

Many peasants were forced to give up their small plots, and move to the cities to find work or join the millions already unemployed. Those who were left found themselves facing higher and higher taxes. The main reason for this was that, by 1900, the government had seen the need to modernise and develop industry. Equipment and experts could only be bought from abroad, and all that Russia had to give in exchange was grain – therefore increasing amounts of grain were taken from the peasants as taxes, and the peasant class grew poorer to pay for Rusia's modernisation. They saw no benefits from this, only less to eat.

The workers in the cities

In 1892 a new minister of finance, Sergei Witte, had come to realise that Russian industry had fallen far behind its rivals. He therefore

A workers' hostel in Moscow before the revolution

introduced a policy of rapid industrialisation. Factories were built, and peasants flocked from the countryside to find work in them. Any hopes of a better standard of living were quickly dashed. Employers were concerned only with profit, and to keep profits high, costs had to be kept low. Therefore the workers were poorly paid and crammed into the poorest of lodgings.

The rapid growth of St Petersburg is shown in the figures:

1881	928 000
1897	1 264 700
1910	1 905 966
1917	2 300 000

A well-researched fictional account describes city life in St Petersburg:

All the large factories were flanked by grey and dejected buildings of several storeys, which were simply warehouses of labour. The same architectural styles were recognisable in all: they were civilian barracks. Inside, a dark and narrow corridor was flanked by thin plank doors, which opened into dormitories for 20 or 30 workers or into minute rooms (*kamorki*), each sheltering several families. Each family strove to mark off its modest domain in the *kamorka* with hangings made of old pieces of cloth. But these flimsy partitions were not enough to ensure the privacy of couples. The beds (simple plank bunks) touched one another. Men, women and children mingled their voices, odours, illnesses, quarrels and reconciliations. The workers did their washing in the room and dried it from lines strung from wall to wall. A sour odour came from these rags as they dripped on the muddy floor.

Henry Troyat, *Daily life in Russia under the last Tsar*, 1961

Working conditions were equally bad. In the capital city, not far away from the palaces of the Tsar and Countess Kleinmikhel, people worked a sixteen-hour day in unhealthy conditions and were in a state of constant, desperate poverty. This class, the industrial proletariat, were thought to be the most dangerous to the government of the Tsar. Some people believed that they could be encouraged to revolt. Then, with the support of the peasantry, they could overthrow the ruling classes and establish a more just society.

Karl Marx, the father of communism. Here, his picture is displayed alongside Lenin, Trotsky and others after the revolution of 1917

The revolutionaries

For many years small groups of people in Russia had discussed the evils of Russian society, and how it could be changed. Some of these adopted the ideas of Karl Marx.

Marx was one of the most important political thinkers of modern times. He saw that nineteenth-century governments were run by and for the few – power lay with the landed, often aristocratic classes. Later, with industrialisation, he saw that power would be taken by the new, wealthy middle classes, such as the factory owners. This class would become powerful because it exploited the working classes. According to Marx it was inevitable that the working classes would rebel against their masters and take power for themselves. The workers would then establish a communist society where all wealth was shared and there would no longer be any private property.

One follower of Marx was Vladimir Ilyich Lenin. In 1895 he had been arrested for his revolutionary activity. He spent two years in prison, and three more in exile in Siberia. During this time he planned and wrote. In 1900 he returned to St Petersburg and joined the Russian Social Democratic Labour Party. Later from a position of voluntary exile in Switzerland, Germany, and England he edited a newspaper, *Iskra*, ('The Spark'). In 1903 Lenin dominated the congress of the Social Democratic Party, which met at Brussels. This domination caused a split in the party. Lenin demanded that the leaders should form a strong central committee which could take decisions and plan revolution; others wanted a more democratic party which would allow events to take their course. Lenin's group was called the Bolsheviks, his opponents were called the Mensheviks. From 1903, each went its own way.

In the early days these revolutionary groups had few successes, although some of them were notable. In March, 1881 an organisation called 'The People's Will' succeeded in the assassination of Tsar Alexander II. However, he was replaced by the more autocratic Alexander III, and revolution still seemed to be far in the future. But in fact, revolution of sorts came unexpectedly in 1905.

Karl Marx (1818–83), author of *The Communist Manifesto* and *Das Kapital*, he spent much of his life in London exiled from his native Germany because of his revolutionary ideas.

Born in the Volga, trained in law, Lenin studied Marx and became a key figure in revolutionary politics.

Thousands of revolutionaries were imprisoned by the Tsar

Autocratic – absolute, uncontrolled rule.

The revolution of 1905

In 1905 Russia went to war with Japan over North Korea. The war was a fiasco, with the Russian fleet defeated in the straits of Tsushima and the army at Mukden. Immediately there was an outburst of criticism at the government's inefficiency in handling the war. At the same time there was a food shortage in the cities, and this caused strikes which developed into a massive workers' movement.

Under the leadership of a priest, Father Gapon, and some revolutionary leaders, demands for a constitution and greater freedom and equality were made in a petition signed by 135 000 people. On Sunday,

Observers were certain that mighty Russia would quickly deal with little Japan in this quarrel over control in the far east. Russia's defeat was a humiliation.

Few gave the Japanese a chance in war with Russia. Little did they know the extent of Japanese military strength

22 January, 150 000 people, carrying portraits of the Tsar and singing hymns, marched peacefully towards the Winter Palace, the home of the Tsar. The police and cossacks, who were waiting for them, opened fire. Possibly one thousand demonstrators died and many more were injured. The strike movement grew, and law and order collapsed in the countryside. The government could not even rely on the armed forces: for example the crew of the battleship *Potemkin* mutinied rather than fire upon the city. Much of this solidarity was spontaneous. However, the revolutionaries were active too, pursuing a more planned campaign, and they succeeded in the assassination of Grand Duke Sergei, the Tsar's brother.

The prime minister, Witte, realised that some demands must be met, or the government and the Tsar might fall. He persuaded the Tsar to issue the 'October manifesto' which promised reform. The constitution outlined in the manifesto served its purpose – to stop the revolution – but for many it was far from satisfactory. Both the reforms, and what Leon Trotsky thought of them, can be seen here:

Two views of Bloody Sunday, 9 January 1905

And so we have been given a constitution. We have been given freedom of assembly, but our assemblies are encircled by troops. We have been given freedom of speech, but there is censorship. We have been given freedom of study, but the universities are occupied by troops. We have been given personal immunity, but the prisons are filled to overflowing with prisoners. We have been given a constitution, but the autocracy remains. Everything has been given, and nothing has been given.

Indeed, the Tsar soon went back on his promises. Leaders of opposition groups were arrested, the parliaments or Dumas were limited in their power by the veto. When the Dumas demanded more than the Tsar was willing to give in only their first session of May 1906 – the Tsar closed them down, and rigged elections to produce a Duma which would co-operate with him.

Only one significant change came out of the revolution of 1905. The new prime minister, Stolypin, realised that the mass of peasants must be helped if further revolution was to be avoided. From 1906–11 he pursued a policy which gave the peasantry greater freedom. Two million families were released from the commune and helped to improve their farming. It was a move in the right direction, but too little to meet Stolypin's aims. Stolypin's other main hope was to repress and stamp out revolutionary movements. In this he clearly failed, as he was assassinated in 1911.

The Potemkin *mutiny, 1905*

Workers at the River Lena gold mines who were shot for striking

Questions

1 Look at the two accounts of court life A and B. What is the attitude of each of the writers to Russian high society? What examples does each writer provide to describe the extremes of wealth?
2 Explain the growing pressures on both peasants and workers which made their standard of living worse.
3 Imagine that you were the foreign guest who attended the Kleinmikhel ball. On the next day despite the protests of your hosts, you demand a tour of the living quarters of the workers. Describe what you see and feel about this.
4 Draw and complete the Marx diagram.

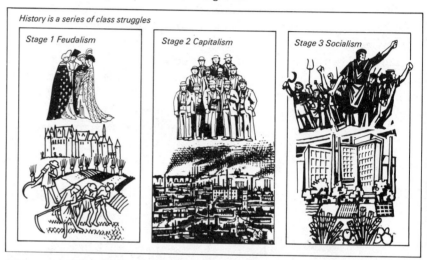

History is a series of class struggles

Stage 1 Feudalism   Stage 2 Capitalism   Stage 3 Socialism

5 Draw and complete the diagram showing long- and short-term causes of the revolution of 1905. Add detail to each box.

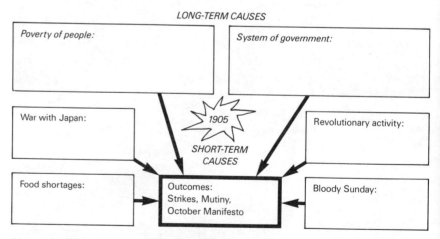

LONG-TERM CAUSES

Poverty of people:

System of government:

War with Japan:

1905
SHORT-TERM CAUSES

Revolutionary activity:

Food shortages:

Outcomes:
Strikes, Mutiny,
October Manifesto

Bloody Sunday:

Note: The following section concerns the revolution of February 1917. As you read the section, establish the long- and short-term causes and enter them on a copy of the diagram in the same way as you have just done for 1905.

Build-up to the revolution of February 1917

In 1914 Russia, with Britain and France, went to war against Germany and Austria (see page 25). At first the Russian people rallied behind their Tsar, but soon things began to go wrong. Defeats at the war front and growing economic problems in the cities put increasing pressure on the government and were to lead to revolution in February 1917.

1 The conduct of the war

The commander of the Russian forces was Grand Duke Nicholas, described as 'a really great soldier and strategist' by the German general, Ludendorff. The Grand Duke found that his advice to the Tsar on the conduct of war was opposed by the Tsarina and her close confidant, the sinister priest Gregory Rasputin.

In June 1915 the Tsarina wrote to the Tsar:

I am haunted by our friend's [Rasputin's] wish and know it will be fatal for us and the country if it is not fulfilled.

I have absolutely no faith in Grand Duke Nicholas. You know Nicholas' hatred for Gregory is intense. Russia will not be blessed if her Sovereign lets a Man of God sent to help him be persecuted.

The Tsar relieved Grand Duke Nicholas of command, making himself responsible for the conduct of the war. In February 1916 he ordered a great offensive against the Germans which sustained massive losses:

No one knows the figures of Russian losses. Five or eight millions? No one knows the figures. All we know is that sometimes in our battles with the Russians we had to remove mounds of enemy corpses before our trenches in order to get a clear field of fire against fresh assaulting waves.

General Hindenburg

Having assumed personal command, the Tsar himself was blamed for the defeats and heavy casualties of 1916.

2 The economy

The war shattered Russia's economy, and the poorer classes found themselves worse off than ever. Demonstrations and strikes took place in the cities and towns, but the shortages of basic foodstuffs and supplies grew worse as the war proceeded, and more men were sent to the front:

	1914	1915	1916	1917
Number of men mobilised (millions)	6.5	11.2	14.2	15.1
Percentage of males of working age	14.9	25.2	35.7	36.7
Grain production (million *poods*)	3509	4006	3319	3185
Inflation (where rouble is 100 in 1913)	130	155 *(Jan)*	300 *(Jan)*	755 *(Oct)*

A letter from a revolutionary, Shlyatnikov, to Lenin and Zinoviev, written in December 1916, states:

Rasputin won the Tsarina's favour by healing the Tsarevich, a boy who suffered from haemophilia. His private life was a scandal, yet he had great influence on people and policies.

Rasputin

Pood – 40 pounds weight.

Zinoviev was a close companion of Lenin, prominent in the revolution, and high in the party until his rivalry with Stalin.

A total absence of patriotic feeling can be seen in the mood of the working masses. The high cost of living, exploitation, and the barbaric policy of the government have proved to the masses the true nature of the war. The cry of 'war till victory' remains the slogan only of the war industries. . . . The workers' movement is marked by an upsurge of strikes throughout the country. . . . Prices have gone up five to ten times compared with last year. Clothing and footwear are becoming unobtainable. And you no longer talk about meat. . . .

At Kremenchug a large crowd of 'queuers' had collected around a shop for sugar. The majority were women. A row broke out. The row led to constables being beaten up and shops looted. Soldiers were called out, but they refused to fire.

This spontaneous mutiny lasted two days but then fresh forces arrived and the crackdown began with customary ferocity.

This report was sent to Shlyatnikov in the same month:

There is an engineering and mining works in the village of Lyudinovo with some 5000 workers. The plant works for the defence industry. On the occasion of a shortage of food products and because of high prices, the workers in September 1916 went on strike demanding a rise of 75 per cent. The strike lasted two days; they settled at 50 per cent.

In October an acute shortage of flour and sugar was experienced. Flour had reached five roubles a pood. The workers struck again, putting forward a demand 'bread and sugar' and pay rises from 25 per cent to 100 per cent. They were out for a day and a half. Flour and sugar were distributed, and wages

A bread line, Petrograd, 1917

raised by up to 75 per cent. In November there was no flour, sugar or paraffin at all. I travelled round the villages: grumbling, discontent and vague apprehension all around.

3 The trigger

By February 1917 the discontent had built up to the extent that one quarter of a million Petrograd workers were on strike. These massive strikes were the trigger which started the revolution itself. Historians still argue as to whether the strikes and the revolution itself were planned, or spontaneous. If the revolutionaries used the bad conditions for their own purposes, it could be said that the revolution was planned. If the bad conditions themselves led to the revolution, it could be called spontaneous. Here are three comments which highlight this problem:

The strikes in the Petrograd factories, which started on 23 February and involved 90 000 workers, spread on the following day. . . .By the 28th, 240 000 workers were out. There is still something about these February strikes which remains unaccounted for. . . . A mass movement on this scale and with this momentum would not have been possible without some sort of directing power behind it. . . . Two important reasons have been advanced for the rapid growth of the strike movement . . . the dwindling bread supply, and the lockout at the large Putilov works. . . . This lockout must have contributed substantially . . . the 30 000 strikers went from factory to factory persuading their comrades to join the strike. Coming at a time when feeling was running high because of wild rumours of a food shortage, the calls were . . . effective. Large crowds gave the agitators unlimited scope for action. . . .

The Bolsheviks played an insignificant part. There was however, another social democratic group, The Mezhrayonka . . . in organisation and ideology this group was influenced by Trotsky . . . it had widespread contacts with soldiers.

In February 1917 the Mezhrayonka had issued a leaflet containing the slogans 'Down with autocracy', 'Long live the revolution', 'Down with war'.

G. Katkov, *Russia, 1917. The February Revolution*, 1969

The Revolution struck like a bolt from the blue, and caught not only the government, the Duma and the existing public organisations by surprise . . . it was also a surprise to us revolutionaries.

V. Zenzinov, member of the Social Revolutionary Party

In every factory, in each guild, in each tavern . . . the molecular work of revolutionary thought was in progress.

Leon Trotsky's *Autobiography*

Questions

1 What evidence is there in these documents that the rising was planned?
2 What evidence is there that the rising was spontaneous?
3 Which of the three documents do you consider to be the more valuable in helping you to answer these questions? Why?

The February Revolution

On Saturday, 25 February, there were massive strikes in Petrograd. The transport system was crippled, and production halted. The Cabinet wrote to the Tsar begging that he return, and offering their resignations. Five hundred miles away, the Tsar failed to understand the urgency and panic in their letter. He sent back a telegram to General Khabalov, military governor of Petrograd, saying,

I order that the disorders in the Capital, intolerable during these difficult times of war with Germany and Austria, be ended tomorrow.

In his turn Khabalov gave the following orders:

The Sovereign has ordered that the disorders be stopped by tomorrow. Therefore the ultimate means must be applied. If the crowd is small, without banners and not aggressive, then utilise cavalry to disperse it. If the crowd is aggressive and displays banners, then act according to regulations, that is, signal three times and fire.

An historian sees this as a moment of great importance:

Up to this point the soldiers had not been forced to commit themselves. Their sympathies were clearly on the side of the demonstrators. Now they were to be made the instrument of bloody repression against people of their own kind. To refuse meant the firing squad. Therefore the only course for those who were not prepared to obey the command to shoot was to mutiny *en masse*.
A. K. Wildman, *The End of the Russian Imperial Army*, 1980

On 27 February the commander-in-chief of the army, General Alekseev, sent this telegram:

On 27 February about midday the President of the State Duma reported that troops were going over to the side of the population and killing their officers.

Russian prisoners after the battle of Tannenberg

After 7 p.m. the Minister of War reported that the situation had become very serious. The majority of the units have betrayed their duty and many have joined the rebels.

With the Cabinet powerless, and the army in a state of mutiny, the Duma had to decide what to do. For a long time this body had been powerless. Now, on 27 February, it met to consider what should be done – to try to uphold the failing government, or to grasp power for itself. The numbers divided in opinion about this, as shown by the actions of the president of the Duma, Rodzyanko, and another member, Kerensky.

On 27 February – this telegram arrived, from Rodzyanko to the Tsar:

The government is absolutely powerless to suppress disorders. The reserve battalions of the guard regiments are in rebellion. Officers are being killed. Having joined the crowd they are proceeding to the State Duma. Order the immediate calling of a new legislative government. Make these measures known without delay. Your Majesty, do not delay. If the movement spreads to the army at the front, the Germans will triumph, and the ruin of Russia and with her the dynasty will become inevitable. Rodzyanko.

A member of the Duma V. V. Shulyin, remembered the rise to importance of Kerensky:

All members of the Duma were present . . .

Rodzyanko, put the question 'What is to be done?' to this quivering human mass. Someone proposed that the Duma should declare itself the government. Milyukov recommended caution, that too hasty decisions should not be taken, especially when we did not yet know what would happen. . . .

Someone spoke and demanded that the Duma declare on which side it was: with the old order or with the people. At that moment there was a commotion at the door and an officer rushed into the room.

'Members of the Duma, I need to be defended. Some soldiers have broken in. My aide has been injured. They want to kill me. Help me!'

Kerensky began to speak at this moment.

'What has happened confirms that we must not lose any time. I am receiving reports constantly that the army is in revolt. They are going on the streets. I am going to the regiments. It is necessary to know what to say to them. May I tell them that the State Duma is with them, that it is taking on itself responsibility and that it is leading the movement?.

Kerensky grew into a man of importance at that very moment.

By 28 February, General Alekseev realised that Petrograd was lost:

At 2 a.m. the rebels occupied the Marinsky Palace. by 8.25 a.m. the number of faithful had dropped to 600 infantrymen and 500 cavalrymen.

We have just received a telegram from the Minister of War stating that the rebels have seized the most important buildings in all parts of the city. Due to fatigue and propaganda the troops have laid down their arms, passed to the side of the rebels, or become neutral.

The Tsar responded with this letter on 2 March to his chief-of-staff:

The internal disturbances which have begun among the people threaten to have a calamitous effect on the future conduct of a hard fought war. The

Kerensky (left) reviewing the troops

The Tsar in captivity at Tsarskoe Selo

destiny of Russia . . . the whole future of our beloved Fatherland, demand that the war be carried to a victorious conclusion no matter what the cost. . . . We have judged it right to abdicate the Throne of the Russian State and to lay down the Supreme Power. We hand over our succession to our Brother, the Grand Duke Mikhail. . . . We call upon all true sons of the Fatherland to fulfil their sacred duty to it by their obedience to the Tsar at this time of national trial. . . . May the Lord God help Russia!

Questions

1 If you have not already done so, refer to the questions about the February Revolution on page 123 and complete this diagram.

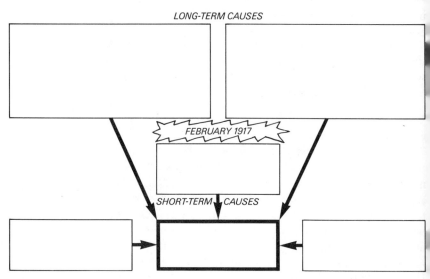

LONG-TERM CAUSES

FEBRUARY 1917

SHORT-TERM CAUSES

2 Explain the attitude of the following people towards the events of 27 February:
(a) a soldier, (b) Rodzyanko, (c) Kerensky, (d) The Tsar.
3 What reasons does the Tsar give for his abdication on 28 February?

Using the evidence: the provisional government at war

At the moment of his abdication, the Tsar did not grasp the real nature and scale of the revolution. He named his brother, Grand Duke Michael, as his successor. Michael refused the throne and abdicated in favour of the Duma, the constitutional assembly. The Duma named Prince Lvov as prime minister, and Kerensky as minister of justice in the new provisional government. However, there was now another organisation which looked for a share in government. During the February Revolution, workers, soldiers and peasants had sent representatives to their own councils or soviets. When the provisional government met, the soviets met too, and for some people the soviet was more representative and important than Lvov's government. For the time being the two worked side by side. Indeed, Kerensky was involved in both.

It was not long before a major disagreement between the provisional government and the soviets emerged – whether or not Russia should continue to fight the war against Germany. Their differing views are shown here:

A Warriors, our country is in danger! Liberty and revolution are threatened. The time has come for the army to do its duty. Your Supreme commander (General Brusilov), beloved through victory, is convinced that each day of delay merely helps the enemy, and that only by an immediate and determined blow can we disrupt his plans.

Officers and soldiers! Know that all Russia gives you its blessing on your undertaking in the name of liberty, the glorious future of the country, and an enduring and honourable peace.

Forward!

Kerensky, Minister of War and Navy, 16 June 1917

B Comrade proletarians and toilers of all countries.

We, Russian workers and soldiers, united in the Petrograd Soviet of Workers' and Soldiers' Deputies send you cordial greeting and inform you of a great event. Russian democracy has overthrown the age old despotism of the Tsar. . . . Our victory is a greater one for universal freedom and democracy.

Appealing to all the people who are being destroyed and ruined in this monstrous war, we say that the time has come to begin a decisive struggle against the ambitions of the governmens of all countries; the time has come for the people to take into their own hands the decision of war and peace.

But we appeal to you – by our united efforts we shall stop the dreadful butchery that is a strain on humanity.

Proletarians of all countries unite.

Petrograd Soviet of Workers' and Soldiers' Deputies
Izvestiya, 15 March 1917

C The situation in the army grows worse every day: information coming in from all sides indicates that the army is systematically falling apart.
1 Desertions continue. Between 1 and 7 April, 7688 soldiers deserted.
2 Discipline declines with each passing day; those guilty are indifferent to possible criminal punishments.
3 The authority of officers and commanders has collapsed, growing to undeserved humiliations and assaults and the removal of their authority.
4 A pacifist mood has developed in the ranks.
5 Defeatist literature and propaganda has built itself a firm nest in the army.

War Minister Guchkov's report to the provisional government, April 1917

D Desertions were perhaps the most alarming form of disorganisation. Trains moving to the rear were jammed with soldiers. The cities teemed with unattached soldiers – at one time it was estimated that 1000 soldiers a day were pouring into Kiev railway station.

General Lukomski estimated that on average each division was losing 5 to 7 men per day, which, if extended to the whole army for March, would amount to 100 000 to 150 000. He put this down to widespread rumours of the impending division of land, which peasant soldiers were so eager to believe. Many of them were also stirred up by horrifying stories that landowners were burning villages and grabbing peasant land to forestall such action by the new government.

A. K. Wildman, *The End of the Russian Imperial Army*, 1980

1 According to document A why should the war effort continue? According to B why should it not?
2 Study documents C and D.
   (a) What reasons can be found to explain the number of desertions?
   (b) Do you consider either or both of the sources to be reliable? Explain your answer carefully.

Using the evidence: the October Revolution

The group most dissatisfied with the provisional government was the Bolsheviks. It has already been seen that the Bolsheviks played little part in the February Revolution. Lenin had been in Switzerland when the Tsar fell, and it seems that the Bolshevik leadership was taken by surprise.

However, their activities increased in the following months, and they worked hard to increase their influence in Petrograd, especially amongst dissatisfied workers and soldiers.

Lenin was allowed to pass across Germany in a sealed train. Germany also helped with money in an effort to do as much damage as possible to the Russian war effort.

At the end of March, Lenin returned from exile, helped by the German government who hoped that he would take Russia out of the war. Soon after his return he published his 'April Theses'. His programme included the withdrawal of support for the provisional government, the creation of a republic of soviets, and the nationalisation of all land. He saw this as a logical step in the process of Marxist revolution:

The specific feature of the present situation in Russia is that it represents a *transition* from the first stage of the revolution – which, owing to the insufficient class-consciousness and organisation of the proletariat, led to the assumption of power by the bourgeoisie, to the *second stage* which must place power in the hands of the proletariat and the poor strata of the peasantry.

To enable this transition to take place the Bolsheviks needed mass support. So far the Bolsheviks were a relatively small group within the Menshevik-dominated soviet.

Several events enabled the Bolsheviks to increase their influence:
1 The war continued to go badly. In June 1917 General Brusilov launched a disastrous offensive which lost 40 000 men. Desertions from the front increased and the cry for peace grew louder.
2 Food was in short supply and prices were high. During the 'July Days' there was rioting in the capital which Kerensky, now prime minister, blamed on the Bolsheviks. He arrested the leaders and

closed down their newspaper *Pravda*, only to find that he needed their help in the crisis of August/September.

3 At the end of August General Kornilov marched an army towards Petrograd with the aim of taking power for himself. Bolshevik supporters stopped him from reaching the capital and enabled his arrest. The Bolsheviks' reputation rose as Kerensky's fell.

4 The Bolsheviks were increasingly well organised. They trained a 'Red Guard' to act as an effective fighting force, and at the same time increased their influence amongst soldiers, workers and peasants. When Kerensky released the imprisoned Bolshevik leaders in September and new elections were held for the soviets, the Bolsheviks gained majorities in the key cities for the first time.

With Trotsky as the chairman of the Petrograd soviet, and Lenin returned once again from exile, the Bolsheviks decided that the time was ripe for revolution. Kerensky hesitated, but finally on 23 October decided to take action against them. He was too late.

Trotsky's key role was in his control of the Red Army

Consider the following documents.

A A letter to the Central Committee of the Petrograd and Moscow RSDLP, dated 12 September, 1917:

The Bolsheviks, having obtained a majority in the soviets of both capitals, can and *must* take state power into their own hands.

It would be naive to wait until the Bolsheviks achieve a formal majority in the constituent assembly. No revolution ever awaits that. Kerensky and company are preparing to surrender Petrograd to the Germans. History will not forgive us if we do not assume power now. . . .

By seizing power both in Moscow and Petrograd *at once* we shall win *absolutely* and *unquestionably*.

B A member of the provisional government remembered discussion right through the night of 24 October. He continues:

Next morning it became clear that events had taken such a turn that the government crisis could not be solved in the usual manner; almost the whole city was in the hands of the insurrectionists. The government and an ever-decreasing number of officers remained in the Winter Palace. I sat down to draft an appeal to the army. All this time, sad and alarming news was coming in by telephone. The railway stations had been occupied. The telegraph and telephone exchanges had been taken over. The Mariinsky Palace had been occupied and the members of the council who had gathered there for a meeting thrown out.

C An eye-witness remembers the storming of the Tauride Palace:

There is disorganised firing around the Palace, several soldiers have just surrendered. Darkness. Shots ring out. The chatter of machine guns. A crowd of sailors, soldiers and red guards rush up the street, and then retreat, hugging the walls, when the cadets open fire.

At this stage there was cannon fire from the Bolsheviks in the Peter and Paul fortress. 'Shouldn't we ask them to surrender?' suggests Chudnovsky. The sound of cannon fire has had its effect. The military school surrenders; the cadets lay their guns on the sidewalk in bundles and leave under escort. With Chudnovsky I went up into the apartments of the Palace. The remains of barricades, arms, cartridge cases, crusts of bread were scattered everywhere. We invaded the upper floors. Suddenly we found ourselves in a vast hall before a door guarded by a row of young people with their rifles crossed. They hesitated for a moment. They seemed petrified. We had trouble tearing their rifles from their grasp.

'Is the provisional government here?'

'It is here', one of the cadets replies, and then he whispers 'I am with you.' This is the last government of old Russia. We entered to arrest them.

D Announcement from the Military Revolutionary Committee of the Petrograd Soviet to the people of Petrograd:

In the interests of the defence of the revolution, commissars have been appointed by us in military units and at strategic points in the the capital. Oppositon to the comissars is opposition to the Soviet.

E Leon Trotsky remembered:

The final act of the revolution seems, after all else, too brief, too businesslike. The reader experiences a kind of disappointment. Where is the insurrection? The events do not form themselves into a picture. A series of small operations, calculated and prepared in advance. No action of great masses. No dramatic encounters.

1 Why did Lenin judge that the time was right for the Bolsheviks to
   seize power? (Document A). What evidence is there in B of careful
   planning?
2 What is the attitude of the various military organisations to the rising,
   according to B and C?
3 (a) What is the main point made by Trotsky in document E?
   (b) What evidence is there in A–D to support this opinion?
4 You have completed two causation diagrams for the revolutions of
   1905 and February 1917. Construct one of your own for October
   1917, clearly showing the balance between long-term causes and
   short-term causes or triggers.

1917–24: the problems of making communism work

The Bolsheviks had taken power. Yet their chances of survival were
slim. The problems they faced were truly daunting.

1 The government of Russia

The Bolsheviks had won the revolution, but the problem of who should
rule Russia, and by what means, still remained. The Bolsheviks had a
majority in the all-Russian Congress of Soviets which met on 25
October, and a council of people's commissars was established with
fifteen Bolsheviks in sole charge. Elections were held for a constituent
assembly, but there the Bolsheviks gained only one quarter of the votes.
When this assembly met and refused to adopt the Bolshevik programme, it was closed down and power returned to the Congress of
Soviets. The constitution was created by this body, and established:

Constitution – the body of rules
by which an organization or
government is run.

1 Russia would henceforth be the Russian Socialist Federal Soviet
   Republic.
2 Supreme power would be held by the all-Russian Congress of Soviets.
3 Delegates to the congress would be elected by the people.

*Lenin leaving Red Square after a
speech to Red Army troops*

4 The congress would elect a powerful executive committee which would appoint a council of people's commissars.

5 The council of people's commissars would be directed by an inner circle of about five leaders who represented the strong influence of the Bolshevik party's Politbureau.

To ensure that Bolshevik control was absolute, a new secret police force, the *cheka* was set up. This carried out the 'Red Terror' which eliminated opposition parties such as the Mensheviks, and groups such as the sailors who opposed the government in the Kronstadt rising of 1921. The *cheka* also murdered the Tsar and his family.

2 The war

Despite the revolution, Russia was still at war with Germany and Austria. On one hand the old allies of Russia, Britain and France, demanded that Russia should continue with her war effort. Trotsky's response to this was simple:

The soldiers, workers and peasants of Russia did not overthrow the governments of the Tsar and Kerensky merely to become cannon fodder for the allied imperialists.

On 15 December 1917 an armistice was declared between Russia and Germany. This was made into the formal Treaty of Brest – Litovsk in March 1918.

Immediately the Bolsheviks found themselves fighting a new war. The enemy was not any one country, but various forces with different motives: 300 000 Czech prisoners of war; supporters of the Tsar (the Whites); Russia's old allies; and nationalist groups which wanted their states to gain independence. What they all had in common was a wish to overthrow Bolshevism. Yet they failed. Look at the map, and use the following documents, to find reasons for this failure.

Politbureau – Soviet supreme governing body.

The *cheka* was set up to defend the revolution by counter-terror.

Sailors at Kronstadt had been the most loyal revolutionary supporters. This was a protest at the way the new government was working. The rising was forcibly put down by the Red Army.

The Tsar and his family were held prisoner at Ekaterinburg. With the White Army drawing near, Nicholas and all his family were shot or bayoneted.

The severity of the Brest–Litovsk Treaty shocked many Russians – Russia lost its satellite states (see map), and one third of European Russia including the people and rich resources there.

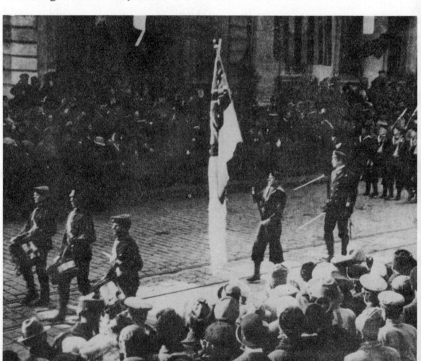

British troops arriving in Vladivostock

Using the evidence: the failure of the counter-revolution

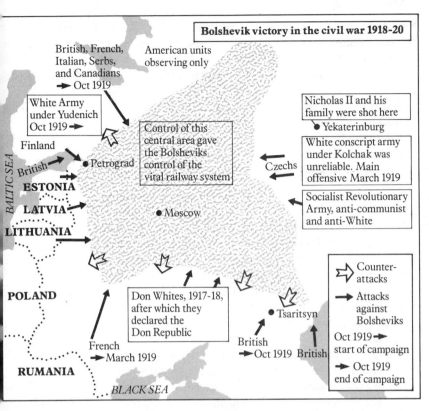

Bolshevik victory in the civil war 1918-20

British, French, Italian, Serbs, and Canadians → Oct 1919

American units observing only

White Army under Yudenich Oct 1919 →

Finland

British

ESTONIA

LATVIA

LITHUANIA

Petrograd

Control of this central area gave the Bolsheviks control of the vital railway system

Moscow

BALTIC SEA

Nicholas II and his family were shot here
● Yekaterinburg

White conscript army under Kolchak was unreliable. Main offensive March 1919

Czechs

Socialist Revolutionary Army, anti-communist and anti-White

POLAND

Don Whites, 1917-18, after which they declared the Don Republic

French → March 1919

Tsaritsyn

British → Oct 1919 British

RUMANIA

BLACK SEA

Counter-attacks

Attacks against Bolsheviks

Oct 1919 → start of campaign

Oct 1919 end of campaign

Recruitment poster for the civil war

A Statement by Kursky, the People's Commissar of Justice, 5 September 1918:

The Soviet of People's Commissars, after having heard the report of the Chairman of the Extraordinary Commission to fight Counter-Revolution . . . finds that, in the present situation, the protection of the rear by terror is an urgent necessity; it is necessary to protect the Soviet Republic from class enemies by isolating them in concentration camps. All those involved in White Guard organisations, plots and revolts are to be shot. The names of all those shot and the reason for their execution should be published.

Japanese troops standing over the bodies of Russians who opposed their intervention in the Far East

B Chairman of Revolutionary Military Council to Red Army defending Petrograd, 20 October 1919:

Red Army men, commanders, commissars. The fate of Petrograd will be decided tomorrow . . . Petrograd must not be surrendered. Even the temporary surrender of Petrograd would mean the loss of thousands of workers' lives and innumerable cultural treasures. Petrograd must be defended, no matter the cost. . . .

Remember: the great honour of defending this city, in which the revolution of workers and peasants was born, has fallen to your lot. Forward!

Take the offensive!

Death to the hirelings of foreign capital!

Long live red Petrograd!

C How could it possibly weather the opposition it aroused and emerge triumphant?

There is no simple answer. A good many factors, however, provide part of it.

On the one hand there was the unity, dedication, and unswerving purpose of the Bolsheviks; and on the other disunity brought about by self-interest and ignorance. The anti-Bolshevik factions could never co-ordinate their strength at the moment when it would have been most decisive. . . . There was no programme, then, acceptable to all the warring anti-Bolshevik factions; neither was there an inspiring leader who might have made up for this deficiency.

There is another factor in the defeat of the Whites, and that is their failure to compromise on issues of vital importance to states which had broken away from Russia following the revolution. . . . Finland, Estonia, Latvia, Lithuania, Poland, and the Ukraine therefore could hardly be expected to help the White leaders who denied their right to independence.

Allied action in Russia in support of the anti-Bolsheviks was a definite part of Anglo-French policy. But they had been bled white on the western front and had garrisons to maintain in other parts of the world.

John Swettenham, *Allied Intervention in Russia 1918–19*, 1967

1 Draw the map, indicating the strengths and weaknesses of the two sides.
2 Summarise, in your own words, why the Bolsheviks won.
3 (a) For each source, A–C, say whether the evidence is primary or secondary.
   (b) What are the advantages and disadvantages of the primary sources?
   (c) How does the secondary source compare with the primary sources in terms of (i) reliability, (ii) value?

3 The economy

Before the end of 1917 the Bolsheviks began their attack on capitalism. Consider the following government decrees on the economy.

A 27 December 1917 –

In the interests of a proper organisation of the national economy . . . the

Central Executive Committee decrees that
1 Banking is declared a state monopoly.
2 All existing private banks and banking houses are merged with the State Bank.

B 3 February 1918 –
1 All state loans negotiated by the governments of the Russian landlords and the Russian bourgeoisie are annulled as from 14 December.
2 All guarantees given by the aforesaid governments with regard to loans are likewise annulled.
3 All foreign loans are annulled unconditionally and without exception.

C 8 November 1917 –
1 Landed proprietorship is abolished forthwith without any compensation.
2 The landed estates, as also all crown monastery and church lands, with all their livestock, implements, buildings . . . shall be placed at the disposal of the *volost* land committees and *uezd* Soviet of Peasants' Deputies.
3 All damage to confiscated property, which henceforth belongs to the whole people, is proclaimed a grave crime to be punished by the revolutionary courts.

In June 1918 this nationalisation of land and banks was followed by large scale nationalisation of industry. Strict measures were taken to maintain the supply of food and essential goods to the urban population. This was known as 'war communism'. To maintain grain supply the government used requisitioning and rationing. In the short-term, the effect was disastrous for the reasons shown in this diagram.

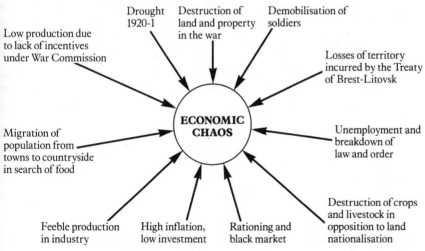

Amongst the greatest suffering was that of refugees in the drought-stricken Volga area. Their plight in August 1921 is described by an eye-witness, C. E. Bechhofer:

The conditions under which they are living are appalling. Their only shelter consists of strips of rags stretched from poles. . . . In these uncouth tents the whole family is herded together – old men with emaciated bodies and eyes that scarcely are to be seen in their deaths-heads of faces, and children sitting listlessly on the ground too exhausted to move, talk or play.

A peasant family

All through the summer they have watched their soil harden to stone under the rays of the terrible sun, and the few scattered shoots blacken and perish. They have been living on the tiny remnants of last year's harvest – which also, it must be remembered, was a failure – eked out with acorns, bark lime tree leaves, pigweed, clay, insects beaten up into a paste, even animal droppings – anything that will cheat them into imagining that they are eating something.

I meet a Tartar soldier. He has come down the river from Kazan, he tells me, where things are much worse even than here. He speaks of mothers killing their children so they may not watch them slowly die of starvation. Typhus had already broken out there, he says, hard on the heels of a cholera epidemic.

The Bolshevik government saw that something must be done to stop widespread famine. In particular the peasants had to be encouraged to grow more. Lenin realised that this could only be done if they were given incentives. In March 1921 he introduced a 'New Economic Policy', Whereas 'war communism' had removed peasant surpluses, NEP took only a fixed proportion: the more a peasant grew, the more he kept. His surplus could then be sold for profit on the open market. This was against the spirit of communism but Lenin justified it by saying,

> Incentives are against the communist tradition because they encourage selfishness instead of work for the common good.

We are now retreating, going back as it were, but we are doing this to retreat first and then run and leap forward more vigorously. We retreated on this one condition alone when we introduced our New Economic Policy – so as to begin a most determined offensive after the retreat.

This was a small step backwards for Lenin. He had achieved much of what he set out to do. The Bolsheviks had gained total power; they had won the civil war, and fought off foreign involvement; and the first strides had been made towards the creation of a socialist economy.

Questions

1 Look at the diagram showing causes of the economic chaos in 1919. Which of these causes stem from Bolshevik policies, and which are beyond their control?

2 How did Lenin justify the 'retreat' to New Economic Policy?
3 Lenin died in 1924. Write a summary of his life in the form of an obituary. In particular you should emphasise his motivation, his 'achievement', and the impact of his work.

Using the evidence: the rise of Stalin

Lenin had been injured in an assassination attempt in 1918, and his health steadily deteriorated until his death in 1924.

Meanwhile a battle had been developing within the party – who should succeed him? The man who had most advanced his position since the revolution was Josef Stalin, who had worked his way up to the post of general secretary of the Communist Party. In 1924, he was prepared for the final struggle against his rivals, Trotsky, Zinoviev, and Kamenev.

Study these three documents which show the relationship between Lenin and Stalin.

Stalin's first influential post was editor of *Pravda*. He led the defence of Tsaritsyn (Stalingrad) and fought Kolchak during the civil war. Admiral Kolchak led a revolt to bring back the government of the Tsar, or Kerensky.

A From Lenin's Testament, written before his death – but suppressed:

Comrade Stalin, having become General Secretary, has concentrated an enormous power in his hands; and I am not sure that he always knows how to use that power with sufficient caution. . . .

Stalin is too coarse, and this fault is insupportable in the office of General Secretary. Therefore I propose to the comrades to find a way to remove Stalin from that position and to appoint to it another man who in all respects differs from Stalin – more patient, more loyal, more polite, more attentive to comrades.

B Stalin's oration on Lenin at his funeral:

In leaving us, Comrade Lenin commanded us to hold high and pure the great calling of party member. We swear to thee, Comrade Lenin, to honour thy command. In leaving us, Comrade Lenin commanded us to keep the unity of our Party as the apple of our eye. We swear to thee Comrade Lenin, to honour thy command.

C A description written as part of Stalin's fiftieth birthday celebration:

During Lenin's lifetime, Comrade Stalin, though he was one of Lenin's pupils, was however his single most reliable aide, who differed from others by never flattering, by always moving hand in hand with Lenin at the crucial stages of the revolution.

Lenin and Stalin in 1922. Good friends?

Stalin allied with Zinoviev and Kamenev to defeat Trotsky at the thirteenth party congress of 1924. Trotsky sought world revolution, rapid industrialisation, and a war against the peasants who were holding back grain production and supply. On all of these issues Trotsky found the opposition too great, and when he attempted to denounce Zinoviev and Kamenev for betraying the revolution of October 1917 he was dismissed from his post as commissar for war. Then Stalin turned on his two allies, whom he accused of favouring the cities against the interest

Kamenev – party leader in Moscow. Trotsky wanted 'world revolution'. Zinoviev and Kamenev opposed him because they had a more realistic view of the problems facing communism within Russia.

of the peasants. Zinoviev and Kamenev too, lost their posts. An attempt
by Trotsky to overthrow Stalin in 1927 failed; he was expelled from the
party and subsequently sent into exile.

The Kirov killing

By 1928 Stalin had total command. He then began his own attack on the
peasantry and on the backwardness of industry. These were years of
consolidation. However, he wanted to make sure that his dictatorship
was unchallenged. In 1934, an assassination occurred which was to
begin the great purge of any possible opponents, and which was
eventually to lead to the death of millions. The victim was the successful
and increasingly popular party secretary for Leningrad, Kirov:

> **D** On 1 December 1934, at about 4 p. m. the young assassin Leonid
> Nikolayev entered the Smolny, headquarters of the Communist Party in
> Leningrad. . . . The outer guard examined Nikolayev's pass, which was in
> order, and let him in without trouble. In the interior the guard posts were
> unmanned and Nikolayev wandered down the ornate passages until he
> found the third-floor corridor on to which Sergei Kirov's office opened.
>
> Kirov was preparing a report. . . . At 4.30 he left his office and turned
> towards the office of the Leningrad Second Secretary. He had gone only a
> few steps when Nikolayev moved from a corner, shot him in the back with a
> Nagan revolver, and then collapsed beside him.
>
> At the sound of the shot Party officials came running along the corridor.
> They were astonished at the complete absence of guards. Even Kirov's chief
> bodyguard, Borisov was nowhere to be seen.
>
> Robert Conquest, *The Great Terror*, 1968

E Various theories have been put forward about the assassination:

> According to the first theory the murder was the result of the combined
> efforts of all the existing opposition groups. Amongst those charged were the
> agents of foreign powers, Trotskyites, left-wing deviationists, right-wing
> deviationists. . . .
>
> The second theory is that the assassination was a crime of passion. Kirov
> had an affair with the extremely attractive wife of Nikolayev. The jealous
> husband surprised them together, and shot Kirov on the spot.
>
> According to the third version Kirov's assassination was planned by the
> Leningrad OGPU on instructions from higher authority. There are reasons
> for the suspicion that the killer of Kirov, Nikolayev, was assisted by
> someone from among the people whose duty it was to protect to person of
> Kirov! The day after the murder Kirov's personal bodyguard was killed in
> suspicious circumstances in a road accident in which no other occupants of
> the car were harmed.
>
> G. Katkov, *The Trial of Bukharin*, 1969

OGPU, NKVD, MVD. The
OGPU replaced the *cheka* in
1922, and was absorbed into the
NKVD, the ministry of internal
affairs in 1934. This was Stalin's
terror machine, later known as
the MVD.

F The official version of the story given during the Stalin years was:

> As the court proceedings have established, the dastardly assassination of S
> M. Kirov on 1 December 1934 was organised in accordance with the
> decision of the 'Bloc of Rights' and Trotskyites.

The official verdict did not stop there:

The materials of the investigation have established that the united Trotskyite-Zinovievite centre, after it had killed Comrade Kirov, did not confine itself to organising the assassination of Comrade Stalin alone.

1 Look at documents A-C. What is the difference between what Lenin thought of Stalin and what people believed Lenin thought of Stalin?
2 Explain the tactics used by Stalin to gain total power.
3 Look at documents D-F.
(a) What is suspicious about the circumstances of Kirov's murder?
(b) Which of the versions of the murder given in E broadly agrees with the official verdict in F?
(c) Which of these theories suggested in E can you dismiss? Explain your answer.
(d) Which theory would the government wish to suppress? Explain your answer carefully.
(e) In summary, who murdered Kirov?

Using the evidence: the Great Purges

Soon after the Kirov murder, arrests of individuals and groups who opposed the government began. All of them were labelled 'wreckers'. The first victims were top party members, including Zinoviev and Kamenev. They were followed by heads of departments, army chiefs and diplomats. Later people from lower down the party ranks were charged. Finally, arrests were made of millons of people in any way associated with those already charged. To tie up loose ends, even the NKVD, the secret police which had carried out the purges, was itself purged.

Senior party members were put on trial with great publicity. One astonishing feature of these trials is that confessions were made by old revolutionaries for crimes of which they were certainly innocent.

Few of those who went through the process of examination and confession lived to tell the tale. Here are the stories of two men who did.

A Suren Gazarian gives account of the techniques used by OGPU investigators:

The torture began . . . The five men beat viciously. They beat with fists, feet, birch rods, tightly braided towels; they beat with anything anywhere. . . . The more they beat, the more brutal they became. . . . How long they beat me I don't know. . . .

My shirt had turned to bloody shreds. I lay on the floor in a pool of blood. My eyes were swollen. With difficulty I raised my eyelids and as if in a fog saw my torturers. . . .

They were smoking, taking a rest.

Someone came up to me and just then something very painful burned my body. I was convulsed with pain. And they laughed. Then it burned again, again, again . . . I understood. They were putting out their cigarettes on my body.

This sort of beating was followed by night after day of ceaseless interrogation on the 'conveyor' – the nickname for the process of continuous 'treatment'. Eventually the victims would say anything to gain sleep, and to have to avoid going through all of that again.

B M. K. Iakubovich tells of his treatment, and why he gave in:

The OGPU investigators did not make the least effort to discover the real political connections and views of . . . any defendant. They had a ready made scheme of a 'wrecker' organisation.

Evidence came from such as Petin. According to his account . . . he calculated that he would gain the most, given his arrest, by actively co-operating in setting up the wrecking trial. For this he would receive a reward from OGPU, that is the restoration of freedom and a job. If he didn't co-operate he could get a long term in prison or even die.

Others who tried to resist were 'made to see reason' by physical methods. They were beaten – on the face and head, on the sexual organs; they were thrown to the floor and kicked, choked until no blood flowed to the face. . . . They were kept on the 'conveyor' without sleep, put in the *Kartser* (half dressed and barefoot in a cold cell, or in an unbearably hot and stuffy cell without windows).

A. M. Ginzburg and I . . . came to the same conclusion: we could not endure the methods used; we would be better off dead. We opened our veins but did not succeed in dying.

After my attempt at suicide they no longer beat me, but for a long time they did not let me sleep. My nerves reached such a stage of exhaustion that nothing on earth seemed to matter – any shame, and slander, if only I could sleep. In such a a psychological condition I agreed to any testimony.

How should I behave at the trial? Deny the depositions I had made? Try to disrupt the trial? Create a worldwide scandal? Whom would that help? I felt I ought not to betray the party and the state. I won't hide the fact that I had something else in mind. . . . What would the investigators, the torturers do to me?

The trial ran smoothly, and from the outside had the look of truth. . . . In my defence speech I said that the crimes I had confessed deserved the supreme penalty, that I was not asking the Supreme Court to spare my life. I wanted to die.

But we were not condemned to death.

Iakubovich spent 24 years in a labour camp followed by a long stay in a home for invalids. Many who were tried and confessed were then shot. Others went on to labour camps where they died in millions.

C V. Shalamov writes:

It took twenty to thirty days to turn a healthy man into a wreck. Working in the camp mine sixteen hours a day, without any days off, with systematic starvation, ragged clothes, sleeping in a torn tent at sixty below zero, did the job. Beatings by the foremen, by the ringleaders of the thieves, by the guards, speeded up the process.

Solzhenitsyn's *One Day In The Life Of Ivan Denisovich* tells of the terrible daily struggle to survive in such a camp. For Ivan, a fish's eye in the soup was seen as an unexpected luxury.

D V. I. Volgin also remembered the great hardship:

They handed out a ration that clearly meant starvation on a ten hour day. The ration was intentionally harmful to health. . . . Prisoners were taken out to work, during the worst frosts. The barracks were not given enough heat, clothing would not dry out. Prisoners were not dressed for the climate in the Kolyma region, for example. They were given third-hand clothing, mere rags, and often had only cloth wrapping on their feet. Their torn jackets did not protect them from the bitter frost, and people froze in droves.

E Not all of the accused men were caught. One, a diplomat, F. F. Raskol'nikov, heard that he was outlawed while he was in France. He stayed there, and wrote this letter to Stalin:

Stalin, you have begun a new stage, which will go down in the history of our revolution as the 'epoch of terror'. No one feels safe in the Soviet Union. No one, as he goes to bed, knows whether he will escape arrest in the night.
   . . . Joseph Stalin!
   With the help of dirty forgeries you have staged trials which, in the absurdity of the accusations surpass the medieval witch trials. You have defamed and shot . . . colleagues of Lenin, knowing very well that they were innocent. You have forced them before dying to confess to crimes they never committed, to smear themselves in filth from head to toe . . . you have forced those who go along with you to walk with anguish and disgust through pools of their comrades' and friends' blood.
   On the eve of war, you are destroying the Red Army.

Here, an historian sums up the consequences of the purges:

Very grievous consequences, especially in reference to the beginning of the war, followed Stalin's annihiliation of many military commanders and political workers during 1937–41. During this time the leaders who gained military experience in Spain and the Far East were almost completely liquidated . . .
   How many were shot, how many arrested, how many perished in camps and prisons? I will resist the temptation to speculate. Various computations exist, and some people have put total losses from Stalinist repression at between twelve and fifteen million, a fantastically high figure which is yet within the bounds of credibility.
R. Nove, Stalinism and After, 1975

1 Why was the murder of Kirov so important for Stalin?
2 Look at documents A and B. What motives help to explain the willingness of the accused to plead guilty at their trial?
3 Look at documents C and D. Why was the sentence of imprisonment in the labour camps the same as a sentence of death?
4 Raskol'nikov was a loyal party member who was horrified by events in Russia. From the freedom of France he was able to tell the truth as he saw it. Compile a full list of charges which he might have made at the time he was writing to Stalin.

Collectivisation of agriculture

1927 was the year of change in Stalin's agricultural policy. Russia was still a land of peasants living at subsistence level on small plots. Stalin wanted a larger scale of production, and greater efficiency in farming:

There are two ways of doing this. There is the capitalist way, which is to enlarge the agricultural units by introducing capitalism into agriculture – a way which would lead to the impoverishment of the peasantry. . . . There is a second way, the socialist way, which is to set up collective and state farms, the way which leads to the amalgamation of small peasant farms into large collective farms, technically and scientifically equipped. . . . We are in favour of the second way.

From 1927 peasants were encouraged to farm collectives, or *kolkhoz*. Peasants in the *kolkhoz* kept a small plot of land and could earn a proportion of the produce of the *kolkhoz* as 'wages'. However, the bulk of their produce went to the government, the local tractor station, and into a communal fund for the purchase of seedcorn. The *kolkhoz* was controlled by a chairman, and people worked at his instructions to meet government targets.

Many peasants did not want to go into collectives. Rather than allow their livestock to go to the collective farm, some peasants began a mass slaughter:

Men began slaughtering their cattle every night at Gremyachy. . . . They slaughtered oxen, sheep, pigs, even cows. . . . Dogs began to drag offal about the streets. 'Kill, it's not ours now! 'Kill, the state butchers will do it if we don't.' 'Kill, they won't give you meat in a collective farm.' And the villagers killed. They ate until they could eat no more. Young and old had the belly-ache. At dinner time the peasants' tables sagged under their loads of meat. At dinner time all mouths glistened with fat and there was belching enough for a funeral feast.

M. Sholokhov, *Virgin Soil Upturned*, 1941

Official livestock figures show an overall decrease of over 65 per cent down, the first five years after Stalin announced the collectivisation policy:

Livestock (millions)	1928	1933
Horned cattle	70	34
Pigs	26	9
Sheep and goats	146	42

Grain was also destroyed, and by 1932 the resulting loss of crops had taken its toll:

In Petrakovska cattle died for lack of fodder, people ate bread made from nettles, biscuits made from one weed, porridge made from another. In Vokhovo, in the little park near the station, de-Kulakised peasants expelled from the Ukraine lay down and died. You got used to seeing corpses there in the morning; a wagon would pull up and the hospital stable hand would pile in

Kulaks – well-to-do peasants, see below.

the bodies. Not all died; many wandered through the dusty mean streets, dragging blue bloodless legs, swollen from dropsy.

V. C. Tendriakov, *Death*

Stalin's response when informed of the famine by a Ukranian was to say:

It seems you are a good storyteller, you've made up such a fable about famine thinking to frighten us, but it won't work. Wouldn't it be better for you to . . . join the Writers Union! Then you can write your fables and fools will read them.

Here are two further views of collectivisation, the first from a Russian history textbook:

Immediately after the end of the Civil War poor peasants showed a desire to work collectively. In the late twenties when the first tractor plants were commissioned, it became possible for the state to allocate more funds and machinery for the development of agriculture. After that not only poor but also middle peasants joined collective farms. . . . By the middle of 1930 six million peasant holdings were united in collective farms, and in the summer of the next year over 60 per cent of peasant families joined collective farms. An end was put to exploitation in the countryside: thanks to collectivisation the last exploiting class in the country – the Kulaks – was eliminated.

Konstantin Tarnovsky, *Illustrated History of the USSR*, 1982

Published by the official Soviet press, Novosti.

Between January and March 1930 the number of peasant holdings brought into collective farms incresed from two million to fourteen million. Over half the total peasant households had been collectivised in five months. And in the countryside the peasants fought back with the 'sawed-off shotgun, the axe, the dagger and the knife.' At the same time they destroyed their livestock rather than let it fall into the hands of the state.

R. Conquest, *The Great Terror*, 1968

Communal farming – the advantages of scale

Resistance to collectivisation came in particular from the middle ranking peasants, the Kulaks. This group had done well under the New Economic Policy, producing large grain surpluses and getting good prices for it. Stalin realised that this group would resist change, and in 1928 he accused the Siberian Kulaks of causing a crisis in grain supply.

I have made a tour of your territory and and have had the opportunity to see for myself that your people are not seriously concerned to help the country emerge from the grain crisis. You have had a bumper harvest. . . . Your grain surpluses this year are bigger than ever before. Yet the plan for grain procurements is not being fulfilled. Why? . . . Look at the Kulak farms: their barns and sheds are crammed with grain. . . . You say the the Kulaks are waiting for prices to rise. That is true . . . the Kulaks are demanding an increase in prices to three times those fixed by the government. . . . so long as there are Kulaks, so long will there be sabotage of grain procurements.

The effect will be that our towns and industrial centres, as well as our Red Army, will be in grave difficulties; they will be poorly supplied and will be threatened with hunger. Obviously we cannot allow that.

In 1929 Stalin made his policy towards Kulaks quite clear:

We must break down the resistance of this class and deprive it of its existence. . . . The present policy of our Party in the rural districts is not a continuation of the old policy, but a turn to the new policy of eliminating the Kulaks as a class.

Any Kulaks guilty of 'political' crimes

were to be isolated at once, by imprisonment and corrective labour camps, and there was to be no hesitation in applying the most extreme measure of punishment against them – shooting.

High technology comes to the commune – the first tractor, 1926

Kulaks being deported from their village, March 1930

Soon mass transportations of Kulaks took place. An historian has tried to assess the extent of the problem:

In unheated railway cars thousands of peasants with their wives and children, went east to the Urals, Kazakhstan, Siberia. Many thousands died on route from hunger, cold and disease. E.M. Landau met a group of these transportees in Siberia in 1930. In winter, during a severe frost, a large group of Kulaks were being taken in wagons three hundred kilometres. One, unable to endure the crying of a baby sucking its mother's empty breast, grabbed the child and dashed its head against a tree. . . .

An American correspondent set at two million the approximate number of those deported and exiled in 1929–30 (*New York Times*, 3 February 1931). . . . But the truth appears far worse if we realise that deKulakisation continued without let-up through the following years, and official figures vary between five and 10 million.

R. Medvedev, *Let History Judge*, 1971

Questions

1 Explain the two main motives for collectivisation.
2 What personal rewards did the peasants in the *kolkhoz* have, compared to their situation under NEP?
3 Compare Tarnovsky's view of the effects of collectivisation with that of Conquest. What are the points of agreement and disagreement?
4 What were Stalin's grievances against the Kulaks?
5 Describe
   (a) Stalin's action against Kulaks.
   (b) The effects on agriculture of this action.

Planning industrial growth

Industrialisation still relied on muscle power – construction work at Magnitka Hill

Since 1921, when the state planning commission, Gosplan, had first set targets for growth, the economy had recovered steadily. In 1927 Stalin ordered that a five-year plan should set new and higher targets for industry and trade. Stalin said of this ambitious plan,

It is sometimes asked whether it is not possible to slow down the tempo a bit, to put a check on the movement. No comrades, it is not possible! The tempo must not be reduced. To slacken the pace would mean to lag behind, and those who lag behind are beaten. We do not want to be beaten.

We are fifty or a hundred years behind the advanced countries. We must make good this lag in ten years. Either we do it, or they crush us.

Stalin could take some comfort from the results of this first plan: 1500 large industrial complexes were built, manufacturing metals, tractors, cars, chemicals, agricultural machinery, and other vital products. Massive industrial plant was created at places such as Dneproges, Magnitogorsk, Stalingrad, and Kharkov. Total expansion of industry under the plan was 118 per cent, which seems a remarkable feat. However, the plan had its failings. In particular, there were shortfalls in the production of iron, steel, and coal. In addition, industry failed to attract the technical expertise and capital from the West which Stalin hoped for.

A second five-year plan sought to make up for these shortfalls. Stalin was not a man to lower his sights. He increased targets still further, and demanded that, by 1937, the 1932 figures should be raised by 250 per cent. Plans were drawn up for 107 new steel-rolling mills, 164 open-hearth furnaces and 45 blast furnaces. Stalin also demanded higher production of consumer goods – textiles, footwear, food processing – and more building.

Furnaces at the great steel works, Magnitogorsk

New centres of production grew up. Karaganda grew from a building site to a city of 166 000 people in six years. Magnitogorsk was regarded as a triumph of Soviet achievement:

Within several years, half a billion cubic feet of excavation was done, 42 million cubic feet of reinforced concrete poured, five million cubic feet of fire bricks laid, a quarter of a million tons of structured steel erected. This was done without sufficient labour, without necessary quantities of the most elementary supplies and materials. Brigades of young enthusiasts from every corner of the Soviet Union arrived in the summer of 1930 and did the groundwork of railroad and dam construction necessary before work could begin on the plant itself. Later, groups of local peasants and herdsmen came to Magnitogorsk because of bad conditions in the villages, due to collectivisation. . . . A colony of several hundred foreign engineers and specialists arrived to advise and direct the work.

From 1928 till 1932 nearly a quarter of a million people came to Magnitogorsk. About three quarters of these new arrivals came of their own free will seeking work, bread cards, better conditions. The rest came under compulsion.

John Scott, an American engineer

Let there be light. Electricity arrives, 1928

Stalin also placed greater emphasis on transport. The railway system was modernised. Waterways were built such as the Baltic–White Sea canal and the Moscow–Volga canal. To improve the road system, arterial highways were built connecting major cities with the newly developing areas. With such great distances involved, Stalin also sought better air transport systems. Propaganda constantly urged higher production, and incentives were used to encourage individual workers. One of the most publicised cases was that of Alexei Stakhanov:

In August 1935, a miner, Alexei Stakhanov, pondered over his highly skilled task of operating a pneumatic drill or coalcutting machine. He had the idea that he could cut more coal if he could concentrate all his effort and attention on

The oil fields at Baku, 1934

cutting, while the subsidiary operations of removing the coal was performed by other members of the team, similarly concentrating on their own particular process.

The result was immediately amazing. Instead of the six or seven tons per shift usual, Stakhanov began to cut 102 tons in one shift. The idea spread to other industries.

Any worker coming up with this sort of idea for improved productivity was given honours and financial rewards.

In 1938 Stalin launched a third five-year plan. This plan again concentrated on consolidation of major industries. However, it was recognised that, for most Russian citizens, life was austere. To boost consumer goods production, higher targets were set.

The plan was interrupted by the outbreak of the Second World War in 1939. As a result of the plans, Russia was now far more important as an industrial nation. This industrialisation had brought little direct benefit to the people of the USSR, and much suffering. However, it did provide a strong backbone to stand against Hitler's Germany, and eventually the strength to overwhelm Nazism.

Questions

1 By what means did Stalin promote industrialisation?
2 What were the various motives of the people who went to Magnitogorsk?
3 Explain the success of Alexei Stakhanov.
4 Use the statistics in the table to show particular strengths and weaknesses of Russian industry and agriculture up to 1946. Draw graphs to show patterns of production for electricity, coal, steel, grain, and cows.

The foreign policy of the USSR, 1922–41

After the revolution the government of the USSR felt very insecure. They looked for an alliance, at times any alliance, to avoid isolation. The timeline opposite explains why the USSR shifted its alliances during these years.

Questions

1 Explain why the line which represents Soviet foreign policy avoids the centre of the diagram.
2 Explain each of the turning points on the diagram.
3 On what grounds might the Western powers criticise the Nazi–Soviet Pact of 1939? On what grounds might Stalin defend it?

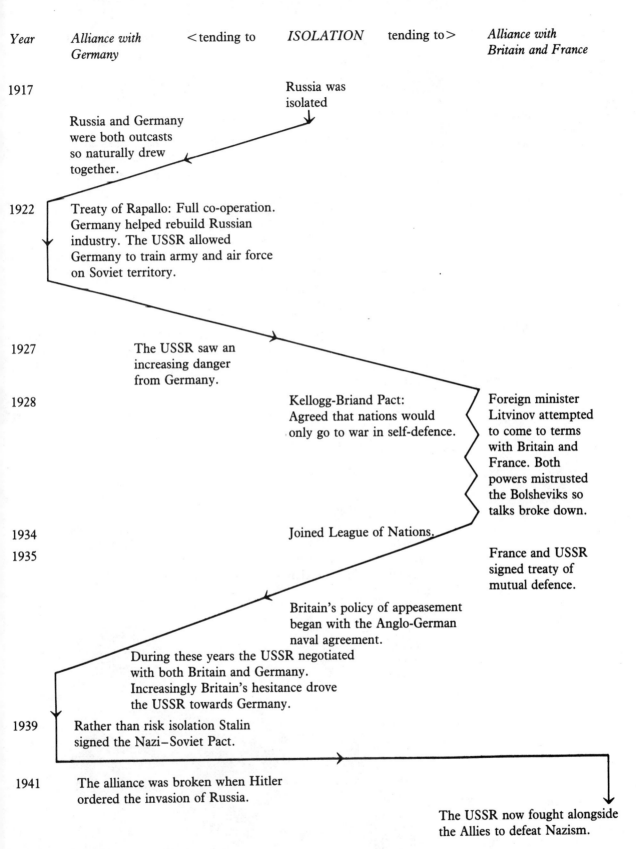

Year	Alliance with Germany	<tending to	ISOLATION	tending to>	Alliance with Britain and France

1917

Russia was isolated

Russia and Germany were both outcasts so naturally drew together.

1922

Treaty of Rapallo: Full co-operation. Germany helped rebuild Russian industry. The USSR allowed Germany to train army and air force on Soviet territory.

1927

The USSR saw an increasing danger from Germany.

1928

Kellogg-Briand Pact: Agreed that nations would only go to war in self-defence.

Foreign minister Litvinov attempted to come to terms with Britain and France. Both powers mistrusted the Bolsheviks so talks broke down.

1934

Joined League of Nations.

1935

France and USSR signed treaty of mutual defence.

Britain's policy of appeasement began with the Anglo-German naval agreement.

During these years the USSR negotiated with both Britain and Germany. Increasingly Britain's hesitance drove the USSR towards Germany.

1939

Rather than risk isolation Stalin signed the Nazi–Soviet Pact.

1941

The alliance was broken when Hitler ordered the invasion of Russia.

The USSR now fought alongside the Allies to defeat Nazism.

9

The Second World War in Eastern Europe

Using the evidence: the invasion of Russia and the siege of Stalingrad

Operation Barbarossa, the invasion of Russia, began in June 1941.

A A Russian textbook describes the invasion:

Early in the morning of 22 June 1941, Fascist Germany treacherously attacked the Soviet Union.

In the very first hours of the war the enemy launched massive air raids. Fascist planes dropped bombs on Soviet towns, aerodromes, and railway junctions. Thousands of guns opened fire on the frontier posts and the areas where Red Army units were stationed. Shock formations of enemy tanks and motorised convoys burst on to Soviet soil. . . .

It was only after an hour and a half of the start of operations that the German consul in Moscow informed the Soviet Government that Germany considered herself to be in a state of war with the Soviet Union.

B A German infantryman remembered:

After short, bitter fights with the surprised but determined frontier troops they were now advancing more quickly. In front of them the assault guns, behind them their own heavy artillery firing deep into enemy lines. German bombers cruised overhead weaving silver trails across the sky.

The hands of the watches had shown 3.05 and they had rushed forward springing in quick steps to reach the Soviet frontier pill-boxes. A few short bursts had been sufficient to beat down the resisting enemy who were only dressed in vest and pants. Only a few were killed.

C Another infantryman remembered the advance:

In between fighting the infantry had marched sometimes 70 kilometres each day, and this they had achieved in enemy territory where cornfields and trees hid the wily sniper. Burning villages, staring bodies of fallen Soviet soldiers, swollen carcasses of dead horses, rusting burned-out and blackened tanks were the signposts of the march. Soviet cavalry, enemy tanks, dive-bombing aircraft and fighters skimming low – all tried to halt the advance but none succeeded.

D Leningrad party members were called to a meeting on 20 August:

Russian citizens who resisted the German advance were dealt with as an example to others

'As you see', said Voroshilov, 'the situation is very difficult but we have the capability not only to halt the enemy's advance, but to smash and destroy him.'

Zhdanov said, 'The moment has come to put your Bolshevik qualities to work. What we have to do in the shortest possible time is to teach the people the main methods of combat – shooting, throwing grenades, street fighting, digging trenches, crawling. We must sign up the younger people for work in labour battalions. The enemy is at the gates. It is a question of life or death. Either the working class of Leningrad will be enslaved, or we must gather all the strength we have, hit back twice as hard, and dig Fascism a grave in front of Leningrad.'

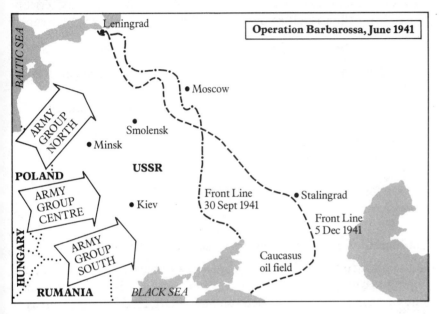

E Führer's GHQ, 7 October 1941:

Supreme Command of the Wehrmacht to Supreme Command of the Army: The Führer has decided that a surrender on the part of Leningrad or later Moscow, will not be accepted even if offered by the enemy.

No German soldiers are to enter these cities. All cities are to be worn down before capture by artillery fire and air attacks and their populations caused to flee. There can be no reason for exposing the lives of German soldiers to enemy fire to save Russian cities or to feed their populations at the expense of Germany.

signed Jodl

The German troops dug in as instructed, and began to pound Leningrad. In the city food soon ran out.

F To fill their empty stomachs and deaden the pains of hunger the inhabitants trapped crows, hunted down the surviving cats and dogs, and prepared soup and jelly from carpenter's glue. During the period of the blockade 632 000 people died of starvation.

Once winter came the only possible supply route was across the ice. For the passage of freight across the ice the thickness must be 200m to support a truck carrying one ton. By 17 November, the ice was 100mm thick.

On the morning of 18 November the longed-for north wind began to blow. By the end of the day the temperature was down to minus twelve and remained there for several days.

And now came the bright day when machines began to move across the ice. On the morning of 22 November 1941, keeping intervals between them, at low speed, one truck after another went to pick up the long awaited supplies.

D. Pavlov, Leningrad, 1941

Throughout 1942 supplies into into the city steadily improved. In January 1943 Soviet troops broke through the enemy blockade, and a year later Leningrad weas completely freed. The city was terribly scarred and the casualties over one million, but Leningrad remained undefeated.

1 Use documents A–C to show why Barbarossa was so successful in its early stages.
2 How do the speakers in source D try to prepare the citizens of Leningrad for the coming ordeal?
3 Explain Jodl's order to the army commander and the reasons for issuing that order.
4 Write extracts from the diary of a citizen of Leningrad, dated 22 June 1941, 20 August 1941, 8 October 1941, 17 November 1941, 22 November 1941.

Stalingrad: The turning point on the eastern front

In the spring of 1942 Hitler launched a new offensive against Stalingrad hoping to capture the city and thereafter the oilfields of the Caucasus. The German 6th Army advanced on Stalingrad, reaching the suburbs in August 1942.

A The Soviet general, Talensky, remembers the disadvantages faced by the Soviet troops at the start of the siege:

In July and August in the Don and Stalingrad areas the Germans had twice as much infantry as the Russians, two and a half times as much artillery, two to three times as many tanks. Their superiority in the air was overwhelming.

Fortunately the tank had ceased, in Stalingrad, to be a decisive weapon. The more the Germans bombed the Russian positions, the more obstacles did they add to their advance. With the accumulation of rubble it became more difficult, and sometimes impossible, for the tanks to move, and at the same time bombing created new 'shelters' for the Russian defenders.

Our losses were very heavy, especially during the first stages of the battle. Later, after we had dug in at Stalingrad, the German casualties began to pile up beyond ours.

Russian soldiers who survived acquired tremendous experience in hand-to-hand fighting. They knew every drainpipe, every manhole, every shell-hole and crater. Among piles of rubble, which no tanks could penetrate, he would turn on his tommy gun the moment he saw any German within firing distance. Seldom anything short of a direct hit could knock him out . . .

B On 1 October the Soviet newspaper *Red Star* ran the following piece:

The surrender of the German 6th Army at Stalingrad

THE HEROES OF STALINGRAD

Every day Rodimstev's men take it upon themselves to repel twelve to fifteen enemy attacks of tanks and infantry, supported by artillery and aircraft. Not only with their brain, but with their heart, do these guardsmen know that no further retreat is possible. They defend to the last every street and every house. In one day alone they destroyed 2000 Nazis, 18 tanks, 30 vehicles.

By September it was obvious to observers that the German army was on the defensive, and that Soviet reinforcements and supplies threatened the German 6th Army. Retreat seemed sensible to the generals, but not to Hitler:

C When a statement was read to him which showed that Stalin would still be able to muster another 1.25 million men in the region of Stalingrad, and which proved that the Russian output of first line tanks amounted to 1200 a month, Hitler flew at the man who was reading, with clenched fists and foam in the corners of his mouth, and forbade him to read such idiotic twaddle.

Franz Halder, German general

D Russian Colonel Zamiatin described the Soviet counter-attack:

Having regained their strength the Soviet army prepared to strike back. By the middle of November preparations had been completed. What was planned was a two-sided concentric blow, a pincer round the Stalingrad group. The main operation was carried out in four to five days. In an area of 1500 square kilometres twenty-two enemy divisions consisting of 330 000 men had been trapped.

On 31 January the German 6th Army of 100 000 men surrendered. The tide of war on the eastern front had turned.

Write a full report to Hitler, including maps and diagrams, to explain why your army failed to capture Stalingrad, and is now on the point of surrender. Knowing Hitler's response, your excuses had better be good!

The fall of Berlin, Spring 1945

From April 1943 the Soviet armies went onto the offensive. By May 1944 almost all the ground that had been lost to the Germans was recovered. Poland, Rumania, Bulgaria, Yugoslavia, Hungary and Czechoslovakia had fallen. By the spring of 1945 General Zhukov was ready to launch the attack on Berlin:

A It seems to me that Eisenhower may be wrong in supposing Berlin to be largely devoid of military and political importance. . . . The dominating fact on German minds of the fall of Berlin should not be overlooked. The idea of neglecting Berlin and leaving it to the Russians to take at a later date does not appear to me correct.

Winston Churchill

B The Russian thrust employed 32 rifle divisions and eight tank corps, the greatest concentration of force in the narrowest circle since the start of the war.

Needless to say I had kept Hitler fully informed of the grave developments taking place. His replies during the early days consisted merely of repetitions of the instructions he had given me on 9 January: The Eastern Front must make do with what it's got.

General Guderian, January 1945

When Guderain told Hitler that he was only thinking of Germany's interests, Hitler replied 'How dare you speak to me like that? Don't you think I'm fighting for Germany? My whole life has been one long struggle for Germany!'

Guderian's principal staff officer had to grip his chief's jacket and pull him out of the range of the Führer's fists.

John Strawson, *The Battle for Berlin*, 1974

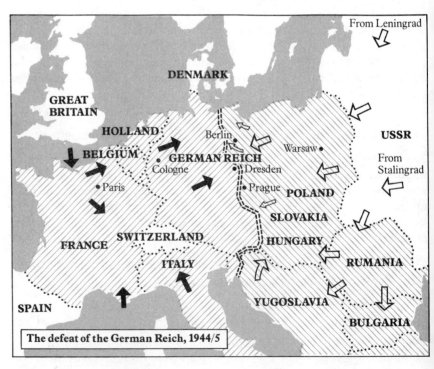

The defeat of the German Reich, 1944/5

C The raid began at 10.45 a. m. and ended at 12.30. Many people had to wade about underground for two hours in icy water. Under the heavy explosions the massive shelter swayed and shivered like the cellar of an ordinary house. Finally the lights went out and we felt as though we had been buried alive . . . Gigantic clouds hung over the whole city.

Von Studnitz, a German in Berlin, quoted in *The Battle for Berlin*

D On 25 April 1945, the last stage of the Great Patriotic War was to begin – the storming of Berlin. On the night before I visited the positions of our artillery. I wanted to see the results of our ranging fire, and at the same time to imprint on my own memory the first shots fired on the den of the fascist beast.

Everything was ready for firing. 'On the fortification of Fascist Berlin – Fire!' The heavy shells flew up, cleaving the air with a whistling sound. The path had been opened.

In the morning I went to my observation post. Somewhere in the middle of the city ragged yellow plumes rose skywards as bombs exploded: the heavy bombers had already started their attack. . . . Suddenly the earth shuddered and rocked under my feet. Thousands of guns announced the beginnings of the storming operation.

The artillery continued to tear into the defence positions of the Berlin garrison. The walls of buildings were collapsing, ramparts and street barricades went flying into the air. I remember thinking then 'Hitler has committed his last and greatest crime against his own people. Why is he dooming thousands upon thousands of Germans to die, putting arms in their hands and sending them out under oath not to give in?'

General Chuikov

Possibly the last photo of Hitler. Here he is shown surveying the damage outside his bunker, c. 20 April 1945

E On the morning of 30 April, Hitler was given the latest reports on the situation in Berlin. Hitler received the news without excitement and took lunch at two in the afternoon. . . . Having finished his lunch, Hitler went to fetch his wife from her room, and they said farewell to Goebbels, Bormann, and others who remained in the bunker. Hitler then returned to the Führer's suite with Eva and closed the door. A few minutes passed while those outside stood waiting in the passage. Then a single shot rang out.

After a brief pause the little group opened the door. Hitler was lying on the sofa, which was soaked in blood. He had shot himself in the mouth. On the right hand side lay Eva Braun, also dead. She had swallowed poison.

A. Bullock, *Hitler*, 1952

On 4 May 1945, German armies began to surrender. On 7 May, General Jodl signed an unconditional surrender. The war in Europe was over.

Questions

1 Why, according to source A was the capture of Berlin important to the Western Allies? What other reasons for Berlin's importance might Churchill have also borne in mind?
2 Why might Guderian have doubted Hitler's confidence at this point?
3 According to C and D what were conditions like for Berliners in 1945?
4 Write a report for Allied readers on the fall of Berlin, including the death of Hitler.

The USA in 1919

The economy of the USA had grown during the First World War. Industry and agriculture had boomed, investment and profits were high, unemployment was low. The war had enabled the USA to move clearly ahead as the world's wealthiest nation. By contrast the year 1919 came as a shock to the American nation. As in Europe, the end of the war brought with it social and economic problems.

There were fewer jobs: soldiers returning from Europe found few opportunities. Furthermore, they blamed this not on the fall in demand for goods which had taken place since the war, but on the blacks and immigrants whose numbers had increased in the cities during the war. The result was increasing racial tension and violence. Even those with a steady income found conditions difficult. Prices were rising steadily, but wages were actually falling:

Average weekly earnings (dollars)
1920   26.30
1922   21.21
1924   24.65

In 1919 four million workers went on strike. Major industries such as steel were affected. More worrying for the government, the Boston police force went on strike. To many Americans this seemed like a breakdown in law and order which could make way for revolution. Employers, state governments, and the US government in Washington took action to break these strikes and force the workers back into line.

Even so, the racial tensions, strikes and economic problems were matters of grave concern to US citizens at the start of the 1920s. One answer was to purify America – to bring it back to prosperity, godliness, and to the ideals for which its white – and mainly Anglo-Saxon – ancestors had fought.

Warren Harding, 1920–3, a Republican whose government was notorious for corruption. Calvin Coolidge, 1923–8, a Republican who loosened control on industry and kept taxes low. Herbert Hoover, 1929–32, honest and a firm believer in American 'freedoms'.

Purification in government: back to rugged individualism

The three American presidents who dominated the 1920s and early 1930s shared the same basic idea about government. Here, the idea is expressed by President Hoover:

[After the war] we were challenged with a peacetime choice between the American system of rugged individualism and a European philosophy of paternalism and state socialism. The acceptance of these ideas would have meant the destruction of self-government, initiative, and enterprise through which our people have grown to greatness.

Rugged individualism harks back to the great pioneering days when America was won by the determination of the settlers.

The American choice, of rugged individualism, argued that government should not interfere in the lives of individual citizens. It saw life as a race. Government, it was believed, should give an equal start through the education system, and then make sure that the race was fairly run. In short, 'The winner is he who shows the greatest ability and the

156   THE USSR AND THE USA

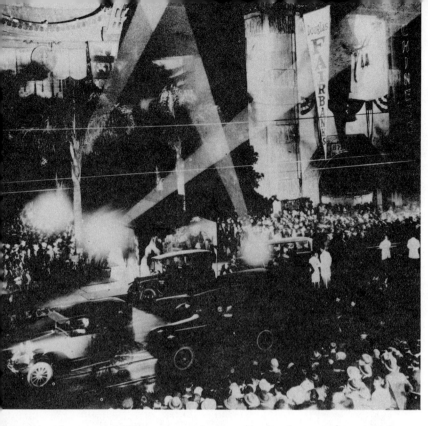

A film premiere at Hollywood – a popular image of the USA between the wars

greatest character.' The prize, of course, was the greatest wealth.

Hoover may have believed that life's race in America was fair, and his view was shared by the prosperous middle classes who shared in the new consumer boom of the 1920s. In practice, the 631 000 people with top incomes received more than the bottom sixteen million put together. These people could not share in the boom in luxury goods – indeed they did not have enough money to pay for basic necessities. More than 10 per cent of the workforce was unemployed, and as much as half of the population may have been living below the poverty line. Some of these people had always been poor – especially black and immigrant comunities. Other groups had become poor in the 1920s. For example, farmers had invested money in growing more grain during the war because they could get high prices for it in Europe. They had began to cultivate poorer land, but found that once the war was over Europeans no longer wanted their grain, and prices were low. Profits fell, and soon many of them were heavily into debt. They could not pay for labour, and the labourers who could not find work drifted into the cities to add to the problems already there. Evidently rugged individualism worked only in times of plenty, and tended to benefit only the few.

This was a time of high spending on new luxury goods such as domestic gadgets and cars.

Poverty line – where income is insufficient to provide basic requirements for good health.

Purification of morals: the prohibition laws

One of the most astonishing stories in US history is that of prohibition. Against the wishes of vast numbers of people, the 18th Amendment, a law which banned alcohol, was passed through congress in 1917. Those

The American constitution was written in 1787. Very occasionally it has been amended – for example, the 19th Amendment gave women the same rights as men.

who favoured the Act saw it as a remedy for many evils. Here is the view of an evangelist preacher:

The slums will soon be only a memory. We will turn our prisons into factories and our jails into storehouses and corn cribs. Men will walk upright now, and women will smile, and the children will laugh. Hell will be forever rent.

What actually happened was an entirely different story:

The American people had expected to be greeted when the great day came, by a covey of angels bearing gifts of peace, happiness, prosperity and salvation. Instead they were met by a horde of bootleggers, moonshiners, rum-runners, hijackers gangsters, racketeers, triggermen, venal judges, corrupt police, crooked politicians, and speakeasy operators, all bearing the twin symbols of the 18th Amendment – the tommy gun and the poison cup.

H. Asbury, *The Great Illusion*, 1950

Bootlegger – transports and sells illegal liquor (named after those who hid the bottles in their boots).
Moonshiner – illegal distiller of alcohol.
Venal – corrupt, easily bought.
Speakeasy – illegal bar.

Evidently most people wanted to drink alcohol, and the law in this case was too poorly thought of and too easily evaded so that drinks were available in plenty in the downtown speakeasies. These illegal bars enabled gangsters to make a fortune by controlling the production and sale of illegal drink. The 'greatest' of these gangsters was 'Scarface' Al Capone. An estimate of his takings in 1927 is as follows:

	$ (millions)
Beer, liquor, home-cooked alcohol	60
Gambling places and dogtracks	25
Brothels, dance halls and inns	10
Miscellaneous rackets	10

Illegal drinks in a New York 'speakeasy'

Capone justified his business by saying,

They call Capone a bootlegger. Yes. It's bootleg while it's on the trucks, but when your host at the club, in the locker room, or on the Gold Coast hands it to you on a silver platter, it's hospitality. What's Al done, then? He's supplied a legitimate demand. Some call it bootlegging. Some call it racketeering. I call it business. They say I violate the prohibition law. Who doesn't?

Capone and the other gangsters were playing for high stakes, and it can be argued that prohibition encouraged violence. One famous case involved Dion O'Banion who used a florist's shop as a cover for his liquor dealing. He was killed by Capone in one of the many incidents of gang warfare. Capone contributed $50 000 worth of flowers at the funeral. Another case was the 1929 Saint Valentine's Day massacre, (14 February), when, in another gang feud, seven members of the Moran mob were line up against the wall of their beer depot, and machine-gunned to death. Prohibition agents worked hard to control the availability of alcohol, but despite their activities, the alcohol continued to flow and after thirteen years the Act was finally repealed.

High stakes in the criminal world – The St. Valentine's Day massacre, Chicago, 1929

Gang warfare hits the headlines

Purification of the spirit: the fundamentalists

Fundamentalism was an influential religious movement. Fundamentalists believed in the absolute authority of the Bible – that every word in it was absolutely true. They were most influential in the southern states, and in several states the teaching of the theory of evolution was banned because it conflicted with the story of the creation in Genesis.

In 1925 a biology teacher was prosecuted and fined $100 for teaching about evolution. Excerpts from the trial are illuminating:

[Howard Morgan aged 14, talking about his teacher's lessons:]
He said that the earth was once a hot, molten mass; in the sea the earth cooled off and there was a little germ of one celled organism formed, and this organism kept on forming and this was man.

The geological evidence offered to prove this was dismissed by the judge, who 'couldn't see the purpose of any evidence by a bunch of imported scientists.' When Darrow, the defence counsel, went on the attack against Bryan, a fundamentalist, the prosecution case was proved to the judge's satisfaction.

Darrow: Do you believe Joshua made the sun stand still?
Bryan: I believe what the Bible says.
Attorney: What is the point of this line of questioning?
Bryan: The purpose is to cast ridicule on everybody who believes in the Bible.
Darrow: We have the purpose of preventing bigots and ignoramuses from controlling the education of the United States.
Bryan: I am simply trying to protect the word of God against the greatest atheists in the States.

Notably at this point, the gallery cheered. Fundamentalism had defeated science.

Purification of race

Ku-Klux Klan – a terror organisation originally set up to persecute freed slaves in the deep South.

The most notorious aspect of the attempt to 'purify' America was the Ku-Klux Klan, whose membership rose to above five million during the twenties. Their attitude can be seen from this statement by Joseph Simmons, who led the KKK until 1923:

We exclude Jews because they do not believe in the Christian religion. We exclude Catholics because they owe allegiance to an institution that is foreign to the Government of the United States. To assure the supremacy of the the white race we believe in the exclusion of the yellow race and the disenfranchisement of the Negro. By some scheme of Providence the Negro was created a serf.

Franchise – freedom expressed in the right to vote.

The Klan terrorised many American people, especially in the South. They paraded through the streets with blazing torches. Flogging and tarring and feathering were common punishments, and in the view of Governor Dorsey of Georgia their purpose was to drive out black people altogether. When a black man broke the law, or was even suspected, he could expect no mercy. In Georgia alone there were 135 cases of

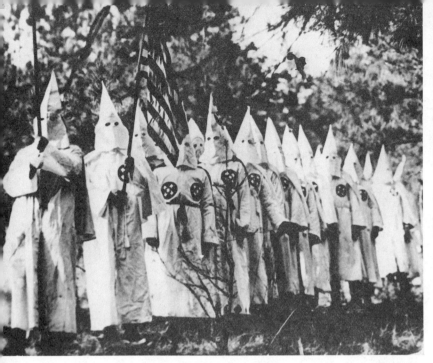

Above: The townspeople of Marion, Indiana, using lynch law on two blacks accused, but not convicted of murder

Left: Knights of the Ku-Klux Klan awaiting the Imperial Wizard in Georgia

lynching in two years. In 1921 the *Washington Eagle* reported the fate of a black man convicted of murdering a white girl:

The negro was taken to a grove, where each of more than five hundred people, in Ku-Klux ceremonial, had placed a pine knot around a stump, making a pyramid to the height of ten feet. The negro was chained to the stump and asked if he had anything to say. Castrated, and in indescribable torture, the negro asked for a cigarette, lit it, and blew the smoke in the face of his tormentors.

The pyre was lit and a hundred men and women, old and young, grandmothers among them joined hands and danced around while the negro burned. A big dance was held that evening in celebration of the burning.

The Washington Eagle, 1921

The 'Roaring Twenties'

All of those who wanted to purify America may have wanted to go back to some past-imagined American ideal. In fact, far from going back, America in the 1920s was roaring forwards. One aspect of this was changing fashions and attitudes.

The representative symbol of the age was the 'flapper', with her bobbed hair and pudding basin hat, her rouge and lipstick, her flattened breasts, her waistless short skirt, her flesh coloured stockings and her undergraduate escort. The two of them went . . . in a car to movies and parties where they probably danced the Charleston and Black Bottom. As likely as not some strong, illegal liquor was served, and by late evening the couple might well have been conducting a spirited and wordless debate as to the amount of 'necking' and 'petting' that 'nice girls' permitted.

Daniel Snowman, *USA The Twenties to Vietnam*, 1968

The Whippet, with new features!

The Hoover – and a familiar advertising line!

The latest in modern electric refrigeration

If attitudes were changing, so too was the quality of life of those who could afford it. Indeed, for them the twenties were roaring. The noise of automobiles in the streets, the sound of jazz on the radio, the advertisements urging the ear and the eye to buy the new consumer luxuries – for cash if you have it – or on credit if you have the status to get it. Hire purchase and catalogues were new ways in which people were tempted to spend their money.

Leading the way in this consumer boom was the automobile industry. At first cars were very expensive. Then, in 1909 Henry Ford launched his 'Model T' range. A Model T Ford was completed under mass production methods every twenty seconds. In 1908 it cost $760, but by 1925 it had fallen to $260, and many prosperous Americans could afford them:

Year	Number of vehicles sold
1904	22 800
1909	127 300
1919	1 876 400
1946	3 089 600

By 1930 there were 30 million cars on the roads. This produced work directly in the motor industry. But, in addition, cars created a demand for 90 per cent of all petroleum products, 80 per cent of rubber products, 20 per cent of steel, 75 per cent of plate glass, and 25 per cent of machine tools.

Another revolution took place in the field of communications. On 2 November 1920, station KDKA in Pittsburg broadcast the election victory of President Harding. Few people heard the broadcast, but the radio industry was soon to expand dramatically. By 1922, there were 220 broadcasting stations and three million houses were tuning in. By 1925 the listening audience was estimated at 50 million.

A host of other electrical goods were also appearing for the first time. Vacuum cleaners and refrigerators, for example, were to have a great effect on ordinary domestic life. however, for many people without a substantial income, these items were as far from reach as the film stars of the new silent movies. Furthermore, things were going to get worse for them before they got any better.

Questions

1 Describe the American way of life which was sought by those who wanted to purify the USA.
2 The American Declaration of Independence states 'that all men are created equal, that they are endowed by their Creator with certain inalienable rights, that among these are life, liberty and the pursuit of happiness'. how do the actions of government and citizens in the 1920s measure against these ideals?
3 How did the twenties gain the nickname 'roaring'?

4 If you assume that everything about the flapper is new, and against the rules, write a list of the rules that her parents might have made, and which she was breaking.
5 Why is the automobile so significant in the development of the economy at this time?
6 Use the text and illustrations to describe how the 'consumer boom' might have affected the wealthier American's home?

The Crash and Depression

In 1929 the USA received a blow which, for a moment, stopped its heart. This was the Wall Street Crash.

Investing in shares had become a regular feature of the lives of many Americans, whether they were wealthy, or whether they hoped to be wealthy:

Shares – vouchers which indicate part ownership of a company. Profits are distributed to shareholders according to the number of shares they hold. There is, of course, a risk of loss.

The volume of trading on the Wall Street Exchange [the total number of shares bought and sold] rose by a series of unprecedented leaps from 451 million in 1926 to over 1.1 billion in 1929. In the same three years the average top price for twenty-five leading industrials rose from $186.03 to $469.49 per share.

A large proportion of the trading, possibly a third or more, was done on the margin. A broker required only about a ten or twenty per cent down payment on a block of stock. This easy payment plan naturally excited the gambling instinct. Under the feverish scramble to 'get into the market' the volume of these loans rose . . . from 3.2 billion in September 1926 to 8.5 billion in September 1929.

Cabell Phillips, *The New York Times Chronicle of American Life 1929–39*, 1969

The upsurge in the market relied on confidence that US industry would continue, to expand and make high profits. People who put down only 10 to 20 per cent of the value relied on selling at high enough profit to cover the rest when they paid the broker what they owed him. Thousands of people who bought 'on the margin' in this way would never have dreamed of having to find the remaining 80 per cent or 90 per cent in any other way, and could not have done so if it had been demanded.

However, share prices could not continue to increase iike this. The economy was not as strong as it seemed. Agriculture had not yet recovered from the depression of 1919–20, and agricultural shares were already weak. The boom area was industry. However new industry had over-expanded in both capacity and production techniques. To take an example, the USA was now producing thousands of vacuum cleaners and fridges every year and production had outstripped demand. Once a family had a new fridge it would not want another. America was spent up. Stocks of unsold commodities started to grow. Demand for goods, and profits, were falling. When profits started to fall, people wanted to sell their shares. When everyone wanted to sell, and no one wanted to buy, panic set in – and the bottom fell out of the market.

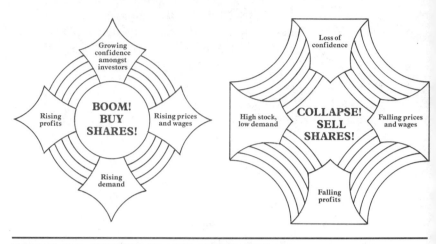

BOOM! BUY SHARES!
- Growing confidence amongst investors
- Rising prices and wages
- Rising demand
- Rising profits

COLLAPSE! SELL SHARES!
- Loss of confidence
- Falling prices and wages
- Falling profits
- High stock, low demand

THE WALL STREET CRASH: TIMELINE

1928–September 1929	Shares gain steadily in value.
3 September 1929	Share prices at peak.
4 September 1929	Slight fall in share value. No panic.
4 September–19 October 1929	Steady fall in share value. Quiet selling.
19 October 1929	Share brokers call on customers who have bought 'on the margin' to pay the full price of their shares. The deadline for payment is Thursday, 24 October. Banks call in money which they have loaned for share purchase.
24 October 1929 (Black Thursday)	Many clients had failed to respond. Their shares were 'dumped' as brokers rushed to sell; 12.8 million shares changed hands at rapidly falling prices.
25 October onwards	Panic selling. 'Around the stock exchange crowds were especially heavy. Persons bruised by the rough milling brought ambulances clanging into Wall Street . . . and started rumours that a trader caught in the market had jumped from a window
29 November	A typical news story read: 'James J. Riordan, President of the County Trust . . . was a victim of the stock market. He died with a bullet through his right temple in his bedroom at 21 West 12th Street. The banker is reported to have suffered heavily in the collapse of radio shares. Radio dropped to 35½ on Friday, a loss of 14½ points.'

An unemployed worker uses his initiative

Americans who had known prosperity in the twenties now joined the great numbers of existing poor in a terrible economic depression. Its effects, of course, were not limited to the USA – it had repercussions throughout the world, and especially on Western Europe (see page 69) Hoover did not think that it was the government's job to deal with the effects of the crash. He called together a group of industrial leaders in December 1929, and made it quite clear where the responsibility would lie:

The cure for such storms is action. The cure for unemployment is to find jobs. You represent the business of the US, undertaking through your own voluntary action to contribute to the advancement of our economic life. . . . And this is not dictation or interference by the government with business. It is a request from the government that you co-operate in prudent measures to solve a national problem. A great responsibility and a great opportunity rests upon the business and economic organisations of the country.

The years 1930–2 show the extent of Hoover's success:

	Unemployment	Failed businesses	Farm income (billion $)	Average weekly earnings in manufacturing
1930	4 340 000	26 355	4.1	$24.77
1931	8 020 000	28 285	3.2	
1932	12 060 000	31 822	1.9	$16.21

Most characteristic of this phase of the Depression was the 'Hooverville'. The unemployed, the evicted, the desperate, built these shanty towns outside Washington and other cities:

Each had built for his family a rickety shelter of salvage lumber, boxes, and tin cans. The entire settlement was a dreary, sodden mess; stagnant rainwater stood three to six inches deep; outdoor privies had overflowed shallow wells; sickness was rampant, half-clad urchins peered through windows or skittered through slop. There wasn't a dollar in the whole settlement.

L. Hewer, *Box Car in the Sand*

They used to tell me I was building a dream
and so I followed the mob –
When there was earth to plough or guns to bear
I was always there – right on the job.
They used to tell me I was building a dream
With peace and glory ahead –
Why should I be standing on line
Just waiting for bread?
Once I built a railroad, made it run,
Made it race against time,
Once I built a railroad,
Now it's done –
Brother, can you spare a dime?

Wealth and poverty. Broadway, New York, with a queue waiting for the relief kitchen to open

A migrant family with their mobile shack

Roosevelt – wealthy Democratic candidate, governor of New York State. He suffered from polio but this proved to be no handicap in a very successful career.

1932 was election year. The Democrats put up a new man with new ideas – Franklin D. Roosevelt. The election was fought over two different philosophies. Hoover and the Republicans stood by 'rugged individualism' – the idea that 'prosperity was just around the corner' and would result from individual initiative without goverment interference. Roosevelt, on the other hand, said,

A freedom of action which might have been justified in the relatively simple life of the last century cannot be tolerated today . . . we have left the period of extreme individualism.

To Roosevelt it was the government's job

to prevent the starvation or the dire want of any of its fellow men who try to maintain themselves but cannot.

Roosevelt won 42 of the 48 states, and as soon as he took office he started to carry out major reforms. He gave America what he had promised – a 'New Deal'.

Roosevelt brings in the New Deal

THE NEW DEAL

Need	'New Deal' Act	Effect
1 Some banks had gone broke and action was needed to restore confidence.	Banking Acts, 1933	Banks were closed and inspected. Sound banks were reopened with a government guarantee. Unsound ones were shut down. In future banks were prohibited from speculating on stock exchange.
2 Many people were in desperate poverty.	Federal Emergency Relief Agency (FERA), 1933	Gave $500 million cash relief to states to solve immediate problems.

3 The government needed to raise money to pay for projects such as FERA.	Economy Bill, 1933	This Bill cut the salaries of war veterans and federal employees. The money saved was then used elsewhere.
	Prohibition Bill, 1933	The government scrapped the prohibition laws and gained in taxes on the sale of alcohol.
4 High unemployment. (a) Amongst the young	Civilian Conservation Corps, 1933	Young people, 18–25, were set to work on conservation and reforestation programmes at $1 a day.
	Civil Works Administration, 1933	Set people to work on community projects. Four million people were involved but what they did was labelled 'trivial' by critics and the CWA was replaced in 1935.
(b) Long-term unemployment	Works Progress Administration, 1935	Major projects included 5900 schools, 2500 hospitals, and other public buildings, and road building. The WPA also supported such people as actors and artists.
	Public Works Administration, 1933	Created major schemes such as the Boulder Dam on the Colorado River.
	Tennessee Valley Authority 1933	This was one of the poorest areas in the USA, covering seven states. Problems included soil erosion, little industry, poor communications. A major works programme made the river navigable, provided irrigation, and hydro-electric power through sixteen new dams.
5 Slump in industry. Poor employer/employee relations.	All above in 4 will have stimulated industry.	
	National Industrial Recovery Act (NIRA), 1933 National Recovery Administration, 1933	Firms agreed to negotiate minimum wages and maximum hours. Those that did were allowed to carry the badge of the Blue Eagle, itself a morale booster which came to symbolise national recovery.
6 In 1935 the Supreme Court declared NIRA to be illegal. Need for new labour laws.	National Labour Relations Act, 1935	Restated the right of workers to join unions. Improved wages and working conditions.
7 Depression in agriculture.	Agricultural Adjustment Administration, 1933	Organised co-operative marketing schemes and gave loans to those in danger of eviction. Gave farmers subsidies. On occasion urged them to produce less to keep prices up. Thus, for example, six million piglets and 200 000 sows in farrow were slaughtered.
8 Fear of poverty.	Home Owners Loan Corporation.	Loaned money at low interest to mortgagees in difficulty.
	Social Security Law, 1935	Provided government support for pensioners, the impotent poor and the unemployed.

Civilian Conservation Corps

Works Progress Administration

National Recovery Administration

Using the evidence: attitudes towards the 'New Deal'

1 Study the following sources which show what people thought of the New Deal. Divide a page into two columns, for, and against the New Deal. In the case of each document decide whether it favours the New Deal or not.

In the appropriate column, write:

(a) whether the source is primary or secondary.

(b) the standpoint or motive of the writer.

(c) why the writer seems to favour or be critical of Roosevelt.

2 Some of these documents are criticisms by small groups or individuals. Some represent the opinion of large numbers of people. Do those which represent large numbers fall in the 'for' or the 'against' category?

3 Use all of the sources to write a balanced summary of responses to the New Deal.

A A young worker said,

There are twenty of us making $15 a week and working 48 hours a week. But without the NRA code all that would change in one day. There would be fifteen of us working and we would do 68 hours a week for $10 – the way it was before the code.

B New Deal Joke 1:

New Deal definitions –
Socialism – If you own two cows, you give one to your neighbour.
Communism – You give both cows to the government, and the government gives you back some of the milk.
New Dealism – You shoot both cows and milk the government.

C Colonel Eugene Sanctuary of the 'American Christian Defenders' said:

The Roosevelt New Deal is not sincere; it is not a recovery movement; it is sabotage with the idea of bringing about the World Jewish State.

D From G. Wolfskill, *All but the People, F.D.R and his Critics, 1969:*

With the amount of criticism the New Deal generated over the years it was easy to forget that the vast majority approved Roosevelt and the New Deal. That approval was expressed clearly, and also at four-yearly intervals, in a blizzard of votes – not once but an unprecedented four times.

E A contemporary newspaper article read:

The Russian newspapers during the election published the photo of F.D.R. over the caption 'The First Communistic President of the US'. Evidently the Russian newspapers had knowledge concerning the intentions of the President which had been carefully withheld from the voters in this country.

F New Deal Joke 2:

Have you heard there's only six dwarfs now?
Dopey's in the White House.

G The communist *Daily Worker* said:

Is not this trickery the hallmark of the Wall Street tool, the President who always stabs in the back when he embraces, spending billions for war profits and trampling on the faces of the poor?

Roosevelt had a landslide victory in 1932. This was repeated in 1936. Despite considerable opposition he was elected for a third term in 1940 and, despite ill health, again in 1944.

A New Deal poster shows the American way

WORLD'S HIGHEST STANDARD OF LIVING

There's no way like the American Way

H From William Leuchtenburg's *Franklin Roosevelt and the New Deal*, 1963:

The New Deal left many problems unsolved and even created some new ones. As late as 1941 the unemployed still numbered six million, and not until the war years of 1943 did the army of jobless finally disappear. The New Deal achieved a more just society but left many Americans – slum dwellers, mostly negroes, outside.

Some of these omissions were promptly remedied. . . . When recovery did come, it was much more soundly based because of the adoption of the New Deal programme.

I A welfare worker remembered:

Every house I visited had a picture of the President. These ranged from newspaper clippings to large coloured prints framed in gilt cardboard.

J New Deal Joke 3:

When a statue is put up of Roosevelt, where should it be placed?
  Not near George Washington, because he never told a lie.
  Not near Lincoln, because he freed the slaves.
  Near Columbus! He didn't know where he was going when he started, didn't know where he was when he arrived, and didn't know where he had been when he returned. Besides, he did it all on borrowed money.

American foreign policy, 1919–41

The 'Fourteen Points' which dominated the peace settlement of 1919 were drawn up by President Wilson. Yet when he returned to America he found that the voters would not support his view of an international role for the USA. He was voted out of office, and America turned to isolationism. This does not mean that the USA wanted no part in world affairs. It meant a withdrawal only from involvement in political affairs and alliances abroad and especially from conflict in Europe.

There were other aspects of international relations in which the USA played an important part during these years. Although the USA turned its back on the League of Nations, it was involved in disarmament talks. In 1928 the Kellogg–Briand Pact was made, condemning war except in the case of self-defence. In 1932, US delegates attended the Geneva World Disarmament talks, although these were unlikely to succeed in an atmosphere of rising aggression.

The USA was also of key importance in the world economy, as an exporter of both goods and credit. In particular, the US was owed vast sums by both victors and vanquished in the Great War. In 1924 the Dawes plan attempted to make sense of German reparations, and in 1929 the Young plan reduced the bill to a more reasonable level (see page 68). The plans were important in aiding the recovery of European economies.

The economic importance of the USA is perhaps best shown by the

Frank Kellogg – US Secretary of State.

effects of the Wall Street Crash, which was a major cause of the depression of the 1930s (see page 46).

Another aspect of US policy during this so called period of 'isolation', was the 'good neighbour' policy with regard to countries in the Caribbean and South America. Instead of interfering, the USA sought co-operation through trade, and mutual assistance. The Declaration of Lima of 1938 provided for joint resistance by the states of the Americas to outside attack.

Roosevelt and the coming of the Second World War

As far as European affairs were concerned, there were many Americans who were strongly isolationist. Of those who thought the USA should be involved, many saw Britain and the Western democracies as natural allies, but there were others who took the opposite view. For example, there were German Americans, and Nazism did have some support in the USA. There were also Irish Americans, including the US ambassador to Britain, Joseph Kennedy, and their feelings were anti-British.

The events of the 1930s therefore affected Americans in a variety of ways. The key person in deciding what the United States would do was, of course the president. However, with elections due in 1940, Roosevelt could not afford to lose the sympathy of the voters by pursuing a policy which they disliked.

Using the evidence: Roosevelt's words and actions

Phase 1, 1937

Fascist powers were increasingly aggressive. Civil war was raging in Spain, Italy had invaded North Africa, and Japan had invaded Manchuria. Roosevelt's words were:

The peace, the freedom, and the security of 90 per cent of the population of the world is being jeopardised by the remaining 10 per cent . . . we are determined to keep out of war, yet we cannot insure ourselves against the disastrous effects of war and the dangers of involvement.

In his actions, Roosevelt tried to oppose the passage of a neutrality law through congress, and to take a moral stand against aggression. He failed for lack of public support.

The opposition said,

STOP FOREIGN MEDDLING. AMERICA WANTS PEACE.

Wall Street Journal

Phase 2, 1939

Negotiations were held over the fate of Czechoslovakia. Hitler showed bad faith both here, and subsequently in the invasion of Poland which started the Second World War in Europe, September 1939.

Roosevelt's words were:

This nation will remain a neutral nation but I cannot ask that every American will remain neutral in thought as well. . . . Even a neutral cannot be asked to close its mind to conscience.

And his actions? In June 1939, Roosevelt asked King George VI of England to visit the USA, privately 'believing that we might all soon be engaged in a life or death struggle in which Britain would be our first line of defence'. He also assured the king 'If London was bombed, the USA would come in.'

In September 1939, while Chamberlain was still attempting to negotiate peace with Hitler, Roosevelt opened private correspondence with Winston Churchill with preparations for war in mind.

The opposition said,

I am more confirmed that ever in my belief that not a dollar should be wasted nor a drop of blood sacrificed over the boundary disputes of the old world.

Senator Luddon

Phase 3, June 1940

France had fallen, and Great Britain stood alone. Roosevelt's words were:

If Great Britain goes down . . . all of us . . . would be living at the point of a gun. . . .

The vast resources and wealth of this empire constitute the most tempting loot in all the world. . . . No man can tame a tiger into a kitten by stroking it. There can be no appeasement with ruthlessness. A nation can have peace with the Nazis only at the price of surrender. . . .

We must be the great arsenal of democracy.

And Roosevelt's actions? Since his first writing to Churchill, a joint intelligence system had been established. Roosevelt had learned that the Nazis were developing 'extremely powerful bombs of a new type', and now ordered the closest possible marriage between the FBI and British intelligence. This remained a close secret.

Roosevelt also made a deal with Britain, swapping fifty destroyers for bases in Newfoundland and the Caribbean. Because no money was involved, Roosevelt was able to do this without asking congress.

The opposition said,

Mr Roosevelt today committed an act of war. He also became America's first dictator. . . . He hands down an edict that may eventually result in the shedding of blood of millions of Americans; that may result in transforming the United States into a goose-stepping . . . slave state.

St. Louis Post Dispatch, 3 September 1940

The most arbitrary and dictatorial action ever taken by a president.

Wendel Wilkie, (Republican candidate for the presidential election)

I call on the British Government to abandon the British Isles. This will end Hitler's ambition for world conquest.

Senator Key Pittman, Nevada

A nation of many parts – American Nazis, 1938

In a Gallup poll 60 per cent of the American people thought that Britain was fighting in the American interest, and should receive more aid. Thirteen per cent were willing to go to war.

Phase 4, 1941

Roosevelt had been elected to serve a third term as president. Britain was fighting on, but grew short of war materials. Roosevelt's words were:

I ask this Congress for authority and funds sufficient to manufacture additional munitions and war supplies of many kinds, to be turned over to the nations which are now in actual war with aggressor nations [i.e. Lend Lease].

The time is near when they will not be able to pay for weapons in ready cash. We cannot, and will not tell them that they must surrender, merely because of an inability to pay.

The 'Lend Lease' Bill was passed by congress.

What were Roosevelt's actions? After top level talks between British and US military staffs, Roosevelt agreed that

1 When war came, Germany must be the first target.
2 Henceforth US ships crossing the Atlantic would be given destroyer escorts.
3 Italian, Danish and German ships were confiscated in US ports.

The Lockheed plant at Burbeck, California. The US war machine rolls into action making Hudson bombers

Roosevelt met Churchill secretly at sea in August 1941, and together they devised the Atlantic Charter. This was a joint statement about the aims of the two countries 'after the final destruction of Nazi tyranny'.

The opposition said,

There will be revolution in this country if the administration gets us into this damnable war.

Senator Burton K. Wheeler, Montana

When polled 70 per cent of US citizens did not want war. Seventy-six per cent of US citizens said they would follow Roosevelt into war.

Phase 5, December 1941

In September 1941 German U boats had attacked the US ships *Greer* and *Kearney*, and sunk the *Reuben James*. On 7 December, the Japanese attacked Pearl Harbour, where the US Pacific fleet was stationed. Roosevelt's words were:

We must abandon once and for all the illusion that we can ever again isolate ourselves from the rest of humanity.

And his actions? Roosevelt declared war on Japan, and soon after on Germany and Italy saying,

The American people in their righteous might will win through to absolute victory!

The 'America First' Committee, previously Roosevelt's greatest critics, responded:

We stand behind you in your endeavour to win this war. We pledge you our support.

America First – an organisation which campaigned to keep America out of the war. Prominent members included the pioneer aviator Charles Lindbergh.

1 Using the documents on 'Roosevelt's words', list the arguments which he used to persuade US citizens that isolation was impossible.
2 Using the documents on 'what the opposition said' list the arguments against becoming involved.
3 On the basis of the evidence here, do you agree that Roosevelt deceived the American people?
4 Draw up a timetable showing America'a growing commitment to help Great Britain.
5 Can we, as historians, say that Roosevelt was right or wrong to carry out these policies?

Winston Churchill on board the Prince of Wales, *returning across the Atlantic after meeting with Roosevelt*

11 The Second World War in the Pacific

Using the evidence: Pearl Harbour

Relations between the USA, and Japan had been deteriorating for some time – over the invasion of China, over Japan's tripartite pact with Germany and Italy (September 1940), over threatening Japanese moves in Indo-China, and over an American trade embargo on Japanese goods. Despite negotiations, no settlement could be reached, and war seemed inevitable. It came on 7 December, 1941, with the attack on Pearl Harbour. The following documents describe the final stages:

A 27 November
TOP SECRET
This despatch is to be considered a war warning. An aggressive move by Japan is expected in the next few days. The number and equipment of Japanese troops and the organisation of naval task forces indicate an amphibious expedition against either the Philippines, Thai or Kra peninsula, and possibly Borneo. Exercise an appropriate defensive deployment.

B At Pearl Harbour weather conditions were ideal for a surprise attack. The American tradition of weekends in port, on which the Japanese were counting so heavily, was being upheld. The vessels were lined up in a row, and officers and men were relaxed.

C Permanent radar stations had not yet been installed on the island. Of the six temporary stations only one was in operation after 7 a.m. At 7.02 Lockard detected signals of approaching aircraft. Unfortunately the watch officer, to whom the information was reported, was inexperienced in the use of radar and confused the aircraft with some B.17s expected from the mainland. Consequently he did not forward the information.

US Diplomatic and Military Documents

Japanese photo of the attack on Pearl Harbour. First strike aircraft are circled. The photo was torn up but retrieved by a US photographic expert

USS West Virginia *and USS* Tennessee *after the attack*

D The Japanese force had been steaming under radio silence from Kure naval base. It consisted of 6 aircraft carriers, 2 battleships, 9 destroyers, 2 cruisers, 3 submarines and supply vessels, 145 dive bombers, 103 bombers, 40 torpedo planes. . . .

The green light to execute the attack was sent by Admiral Yamamoto on December 2nd. The message was NIITA KAYAMA NOBORE – This was the code phrase meaning 'proceed with the attack.

(From the interrogation of Captain Minoru Genda)

E Tora Tora Tora! We have succeeded in a surprise attack.

Admiral Fuchida

F The toll:
2403 dead.
Battleship *West Virginia* sunk (7 torpedo hits, 2 bombs)
Battleship *Arizona* sunk by bombs
Battleship *Nevada* heavily damaged by 5 bombs
Battleship *Oklahoma* capsized with 3 torpedo hits
Battleship *California* sunk (2 torpedo hits, 2 bombs)
Battleship *Pennsylvania* minor damage
Battleship *Utah* (now a target ship) sunk

F The result of the attack on 7 December was a strategic success for the Americans rather than the Japanese. Yamamoto's coup, the desperate throw of the gambler that he was, failed because by a miracle the American aircraft carriers were at sea, and because his attack plan left out the fuel stocks and workshops, so that in spite of terrible damage Pearl Harbour continued an unbroken record as a great fleet anchorage and a naval base.

R. Lewin, *The American Magic*, 1983

G If the 4 500 00 barrels of fuel oil in storage had been destroyed, the US Pacific fleet would have had to retreat to the west coast and fight the early part of the war from there.

J. Winston, *The War in the Pacific*, 1978

H The political effect of Pearl Harbour far outweighed the military and naval. Nobody understood the effect of Pearl Harbour upon the American nation and on long-term strategy better than Winston Churchill. He did not conceal his jubilation. 'So we have won after all', he wrote, 'We had won the war, England would live, Hitler's fate was sealed. As for the Japanese, they would be ground to a powder. I went to bed and slept the sleep of the saved and thankful'.

1 What mistakes were made by the Americans which help to explain why they were caught napping on 7 December? Use the documents to explain your answer in detail.

2 Why was Churchill so pleased? Answer in detail, looking at both the short-term and long-term effects of Pearl Harbour. Look back to pages 172–75. Would Roosevelt have shared his view?

The Japanese advance, 1941–42

Immediately after the attack on Pearl Harbour the Japanese struck at key points across the Pacific Ocean. British possessions such as Hong Kong were key targets. So were US bases in the Philippines, starting with Wake Island and ending at Bataan. Even the pride of the Royal Navy, the battleship *Prince of Wales* and the battlecruiser *Repulse* had no answer for the Japanese:

A By late October 1941 there were about 400 marines at Wake. The twelve Grumman Wildcat aircraft had bomb racks which did not fit the bombs in supply on the island. The marines, a fifth of whom had no arms and equipment, had partly completed placement of guns, but there had been no time to fire them. There was no radar.

    A. Russell Buchanan, *Military and Diplomatic Documents*, 1964

B At Bataan the charge began with machine guns. When you heard the rat-a-tat-tat you knew that attack was about to begin. Then we waited, crouched along our fronts behind our protective land-mines. The Japanese knew the position of the mines. The shock troops charged, crouching, running and

The Rising Sun over Wake Island

Aircraft carriers Cabot *and* Ticonderoga *lead a line of battleships*

crawling along with lifted guns waiting for their chance to fire. Their faces behind their guns were terrible – muscles strained and lips were stretched over bare teeth. No doubt we looked as hideous to them. The nervous strain of fighting for one's life makes the gentlest man look inhuman.

The shock troops threw themselves on our mines. They exploded under their bodies. Then came the lines not in straight advance but in zig-zag formation, jumbing from fox-hole to crater. In the fox-holes our machine gunners tried to pick off the broken lines. Our officers looked for machine-gun nests to concentrate upon.

More Japanese soldiers came on. No matter how many died there were always more. When they were over the land-mines they knew they would meet the electrified barbed wire. Japanese soldiers flung themselves on the wire. Other waves of Japanese coming up from behind walked over the bodies spitted on the entanglements, to drop upon us – waiting or running to meet them with lowered bayonets.

Fight or die, it was all one to the Japanese soldier. By crucifying himself on barbed wire, by blowing himself to bits on a mine, he robbed us of one jot more of our diminishing defences.

Carlos P. Romulo, *Last Man off Bataan*, 1943

Japanese convoys were detected transporting an invasion force to Malaya. The Royal Navy ships *Prince of Wales* and *Repulse*, with four destroyers, set out to meet them.

Cecil Brown, who was on the *Repulse*, remembered:

I gape open-mouthed at those aircraft coming over us, flying so low that they will pass from bow to stern over the *Repulse*. The sky is filled with black puffs from our ack-ack.

A plane is diving straight for the middle of the ship off the port side, five hundred yards away, and tracers are rushing to meet it, but it comes on. Now it seems suspended in the air above the water, and the torpedo drops.

It is streaking for us. The torpedo strikes the ship about twenty yards astern of my position. It feels as though the ship has crashed into dock. I am thrown four feet across the deck, but keep my feet. Almost immediately, it seems, the ship lists.

The command roars out, 'Blow up your lifebelts!'.

The *Repulse* is going down.

The torpedo-smashed *Prince of Wales*, half a mile ahead, is low in the water, half shrouded in smoke, a destroyer by her side.

Japanese bombers are still winging around like vultures, still attacking the *Wales*.

Men are tossing overboard rafts, lifebelts, benches, anything that will float. Fifty feet from the ship, hardly swimming at all now, I see the bow of the *Repulse* swing straight into the air, like a church steeple.

Singapore was prepared for an attack from the sea. In fact the attack came by land, from Malaya. Allied troops withdrew to Singapore and destroyed the causeway linking the island to the mainland. The Japanese bombarded Singapore, then the invasion began. By mid-February the governor reported:

There are now one million people within a radius of three miles. Water supplies are very badly damaged, and unlikely to last for more than twenty-four hours. Many dead are lying in the streets and burial is impossible. We are faced with total deprivation of water which must result in pestilence.

He had little option but to surrender.

Questions

1 Use documents A and B to show why the Japanese attacks were so successful.
2 The news from the Pacific came as a terrible blow to the British. Write a frank report for the benefit of the Cabinet (but not the public) to inform them of the naval action and the fall of Singapore. How might the Cabinet change this information before releasing it to the press?

The war in the Pacific, 1942–4

The war in the Pacific turned against Japan in 1942 with US victories in aircraft carrier battles in the Coral Sea and at Midway, where four Japanese carriers were sunk. From that moment the US forces captured base after base until, in 1943, General MacArthur was ready to recapture the Philippines, which the Americans had evacuated from Bataan in 1941. Victory in the battle of Leyte Gulf gave the US navy control of the Pacific, and it remained to clear up pockets of opposition on the islands before attacking Japan itself. The following documents show the tenacity of the opposition, and the nature of warfare on the Pacific islands.

Using the evidence: the struggle for the islands

A With the USA winning the carrier war, the Japanese found themselves with fewer, less experienced pilots. They then began to adopt desperate tactics including the use of kamikaze pilots:

Dear Parents,
Please congratulate me. I have been given a splendid opportunity to die. This is my last day. The destiny of our homeland hinges on a decisive battle in the seas to the south where I shall fall like a blossom from a radiant cherry tree.

Our goal is to dive against the aircraft carriers of the enemy. Movie cameramen have been here to take our pictures. It is possible that you may see us in the newsreels at the theatre.

We are sixteen warriors manning the bombers. May our death be as sudden and clean as the shattering of crystal.

Isao.

B Japanese bombers were also used to attack recaptured US bases. Here is an account of 'Tojo time', the daily bombing of Guadalcanal:

Japanese kamikaze plane attacks a US aircraft carrier

The assault on Luzon – against enemy fire, sand bars, and treacherous currents

US marines plant the flag on Iwo Jima – a famous moment now remembered in a Washington sculpture

There was a routine of noises at Tojo time. Every airplane that could fly would start up immediately and would rush for the runway, dodging bomb craters. Often through the swirling dust the ground crews would see a wing drop – another bomber had taxied into a small crater. The Grummans would climb for altitude, test firing on the way. The whining engines at high r.p.m., the chattering machine guns, the settling of dust. . . . Then the high singalong whine of the approaching enemy bombers. Only a few moments now. The sing-song would grow louder. Then swish swish swish and the men would pull their helmets tighter and tense their muscles and press harder against the earth in their foxholes and pray.

Then WHAM! (the first one hit) WHAM! (closer) WHAM (walking right up to your foxhole) WHAAM (Oh Christ!) WHAM (thank God they missed us) WHAM (the bombs were walking away) WHAM (they still shook the earth and dirt trickled in) WHAM.

C These two accounts show the nature of fighting as US troops recaptured Pacific islands from the Japanese. At Iwo Jima

the enemy remains below ground in his maze of communicating tunnels throughout our preliminary artillery fire. When the fire ceases, choosing a suitable exit he moves as many men and weapons to the surface as he can, depending on the cover, often as close as 75 yards from our front. As our troops advance towards this point he delivers all the fire at his disposal. He then withdraws through his underground tunnels and the cycle continues.

At Peleliu, a civilian war correspondent remembered:

. . . a horrible place. The heat is stifling and rain falls intermittently – muggy rain that brings no relief, only greater misery. The coral rocks soak up the heat during the day and it is only slightly cooler at night. Marines are in the finest possible physical condition, but they wilted on Peleliu.

Peleliu is incomparably worse than Guam in its bloodiness, terror, climate and the incomprehensible tenacity of the Japanese. For sheer brutality and fatigue I think it surpasses anything yet seen in the Pacific.

By the end of 1944 the Japanese were also being driven back by British and Commonwealth troops in an equally dreadful theatre of war – Burma.

With the fall of Okinawa to US troops in July 1945, the way was open to an attack on Japan itself.

1 'A savage war in dreadful conditions against a fanatical enemy'. An American veteran of the Pacific war made this statement. Use all of the documents to show why he did so.
2 Describe the phases by which the Japanese were forced onto the defensive.

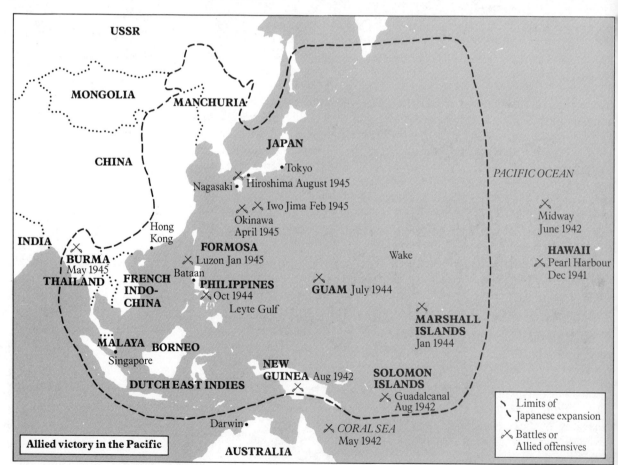

Allied victory in the Pacific

Hiroshima after the bomb

August 1945: the atom bomb

By early August 1945 Japan was on its knees. Its industrial areas, air bases and harbours were destroyed. It was short of raw materials and food. Yet Japan still controlled many islands and it seemed that thousands more Allied lives must be lost before the Japanese accepted defeat.

In July, after the successful testing of 'Fat Boy', the first atom bomb, the Allied powers issued the Potsdam Declaration:

We call upon the government of Japan to proclaim now the unconditional surrender of all Japanese armed forces and to provide proper and adequate assurances of good faith in such action. The alternative for Japan is prompt and utter destruction.

On 30 July Japan gave its response – a rejection of this ultimatum. However at the same time Japan began negotiations with Russia in hope of better terms. President Truman now had to make the decision – should he use this terrifying new weapon? Some advisers recommended a demonstration of the power involved:

It is not at all certain that American public opinion would approve of our own country being the first to use such an indiscriminate method of wholesale destruction of civilian life. From this point of view a demonstration of the new weapon might best be made, before the eyes of the representatives of all the United Nations on the desert or a barren island.

After such a demonstration the weapon might perhaps be used against Japan, after a preliminary ultimatum.

Truman disagreed: 'I regard the bomb as a military weapon and never had any doubt that it should be used.'

On 6 August the bomb was dropped on Hiroshima. The US government made the following statement:

It is an atomic bomb. It is a harnessing of the basic power of the universe. The force from which the sun draws its power has been loosed against those who brought war to the far east.

It was to spare the Japanese people from destruction that the ultimatum of 26 July was issued at Potsdam. Their leaders promptly rejected that ultimatum. If they do not now accept our terms, they may expect a rain of ruin from the air, the like of which has never been seen on this earth.

Japan still hesitated. Then, on 8 and 9 August, they received a double blow. First Russia declared war on Japan; and secondly another bomb was dropped, this time on Nagasaki. Finally, after further quibbling about the fate of the emperor, Japan surrendered on 14 August.

Futaba Kitayama remembered the effects of the bomb:

Someone shouted 'A parachute is coming down' I responded by turning in the direction she pointed. Just at that moment the sky I was facing flashed. I do not know how to describe that light. I wondered if a fire had been set in my eyes. The next moment I was knocked down flat on the ground. Immediately things started falling down around me. I couldn't see anything.

Soon I noticed that the air smelled terrible. Then I was shocked by the feeling that the skin of my face had come off. Then the hands and arms too, from the elbows to the fingertips, all the skin of my right hand came off and hung down grotesquely.

M. Kazuo was another victim:

I ran to the railway bridge. On the far side crowds of maddened people were running like demented lemmings, trying to get across the river. In the middle of the bridge lay four or five bodies, unrecognisable as human beings, but still moving. Their skin hung from them like strands of seaweed! Instead of noses, holes! Their ears and hands were so swollen as to be shapeless.

There were still fifty or sixty clinging to red hot rails. In their terror of dying they clawed their way, over one another, their eyes hanging from their sockets, pushing one another into the river, and screaming all the time.

A *Daily Express* reporter visited the area soon after:

In these hospitals I found people who, when the bomb fell, suffered absolutely no injuries, but are now dying from uncanny after-effects. For no apparent reason, their health began to fail. They lost appetite. Their hair fell out. Bluish spots appeared on their bodies. And then bleeding began from the ears, nose, and mouth.

Hiroshima: population 340 000. 30 per cent of doctors dead. 42 out of 45 hospitals destroyed. Total dead, 70 000.
Nagasaki: Causes of death: flashburns 20–30 per cent; radiation sickness 15–20 per cent; other injuries 50–60 per cent. Total dead, 40 000.

Questions

1 Do you agree that the dropping of the bomb was necessary? Do you agree that the Potsdam Declaration gave fair warning? Explain your answer carefully.
2 Describe both the short-term and long-term effects of human exposure to this type of weapon.

Superpower Confrontation

12 East versus West: the boundaries of post-war Europe

Even before the victory of 1945 it seemed likely that the alliance between the USSR and the Western powers would collapse. Indeed, it has been suggested that the dropping of the 'A' bombs on Hiroshima and Nagasaki were as much a beginning as an end: while finishing off Japan, the explosions were also a warning to the USSR of the power of the USA. There were deep-seated reasons why a new confrontation was likely:

1 The Alliance had not always been harmonious. For example, the USSR, had suffered by far the greatest number of casualties and damage during the war. As early as 1941 Stalin had asked the Allies to set up a second front to relieve pressure on the Soviet Union. In his eyes they had been slow to act, causing his country to make an even greater sacrifice.

2 The Western powers feared the expansion of communism, and especially Stalin's brand of communism with its theoretical commitment to world domination.

3 The Soviet Union feared the expansion of capitalism, especially in the light of Europe's post-war weakness and the power of the USA, with its strong economy and its atomic bomb.

Stalin, Roosevelt and Churchill at their first wartime conference, Tehran 1943

The USSR and its neighbours

The Cold War begins

The shape of post-war Europe was discussed by the Allies at Yalta in 1944. Churchill and Stalin agreed on broad areas of influence in the post-war world, but Roosevelt opposed any formal arrangement. Nonetheless Churchill was content that the USSR should maintain influence in Bulgaria, Rumania and Hungary, and that the USSR, with the USA and Britain, had signed the Declaration for Liberated Europe – which promised support for democratically elected governments in all European countries.

However, Churchill's calculations for the shape of Europe were upset by the rapid pace of the the Soviet advance in 1945. As well as Bulgaria, Rumania and Hungary, the USSR had armies in Poland, Czechoslovakia, Austria and Germany. Churchill wanted an immediate stand to make

a settlement . . . on all major issues between the West and East in Europe before the armies of democracy melted, or the Western Allies yielded any part of the German territories they had conquered.

In fact communist governments were imposed on Hungary, Bulgaria, Rumania and Poland, a communist government was elected in Czechoslovakia, and Austria and Germany were each divided into four parts, one of which was under Russian control, pending further discussions on their future.

Churchill had no doubts that this was the first stage of a new war against communist expansionism. In March 1946 he made his famous 'Iron Curtain' speech:

From Stettin in the Baltic to Trieste in the Adriatic, an iron curtain has descended across the continent. Behind that line lie all the capitals of the ancient states of central and eastern Europe. Warsaw, Berlin, Prague, Vienna, Budapest, Belgrade, Bucharest and Sofia, all these famous cities and the populations around them lie in the Soviet sphere and are all subject, in one form or another, to a very high and increasing measure of control from Moscow. In other countries communist parties or fifth columns constitute a growing challenge and peril to Christian civilisation.

From what I have seen of our Russian friends and allies during the war, I am convinced that there is nothing they admire so much as strength, and there is nothing for which they have less respect than for military weakness. If the Western democracies stand together in strict adherence to the principles of the United Nations Charter . . . no one is likely to molest them. If, however, they become divided or falter . . . then indeed catastrophe may overwhelm us all.

US Congressional Record

United Nations – see Chapter 23.

Stalin replied:

Mr Churchill now takes the stand of the warmongers, and he is not alone. He has friends not only in Britain, but in the US as well.

The following circumstance should not be forgotten. The Germans made their invasion of the USSR through Finland, Poland, Rumania, Bulgaria and Hungary. . . . Governments hostile to the Soviet Union existed in those countries. As a result of the German invasion the Soviet Union has lost irretrievably in the fighting against the Germans . . . and also through the German occupation. In other words, the Soviet Union's loss of life has been several times greater than that of Britain and the United States put together. . . . And so what can be surprising about the fact that the Soviet Union, anxious for its future safety, is trying to see to it that governments loyal in their attitude to the Soviet Union should exist in these countries? How can anyone, who has not taken leave of his senses, describe these peaceful aspirations of the Soviet Union as expansionist tendencies on the part of our state?

As for the form of government in those states Stalin said,

Whoever occupies a territory also imposes on it his own social system. Everyone imposes his own system as far as his army has the power to do so.

To the Western powers, the cause of this new cold war was Soviet expansion into central Europe. To the USSR this expansion was justified, and it was the capitalist West which was trying to dominate the new Europe. Soviet fears about the expansion of capitalism were apparently borne out in two US initiatives of 1947.

The first of these came at a time when the governments of both Greece and Turkey, with British support, were fighting against communist 'rebels'. Britain, because of economic problems, was forced

PEEP UNDER THE IRON CURTAIN

o back out of these conflicts. In March 1947 the USA stepped in, and he principle on which they did so became known as the 'Truman doctrine'.

At the present moment in world history nearly every nation must choose between alternative ways of life. The choice is too often not a free one.

One way is based upon the will of the majority, and is distinguished by free institutions, representative government, free elections, guarantees of individual liberty, freedom of speech and religion, and freedom from political oppression.

The second way of life is based upon the will of a minority forcibly imposed upon the majority. It relies upon terror and oppression, controlled press and radio, fixed elections and the suppression of personal freedoms.

I believe that it must be the policy of the United States to support free peoples who are resisting attempted subjugation by armed minorities or by outside pressures.

In June a second major policy statement was made by secretary of state George Marshall. This was the announcement of 'Marshall aid':

The United States should do whatever it is able to do to assist in the return of normal economic health in the world, without which there can be no political stability and no assured peace. Our policy is directed not against any country or doctrine, but against hunger, poverty, desperation and chaos. Its purpose should be the revival of a working economy in the world so as to permit the emergence of political and social conditions in which free institutions can exist.

The Truman doctrine was seen as a direct threat to Soviet Union. Even though 'Marshall aid' was offered to East European countries, this too was seen by the Soviet Union as an American attempt to increase its influence:

The United States attempts to impose its will on other independent states, while at the same time obviously using the economic resources distributed as relief . . . as an instrument of political pressure.

The United States also counted on making all these countries directly dependent on the interests of American monopolies, which are striving to avert the approaching depression by an accelerated export of commodities and capital to Europe.

Implementation of the Marshall plan will mean placing European countries under the economic and political control of the United States. and will split Europe into two camps . . . to complete the formation of a bloc of several European countries hostile to the interests of the democratic countries of Eastern Europe.

NEIGHBOURS
"Come on, Sam! It's up to us again."

According to this cartoonist, is US aid unselfish?

The Soviet response to the Marshall plan was to reject economic contact with the West. Instead, a new organisation, COMINFORM was established in October 1947. This linked together communist parties both within the Eastern bloc and in Western European countries such as Italy and France. This bloc was further consolidated when, in 1948, a coup in Czechoslovakia confirmed the rule of the Communist Party, which had been losing popularity. In 1955, the USSR organised its European allies into the Warsaw Pact and tightened its grip.

Warsaw Pact countries – Albania, Czechoslovakia, East Germany, Hungary, Poland, Rumania, USSR.

NATO is dominated by the USA which provides most of the cost and controls the nuclear armoury.

By this time the Western powers had also formed into a strategic bloc. In March 1948 Britain, France, Belgium and the Netherlands and Luxembourg signed the Treaty of Brussels, a mutual defence treaty which was fully supported by President Truman. In April 1949 the Brussels countries were joined by the USA, Canada, Denmark, Norway, Iceland, Italy and Portugal in the North Atlantic Treaty Organisation. They were joined by Greece and Turkey in 1952 and West Germany in 1955. The first trial of strength between the two sides was in Berlin, 1948.

By 1948 the British, French and American zones in West Germany and Berlin had been merged into one, and the Western powers were willing to see the formation of an independent West Germany. The Soviet Union had hoped for a reunited and independent Germany, but when the Treaty of Brussels was signed the Soviet Union walked out of the joint council which had controlled Germany, and began to create an independent state. The problem was that Berlin lay at the heart of East Germany. Traffic from the West into Berlin was already restricted. When, in June 1948, a new currency was introduced which threatened to undermine the economy of East Germany, the corridors into Berlin were closed.

Konrad Adenauer had been imprisoned by the Nazis. Elected to power in 1949, he was determined to bring about the recovery of Germany's political and economic systems and her friendship with other powers.

The Western powers were determined that Berlin should not be lost and an Anglo-American airlift was organised which supplied the 2.5 million Berliners with essential supplies for ten months. In May 1949 the blockade was ended, but the basic problem remained. The immediate outcome was the foundation of West Germany (the Federal Republic of Germany) led by Konrad Adenauer, and the East German state, (the German Democratic Republic) under a communist government. The Cold War was now to focus on other parts of the world (see page 220).

A Globemaster and a Dakota bringing supplies to Berlin. The Globemaster could carry 20 tons of flour

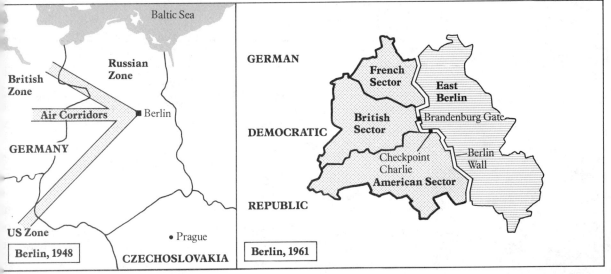

Berlin, 1948 — Berlin, 1961

Roads and railways being closed,
West Berlin could only be supplied
by air. With the building of the
wall, West Berlin was totally isolated.

Questions

In many ways the early stages of the Cold War was a war of words.
(a) How would the West describe the USSR occupation of Eastern Europe at the end of the Second World War?
(b) How would Stalin defend the Russian occupation of Europe?
(c) What words show the Truman doctrine's hostility to the USSR?
(d) At the time of the Marshall plan, in what sense did the USSR see the USA as an 'invading force'?

2 Describe the formation of the two power blocs.
3 Why was Berlin so important to both sides?
4 Make a timeline to show the deterioration in relations between East and West.

The Warsaw Pact countries, 1945–85

The internal development of post-war Russia

Russia had suffered dreadfully in the Second World War, with twenty million people dead and its cities, industries, agriculture and communications devastated. Stalin's immediate task was to rebuild, and in August 1945 he launched a fourth five-year plan. Industry was renewed and rebuilt on a massive scale. By 1948 Russia was back to pre-war production levels. Not only were heavy industries leaping ahead, but there was also a new emphasis on light industries producing consumer goods.

Industry and agriculture were back on their pre-war course. But so too was political repression. Soldiers returning to Russia with western ideas were suppressed. Purges began once more, although on a much smaller scale than in the thirties.

Stalin and Khrushchev in 1938

In March 1953 Stalin died. He remains one of the most controversial figures in modern history:

STALIN: A BALANCE SHEET

For	*Against*
He took over with Russia weak and in ruins. He made Russia into a superpower.	Stalin limited Russia's growth and power, by carrying out the great purges, making it dreadfully weak in 1939.
He consolidated Russia's borders and made them secure.	Russia's neighbours felt threatened. This led to cold war.
He played an important part in the defeat of Nazi Germany. He gave Russia the forceful leadership which it needed.	Stalin encouraged Hitler to be more ambitious in the 1930s. Nothing can justify the purges and Stalin's tyrannical government.
He made communism work in Russian agriculture and industry.	Agriculture suffered, especially the Kulaks. Mistakes were made in the five-year plans including over-centralisation.
He created an effective system of education and social security.	True education was not allowed. Social security is not as important as personal liberty.
He made communism strong.	He destroyed the party.

Questions

Facts, opinions or judgements? The Stalin balance sheet shows the difficulties faced by historians in writing about controversial leaders.

Either as a class, or on your own, consider the difference between fact, opinion and judgement:

1 With reference to pages 137–49, write a purely factual account of Stalin's life.
2 Decide whether you would like to defend or attack Stalin. Most Westerners would attack, and so would some Russians (see page 193). But others have defended his actions. Write an account which states the opinion of Stalin you have chosen, using the balance sheet to help you.
3 Finally, present a balanced view of Stalin's life, expressing your balanced judgements. (If this is a class exercise tasks from the Stalin balance sheet could be allocated and opinions read back to the whole class.)

4 In the light of your answer, define the difference between fact, opinion and judgement. Which of these is a characteristic of good historical writing, and which should the historian avoid?

The USSR under Khrushchev

When Stalin died the leaders of the Communist Party made it clear that there would be changes. For example, the head of the secret police, Beria, was removed from office. It was also said that, in future, there would be collective leadership – not rule by one man. Despite this idea, one man did emerge to take over from Stalin – Nikita Khrushchev. Khrushchev was altogether a different type of leader. He was sometimes coarse, often witty, rather informal, and very much a colourful individual with the power to shock others by his words and actions. One such shock came in his 'secret speech' to the 20th Congress in 1956. This was an exposé of the facts behind the Kirov killing (page 138) and a devastating attack on Stalin. These are some extracts to show how Khrushchev mentioned the unmentionable:

Of peasant stock, Khrushchev rose through the party to become first secretary of the Moscow party in 1935, Politburo member in 1939, party secretary in 1954.

Of the 139 members and candidates of the Party Central Committee who were elected at the 17th Congress, 98 persons, i.e. 70 per cent were arrested and shot. [Indignation in the hall.]
    Eighty per cent of these joined the Party before the revolution or during the civil war. By social origin the basic mass of the delegates were workers . . . the only reason why 70 per cent were branded enemies of the Party was that honest communists were slandered, accusations against them were fabricated, and revolutionary legality was gravely undermined.

Khrushchev's speech placed all the blame on Stalin, and ignored the part played by other party members in the purges. One story tells of how Khrushchev defended himself when asked, 'And what were you doing?' He snapped back 'Who said that?' Silence. 'Well', he replied, 'That is what I was doing. Keeping silent' The 'secret speech' was one aspect of the process of de-Stalinisation. Those who had been imprisoned by Stalin were released. Those who had died in disgrace at least had their reputations restored. Furthermore, it was now possible to criticise Stalin and his mistakes, and to make changes for the future.
    The power of the secret police was substantially reduced. Censorship was loosened. Certain books, including Solzhenitsyn's story about the labour camps, *One Day in the Life of Ivan Denisovich*, were now permitted. Even so, only officially approved news items were allowed, and books critical of the revolution, such as Pasternak's *Doctor Zhivago*, were still banned. Intellectuals who criticised the government were still persecuted.
    Khrushchev made important changes in economic policy. In industry he moved towards greater production of consumer goods, pledging that the seven-year plan 1959–67 would ensure the USSR 'the world's highest standard of living.' To this end he allowed greater incentives

(the profit motive!) to put money into people's pockets so that they could buy such consumer products. He believed that Russian industry was over-centralised, so in 1957 he created the *zovnarkhozy* – regional economic councils – which would handle planning, production, and distribution of goods. Technical advancement was another priority, and the launching of Sputnik I into space in 1957 was a signal to the world that the USSR had caught up.

In agriculture too Khruschev moved towards greater incentives. Private plots were allowed to peasants on the collectives, and they could keep or sell what they produced there. The 'virgin lands scheme' was a plan to farm previously untilled lands in Siberia. In all cases he sought to modernise agriculture by greater investment, especially in machinery.

Product and unit	1913	1921	1928	1933	1940	1945	1952	1963
Industrial								
Electric power, bill. kwth.	2·0	0·5	5·0	16·3	48·3	43·2	119·1	412·0
Crude oil, mill. tons	9·2	3·8	11·6	21·5	31·1	19·4	47·3	206·1
Coal, mill. tons	29·1	9·5	35·5	76·3	165·9	149·3	300·9	532·0
Steel, mill. tons	4·2	0·2	4·2	6·9	18·3	12·2	34·5	80·2
Machine tools, 1000 units	1·8	0·8	2·0	21·0	58·4	38·4	74·6	183·0
Turbines, mill. kw.	—	—	0·04	0·3	1·2	0·2	3·4	11·9
Locomotives, units	477	78	479	948	928	8	439	2162
Trucks, 1000 units	—	—	0·7	39·1	136·0	68·5	243·5	414·0
Tractors, 1000 units	—	—	1·3	73·7	31·6	7·7	98·7	325·0
Grain harvesters, 1000 units	—	—	—	8·6	12·8	0·3	42·2	82·9
Excavators, 1000 units	—	—	—	0·1	0·3	—	3·7	17·9
Fertilizers, mill. tons	0·09	—	0·1	1·0	3·2	1·1	6·4	19·9
Timber, mill. cu. meters	67·0	6·5	61·7	173·3	246·1	168·4	291·4	352·7(a)
Cement, mill. tons	1·8	0·06	1·8	2·7	5·7	1·8	13·9	61·0
Consumer								
Automobiles, 1000 units	—	—	0·1	10·3	5·5	5·0	59·7	173·0
Washing machines, 1000 units	—	—	—	—	—	—	4·3	2282·0
Bicycles, 1000 units	4·9	7·7	10·8	125·6	255·0	23·8	1650·4	3352·0
Cameras, 1000 units	—	—	—	29·6	355·2	0·01	459·1	1432·0
Radio sets, 1000 units	—	—	—	29·0	160·5	13·8	1294·5	4802·0
Television sets, 1000 units	—	—	—	—	0·3	—	37·4	2474·0
Cotton fabrics, bill. meters	2·7	1·5	2·7	2·7	3·9	1·6	5·0	6·6
Leather shoes, mill. pairs(e)	60·0	28·0	58·0	90·3	211·0	63·1	237·7	463·0
Sugar, mill. tons	2·2	0·06	1·9	1·4	2·8	0·5	4·1	6·2
Canned food, billion cans	0·1	0·1	0·1	0·7	1·1	0·6	2·1	6·4
Alcohol, mill. decaliters	55·2	10·2	23·3	38·8	89·9	26·5	89·1	184·0(b)
Agricultural								
Grain, mill. tons	86·0	36·2	73·3	69·1	95·5	75·0(d)	82·5(c)	138·0(b)
Cows, mill.	28·8	24·8	29·2	19·0	27·8	22·9	24·3	38·3
Hogs, mill.	23·0	13·1	19·4	9·9	27·5	10·6	28·5	40·8
Vegetable oil, mill. tons	0·5	0·03	0·5	0·3	0·8	0·3	1·0	2·2
Fish caught, mill. tons	1·0	0·3	0·8	1·3	1·4	1·1	2·1	4·7
Freight transport, bill. t/km	126·0	42·3	119·5	218·3	487·4	374·6	877·6	2300·0

Production of selected goods in the USSR

These were all ambitious plans, and there were a number of setbacks. In industry the *zovarkhozy* proved to be cumbersome, duplicating many tasks but not working well together. In agriculture, targets for growth were set too high, and the emphasis on production of meat and maize, for example, led to a grain shortage.

These failures, added to foreign policy setbacks such as Cuba (see page 220), were enough to bring Khrushchev down. In 1964, while he was on holiday, the Politburo met and deposed him. However, it was a sign of the much lighter political climate that Khruschev did not 'disappear'. He merely became a private citizen, and was succeeded by Leonid Brezhnev.

When Khrushchev fell, he was replaced by Brezhnev, Kosygin, and Podgorny. However it soon became obvious that Brezhnev would dominate, and he was made both party secretary and president.

The USSR after 1964

Leonid Brezhnev became general secretary of the Communist Party in 1966, and his hold on power became almost total by 1977, when he became head of state and chairman of the praesidium. The new view was that Khrushchev had gone too far, and that liberal policies were undermining the state. There was a return to strict censorship, the power of the KGB was increased, dissidents were dealt with more harshly, and criticism of Stalin was stopped.

Krushchev's agricultural policies were continued, with greater emphasis on rewards for high production, and lower taxation to give farmers more spending power. However, organisation of industry changed. The *zovnarkhozy* were disbanded and responsibility for planning was returned to large central ministries and Gosplan (the state planning commission). Once more the emphasis was on heavy industry. Khrushchev's promises were forgotten, and production of consumer goods declined. The 1976–80 plan allowed 750 000 million roubles for investment, of which only 50 000 million were for light industry producing consumer goods.

Brezhnev and his generation of elderly statesmen were followed in 1984 by the stylish and relatively youthful Mikhael Gorbachev. He has been highly critical of the inefficiency of agriculture, industry, and the workforce. The signs in 1986 are that there will be a return to more liberal policies, greater incentives, and a new emphasis on consumer goods. The release of the dissident Andrei Sakharov in February 1986 was seen as another sign of goodwill from inside the USSR.

Praesidium – The top governing body of the Soviet Union.

Andrei Sakharov – Traded in a 'spy swap' in 1986, he joined his wife in Israel.

L. I. Brezhnev at a May Day celebration, 1980

Satellite states of the USSR

Since 1945 the USSR has kept close control over its satellite states. Relations with some of them – in particular Rumania and East Germany – have remained cordial. Others, especially Poland, Hungary, and Czechoslovakia have experienced interference in their internal development because they have strayed in one way or another from the Soviet path of development.

Poland, 1956

Until the death of Stalin, Poland was governed on strictly Stalinist lines. Leaders who showed liberal ideas, such as Gomulka, were imprisoned. After Stalin's death things quickly changed. Polish leaders were released from prison and returned to power, while those who had followed Stalin's policies were dismissed. The powers of the security police were curbed, and proposals for greater democracy were in the air. In this atmosphere a group of workers travelled to Warsaw to protest about low wages, high prices and poor living conditions. Their mission failed, and an uprising began.

A Western view of the Eastern bloc

Here is Khrushchev's account of what happened:

We learned from our Ambassadors that the tensions which had been building up had boiled over. Anti-Soviet demonstrations had broken out at factories in some cities. Some Poles were saying the treaty signed after World War II was unequal and that the Soviet Union was taking advantage. In particular they complained that Poland was being forced to supply coal at prices lower than those in the world market.

The demonstration also demanded the withdrawal of Soviet troops from Polish territory. They said nothing about how much Soviet blood had been shed and how many Soviet lives have been sacrificed for the liberation of Poland. No one mentioned how much bread the Soviet Union has given Poland, bread taken from the months of the Soviet people to feed the Poles. Some of the criticisms against us were justified, but many were fabricated. The propaganda machine of our enemies began churning out slander against us. We began to calculate which Polish regiments we could count on, the situation looked somewhat bleak. We didn't want to resort to use of our own troops if at all avoidable. On the other hand, we didn't want Poland to become a bourgeois country, hostile to the Soviet Union.

In fact there was no need to send in troops. Polish troops restored order, but at a cost of 53 dead. The politicians then came to a compromise, and Gomulka was restored to the post of first secretary. Unhappy with this, Khrushchev flew to Warsaw, but he took no further action when he learned that Gomulka wanted only internal reforms, and intended to maintain Poland's ties with the Soviet Union. Within the broad framework of the Warsaw Pact, Poland was allowed to move in its own direction.

Question

1 Why, according to Khrushchev, did the disturbances in Poland break out?
2 What is Khruschev's attitude towards the motives of the Poles?
3 Khruschev accuses his enemies of making propaganda. Is he guilty on the same charge in this passage? Explain your answer carefully.

Hungary

Events in Poland played a part in triggering a rising in Hungary. As a defeated power in 1945, Hungary had harsh conditions imposed upon it. Hungary did not take well to collectivisation of farms or large-scale economic planning, and the early 1950s saw food shortages and a falling standard of living.

When Stalin died, the new premier of Hungary, Imre Nagy, started to dismantle the collective farms and introduce other reforms. He was removed from office. When in 1956 the Poles succeeded in making Gomulka their leader, the Hungarians hoped to bring back Nagy and introduce liberal reform.

Using the evidence: the 1956 Hungarian rising

A Budapest, 22 October:
The students of the Engineering University called a parliament for October 22nd. Long before the appointed time the students crowded into the big hall.

A student jumped to the platform and shouted 'The truth is that the Russians exploit us worse than a colony!' The 4000 students crammed in the hall howled their approval.

Now the university Communist Party secretary pushed his way to the rostrum and tried to say that the Russians were Hungary's friends and liberators. He was hustled out of the hall. . . . Then, at last one of the students shouted 'We want to be rid of the Russians.' The roar of approval was deafening.

Judith Listowel, Saturday Evening Post, Philadelphia

Soviet tanks on the streets of Budapest, 1956

His statue toppled, his head removed, Stalin in Budapest, 1956

B 23 October:

The revolt began as a series of demonstrations that remained peaceful until about 10.30 Tuesday evening (23rd). The trouble began in front of the Budapest radio station when a delegation that had entered it to request the broadcasting of its sixteen points was arrested by political policemen who were guarding the building.

The crowd demanded their release and tried to storm the doors. At first the policemen tried to drive the demonstrators back with tear gas. Then they opened fire.

When this correspondent arrived at midnight the radio station had been stormed. Its lower floors had been occupied by demonstrators. A group of students had mounted a balcony in front of the building, and hung out Hungarian flags.

Shortly before midnight seven heavy Hungarian tanks rumbled into the area. Some of the demonstrators fled. But the leading tank displayed the national flag. Its crew cheered the demonstrators, a number of them mounted to shake hands with the soldiers. . . . It was obvious that the army was refusing to make cause with the political police. An hour later several insurgents were observed with tommy guns in their hands. They said they had obtained them from the soldiers.

Meanwhile, the crowd was beginning to grow more violent. At 1.30 a. m. the crowd stormed the plant of the principal communist newspaper . . . others stormed a Soviet bookstore.

John MacCormac, *New York Times*, 27 October

C 23 October:

The 5000 students who were meeting in front of the Petofi monument in Budapest were joined shortly after dusk by thousands of workers and others. The great crowd then marched to the Stalin monument. Ropes were wound around Stalin's neck, and, to cheers, the crowd attempted to topple the statue.

But it would not budge. They finally managed to melt Stalin's knees by using welding torches.

I have never seen more determination in the faces of a crowd . . . I'm sure they were all ready to risk their lives for the cause.

Reported in the Manchester Guardian, 25 October

D 24 October, Radio Kossuth:
(4.30 a. m.) Dear Listeners, we wish you good morning! Listen please, to our morning broadcast.

Fascist reactionary elements have started an armed attack against our public buildings and have also attacked our police. In the interest of restoring order, and until further notice is given, we announce that it is forbidden to hold any meetings, rallies and parades.
(6.30 a. m.) The suppression of looting counter-revolutionary groups is still under way.
(9 a. m.) Attention! Attention!

The dastardly armed attack of counter-revolutionary gangs during the night has created an extremely serious situation. The bandits have broken into factories and public buildings and have murdered many civilians.

The Government was unprepared for these attacks and has therefore applied for help to the Soviet formations stationed in Hungary under the terms of the Warsaw Treaty.

E 25–6 October:
During the night from Thursday to Friday the guns thunder. Machine guns and carbine shots ring out. Underneath the window of my hotel room 20 to 25 Soviet tanks drive past. From the south, one can hear dull booms – artillery fire. Curfew since 6 p. m. In spite of that, youths and civilians, pistols in hand, slink along the walls.

I spoke with some of the rebel leaders . . . They are communists. They are burning patriots. They want the Hungarian way to socialism.

Eugen Gezapogany, Deutsche Presse, 27 October

F 28 October:
Nagy formed a Cabinet to govern Hungary. He said 'The Hungarian Government is initiating negotiations to settle relations between the Hungarian People's Republic and the Soviet Union, including the question of the withdrawal of the Soviet troops stationed in Hungary.'

Radio Budapest

G 29 October:
Soviet tanks and troops crunched out of this war-battered capital today carrying their dead with them. They left a wrecked city where the stench of death already rises from the smoking ruins.

United Press

H 1 November:
In the next room Nagy was arguing with Soviet ambassador Andropov. The assistant told me that in half an hour's time Nagy intended to declare Hungary a neutral country and ask the UN for protection. 'Russian troops are pouring in from the Ukraine. They are digging in around Budapest. I am very pessimistic! He advised me to leave Budapest at once.

An English journalist waiting for an interview with Nagy

I 4 November:

Since the early morning hours Russian troops have been attacking Budapest and our population. Please tell the world of the treacherous attack against our struggle for liberty. Our troops are already engaged in fighting HELP – HELP – HELP –

Message received by Vienna Associated Press Office

J 4 November:

People are jumping up at tanks, throwing hand grenades inside, and then slamming the driver's windows. The Hungarian people are not afraid of death. It is only a pity that we can't stand for long. Our building has already been fired on.

Hungarian News Agency

On 7 November, order was restored, 25 000 Hungarians and 3500 Russians lay dead in Budapest. Nagy was taken to Rumania and shot.
Khrushchev remembered:

K We had strength and right on our side, but it was difficult to make a decision because part of the workers were on the side of the counter-revolution. . . . Bullets do not choose between striking enemies or misguided workers. Believe me, my friends, we spent painful days and nights before coming to a decision.

1 The accounts concerning the Hungarian rising all come from newspapers or radio. What are the advantages and disadvantages of these types of source? Give examples from these accounts to explain your answer.
2 Draw up a timeline of the rising.
3 How do you explain the strength of feeling in this rising? What events best demonstrate that strength of feeling?
4 Why, compared to Poland, was Hungary dealt with so harshly?

Czechoslovakia, 1968

Czechoslovakia's development as a communist state had been disturbed in 1953 by a major strike at the Skoda works at Pilsen. This was broken, and was the only real display of protest in years which showed steady economic growth:

Year	National Income	Real Wages
1948	100	100
1958	219	123

Other features of the Czech economy were collectivisation of agriculture and increased social benefits. The early 1960s saw poor harvests, but by 1968 economic growth was back on course. In political terms, Czechoslovakia had followed a Stalinist line until 1967 when Alexander Dubcek became party secretary. He introduced 'socialism with a human face'.
The main features of this programme were:
– Freedom of assembly.
– Release from prison of purge victims.
– Freedom of travel.

One version of Czechoslovakia, 1968 – resistance to the Russian 'terror' in Prague

Another version of 1968. Russian troops in conversation with Czechs

- Security police to keep to security rather than interfere in everyday life.
- Political differences to thrashed out in a new asssembly called 'The National Front'.
- Party to earn respect, not impose on people.
- Press censorship abolished.

In this atmosphere of reform, the other Warsaw Pact countries invaded, and quickly crushed any opposition. The movement of tanks into Prague closely resembled the events of Budapest in 1956. There was resistance, and loud protest from the Western powers. Dubcek was arrested and taken to Moscow, but finally he managed to negotiate a settlement. Czechoslovakia lost its reforms, the Warsaw Pact armies remained, and the 'liberals' were dismissed. The 'Prague spring' was over.

Poland in the 1970s and 1980s

By the end of the 1960s Poland's economy was in severe difficulty. Living standards were low, working conditions poor, and the agricultural system dreadfully inefficient:

All the time we come across carriages. Like in old landscape paintings, there are hills on the horizon, peasants ploughing work horses, a kind of scene which has almost disappeared from our minds. . . .

As any visitor to Poland can see, fields are small, many peasants have five hectares of land or less, which is scarcely conducive to mechanisation, and I saw myself dozens of peasants sowing by throwing seed in the wind by hand. Productivity per head cannot be other than low.

Harold Laven, *Osteuropa*, 1973

To modernise, Poland borrowed heavily from abroad, but could hardly pay the interest. Much of what it borrowed was spent on heavy subsidies on meat and other products to keep prices down. When the government attempted to cut their subsidies, and raise the prices to the consumer, they met with heavy opposition. This was the case in 1970 when Gomulka announced price rises ranging from 8 per cent to 60 per cent. Riots followed, and 36 workers were killed in fighting with police and armed forces. Gomulka was dismissed, and replaced by Gierek. His answer was to make changes including a new emphasis on consumer products. With the help of foreign loans, production was increased, but the government remained bankrupt. Attempts to increase prices in 1976 provoked further riots and disturbances.

Since 1978 Poland, more than any other East European state, has hit the headlines in the West. There are two reasons for this. The first appeared in October 1978 when a Polish archbishop was elected Pope John Paul II. In 1979 he returned to his home country:

This Pope was not only unusual in his nationality, but also in the way he took his religion to the world – In Britain he toured in a 'popemobile' so that more people could see him.

The night before his arrival it seemed as if half Warsaw was on the streets. People strolled in the evening sunshine, smiling and gazing in awe at the wooden cross that dominated Victory Square. No one had seen a giant cross in a capital square anywhere in the Eastern bloc.

As the Pope's motorcade travelled through the cities, buses and trams would stop in the middle of the road. Lorries would be left where they stood. Normal life was suspended.

The people spent ten days of that year laughing and crying with their Pope. They sang to him and he sang along with them.

It became almost a cliché but the Poles use to say it all the same 'Our country will never be the same after this.' No one promised them change. No one spoke of revolutions. No one hinted at the vast upheaval that was to take place just a year later. . .

This upheaval took place when Polish workers joined together to form the trade union Solidarity. This union has campaigned not only for higher wages and better working condition, but also for greater freedom. Its leader, Lech Walesa, has attracted world-wide attention:

Walesa's movements were carefully watched by the Western press, who saw his freedom or lack of it as a measure of the political climate in Poland.

It is impossible to overestimate the importance of Lech Walesa in beginning

Pope John Paul II in front of the cathedral at Krakow, where he had once been Archbishop

Lech Walesa waving the permit which enables him to leave the Lenin shipyard for three days to meet the Pope

Solidarity's revolution. No one else had his popularity. No one else was instantly commercial. He didn't always talk sense. He could be coarse.

In the summer of 1981 I asked him 'Are you worried about Soviet tanks massing on the border?'

'I don't see any tanks' he replied curtly.

'What do you think is your biggest failing?'

'I simply haven't got enough time.'

'Was there ever an attempt on your life?'

'Not until now. But I only get three hours sleep at night and that's murder isn't it?'

Tim Sebastian, Nice Promises, 1985

Solidarity was greeted with enthusiasm in the West, although one observer has pointed out:

The formation of Solidarity and subsequently the principle of its right to exist, soon became an emotional catchword for conservative Western statesmen who in their own country have a reputation as 'union bashers'.

Finally it was decided that Solidarity would have to be suppressed. Under a new head of government, Marshal Jaruzelski, Solidarity was banned and martial law declared to enforce orders. Even so, Solidarity leader Lech Walesa was free in 1985 and there are signs that, in the latest round of price rise proposals, there have been more consultations than on previous occasions.

Questions

1 Why do you think that Western powers were so outraged by the invasion of Czechoslovakia?
2 Why did the visit to Poland of Pope John Paul II and the subsequent development of Solidarity gain so much attention from the West?
3 Look back over the whole of this chapter. Draw up a summary pattern note to show methods of intervention used by Warsaw Pact countries to keep their members in line.

East Germany

The Democratic Republic of Germany has always been the communist state most in the spotlight, particularly because it surrounds Berlin and is always compared against West Germany.

The economy of East Germany was ruined by the war. Despite a steady growth rate, there were strikes and protest marches when, in 1953, demands were made by the government for higher productivity at the same wages. The protests were silenced. Productivity was raised, and by 1955 the standard of living was one third higher than in 1950. The target for economic growth 1955–60 was achieved by 1958.

Even so, East Germany lagged behind West Germany. The main reason for this was loss of labour, especially skilled labour. Between 1949 and 1960 two million people left East Germany. In 1960 alone 688 doctors, 296 dentists, 2648 engineers, and 200 000 farmers crossed to the West.

On 13 August 1961, this drift was stopped. The border was closed, and in particular, Berlin woke up to see that it was divided by a wall (see page 221).

The Berlin wall has come to symbolise the East–West divide. When visiting the city in 1961 President Kennedy said, 'Ich bin ein Berliner', to assure Westerners of American support.

For many people in the West the Berlin wall has come to symbolise the great divide between the tyranny of the Soviet bloc and the democratic West. Certainly many people scoff at the official title of East Germany – the German Democratic Republic. An East German would defend this by saying that it is a different use of the word democracy. There, democracy is the representation of workers through their factory organisations and unions, and through the party. Thus there is representation of a type, though few of the freedoms normally associated with democracy.

Since 1961 the GDR has experienced what has been described as an 'economic miracle'. By the mid–1970s it had a higher per capital income than the UK. This does not mean that individuals have a higher standard of living. In the GDR this money is spent in other ways in accordance with the communist ideal. The defence budget is very high. However, the GDR also boasts the best child-care facilities in the world. As for education:

The GDR has 70 per cent more teachers than the West Germany. The GDR invests more than 7 per cent of national income in education, as against 5 per cent in West Germany. In 1972 more than half the students at technical colleges are women.

J. Tampke, *The People's Republics of Eastern Europe*, 1984

Another main item of expenditure is house building, with 1.3 million flats constructed between 1970 and 1980.

Thus economic progress has brought collective wealth. Western observers would dislike many aspects of life in East Germany, and especially the shortages of consumer goods, but this difference of opinion reflects the opposing ideals between the two systems.

Reduced to total ruin by Allied bombing in 1944, the city of Dresden was entirely rebuilt after the war

13 Domestic problems in the USA, 1945–80

20 and 22.

McCa.. y was senator for Wisconsin, and was little-known until he brought accusations before the Un-American Activities Committee.

McCarthyism and the communist scare

In 1945 the USA prepared itself for peace. Demobilisation took place with few problems. Roosevelt had died in April 1945, and was succeeded by his vice-president, Truman. The spirit of Roosevelt's New Deal was continued by Truman's Fair Deal, and with a greatly strengthened economy, the future looked bright.

However, the peace brought new problems. The division of Europe, the tension of cold war, and growing mistrust of socialism contributed to a Republican victory in the 1946 elections for congress which killed the Fair Deal programme.

The worst fears of many US citizens were confirmed by the victory of communism in China, the Korean war, and the trial of Alger Hiss, a State Department official accused of passing secrets to Russia. In a fever of anti-communism, an Un-American Activities Committee was set up in 1949. Its chairman, Joseph McCarthy, burst onto the political scene as the scourge of communists.

Using the evidence: McCarthyism

Read the following documents on McCarthyist tactics:

A Telegram sent by McCarthy, February 1950:

In a Lincoln Day speech in Wheeling, Thursday night, I stated that the State Department harbours a nest of communists and communist sympathisers who are helping to shape our foreign policy. I further stated that I have in my possession the names of 57 communists who are in the State Department at present.

B Speech to the US senate 1950:

I shall submit quite a large number of names. I think they are of importance. They all worked for the State Department at one time or another. I shall not attempt to present a detailed case on each one.

The names are available. The senators may have them if they care for them. I think however, it would be improper to make the names public.
[Example]
Case No. 9. This individual, after investigation, was not given security clearance by the State Department. After failing to obtain clearance he secured a job in the office of the Secretary of Defence. And where do you think that man is today? He is now a speech writer in the White House.

C Speech to the US senate, at the time of the Korean war 1950:

Mr President, at this very moment GIs are consecrating the hills and valleys of Korea with American blood. But all that blood is not staining the Korean hills and valleys. Some of it is deeply staining the hands of Washington politicians. . . . Highly placed Red counsellors in the State Department are far more dangerous that Red machine gunners at Suwon. Those Red counsellors, by blending treachery into policy, can enslave entire nations while the Red machine gunners can at most kill hundreds or thousands.

I agree with the historian who once said 'If this nation is ever destroyed, it will not be by enemies from without, but enemies from within.'

We can successfully fight a war abroad and at the same time can dispose of the traitorous filth and the Red vermin which have accumulated at home.

D Letter from McCarthy to the US High Commissioner, concerning library books:

Our Committee has recently exposed the fact there are some 30 000 publications by authors on information shelves concerned with the furthering of the communist conspiracy.

Would you burn them?

E Speech by McCarthy, November 1953, concerning his critics:

Well my good friends, this gives you some of the picture why the communists, the fellow travellers, the Truman type Democrats who place party above country, scream so loudly about McCarthyism, why their hatred and venom knows no bounds.

What others thought of McCarthy:

F With perseverence, with brazenness, with pugnacity, with lies and deception, with criticism, with irresponsibility, with zeal for any handy issue, with a rascality that he relished . . . and with mastery in using press, radio and TV to trumpet his charges, McCarthy made himself the talk of America, and soon the world!

R Donovan, *Tumultuous Years, the Presidency of Truman*, 1982,

G He is the most dangerous menace to America. When I think of McCarthy I automatically think of Hitler.

Arthur Eisenhower, *Progressive* Magazine, 1954

H In the library of the US Embassy there is a book called *The ABC of American Wines*. It contains a long section on red wines. While I do not believe that there is a strong enough case for removing this book, I suggest that everyone who reads it should be carefully watched.

British reporter in the *Daily Telegraph*, 1953

I What is indisputable is that he was a courageous man who fought a monumental evil.

Since his day Cuba has fallen to the communists. The Free World was rocked in 1967 by the Harold Philby revelation of communist infiltration in high government security posts. Nuclear explosions echo over China and the Soviet Union. American men are defending the borders of South Vietnam against communist aggressors.

Has not history already begun his vindication?

Roy Cohn, *McCarthy*, 1968

Kim Philby – A British senior civil servant who defected to the Soviet Union taking important secrets with him.

McCarthyism was a major influence in politics until 1954, and many Americans were dragged down by this campaign. These included scientists, for example Robert Oppenheimer, film stars, artists, and anyone who criticised either McCarthy or government policy. In particular the Democrats suffered for being more moderate that Republicans.

Some famous stars of the day campaigned against the work of McCarthy's Un-American Activities Committee. Included here are Humphrey Bogart, Lauren Bacall, Danny Kaye, and Larry Adler

The end came when, in 1954, McCarthy accused army chiefs of favouring communism. The televised hearings cleared the army, but revealed McCarthy as an unscrupulous bully. He was censured by the senate and thereafter his influence dwindled. McCarthyism had done considerable damage both within America and to the country's reputation abroad.

1 The Wheeling speech, and subsequently McCarthy's senate speech, brought him to fame. On what grounds might you be unhappy with the evidence which McCarthy offers in the first three documents? Why do you think so many Americans believed him?

2 Use documents A–E to show the methods by McCarthy to make his case against communists.

3 Read documents F–I, showing what others thought of McCarthy. For each:
   (a) Show the standpoint of the writer.
   (b) State what reasons the writers give in support of their view of McCarthy.

Civil rights in the USA

America's black population can broadly be divided into three groups: blacks living in the south, where the abolition of slavery in 1862 did not end the lowly status of the ex-slaves and their descendants; blacks living in the major cities, whether in the south or north, where social problems such as unemployment, poverty and crime go hand in hand; and the small minority of blacks who have escaped the plight of the majority by achieving wealth and recognition.

The southern states had been the homes of slavery in the USA, and the desire of the plantation owners to keep slaves had contributed to the American Civil War in 1861.

People in all three categories have found themselves the victims of prejudice at the hands of both government and people. The civil rights campaigns in the USA have been attempts to correct those prejudices and obtain equality in politics, at work, and in everyday life.

Study the following documents, which show some of the problems of the black community in the USA:

A In Montgomery, Alabama, the medium annual income for the average black worker was under $1000 in 1956. Only 2000 black adults were entitled to vote.

In early 1956, five southern legislatures passed at least 42 Jim Crow laws reinforcing separate black public schools.

> Manning Marable, *Race, Reform and Rebellion*, 1984

Jim Crow – an insulting term for black people, which came to be used for laws which discriminated against blacks. One Jim Crow law was passed in Louisiana in 1892. The law, which provided separate transport for black and white, was challenged in the famous court case Plessey v. Ferguson. Plessey lost, and segregated transport continued for another 60 years.

Segregation, US style, A 'blacks only' shack in Forida, 1945

B We have waited more than 340 years for our constitutional and God-given rights. The nations of Asia and Africa are moving with jetlike speed towards gaining political independence, but we still creep at horse-buggy pace toward gaining a cup of coffee at a lunch counter. Perhaps it is easy for those who have never felt the stinging darts of segregation to say, 'Wait'. But when you have seen vicious mobs lynch your mothers and fathers at will and drown your sisters and brothers at whim; when you have seen hate-filled policemen curse, kick, and even kill your black brothers and sisters; when you have seen the vast majority of your twenty million negro brothers in poverty in the midst of an affluent society, when you find your tongue twisted and your speech stammering as you seek to explain to to your six-year-old daughter why she can't go to the public amusement park that has just been advertised on television, and see tears welling up in her eyes when she is told that Funtown is closed to coloured children; when you take a cross country drive . . . and find it necessary to sleep in your automobile because no motel will accept you; when you are humiliated day in and day out by nagging signs rending white and coloured; when your first name becomes nigger, and your middle name becomes boy – then you will understand why we find it so difficult to wait.

From a speech by Martin Luther King, 'Why we Can't Wait', 1964

C In 1967, in the Marine Corps, 9.6 per cent of all enlisted men were black, while only 0.5 per cent were officers; in the army 13.5 per cent of enlisted personnel were black, and only 3.4 per cent of the army's officers.

Afro-Americans comprised one out of every seven US soldiers stationed in Vietnam, and because blacks tended to be placed on 'combat units' more often than middle-class whites, they also bore unfairly higher risks of being killed and wounded. From January to November 1966, 22.4 per cent of all army casualties were black.

Manning Marable, *Race, Reform and Rebellion*, 1984

D US Census statistics for 1974 (Deaths per 100 000):

	Blacks	Whites
Deaths from tuberculosis	4.1	1.3
Syphilis	0.5	0.1
Infancy diseases	29	11.3

F The negro baby born in America today has about one half as much chance of completing high school as a white baby, one third as much chance of completing college, twice as much chance of becoming unemployed, a life expectancy which is seven years less, and the prospect of earning half as much.

From a speech by President John F. Kennedy, 1963

Martin Luther King on the steps of the Lincoln memorial as crowds assemble to hear him speak

Questions

1 Documents A–E show discrimination in a number of ways: social; economic; political; military; educational. Use each of these as a sub-heading and list the examples you can find of each.
2 Martin Luther King was famous as a great speaker. What aspects of his speech might be particularly effective in influencing a crowd? If you can, make a recording of this speech – it will sound more effective than it may seem in print.

The campaign for equality

Protest against these inequalities has taken many forms, but can broadly be divided into two types: non-violent and violent protest.

Non-violent protest has been pursued since the Second World War by groups such as the Congress of Racial Equality founded in 1942. CORE fights through non-violent direct action, such as boycotts and legal battles against discrimination. CORE faded in the 1950s, being tarred by McCarthy's communist brush (see page 206), but non-violent direct action revived in the 1960s. The form it took was the desegregation protest, begun in February 1960 when four black students sat at a lunch counter in a 'white only' section and refused to move. By April, 50 000 black and white students were involved in sit-ins. The next target was transport, and students took 'freedom' rides, using white-only buses as a protest. The movement continued to grow until 1963, when 250 000 people, black and white, gathered in front of the Lincoln memorial in Washington to voice their support for Kennedy's civil rights Bill.

In fact the Bill was a disappointment to many. Peaceful protest continued, and in 1964, Martin Luther King was awarded the Nobel Peace prize for his leadership of the movement. However, by this time

One of the most controversial aspects of desegregation has been bussing – to bring together black and white children from different neighbourhoods who would otherwise only mix with their own kind.

President Lincoln led the USA into civil war to free the slaves, and still symbolises racial harmony for many Americans.

Freedom Riders failed on this occasion. Their bus was set on fire by angry whites

King was shot in Memphis, Tennessee, while attending a civil rights rally.

more black people were supporting the use of force. When King was assassinated in 1968 many remembered him as a man of peace, but it confirmed the view of others that violence should be met with violence. Since 1964 black power movements had been gathering force. Malcolm X linked black power with Islam. He was assassinated in February 1965, but Stokely Carmichael and the Black Panthers continued to pursue the struggle by use of force. However, Republican presidents pushing a strong law-and-order line suppressed this extreme wing of the civil rights movement.

Protest had some effect. King and his supporters had won over many whites to the cause of racial equality. Far more black people were elected to government office, especially at a local level. Perhaps most important of all, politicians in Washington had been persuaded or forced to act.

Below are listed the major landmarks in US government intervention on race:

1954   Brown v. Board of Education of Topeka, Kansas.
        This Act overturned the ruling of 1896 that allowed segregation of education. The Chief Justice said 'we cannot turn the clock back to 1896 when Plessey v Ferguson was written. We must consider public education in the light of its full development and its present place in American life. In the field of education the doctrine of "separate but equal" has no place. Separate educational facilities are inherently unequal.'

The US constitution is a federal one, creating a balance between central government and state governments. The two have often quarrelled over their rights.

1957   Little Rock, Arkansas put forward plans to desegregate its schools. The state court ordered them not to put the plan into action. The federal court ordered that it should. State troopers stopped nine black children from entering the school. President Eisenhower ordered in US army troops to enforce the federal ruling.

Troopers escort black students to classes at Central High School, Little Rock, 1957

1957	Civil Rights Act. Guaranteed black voting rights and desegregation of schools.
1960	Civil Rights Act. Set up a mechanism by which local obstacles to black voting rights could be bypassed. Brought in federal backing against racists who resisted black voting or desegregation.
1962	A black student, James Meredith, was refused access to the University of Mississippi. The state governor of Mississippi ordered the university to defy a federal ruling, and personally stopped Meredith from entering. President Kennedy sent in federal marshals, and later 1400 troops to escort Meredith and disperse rioters.
1964	Civil Rights Act. Outlawed 'Jim Crow' in public accommodations of every kind.
1965	Voting Rights Act. Enforced the democratic right of all to vote.

The results of these Acts should have been equality of education, an end to segregation, and democracy. They should also have made it clear that the southern states could not defy federal law. However, in the end the success of any civil rights act depends on the day-to-day attitude of ordinary people. President Eisenhower said that ' you cannot change people's hearts entirely by laws'. The law was only a first step, and Martin Luther King's most famous speech revealed that, for him, racial equality was still a dream:

I have a dream that one day this nation will rise up, live out the true meaning of its creed . . . that all men are created equal. I have a dream that one day on the red hills of Georgia the sons of former slaves and the sons of former slave owners will be able to sit down together at the table of brotherhood. I have a dream that one day the State of Mississipi, a state sweltering with the heat of oppression, will be transformed into an oasis of freedom and justice. I have a dream that my four little children one day will live in a nation where they will not be judged by the colour of their skin, but by the content of their character.

According to King:

The greatest stumbling block in the stride towards freedom is not the Ku-Klux Klanner but the white moderate who is more devoted to 'order' than to justice.

Manning Marable offers other reasons for the failure of the civil rights movement:

The mob hates the black man and woman because it fears the strength of united black political power, the danger of being replaced on the job by a black person, the threat of blacks living next door and undermining property values. . . . Leaders of the 'mob spirit' from the hoodlums to the firebombers . . to the President himself will distort the lessons of the past to ensure racial inequality in the future.

In some ways the problem is still as great as it was earlier in the century, and the examples of racial hatred just as shocking:

Mississippi whites were responsible for at least twelve separate lynchings of blacks in 1980. On 12 October 1981 the body of Douglas McDonald was pulled from a lake in Eastover, Mississippi, the black man's ears were removed and his sex organs had been hacked off. In Social Circle, Georgia, the cousin of my wife, Lynn Jackson, was lynched on 8 December 1981 . . . random violence against blacks occurred in Buffalo and Atlanta. Several blacks were executed on street corners. Two black men were savagely beaten to death and amazingly had their hearts removed from their corpses by their killer or killers. Twenty-eight black youths were methodically murdered in Atlanta between 1979 and 1982.

Manning Marable, *Race, Reform and Rebellion*, 198

Governments have also failed to deal successfully with the other problem most associated with black communities – urban decay. In 1967, the year of the worst urban riots, 40 per cent of US cities were were affected by race riots, 86 people were killed, and 11 094 arrested. In December 1981 half of the people in US jails, and half of the 103 awaiting execution were black.

Yet a newspaper headline of 16 August 1985 reads:

WHITE HOUSE PLANS CIVIL RIGHTS U TURN

Rules concerning equal rights in employment which were made by Lyndon Johnson are to be repealed, making higher black unemployment a probability.

Questions

1 Manning Marable has been used as a source of evidence three times in this section. What evidence is there of Marable's personal involvement in this problem? Does that evidence cast doubts on his reliability? Answer the question with reference to the given extracts.
2 What evidence is there that central government in the USA was more enthusiastic about civil rights than some southern states?
3 What progress was made by the central government towards racial equality 1954–65?
4 Why, according to the sources, are laws insufficient? What else is required before there can be genuine equality?
5 Is this problem particular to the USA?

The plight of the presidency

Kennedy was a war hero, extremely wealthy, and came from a powerful political family. He captured the imagination of his generation.

In 1960 the people of the USA elected the Democratic candidate, John F. Kennedy, as their president. He brought new qualities to the office and most important of these were youth – his ministry of 'the best and the brightest' – and idealism. At his inauguration he expressed the philosophy of the new government when he said, 'Ask not what your country can do for you. Ask what you can do for your country.'

Some of the hopes of the Kennedy programme were realised: many young Americans joined the Peace Corps to serve on development projects overseas. The imagination of the world was captured when in 1961, Alan Shepard became the first American in space, and in 1962 John Glenn orbited the earth.

However, there was much that went wrong. Involvement in Vietnam and Cuba and poor relations with the USSR clouded foreign affairs (see page 220). At home Kennedy's 'New Frontier' fell far short of its promise. His plans for civil rights, aid to farmers, medical care for all, and an end to poverty were defeated by congress.

Then, on 22 November 1963, while driving through the streets of Dallas, Texas, Kennedy was shot down. The assassin was Lee Harvey Oswald. Whether he was alone or backed by others remains a mystery, but it has been seriously suggested that Oswald was working with the Soviet Union, the Ku-Klux Klan, and even the CIA. With Kennedy died the hopes of many Americans, and their fears were borne out in the following years.

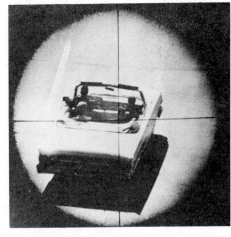

What the assassin saw – a reconstruction from the scene of the President's killing

The news that stunned the world

EXTRA
PRESIDENT SLAIN

Texas Assassin Hits Kennedy in Automobile

PRESIDENT JOHN F. KENNEDY

News Call Bulletin
SAN FRANCISCO'S EVENING NEWSPAPER

Volume 5, No. 90   FRIDAY, NOVEMBER 22, 1963   Phone EX 7-5700   Price 10c

DALLAS---President John F. Kennedy is dead. He died after an assassin fired on his car leading a motorcade into Dallas, third stop on his Texas tour.

DALLAS (UPI)—President John F. Kennedy and Gov. John B. Connally of Texas were cut down by an assassin's bullets as they toured downtown Dallas in an open automobile today.

Mystery San Carlos Gun Battle

Gunfire blazed in a quiet residential section of San Carlos early this morning as an apartment house dweller

The vote losers

In this section the performance of the presidents since 1964 are judge
in terms of the 'credits' which might have won them votes, and 'debit:
for the vote losers.

Johnson's period of office 1963–8

Kennedy's vice-president, Lyndon Johnson, was sworn in immediatel
after the assassination, and he was re-elected in 1964 in preference t
the extreme right-winger Barry Goldwater, who frightened man
voters by advocating use of nuclear bombs in Vietnam.

Credits Johnson's domestic programme, 'the Great Society', whic
promised 'to eliminate the paradox of poverty in the nation by openin
to everyone the opportunity to live in decency and dignity'. Thi
involved:

> Civil Rights Act 1964
> Economic Opportunity Act 1964 ($1 billion to fight poverty)
> Medicare for the elderly 1964
> Elementary and Secondary Education Act
> Voting Rights Act – 1965 which raised number of registered blac
> voters from 25 to over 60 per cent by 1969
> War on Poverty – to teach skills to the unemployed, and help th
> lower income families
> Model Cities Programme

With support from the houses of congress, both now controlled by th
Democrats, and the supreme court which upheld government policy
the numbers of people in poverty dropped from 42.5 million in 1962 t
25 million in 1967.

Debits Johnson was brought down by Vietnam and problems associate
with it. The war was going badly, and protest was rising at home
especially on the university campuses. Possibly half a million Ameri
cans committed draft offences i.e., illegally avoided conscription. A
the same time, the black power movement was growing, taking muc
support from the Democrats. The assassination of Martin Luther Kin;
was a further blow to Johnson's government, and in that year h
announced that he would not stand for re-election. His potentia
Democratic successor, Robert Kennedy was assassinated, and the fina
Democratic presidential candidate, Hubert Humphrey, split the part
with his support for the Vietnam war.

Victory in the 1968 election went to the Republican, Richard Nixon

Nixon in office, 1968–74

Debits Protest against the Vietnam war continued, with half a millio
people marching in Washington. Campus protests grew, until in Ma
1970 four students were killed by national guardsmen at Kent Stat
University.

Violence was growing in American cities. Unemployment stood at
per cent and inflation at 5.3 per cent. Nixon's attempts at price an

Thousands of young Americans who did not want to be conscripted and sent to Vietnam became draft dodgers – often by 'hiding', or going abroad.

age controls were destroyed by business and the unions. His policies
were also opposed by a Democratic congress.

A leak of information, the 'Pentagon Papers', revealed that Johnson
and Nixon had lied about policy in Vietnam, which further discredited
the presidency.

Credits Despite all this Nixon was re-elected in 1972. He won the white
vote by stopping the bussing of children to desegregated schools. He
won confidence by his visit to China in February and the USSR in May.
The activities of his secretary of state, Henry Kissinger, brought the
prospects of peace in Vietnam much closer.

Nixon successfully attacked the Democrats, whose weak candidate,
George McGovern, was pledged to cut defence spending; he was re-
elected with over 60 per cent of the votes – but already his second term
was doomed by the Watergate raid.

Watergate: what happened and when

17 June, 1972	Five men were arrested inside the Watergate building, Washington. They were attaching listening devices in the offices of the Democratic national committee. Four of them were anti-Castro Cubans, the fifth James McCord, ex CIA, then security co-ordinator of CREEP (Committee to Re-elect the President).
	President Nixon announced after 'a complete investigation' that no one in the administration was involved. In the meantime $460 000 was paid out in 'hush money' to stop anyone talking.
Spring 1973	James McCord confessed, implicating both CREEP and the White House.
April 1973	The Director of the FBI resigned, having tried and failed to organise a cover-up.
	White House aide John Dean implicated the President.
	It became known that the President taped all conversations, and proof could be found on the tapes.
	Nixon denied complicity and refused to release the tapes.
April 1974	Nixon released the tapes, but crucial parts had been wiped off.
24 July	Hearings began. Nixon was found guilty on three of five counts:
	1 Obstruction of justice: lying, withholding evidence paying hush money
	2 Defiance of a congressional subpoena.
	3 Use of the CIA and FBI to deprive Americans of their constitutional rights.

Nixon resigned. Never had the reputation of the presidency fallen s
low. His successor, Gerald Ford, added to this feeling when h
pardoned Nixon.

Ford in office

Debits Congress immediately passed a series of Acts to cut the power c
the president and stop a repetition of Watergate. These Acts limited th
president's power to make war without consulting congress, to us
federal money, to spend heavily on election campaigns, and to ensur
freedom of information.

Ford was much liked, but not respected. His greatest problem wa
the economy. US productivity was low, but wages were rising fast. S
too was the price of oil due to middle eastern problems, the rise bein
350 per cent between January 1973 and January 1974.

Ford's answer was a voluntary curb on wage and price rises – 'Whi
Inflation Now'. The campaign didn't work, so he cut governmen
spending. The result was deeper recession, with unemployment at 8.
per cent.

Carter in office

Debits Jimmy Carter came to the presidency in 1976 with a new appea
he claimed that he would sweep the cobwebs out of Washington
bringing a new style of open and honest government. He was elected i
1976 on a very low turnout, and disillusionment followed. He did littl
for human rights, and this was at a time when Ku-Klux Kla
membership was rising towards 10 000. Far from helping the poor an
urban dwellers, he cut spending and gave industry more freedom. H
proposed a new energy policy to cut oil consumption, but it was rejecte
in Congress. By 1980 inflation had risen to 12.4 per cent, interest rate
reached 20 per cent and unemployment stood at 7.5 per cent. Instead c
honesty, there were smears of corruption – Carter's businessma
brother Billy confessed to taking a $200 000 'loan' from Libya. I
Carter's final year, his foreign policy was totally undermined by th
capture of American hostages in Iran.
Credits Carter's strength was his foreign policy. He ended America'
promise to defend Taiwan, thus improving relations with China. H
also played an important role in getting Begin and Sadat together at th
Camp David talks in 1978 and 1979 (see page 282).

By 1980 a conservative movement was widespread. This was partl
religious – the 'born again Christians' – and it was partly economic –
wish to cut spending on social problems. Yet at the same tim
Americans wanted more spent on defence. In this atmosphere Ronal
Reagan was their ideal candidate. Has he raised America from th
plight of the presidency?

Jimmy Carter proclaimed himself
a peanut farmer from Georgia.
He promised that, with his
simple background, he would
sweep Washington clean and give
people the government they
wanted.

When the Shah of Iran went in
exile to the USA, Iranian
students stormed the US embassy
in Tehran and took 50 hostages
to trade for the Shah. Carter
ordered a raid to rescue them
which went disastrously wrong.

Ronald Reagan was an actor who
became governor of California
before running for president.

Unashamed? Nixon boards the White House helicopter after his resignation, September 1974

The future President of the USA . . .

14

Superpower rivalry and the nuclear arms build-up

Cold War crisis: Cuba

The Cold War was, at first, a war of words fought over Soviet borders i Eastern Europe, and over the fate of Berlin (see page 204). In 1950 th focus of the Cold War moved away from Europe on to a new stage Korea (see page 328). By the time that conflict was over, both the US, and the Soviet Union had gained new governments. With the death Stalin in 1953, a new leader was found in Khrushchev. In the US.

Khrushchev displays the evidence of the Gary Powers spying mission

Eisenhower ran as a Republican candidate, but his war record, his command of NATO, and his strong character gave him a broad appeal.

Dulles is remembered for the Domino theory – that if one state fell to communism, others would follow. He believed in a firm stand – see Chapter 22.

Truman was replaced by Eisenhower, whose foreign policy was closel identified with his secretary of state, John Foster Dulles. At the outse Dulles made a strong commitment to continue the Truman doctrine

> To all those suffering under communist slavery . . . let us say: you can cour on us.

Eisenhower offered the promise of better relations:

> The new Soviet leadership now has a precious opportunity to awaken, with th rest of the world, to the point of peril reached and help to turn the tide history. . . . We welcome every honest act of peace.

Khrushchev agreed that peace must be sought:

> There are only two ways: either peaceful co-existence or the most destructiv war in history. There is no third way.

Despite the confirmation of the two power blocs seen in NATO and th Warsaw Pact, the 1950s saw positive moves in pursuit of peaceful cc existence. Both power blocs were involved indirectly in conflict but visit by the British prime minister, Harold Macmillan, to the Sovie Union and Khrushchev's visit to the USA promised diplomati resolution of problems rather than threats. Khrushchev said,

> When I talked to President Eisenhower my impression was that the Presiden . . . is aware of the need to relax international tensions. We for our part mus do everything possible to preclude war as a means of settling outstandin questions.

However, talks of peace were shattered when, on 1 May 1960, a US U2 spy plane was shot down on a reconnaissance mission over the Soviet Union. When this was announced by the USSR no further information was given. Assuming that the plane was destroyed, the USA stated that it had been involved in high altitude weather observation, and had strayed from its course because the pilot had oxygen trouble.

Khrushchev then played his trump card, giving this statement to the Soviet News:

Comrades, I must tell you a secret. When I was making my report I did not say that the pilot was alive . . . and that we have got parts of his plane.

The name of the pilot is Francis Harry Powers, First Lieutenant of the USAF (and) Central Intelligence Agency. . . . he was flying along his assigned course, accurately carrying out the orders of his chiefs . . . to glean intelligence of the Soviet Union's military and industrial establishments . . . the plane at an altitude of 20 000 metres.

Not only do we have the equipment of the plane, but we also have the developed film showing a number of areas of our territory. . . . No concocted story, therefore, can save the reputation of those who bear the responsibility for this treacherous act.

I believe this is a bad preparation for easing international tension.

Khrushchev called off the plans to attend the Paris summit, and demanded an apology. When Eisenhower attempted to defend the U2 flights, Khrushchev responded:

It is not the burglar who is guilty, but the owner of the house he broke into, because he locked it, therefore compelling the burglar to break in. But this is the philosophy of thieves and bandits!

Soon afterwards Eisenhower was replaced by the much younger John F. Kennedy. One of the immediate problems facing him was Cuba, a communist outpost close to the United States. Kennedy inherited a plan, sponsored by the CIA, to assist Cuban exiles in the overthrow of communist President Castro. Kennedy refused to involve the USA directly in the plot, but reluctantly agreed that the invasion by an army of 14 000 should go ahead. The outcome, in April 1961, was a disaster. Unmarked US planes were supposed to destroy Castro's air force on the ground. When this failed, and Kennedy still refused to escalate the attack, ammunition ran out, supply ships were destroyed by aircraft, and the small force was easily defeated. To his credit, Kennedy said,

This is known as the Bay of Pigs incident after the place where the disastrous landing was attempted.

They couldn't believe that a new President like me wouldn't panic and try to save his own face. Well, they had me figured all wrong.

Twice, in the U2 incident and the Bay of Pigs, the USA had been caught out. The building of the Berlin wall in 1961 was a further humiliation for the Western powers.

What followed was the height of the Cold War – the Cuban missile scare. Kennedy had been watching ship movements to Cuba with interest. On 13 September he issued this warning:

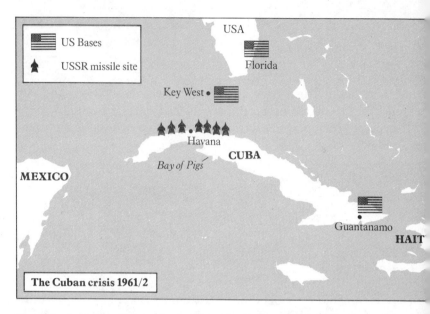

US Bases

USSR missile site

USA

Florida

Key West

Havana

CUBA

Bay of Pigs

MEXICO

Guantanamo

HAIT

The Cuban crisis 1961/2

If at any time the communist build-up in Cuba were to endanger or interfer with our security in any way, or if Cuba should ever become an offensiv military base for the Soviet Union, then this country will do whatever must b done to protect its own security and that of its allies.

During the week Kennedy assembled his intelligence information Aerial photographs clearly showed the building of launching sites fo medium-range ballistic missiles. Yet when Kennedy spoke to the Sovie foreign minister, Andrei Gromyko, he was told:

As to Soviet assistance to Cuba, I have been instructed to make it clear . . . tha such assistance pursues solely the purpose of contributing to the defenc capabilities of Cuba and to the development of its peaceful economy.

LAUNCH STANDS

17 MISSILE ERECTORS

Official US photos showing missile launching sites in Cuba

Kennedy remembered:

told him that there had better not be any ballistic missiles in Cuba. And he told me that such a thought had never entered Khrushchev's mind. It was incredible to sit there and watch the lies coming out of his mouth.

Three possible strategies were considered – to give in, to strike, and to blockade.

On 22 October, Kennedy broadcast an address to the nation:

The urgent transformation of Cuba into an important strategic base by the presence of these large, long-range, and clearly offensive weapons of sudden mass destruction constitutes an explicit threat to the peace and security of all the Americas . . . all ships of any kind bound for Cuba from whatever nation or port will, if found to contain cargoes of offensive weapons, be turned back.

It shall be the policy of this nation to regard any nuclear missile launched from Cuba against any nation in the western hemisphere as an attack by the Soviet Union on the United States, requiring a full retaliatory response upon the Soviet Union.

I call upon Chairman Khrushchev to halt and eliminate this clandestine, reckless and provocative threat to world peace. He has an opportunity now to move the world back from the abyss of destruction by . . . withdrawing these weapons from Cuba.

When the blockade went into force, Russian ships suspected of carrying missiles were only half an hour from the boundary line, with a submarine in escort. How close was the world to nuclear war? Kenneth O' Donnell, Kennedy's closest adviser, remembered:

All of us in the room assumed that the Soviet ships would refuse to stop, that our navy ships and planes from the carrier *Essex* . . . would be forced to open fire, and the Russians would then respond with missiles from Cuba or long range ICBMs from Eastern Europe, or perhaps by seizing West Berlin.

ICBM – Inter-continental ballistic missile.

A US warship alongside a Soviet merchant vessel approaching Cuba

American nuclear missiles were on the alert when a messenger handed in a note:

Mr President, we have a preliminary report that some of the Russian ships are stopping.

Twenty ships had stopped. Dean Rusk said ' We're eyeball to eyeball and I think the other fellow just blinked'. Indeed, the ships turned back.

Khrushchev's answer came on 26 October. He would withdraw the missiles if the USA would undertake not to invade Cuba. Kennedy accepted, the ships turned back, the blockade was ended, and the world breathed a sigh of relief.

Cuba was an important turning point in the Cold War. Although the East and West were at odds in other parts of the globe, steps were taken to avoid further confrontations. Specific conflicts have been avoided since, although the far greater problem of a nuclear arms build-up remains.

Questions

1 (a) On what grounds could Khrushchev be described as the offended party in the U2 incident? How did Khrushchev make the most of the incident?
   (b) What do you think Kennedy meant when he said, 'They couldn't believe a new President like me wouldn't panic and try to save his own face'?
2 (a) Why do you think that the outcome of the Cuban missile crisis is regarded as a triumph for President Kennedy's judgement?
   (b) In what way can this be described as the reverse of the U2 incident?
   (c) It has been said of the Cuba crisis that 'The world stood still'. Rewrite the Cuba story and try to recapture the tension of those days.

The nuclear build-up

The development of the nuclear bomb began before the Second World War. In 1938 two German scientists split the atom. This demonstrated the possibility of tapping a vast new source of energy for peaceful or military purposes. When news of this reached President Eisenhower in the USA he started his own research programme. This was called the Manhattan Project, and it took place in strictest secrecy. The main research centre was at Los Alamos, New Mexico, and the scientists had created and tested the first atom bomb by 1945. The test took place at Alamorgardo. The first actual use of the bomb was at Hiroshima. The effects of this explosion can be seen on page 183.

The Soviet Union, urged on by the climate of the Cold War, developed and tested its own atom bomb by 1949. This came as a shock to the USA, which immediately revived an earlier plan of its own: this was to develop a much more powerful hydrogen bomb, or 'superbomb'. In November 1952 the first hydrogen bomb was exploded at Eniwetok Atoll with extraordinary results. Flames from the explosion were two miles wide and five miles high. The mushroom cloud was a hundred miles long. The test proved that the USA could now destroy a great city with one bomb. In August 1953 the USSR, too, had developed a superbomb. In the race for nuclear power, there were only a few months separating the two sides.

Having the bomb was one thing. There was also the question of how to deliver that bomb to its target. The USA already had the B52 bomber with a range of 6000 miles, and the advantage of bases in Europe from which it could attack the Soviet Union. By 1955 the Soviet Union had developed its own long-range bomber, but by that time both sides were designing rockets to carry nuclear warheads from continent to continent (inter-continental ballistic missiles, or ICBMs) and missiles which could be launched from submarines close to enemy targets.

Early missiles were slow to launch, easy to intercept, and inaccurate. Since the 1960s both superpowers have introduced a number of improvements: fast, accurate, long-range missiles such as the Soviet Titan and the US Minuteman 111, with multiple warheads which scatter to hit various targets. At first these were inaccurate, but now there are multiple independently targetable re-entry vehicles (MIRVs) which release warheads at separate and precise targets. Trident is an example of a MIRV. In addition, there are now shorter-range missiles (e.g. Cruise) which avoid interception by staying close to the ground and following a variable course – rather like a pilotless aeroplane – before hitting their target with precision.

Russia's progress towards the bomb was helped by German atomic scientists, some of whom worked for the Soviet Union after the war, and Dr Klaus Fuchs, who worked for Britain but passed on secrets to Russia.

Four Soviet surface-to-air missiles

These are only a few of the major nuclear weapons projects which have cost billions of dollars and roubles. Both powers acknowledge that they have built far more nuclear weapons than they need.

The Soviet leader Nikita Khrushchev remembered:

President Kennedy once stated . . . that the United States had the missile capacity to wipe out the Soviet Union two times over, while the Soviet Union had enough atomic weapons to wipe out the United States only once. . . . When journalists asked me to comment . . . I said jokingly, 'Yes, I know what Kennedy claims, and he's quite right. But I'm not complaining . . . we're satisfied to be able to finish off the United States first time round. Once is quite enough. What good does it do to annihilate a country twice? We're not a bloodthirsty people.

J. Cox, *Overkill. The Story of Modern Weapons*, 1981

In summary:

The world's arsenals contain tens of thousands of nuclear weapons. The total explosive power of these weapons is equivalent to about one and a quarter million Hiroshima bombs, or about four tons of TNT for every man, woman and child on earth.

F. Barnaby, *Prospects for Peace*, 1980

How can we account for this arms build-up? Here are some answers.

1 Mistrust between the superpowers

In Korea (see page 328), and more dangerously at the time of the Cuban missile crisis (see page 220), the use of nuclear weapons was considered, and the world held its breath. Since the Cuban missile crisis there has been no direct confrontation between the superpowers. In fact, after Cuba there was a relaxation of tension, a period of detente. Even so there have been many occasions when the two sides have attacked each other's policies, and have been indirectly in conflict. Both the USSR and the US accuse the other of wanting world domination. American involvement in Vietnam (page 333) and the Soviet invasion of Afghanistan (page 342) are seen as two blatant examples, but there are many instances of their activity on other countries.

Detente – the easing of strained international relations.

US involvement in foreign states

Central America and the Caribbean: Support for government terror in El Salvador involving 38 000 civilian deaths since 1978; support of slaughter of communists in Guatemala; interference in Honduras and Nicaragua; invasion of Grenada in 1983.

The Middle East: Support for the Shah of Iran before his downfall (see page 242); support for Israel's invasion of the Lebanon in 1982.

Asia: Support for the Lon Nol government in Kampuchea; interference in the affairs of the Philippines and Indonesia; increased naval activity in the Indian Ocean.

Europe: Domination of Western Europe, some would say in the interests of the USA:

It is now possible to see Britain emerging as part of America's nuclear front fire, defending US interests in a nuclear war rather than enjoying protection under the NATO/US umbrella.

. . . American military independence is such that the USAF could actually initiate a nuclear war against the USSR from British soil without the involvement of parliament.

'Facts Against the Nomb', Nottingham Group for Nuclear Disarmament

Soviet involvement in foreign states

Central America: Giving aid to Sandanistas in Nicaragua and communists in El Salvador.

Africa: supporting communist movements in Ethiopia and Angola.

Asia: support of Cambodia. Massive fleet build-up in the Pacific.

Middle East: Continued if rather frustrated attempts to influence Middle Eastern affairs. Increased naval activity in the Mediterranean.

Europe: crushing of trade union and liberal movements in Poland.

The Warsaw Pact has over the years developed a large and growing capacity in nuclear systems that directly threaten Western Europe.

NATO Review, 1980

Individual 'strikes'

Particular incidents have also brought forth criticism – for example the disastrous attempt by the USA to rescue hostages from Iran in 1980, and the shooting down of the Korean Jumbo Jet 007 over Soviet airspace in 1983 have brought hostile accusations from the other side. Official speeches by the two sides reveal the deep mistrust created by such policies and incidents:

This remains a mystery. Some suggest that this plane was being used by the Koreans on behalf of the USA to film, or test, sensitive military areas of the USSR.

On one hand the Soviets are beset by profound problems. They are barely able to feed their people . . . spiritually they are bankrupt . . . and they have succeeded in generating the fear and hostility of every other major power. On the other hand the Soviets have concentrated on building a military capability well beyond any need for self-defence.

US Secretary of State L. Eagleburger, June 1981

The US administration continues to pursue a military course which poses a grave threat to peace. It tries to assure for the United States dominant positions in the world without reckoning the interests of other states and peoples.

American military presence thousands of kilometres from US territory has increased tension the world over.

Yuri Andropov, *Pravda*, September 1983

2 The arms race

These documents show how the two sides see the arms race:

The Soviet Union was not the first to make the atomic bomb. It did not threaten anyone with nuclear destruction and did not surround Western Europe with military bases, although it was itself encircled. The Soviet Union has no forward based system spearheaded at the very heart of a foreign country, whereas the US does have such a system. The fact is that the Soviet

Union has been compelled to do no more than . . . catch up with the US to maintain the balance of forces. . . . Is it surprising that the USSR has found it necessary to create its own military potential in Europe to counter everything that threatens it?

D. Proekter, *The Choice facing Europe*, Moscow 1981

There is no question that Soviet momentum has brought then from a position of clear inferiority to their present status of at least strategic equality with the USA. It is essential to proceed with our modernisation programme.

General D. Jones, US Military Posture 1981

Professor Vadim Zagladin claimed yesterday that the introduction by Moscow of SS20 missiles was a modernisation measure and served only to establish parity with the West.

The Times, 14 October 1981

The Warsaw Pact . . . have deployed the SS20 missile which offers significant improvements over previous systems. Accordingly ministers have decided to modernise NATO Long Range Theatre Nuclear Forces by the deployment in Europe of Pershing and Cruise missiles.

NATO Review, February 1980

American military aims are served by the unprecedented build-up of weapons of all types – nuclear, chemical and conventional. Now it is planned to project the unrestricted arms race into outer space as well.

Y. Andropov, *Pravda*, September 1983

The American Administration is still tempted to try for the possibility of gaining military superiority. By launching an arms race into space they hope to overcome us with electronics and computers. We will find a response, just as we did in the past. To restore the balance the Soviet Union will have enhance the efficiency, accuracy, strike power of its arms in order to neutralise, if we must, the electronic space machine of star wars.

Speech by Mr Gorbachev to the Supreme Soviet, 27 November, 1985

The 'strategic defence initiative', or 'star wars', is claimed by President Reagan to be a system which will render nuclear weapons obsolete.

3 Deterrence

The principle of deterrence is explained here by Caspar Weinburger, the US defence secretary:

The policy of deterrence is difficult for some to grasp because it is based on a paradox. But this is quite simple: to make the cost of nuclear war much higher than any possible 'benefit' to the country starting it. If the Soviets know in advance that a nuclear attack on the United States could and would bring nuclear retaliation they would never attack in the first place. They would be deterred from ever beginning a nuclear war.

Deterrence therefore relies on the ability to retaliate, despite being hit by a first strike. In times of crisis in the late 1950s squadrons of US B52 bombers were kept in the air in a state of consant readiness so that they could mount a counter-attack if necessary. Since the development of highly accurate missiles, new systems have been produced by both sides to ensure that their own missiles cannot be destroyed in a first strike. Submarines and mobile land-based missile launchers have been seen as solutions. The USA has also planned a complex silo system for its MX missiles, This involves a massive network consisting of miles of roadways containing 4 600 possible launching sites for missiles. The 200 missiles will move around the system so that the enemy will never know which silos they must destroy in a first strike.

Such systems would enable a superpower under attack to strike back, ensuring the destruction of both sides – 'mutually assured destruction' (MAD). It therefore assumes that neither side would dare to strike first, and thus that nuclear weapons are defensive, not offensive.

Not everyone agrees that MAD is sane:

Nuclear weapons may not have been used in war since 1945 but things have changed. Deterrence used to rely on the threat of automatic retaliation and mutually assured destruction. But advances in missile technology now mean greater accuracy and independent targetability of nuclear warheads. These advances will offer a chance of wiping out nearly all an enemy's missiles in a single devastating 'first strike'. And so peace depends not on deterrence but on politician's good intentions. Are they reliable enough?

The Peace Pack, 1983

4 Horizontal nuclear proliferation

The possession of nuclear weapons is no longer confined to the two superpowers. China has assumed superpower status since it developed a bomb in 1964. Britain and France also have the bomb. Continued French testing in the Pacific has caused increasing levels of protest from Pacific states and international organisations such as Greenpeace. In 1985 Greenpeace sent a ship 'Rainbow Warrior', to monitor and disrupt testing. The ship was blown up by the French secret service while in port in New Zealand, itself a strongly anti-nuclear state.

Greenpeace – an environmental movement particularly determined to put a stop to nuclear testing and other threats to the ecological balance.

Other states are also nearing the development of their own bomb, or have the capability to do so. India is a potential nuclear power but has held back from the development of the bomb. However, in 1985 growing concern about the threat from Pakistan led the Indian prime minister, Rajiv Gandhi, to say,

At the moment we do not have a nuclear weapon programme and our intention is clear not to make a bomb. But we will not let our security be compromised.

Other powers which could develop nuclear weapons include the world's foremost troublespots – Israel and South Africa. Nuclear watchers feel that, for every power that gains the bomb, the security of the world becomes a little more threatened.

5 The failure of attempts to limit arms control

Politicians from East and West have spent a great deal of time emphasising their hopes for world peace.

During the years of detente, Leonid Brezhnev said,

The struggle to consolidate the principles of peaceful co-existence, to assure lasting peace, and to reduce and in the long term to eliminate the danger of world war has been and remains the main element of our policy towards the capitalist states.

Congress Report, 1976

The US secretary of defence has said of President Reagan's star wars scheme:

The result is extremely worthwhile because you would simply free mankind from these nuclear missiles, and that's the President's great hope and dream.

Caspar Weinberger, March 1983

Similar words have been spoken over the last three decades. What has actually been achieved to limit nuclear proliferation? These are the principal agreements:

Tension over the Cuban crisis persuaded leaders of both sides that there should be a hot line for instant communication.

1963   Hotline agreement, which established a direct link between superpower leaders in order to make communication easy in an emergency.

1963   Ban on certain types of nuclear testing – in the atmosphere in space, underwater.

1967   Ban on placing nuclear weapons in orbit.

1968   Non-proliferation treaty. Existing nuclear powers agreed not to help non-nuclear states to develop weapons. Non-nuclear states agreed not to develop them on their own, but some which did not sign, such as India, have ignored the terms of this treaty.

1972   SALT I (Strategic Arms Limitation Talks). This limited the development of anti-ballistic missiles by both the USA and the USSR, and limited the maximum number of inter-continental ballistic missiles.

1974   Nixon met Brezhnev at Moscow, and further limitations were put on the deployment of ABMs.

1979   SALT II. Placed limits on the number of strategic bombers and missiles. This treaty was signed by President Carter at the Vienna summit but has not been ratified by the US senate.

Detente in action. Brezhnev and Carter in Vienna before the SALT II talks

1985   There was much talk about the Reagan–Gorbachev summit in Geneva. They agreed to the principle of a 50 per cent cut in arms as the basis for negotiations. However, any progress was subject to an agreement on the strategic defence initiative (star wars). No such agreement is in sight.

6 The failure of the peace movement

Arguments put forward by the peace movements have both moral and scientific foundations

The moral argument:

The damage to non-combatants, even indeed to neutral countries; the havoc made of the environment; and the dangers to generations yet unborn; these things make nuclear weapons indiscriminate and nuclear war disproportionate. The evils caused by this method of making war are greater than any conceivable evil which the war is intended to prevent, and they affect people who have nothing to do with the conflict.

CND marchers stepping out from London to Holy Loch, 1961

The scientific argument:

Possible consequences of a nuclear war include the blinding of insects, birds and beasts all over the world; the extinction of many ocean species, among them some at the base of the food chain; the alteration of the climate of the globe; the incapacitation and blinding of people who go out into the sunlight, the scalding and killing of many plants and crops, increase in the rates of cancer and mutation around the world but especially in targeted zones, and the risks of global epidemics; the poisoning of animals by ultraviolet light; the outright slaughter on all targeted continents of most human beings and other living things by nuclear radiation, fireballs, thermal pulses, blast waves, mass fires and fallout. These will all react together in unguessable ways, and one must conclude that a full scale nuclear holocaust could lead to the extinction of mankind.

J. Schell, *The Fate of the Earth*, 1982

Greenham Common. Protesting for the future

CND – Campaign for Nuclear Disarmament.

Some parts of the peace movement have concentrated on specific issues – for example, the Greenham Common Peace Women have protested about siting of Cruise missiles in England. Yet from the days of the Aldermaston marches in the 1960s to the revival of the CND in the 1980s there has been little or no effect on the actions of governments. Other European peace movements have similarly failed to make an impact. Indeed in December 1985 the British government signed an agreement to join research into the star wars programme, and other European states seem likely to follow, despite the fact that this programme is a major stumbling block to further peace negotiations.

Questions

1 Draw a flow diagram to show the development of nuclear weapons and delivery systems.
2 In what ways would a member of the government of the USA or the USSR justify the arms build-up? Explain your answer carefully and give examples.
3 Both sides say that they want peace. How much have they achieved in arms talks since 1963?
4 What are the main arguments against nuclear weapons? Why have these arguments had such little influence on governments?

The Middle East

15

Westernisation and Islamic reaction: Iran and Libya

The crusades of the Middle Ages saw the Middle East as a battleground between Christians and Turks over Jerusalem.

The Suez canal was completed in 1869 by the French engineer Ferdinand de Lesseps. Britain became a major shareholder, realising the importance of the canal on the sea route to India.

The problem of the Middle East

During the twentieth century the Middle East has been in a continual state of turmoil, so much so that people in the West have found the changing situation almost impossible to understand. Why are they fighting each other? What do they hope to achieve? What is the difference between the many groups who seem to be at each others' throats?

In part, the Middle Eastern problem is the result of its geographical position. Looking at the following map, and it is not difficult to see why the region is of such interest to outsiders. It is a crossroads between three continents, and the borders of the Middle East have often been the borders of a world divided over religion, political alliances, and rival doctrines. The route to the Far East though the Suez canal has also made the region one of key strategic importance.

The region has been particular place of strife since the collapse of the Turkish Empire in the early part of this century. As long as Turkey held control in this area, other growing nations such as Russia, could be satisfied that no rival would take over. With the decline of Turkey, rival countries rushed in to take her place. As for the native Arabs and other

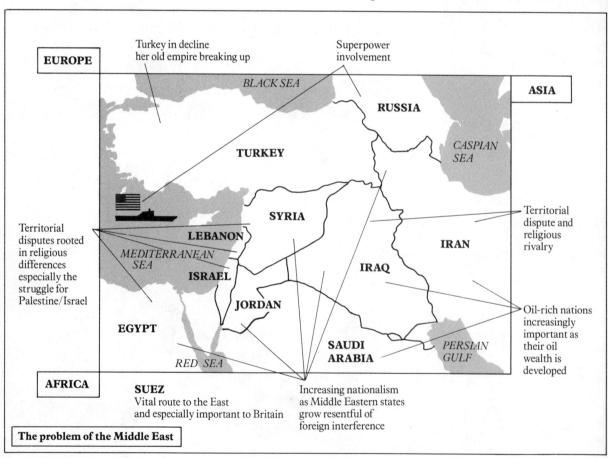

EUROPE

Turkey in decline her old empire breaking up

Superpower involvement

ASIA

BLACK SEA

RUSSIA

CASPIAN SEA

TURKEY

Territorial dispute and religious rivalry

SYRIA

IRAN

LEBANON

MEDITERRANEAN SEA

IRAQ

Territorial disputes rooted in religious differences especially the struggle for Palestine/Israel

ISRAEL

JORDAN

Oil-rich nations increasingly important as their oil wealth is developed

EGYPT

SAUDI ARABIA

PERSIAN GULF

RED SEA

AFRICA

SUEZ
Vital route to the East and especially important to Britain

Increasing nationalism as Middle Eastern states grow resentful of foreign interference

The problem of the Middle East

groups in the Middle East, they merely lost one master and gained others. Not surprisingly therefore, a major trend there has been the rise of Arab nationalism. Various movements in different countries have set out to rid themselves of foreign control and to become masters of their own destiny.

A further cause of conflict has been religion. The Middle East contains the homes of religions at Jerusalem and Mecca. The Arabs of the region are Muslim – but broadly they follow one of two paths, the Sunnite, or the Shi'ite. Jerusalem is the holy city of the Jews, and although their numbers were small at the start of the century, the struggle to create a Jewish homeland has been one of the greatest causes of strife since then. While religion has been a cause of Middle Eastern conflict for centuries, oil is a new source of trouble, as well as wealth, as nations outside have rushed in to take a share.

Mecca – the holy city of Islam.

All of these factors – strategic location, the international power struggle, religion, and resources, have brought outsiders into the region. Problems which already existed there have been magnified to the extent that the Middle East is now seen as the most likely point of origin of a third world war.

Iran under the Shah

Mohammed Reza Khan, Shah of Iran 1925–44

At the end of the First World War, Iran was ruled by a weak government that was dominated by Britain. In February 1921 the government was overthrown in a coup led by a cossack commander, Reza Khan. In 1925 he was proclaimed Shah, and was crowned Reza Shaha Pahlavi. The new Shah was determined that Iran should become a modernised Western-style state. These are examples of some of his reforms:

1 Government administration: he established a strong central government backed by an army of 40 000. Improved efficiency and increased revenue from oil helped to pay for this.
2 Industrialisation: this programme was aimed at developing Iranian industry and improving road and rail communications.
3 Education and health: there was a new emphasis on technical education to help industry, and more hospitals to provided basic health care.
4 Westernisation: the Shah wanted to end the grip of Islam on his people. Some land was confiscated from the mosques, and Muslim customs such as the wearing of the veil and traditional Iranian dress were banned. This would have a particular effect in raising the status and potential of women.

Many people applauded this programme. However, others among the Shah's subjects were annoyed, They disliked his personal power, his use of force, and his 'corrupt' Western ideas which were destroying traditional values. During the 1930s, the Shah moved towards friend-

The Shah and his family in bejewelled splendour in the Throne Room of their palace in Tehran

Mossadeq, for a moment the popular hero in Tehran

ship with Germany. When the Second World War began in 1939, the Shah declared Iran to be a neutral country, but he retained German advisers. This led to British and Russian occupation of Iran in 1941. Reza Shah abdicted in favour of his son, Mohammed Reza Shah, who ruled with the help of a stronger parliament. At the end of the Second World War, the new Shah found that the British, the Russians and the USA were all seeking his friendship and Iran's oil wealth. He rejected the Russians, and suppressed the communist party (Tudeh) in Iran. Britain maintained some influence until May 1951, when the leader of the Iranian parliament, Dr Mohammed Mossadeq, announced the nationalisation of the Anglo-Iranian Oil Company. He justified it by saying,

Our long years of negotiations . . . have yielded no results thus far. With the oil revenues we could meet our entire budget and combat poverty, disease and backwardness among our people. Another important consideration is that by the elimination of the power of the British company, we would also eliminate corruption and intrigue, by means of which the internal affairs of our country have been influenced. Once this tutelage has ceased, Iran will have achieved its economic and political independence.

The Iranian state prefers to take over the production of petroleum itself. The company should do nothing else but return its property to the rightful owners. The nationalisation law provides that 25 per cent of the net profits on oil be set aside to meet all the legitimate claims of the company for compensation.

Britain immediately rejected the nationalisation. The case was taken to the United Nations and in the meantime British troops and naval presence in Iran and the Persian Gulf was increased. In the final event,

Britain avoided force, and instead imposed an oil boycott, which almost brought Iranian production to a standstill. During the crisis which followed, Mossadeq attempted to gain total control over Iran, including the armed forces. The Shah was forced into exile for a few days. Then, on 19 August, another coup occurred. These accounts differ as to its cause:

A General Zahedi with 35 Sherman tanks surrounded the Premier's residence, and after a nine-hour battle captured Mossadeq. Accoustical effects for the event were provided by Sha'yban 'the Brainless' who led a noisy demonstration, and by the gendarmerie who transported some 800 farm hands from the royal stables to central Tehran.

Ervand Abrahamian, Iran between two Revolutions, 1982

B Among other measures Kermit Roosevelt (an American) hired the services of a famous mobster named Shaban ('Brainless') Jafari, leader of a sort of mafia sports club in Tehran. Early on the morning of 19 August Brainless's men danced northwards to Parliament Square, 'Long live the Shah' they shouted. Elsewhere other young men passed out ten rial (15 cent) bills, American bribes for anyone who would raise the same shout. The shouts encouraged the Shah's real partisans . . . without opposition from civilians, Zahedi's troops attacked Mossadeq's house.

W. H. Forbis, Fall of the Peacock Throne, 1980

C The CIA, in conjunction with the American embassy, rallied thousands of non-partisan Iranians by distributing thousands of dollars to them to support the Shah's loyal colleague, General Fazlollah Zahedi. The people who played a major role in the operation were Allen Dulles, head of the CIA . . . and Loy Henderson, American ambassador to Tehran.

Amin Saikal, The Rise and Fall of the Shah, 1980

Questions

1 Explain why Reza's reforms made him unpopular with some people, but popular with others.
2 (a) According to Abrahamian who was the real force behind the Mossadeq coup? What indicates that part of the coup was artificial?
  (b) According to Forbis, who was behind the coup, and what made it effective?
  (c) Who was responsible for the coup according to Saikal?
  (d) Do the documents agree about the extent of genuine popular support for the Shah?
  (e) Why might these accounts differ?
3 Try to piece together the three accounts A–C to give a view of what really happened.

The White Revolution

The Shah, restored to power, wanted to continue his father's programme of westernisation to make Iran one of the world's foremost powers. On one hand he wanted to build up massive military strength.

On the other he wished to modernise Iran's industry and improve its agriculture. He thought both could be achieved by using Iran's oil wealth.

By 1961 he was spending so heavily that he was approaching bankruptcy. This was to cause Iran to move even closer towards the Western powers:

When the Shah's regime was facing severe financial difficulties, the USA promised the regime $35 million with 'special strings' attached, including that a 'particular individual' be appointed as prime minister of Iran. This was to be Ali Amini, who had previously served as Iran's ambassador to Washington, and had special ties with the Kennedys.

R. Graham, *The Illusion of Power*, 1978

The Shah had no choice but to name Amini as Iran's prime minister in May 1961. By 1963 it was increasingly obvious that he had failed to improve the Iranian economy, and opposition to his policies was rising. His answer was a complete new programme, the 'White Revolution':

We will base our future actions on far-reaching social reforms, economic development within the framework of free enterprise, cultural progress, and international co-operation; and at no time must the means of attaining that goal be in conflict with the individual's right of belief and freedom.

The programme was wide ranging and included:
- land reform
- public sale of state-owned factories
- workers' profit-sharing in industry
- voting reform, including votes for women
- encouragement of literacy, and free education
- health and welfare provision
- improvement of water supply
- child care
- improvement in transport and communication

The White Revolution was launched with a five-year development plan, including targets of high government spending to be met from oil profits and foreign loans. Immediate action was impressive: the government purchased 16 000 villages from rich landowners and transferred them to 743 406 families. The number of industrial plants rose from 8500 to 112 500. However, critics noticed that the reforms did not reach the mass of the poorest in the population. Also, despite promises, there was no political reform.

By 1977 the opposition to the Shah was gathering force. The communist Tudeh, the anti-monarchist National Front, and particularly religious opponents led by the Ayatollahs gained a following amongst the poorer classes and intellectual groups. These Muslims in particular wanted a return to the principles of Islamic law – their programme included a rejection of Western ways, extravagance, alcohol, gambling and female equality.

Ayatollahs – Shi'ite priests who are charged with ruling the people of Mohammed until, according to their belief, the heir of Mohammed returns.

Using the evidence: the rule of the Shah

Consider the following documents which relate to Iran under the Shah's rule:

A In September 1978 the worst protests occurred in southern Tehran, where the working class residents set up barricades and threw Molotov cocktails at army trucks; in Jaleh Square, at the heart of the bazaar; and in residential areas in eastern Tehran, where some 5000 residents staged a sit-down demonstration. In the southern slums, helicopter gunships were used to dislodge the rebels, and left a 'carnage of destruction'. In Jaleh Square commandos and tanks surrounded the demonstrators, and, unable to persuade them to disperse, shot to kill . . . the scene resembled a firing squad. . . . That night the military authorities announced that the day's casualties totalled 87 dead and 205 wounded. But the opposition declared that the dead numbered more than 4000.

Whatever the true figures, September 8th became known as Black Friday. . . . It placed a sea of blood between the Shah and his people. Black Friday ended the possibility of gradual reform and left the country with two choices: a drastic revolution, or a military counter-revolution.

Guardian, 17 September 1978

B The Shah's own wealth was – and is – obscenely large. . . . Upon taking the throne the Shah found himself to be the lord of 236 000 virtual serfs in the crown lands, which were worth $60 million. . . . This money went into a new Bank, later known as the Shah's Bank. The Shah got into cement factories, oil

The Shah celebrates 2500 years of Persian monarchy. The parade contained thousands of horsemen, footsoldiers and camels acting out scenes in Persian history

tankers and hotels. In 1961 he put most of his assets into the newly created Pahlavi foundation. This charitable endowment . . . seemed chiefly concerned with defending and enlarging its assets. Its investments included a tyre factory, publishing, sugar factories, computer marketing, oil-well drilling, hotels and two casinos.

E. Abrahamian, *Iran Between Two Revolutions*, 1982

C The brutal intervention of the military in the political sphere became a pervasive characteristic of the Shah's rule. . . . The military and SAVAK were used effectively in crushing and demoralising opposition . . . manipulating the behaviour of citizens, and controlling public opinion. . . . In this the military and secret police executed, imprisoned and exiled hundreds almost indiscriminately. . . . One of the most serious cases was the army purge in late 1954. About 600 officers, alleged to have been Tudeh supporters, were purged and tried by a military tribunal that resulted in massive executions and imprisonment.

A. Saikal, *The Rise and Fall of the Shah*, 1980

D In 1976 Amnesty International estimated that 25 000 to 100 000 political prisoners were being held in Iran.

Time Magazine, 10 December 1979

E The novelist Reza Baraheni was whipped: 'It was like a huge, hot charcoal, live, burning and tearing at the soles of the feet, crippling the whole legs'. He also saw electric prods for use on the genitals, skull squeezers, shoulder-breaking weights, and the notorious Iranian bed-spring torture device, on which the victim lay tied, while the wires were heated from warm to hot to searing.

W. H. Forbis, *Fall of the Peacock Throne*, 1980

F STATE REVENUE AND EXPENDITURE: SELECTED ITEMS

Year	Oil revenue ($ millions)	Year	Defence expenditure ($ millions)
1954/5	34	1953	80
1956/7	358	1963	293
1962/3	437	1973	1800
1970/1	1870	1977	7300
1978/9	20786		

Year	US aid	
1953–63	500	

By 1977 the Shah had purchased:
20 F.14 Tomcat fighters
190 Phantom fighters
208 helicopters
1870 tanks
He had also put aside $206 for the development of nuclear plant.

Year	No. of armed forces personnel
1953	120 000
1963	200 000
1977	410 000

The Shah's troops, some in gas masks, enforce martial law to stop demonstrations against the Shah

G Percentage of total consumption:

	1959–60	1973–4
Top 20 per cent ('the rich')	52	55.56
Bottom 40 per cent ('the poor')	13.9	11.96

Percentage of urban families living in one room:

1967	1977
36	43

Percentage of families with no electricity: 96
Ratio of doctors to people 1977:
  Tehran 1:974   Kurdistan 1:6477

H Glittering apartment houses rose in big cities, but 63 000 of Iran's 66 000 villages still have no piped water. Tehran, a city of five million, boasts traffic jams rivalling those of Tokyo, but it still has no sewer system.

Time magazine, 10 December 1979

A contrast to the Shah's wealth – villagers in Central Iran

I When you think I [the Shah] have been wounded by a good five bullets, one in the face, one in the shoulder, one in the head, two in the body, and another stuck in the barrel because the trigger jammed, you have to believe in miracles. I've had so many air disasters, and yet I've always come out unscathed – thanks to a miracle willed by God and the prophets.

1 What aspects of the Shah's policies would have appealed to Western governments?
2 What aspects of the Shah's promise in his 'White Revolution' programme were not carried out?
3 (a) Look carefully at A–C, secondary sources very critical of the Shah. Does the fact that they are critical mean that they are biased? Use the content of these three sources to help with your answer.
(b) Use sources A–I to show why the Shah was so unpopular with many of his people. The following may be used as sub-headings: (i) lack of freedom, (ii) secret police, (iii) personal spending, (iv) misuse of national wealth, (v) increasing poverty, (vi) offences against Islamic law.

The fall of the Shah and the Ayatollah's return

Khomeini had led the opposition to the Shah in the 1960s, but was forced to leave the country. He went to Paris and led the movement from exile.

By January 1979 the Shah's regime was tottering. The opposition was centred on the Ayatollah Khomeini, who had been exiled in France. On 16 January the Shah left Iran for a 'holiday', but he was never to return. With the Shah gone, many members of the armed forces deserted and the regency council lost control. On 1 February the Ayatollah Khomeini flew in from France, and within two days the Shah's government was toppled. Iran was proclaimed an Islamic republic on 1 April 1979.

Revolution in action – barricades on the streets of Tehran

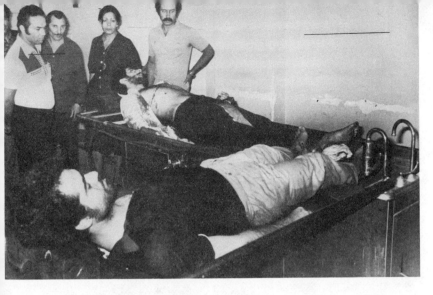

Two torturers, members of SAVAK, after their televised trial, and their execution by firing squad

Since the overthrow of the Shah, the government of Iran has effectively been controlled by the Revolutionary Council at Qom. The prime minister has been sympathetic to Islamic laws, and the Islamic republic has had a majority in parliament since 1980.

The policy of the revolutionary government has been violently anti-Shah and against his chief supporter, the USA. The army and civil service were purged, and in the first six months of rule 300 members of both services, including SAVAK officers, were executed. The Shah himself was sentenced to death in his absence, and when in 1979 he was admitted to a US hospital for treatment, young Iranians stormed the US embassy in Tehran. American hostages were taken to be exchanged for the Shah. In April 1980, President Carter attempted to release them by force. The mission was a failure, and played a part in his defeat in the 1980 presidential election (see page 218).

The Iranian regime is also hostile to the USSR. For Iran, the future lies in the unity of the Arab world, free from outside interference, and it

The Ayatollah Khomeini leads prayers in his Paris villa

Above: Soldiers and civilians combine in support of the Ayatollah

Right: Iran – Iraq war. The image of the Ayatollah inspires his soldiers

has supported groups such as the PLO and Shia Muslims in Iraq.

The regime has to combat severe problems. It is very strict in the application of Islamic law – by its interpretation, this means no alcohol, no Western fashion, the subordination of women, and a lack of political freedom. Opposition at home has been brutally crushed, and the Iranian prisons are as full as they were under the Shah. Many Iranians in exile still seek the overthrow of the Ayatollah, as shown by protest marches in London in the summer of 1985.

Iran and Iraq: Islam divided

Iraq developed in a different way from Iran. Mandated to Britain in 1918, it soon achieved independence under King Faisal, and remained closely tied to Britain (see page 251). The 1950s saw increased protest at the pro-Western dictatorship, and in 1958 King Faisal II and his prime minister were brutally murdered in a revolution.

The new republic faced severe problems with both the economy, and with the Kurdish tribesmen who wanted a self-governing state in northern Iraq. Furthermore Iraq's attempts to wrest control of its oil wealth away from the foreign-controlled Iraq Petroleum Company became a struggle lasting from 1961 to 1973.

A second coup by the Arab nationalist Ba'ath movement put Saddam Hussein Takriti in power as president. Hussein wanted to make Iraq the greatest Gulf power, and quarreled with Iran over two issues: in 1975 Iran was awarded the Shatt-al-Arab waterway by the terms of the Treaty of Baghdad. This had always infuriated Hussein, who wanted a revision of the treaty; secondly the Ayatollah had called upon Shi'ites in Iraq to overthrow Hussein.

Kurds – a fiercely proud and independent people who have struggled against rule by Turkey and Iraq.

On 17 September 1980, Iraq forces mobilised and crossed the Iranian border. Their early offensive soon broke down, and superior Iranian forces drove them back. By 1982, with help from abroad, including the Soviet bloc, Syria and Libya, the Iranians advanced, recapturing the ground which they had lost in 1980. So far, the war has cost more than 100 000 battle casualties to each side and has divided the Arab world.

An Iraqi tank near Khorramshahr, the victim of Iranian gunfire

Libya and the revival of Islam

In the 1980s the most outspoken state in the revival of Islam has been Libya. Libya was an Italian colony from 1914 to 1951 and by the outbreak of the Second World War 10 per cent of the population was Italian. During the Second World War there was fierce fighting in Libya (see page 106). Britain and France remained in occupation until, by UN agreement, it became independent in 1951 with King Idris as ruler. Idris allowed Libya to be dominated by Western states. Not only was Libyan oil exploited by foreign companies, but Britain and the USA kept military bases there. On 1 September 1969 a military coup occurred, replacing Idris with Muammar Gaddafi, a young army officer. He and his revolutionary council immediately took steps to turn Libya into an Islamic state. This meant:

Political parties were banned.
Foreign businesses were nationalised.
Military bases were taken over.
Arabic language was emphasised.
Oil wealth was developed for the people.
A welfare state of schools and hospitals was provided.
A housing programme was developed.
Alcohol was banned.

Gaddafi – ogre to some, inspiration to others

Libya is not a democracy in the Western sense, and claims to be neither capitalist nor communist. Gaddafi has developed what he calls the 'Third Theory', a form of government by which power is delegated from the people through various groups to the leadership. The structure is shown below:

Popular Congresses
↓
Peoples Committees
↓
General Peoples's Congress
↓
General Popular Committee
↓
General Secretariat

Supporters see this as a revolutionary way of turning government around and putting it into the hands of the people. Critics see it as a confidence trick by which Gaddafi centres power on himself while paying lip-service to popular rule.

The most outspoken face of Libyan policy has been in foreign affairs. Gaddafi has struggled for Arab unity, trying to unite Libya, Egypt and Sudan in 1969, and including Syria in 1971. In fact the outcome has been mutual mistrust, and Gaddafi's attempts to gain domination over the Sudan have contributed to conflict there.

Libya is also committed to victory for the Arabs over the Jews in Palestine, and supports the PLO. It also supports other terrorist organisations against European powers, such as the IRA. Libyan diplomats have also been accused of terrorist crimes. In 1984 the whole embassy staff was expelled from Britain after a policewoman was shot by a marksman from inside the embassy building in London.

Gaddafi is the hero of many people in the Arab movement: to the West he has become an ogre, possibly because he has been at the forefront in rejecting Western ways. In 1986 President Reagan tried to organise an international boycott against Libya. When this failed, and in response to further Libyan terrorist activity, in April 1986 Reagan ordered an airstrike on Tripoli and Benghazi. F111 bombers flew from bases in Britain and attacked military targets with cluster bombs. There were some civilian casualties, including Gaddafi's adopted daughter, who was killed. Gaddafi called for retaliation, and a new wave of bombings and attacks on American and British targets began. Libya remains a powder keg in Middle Eastern politics.

Oil wealth and the Middle East

The economy of the Middle East has been increasingly affected by the development of oil wealth during the twentieth century. Saudi Arabia still has the largest oil reserves, and this guarantees the continued importance of the region in world affairs.

The Anglo–Iranian Oil Company refinery at Abadan, in 1951 the largest oil complex in the world

Oil is big business. Looking back on oil exploitation, there seems to have been a continuing struggle between two sides in a rather desperate game for control of the industry.

'The Oil Game'

Players

Consumers of oil: Western powers represented by companies such as Shell, Texaco, Mobil, Gulf, BP, Occidental, Standard Oil.

Producers of oil: (in the Middle East) Iran, Iraq, Saudi Arabia, Kuwait, other Gulf states, and Libya.

Object of the game

Consumers must try to use their superior technology and capital to take hold of oil production in the Middle East. Failing that, they must keep prices as low as possible.

Producers must try to gain control of oil production in their own state, and raise prices to a sensibly high figure.

The game has been played in phases. As both oil and profits are quickly consumed, the winner is the side which has gained the advantage at whatever time the game stops.

Phase 1

1901	Discovery of oil.
1912	Production starts in Iran. Generous terms of control go to the Anglo-Iranian Oil Co.
1918	Production starts in Iraq controlled by Britain, France and Belgium.
1930	Production starts in Kuwait, under British control.
1938	Production of oil in Gulf states is controlled first by Britain, then the USA.

Phase 2

1939–45	Sees much higher demand for oil. Prices and profits rise.
1950	Saudi Arabia, Kuwait and Iraq demand 50/50 shares in oil profits with consumers.
1951	Iran nationalises its oil industry.

Phase 3

1951–54	Consumers refuse to buy Iranian oil. The Iranian economy is in a state of collapse.
1954	Attempts by Arab countries fail to force better terms by starving the West of oil.

Phase 4

1956–60   Arab states give far less generous concessions to consumers, reducing shares to 75–25.

1960   Organisation of Petroleum Exporting Countries (OPEC) is formed to deal with problems arising from overproduction and competition between Arab states. This stops a fall in prices.

1961   Development of oil industry in Libya begins. Concessions are given to small companies with tough limits on profits.

1968   Organisation of Arab Petroleum Companies is formed.

Phase 5

1970   Prices start to rise to keep up with Western inflation, which has reduced the value of oil. Prices level at $2 a barrel.

1971   Libya demands increasingly high prices from its consumers. Others states follow suit.

1971   Britain withdraws from Gulf states.

1973   Iranian oil industry nationalised again.

Phase 6

1973   Oil producers cut off supplies to USA and other states which supported Israel in the Yom Kippur war (see page 260). Israel is pressurised into withdrawing from occupied areas. Oil supply resumes.

1973–80   Prices rise steadily, reaching $32 a barrel.

Phase 7

1981   Depression in West brings fall in demand for oil. Prices are threatened and supply has to be cut.

1985–86   Depression deepens. Oil producers disagree over tactics. Some oil producing countries find their economy badly undermined.

Which of the two sides, producers or consumers, 'won' in each of these phases?

Palestine

Palestine is the area now known as Israel. The Palestinians are the Arabs who live or have lived there and their descendants, many of who now live in neighbouring states.

At the start of the century Palestine was part of the Turkish Empire. During the First World War Turkey fought on the side of Germany, and so Britain became involved in the fighting there, and in the problem of who would control the area after the war (see page 38). Britain was in a difficult position in 1916: no end to the war was in sight, and it was important to open up new fronts and gain new allies, as well as to look to the future. These difficulties may explain the contradictory promises which were made.

Using the evidence: British promises to the Arabs and the Jews

A A letter from Sir Henry McMahon, the British High Commissioner for Egypt, to Sherif Hussein of Mecca, an Arab nationalist leader who had demanded independence, March 1916:

Subject to modifications, Great Britain is prepared to recognise and support the independence of the Arabs in all regions within the limits demanded by the Sherif of Mecca. . . .   When the situation admits, Great Britain will give to the Arabs her advice, and will assist them to establish what may appear to be the most suitable forms of government in those various territories.

I am convinced that this declaration will assure you beyond all possible doubt of the sympathy of Great Britain towards the aspirations of her friends the Arabs and will result in a firm and lasting alliance, the immediate result of which will be the expulsion of the Turks.

B An agreement between the British and French diplomats Sir Mark Sykes and Charles Georges Picot, made in May 1916:

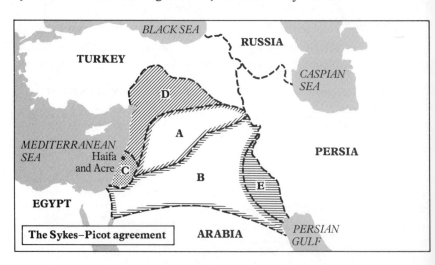

The Sykes–Picot agreement

1 That France and Britain are prepared to recognise and protect an independent Arab state or states in the areas A and B.
2 That in area A France and area B Great Britain shall have priority of right of enterprise. . . .
3 That in area E Great Britain shall be allowed to establish such direct or indirect administration or control as they may think fit.
4 That in the area C there shall be an international administration.
5 That Great Britain will be accorded the ports of Haifa and Acre.

C A letter from the British foreign secretary, A. J. Balfour, to the Zionist leader Lord Rothschild, November 1917:

Dear Lord Rothschild,
I have much pleasure in conveying to you, on behalf of His Majesty's Government, the following declaration with Jewish Zionist aspirations which has been submitted to and approved by the Cabinet.

'His Majesty's Government view with favour the establishment in Palestine of a national home for the Jewish people . . . it being clearly understood that nothing shall be done which may prejudice the civil and religious rights of existing non-Jewish communities in Palestine.

Zionism – the movement to create a Jewish state in the Holy Land, named after a hill in Jerusalem where King David's palace stood.

1 Use the documents and map to establish the contradictions in these promises.
2 Which promise seems to you to be the firmest? Why do you think that others are less firm?
3 What motives can you find behind (a) promise A, (b) promise B.
4 Who do you think the British might hope to influence by promise C?
5 Is there a contradiction within promise C itself?

These promises bore fruit for Britain in two main ways: the Sherif of Mecca launched a revolt against the Turks with the leadership of T. E. Lawrence; and the Zionists, especially in America, now came out in support Britain's war effort.

With victory in 1918 came the moment of decision: despite the sentiments of Wilson's Fourteen Points, by the terms of the San Remo conference of 1920, the Middle East was divided up between Britain and France as 'mandated territories' – that is, full control until the countries were ready for self-government. Other promises were not fulfilled.

Lawrence of Arabia. T. E. Lawrence was an archaeologist who joined British army intelligence in 1914. Lawrence helped to persuade the Arabs to join Britain's side, then taught them guerilla war. He later felt betrayed by British policy.

Jewish settlement and British withdrawal

Britain thus maintained a tight hold on Palestine. Arab hopes for independence were dashed. The Jews, who were increasingly subject to prejudice and discrimination in the period after the First World War, were encouraged to migrate from all over the world, and especially

Europe, into Palestine. Britain was happy to allow this, although still committed to 'ensuring that the rights and positions of other sections of the population are not prejudiced'.

As Jews continued to arrive in large numbers during the 1920s and 1930s, Arab protests grew. These did not go unheeded by Britain. The increasing importance of oil, and the need to keep close ties with the Middle Eastern states to prevent them drifting towards Hitler, brought a change in British policy. Also, the difficulty of Palestine's circumstances was now crystal clear. This is shown in the wording of the Peel report, 1937:

> The problem cannot be solved by giving either the Arabs or the Jews all they want. The answer to the question 'which of them in the end will govern Palestine? must surely be 'Neither'. We do not think that any fair-minded statesmen would suppose that Britain ought to hand over to Arab rule 400 000 Jews; or that a million or so of Arabs should be handed over to their rule.

In line with this view, and increasing sympathy with the Arabs, the MacDonald White Paper was published in 1938. It proposed a limit of 75 000 more Jewish immigrants, after which further immigration would be prohibited. There would follow a transition period of ten years before the creation of a new state with an Arab majority.

The British troops in Palestine were already subject to terrorist raids by Arab groups, furious at the betrayal of San Remo. Now the British were also attacked by Jews. When the war broke out in 1939, many Jews were prepared to fight with Britain against Hitler, but some extremist groups such as the Stern gang saw Britain as the greater enemy, and attacked British targets.

At the end of the war Britain continued to pursue the terms of the MacDonald White Paper. This united moderate and extremist Jews against Britain. The organisation responsible for the most effective raids was the Irgun, led by Menachem Begin. There were attacks on railways and army buildings, but the most notable was the assault on the British headquarters and army command at the King David Hotel in Jerusalem. A Cabinet report on the following day was given by the secretary of state for the colonies:

> It appeared that a lorry had been driven into the tradesmen's entrance of the hotel, and the occupants, after holding up the staff at pistol point, had entered the kitchen premises carrying a number of milk cans. They had shot and seriously wounded a British soldier who had challenged them; and after placing a bomb in the basement of the building, had made good their escape. The subsequent explosion had destroyed a substantial part of the building. The casualties so far reported were 41 killed, 52 missing, 53 injured.

Another version, by Menachem Begin:

> The Assault Unit, under the command of the Jerusalem Gideon . . . executed the attack with great bravery. . . . They brought the milk-cans as far as the approach to the hotel. They then divided into two groups. The first group took

Jewish immigration into Palestine:
1919–23: 330 000
1924–31: 84 000
1932–8: 215 000

The Stern gang was exceptional in fighting the British during the war. The more powerful terrorist movement Irgun did not take violent action until after Hitler's defeat.
Menachem Begin later became prime minister of Israel, with a hawkish reputation for standing up to any threat against the security of Israel.

A wounded soldier being stretchered from the ruins of the King David Hotel

Top ranking 'Jewish terrorists' wanted by the British authorities

the milk-cans into the basement by way of the Regency Cafe. But our men were surprised by . . . two British soldiers. A clash was unavoidable. Both sides suffered casualties.

The last man out was Gideon. . . .

At ten minutes past twelve our telephonist warned the King David Hotel that explosives had been placed under the hotel and would go off within a short time. 'Evacuate the whole building,' she cried to the telephone operator. She then telephoned the *Palestine Post* and announced –as was later testified – that 'bombs' have been placed in the King David Hotel and the people there have been told to evacuate the building.

Twelve thirty-seven. Suddenly the whole town seemed to shudder. There had been no mistake. As the BBC put it – the entire wing of a huge building was cut off as with a knife.

For some reason the hotel was not evacuated. Instead the toll of lives was terrible. Again we went through days of pain and nights of sorrow for the blood that need not have been shed.

Questions

1 Explain why Britain was unpopular with both Jews and Arabs by 1937.
2 Refer to the documents on the King David Hotel incident.
  (a) On what facts do the two accounts agree?
  (b) Why is the first account so brief?
  (c) What points from the second account would Begin particularly wish to publicise. Why?
  (d) Do you believe this account to be reliable? What are the advantages and pitfalls of this type of evidence?

In the increasingly bitter atmosphere both sides made accusations: The British were accused of floggings and other 'degrading and bestial' punishments; the British were furious at attacks on their own troops, some of whom were also flogged by the Jews. When Jews were captured, tried for terrorism and executed, there were reprisals.

On 30 July 1947 two British sergeants, Martin and Paice, spending the afternoon innocently on the beach in the Jewish town of Natanya, were dragged away and hanged in a eucalyptus grove on the outskirts of the town and their bodies made into a 'booby trap'. A notice reading 'This is the sentence of Irgun's High Command' was attached to the bodies.

From a Contemporary Report

By 1947 the British government had decided that the mandate was unworkable, and that the problem should be dealt with by the United Nations. The UN now proposed a partition of Palestine into seven parts – three Arab, three Jewish, with Jerusalem as an international zone.

Both sides were unhappy with the plan, and as the British troops

prepared for final evacuation, fighting between Arabs and Jews began to escalate. The worst fighting was for control of the road to Jerusalem, and it was here, at the village of Deir Yassin, that one of the most controversial incidents in the history of Palestine occurred.

Left: 2 700 illegal refugees aboard the Theodor Herzl. *Two were killed, twenty injured, when they resisted a Royal Navy boarding party after interception near Tel Aviv*

Above: Little comfort for two young illegal immigrants

Using the evidence: Deir Yassin

A The campaign for Jerusalem in 1948 involved the battle at Deir Yassin. How many lies have been published about this battle, from then until today, by Jews and non-Jews.

But the truth cannot be supressed. On 16 March 1969 the Foreign Minister of the State of Israel published a booklet, *Background Pages*, dedicated to the capture of Deir Yassin.

When the full-scale invasion of Israel's territory by the armies of the Arab States began on 15 May 1948, Azzam Pasha, General Secretary of the Arab League declared, 'There will be a war of extermination and a momentous massacre which will be spoken of like the Mongolian massacres and the Crusades.'

As its share in the battle for Jerusalem's approaches, the Irgun decided to assault Deir Yassin.

A small open truck accompanied them, fitted with a loudspeaker. In the early dawn light of 10 April 1948 it was driven close to the village entrance and a warning was broadcast in Arabic to civilian non-combatant inhabitants to withdraw from the danger zone. Some two hundred villagers did come out and took shelter. None of them, during or after the fighting, were hurt or molested in the slightest.

The actual battle of Deir Yassin began with a typical Arab subterfuge . . . white flags from houses near the village entrance. When the advance party of the Irgun unit advanced . . .it was met by a hail of fire. . . . Fierce house to house fighting followed. . . . Most of the stone buildings were defended hotly, and were captured only after grenades were lobbed through their windows.

Israeli soldiers attack a village in advance of the 1949 declaration of the state of Israel

Some of the garrison, as battle neared its close, attempted to escape in women's dress. When approached, they opened fire.

When the fighting ended, the Irgun unit found that it had sustained 41 casualties, four of them fatal. In the captured house they were horror stricken to find that, side by side with those combatant Palestinians and Iraqis, were the bodies of women and children. Either these luckless villagers had trusted the Arab soldiers to beat off the attack, or had been prevented from leaving; whatever the reason, they were the innocent victims of a cruel war, and the responsibility for their deaths rests squarely upon Arab soldiers.

Menachem Begin

A second version of what happened was written by a young Jew who was not a member of the Irgun. He wrote the report immediately after the event, but it was not published until after he had left the Israeli forces in 1972.

B At dawn the two forces reached the outskirts of the village:

The people of the village discovered that members of the secret movements had entered Deir Yassin before the attackers fired their first shot, so that it was the inhabitants of the village who fired first. The attackers burst into the village and met with violent opposition. Most of the male inhabitants fled from the village . . . a small number of men and a large number of women and children remaining in the houses. . . .

It was noon when the battle ended, and the shooting stopped. Things had become quiet but the village had not surrendered. The irregulars 'started carrying out cleaning-up operations'. . . . They fired with all the arms they had, and threw explosives in the houses. They also shot everyone they saw in the houses, including women and children. In the meantime some 25 men had been brought out of the houses; they were loaded onto a truck and led in a victory parade. At the end of the parade they were taken to a stone quarry and shot in cold blood.

Sami Hadawi, *Bitter Harvest*, 1979

1 Why do you think that the events of Deir Yassin have aroused such strong feelings on both sides?

2 What are the significant points of difference between these documents?

3 How do you account for these differences?

4 How would you attempt to establish the truth beyond doubt?

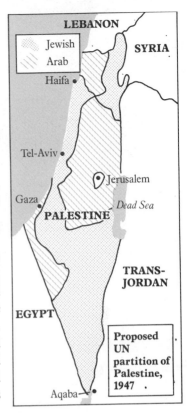

The main effect of Deir Yassin was that

Arabs throughout the country, induced to believe wild tales of Irgun butchery, were seized with limitless panic and started to flee for their lives. The mass flight soon developed into a massive, uncontrollable stampede.

J. Dimbleby and D. McCullin, *The Palestinians*, 1979

An estimated 400 000 Palestinians fled from their homes at this time, to become refugees in neighbouring countries. When, on 14 May 1948, the British withdrew their last forces, the Jews took the initiative and proclaimed the state of Israel. David Ben Gurion was the first prime minister, and the new nation was immediately recognised by the USA. In retaliation, the Arab states invaded. The first of the full-blooded Arab-Israeli wars had begun. With enemies on three sides who would not recognise the Jewish state and with Israel's determination to defend and expand its borders, war was inevitable and continued in phases until 1973.

The diagrams and maps here, and on the following pages, show the immediate causes, course and results of each of the wars.

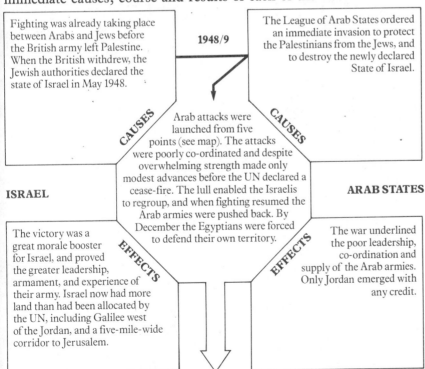

1948/9

CAUSES

ISRAEL: Fighting was already taking place between Arabs and Jews before the British army left Palestine. When the British withdrew, the Jewish authorities declared the state of Israel in May 1948.

ARAB STATES: The League of Arab States ordered an immediate invasion to protect the Palestinians from the Jews, and to destroy the newly declared State of Israel.

Arab attacks were launched from five points (see map). The attacks were poorly co-ordinated and despite overwhelming strength made only modest advances before the UN declared a cease-fire. The lull enabled the Israelis to regroup, and when fighting resumed the Arab armies were pushed back. By December the Egyptians were forced to defend their own territory.

EFFECTS

ISRAEL: The victory was a great morale booster for Israel, and proved the greater leadership, armament, and experience of their army. Israel now had more land than had been allocated by the UN, including Galilee west of the Jordan, and a five-mile-wide corridor to Jerusalem.

ARAB STATES: The war underlined the poor leadership, co-ordination and supply of the Arab armies. Only Jordan emerged with any credit.

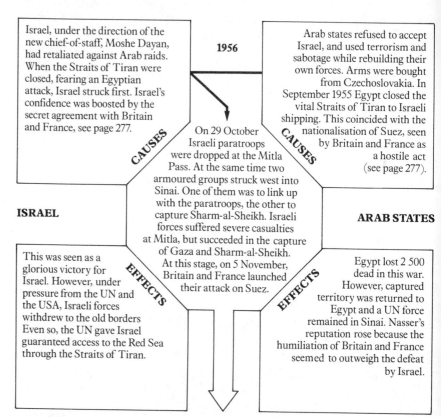

1956

Israel, under the direction of the new chief-of-staff, Moshe Dayan, had retaliated against Arab raids. When the Straits of Tiran were closed, fearing an Egyptian attack, Israel struck first. Israel's confidence was boosted by the secret agreement with Britain and France, see page 277.

Arab states refused to accept Israel, and used terrorism and sabotage while rebuilding their own forces. Arms were bought from Czechoslovakia. In September 1955 Egypt closed the vital Straits of Tiran to Israeli shipping. This coincided with the nationalisation of Suez, seen by Britain and France as a hostile act (see page 277).

CAUSES

CAUSES

On 29 October Israeli paratroops were dropped at the Mitla Pass. At the same time two armoured groups struck west into Sinai. One of them was to link up with the paratroops, the other to capture Sharm-al-Sheikh. Israeli forces suffered severe casualties at Mitla, but succeeded in the capture of Gaza and Sharm-al-Sheikh. At this stage, on 5 November, Britain and France launched their attack on Suez.

ISRAEL

ARAB STATES

EFFECTS

EFFECTS

This was seen as a glorious victory for Israel. However, under pressure from the UN and the USA, Israeli forces withdrew to the old borders Even so, the UN gave Israel guaranteed access to the Red Sea through the Straits of Tiran.

Egypt lost 2 500 dead in this war. However, captured territory was returned to Egypt and a UN force remained in Sinai. Nasser's reputation rose because the humiliation of Britain and France seemed to outweigh the defeat by Israel.

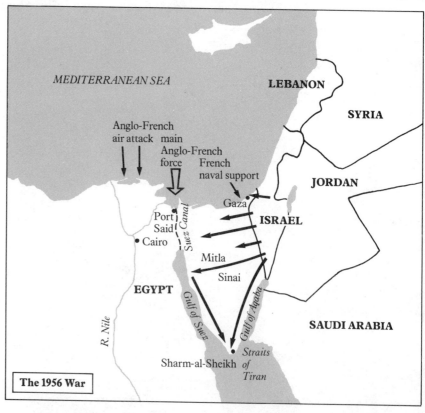

The 1956 War

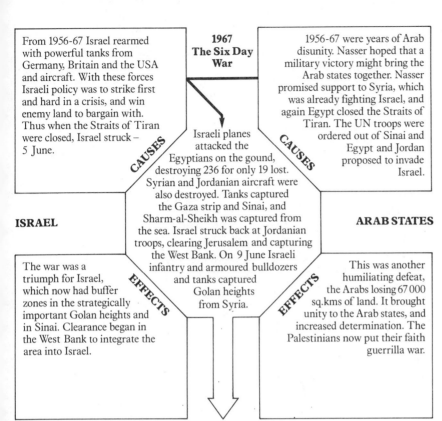

**1967
The Six Day
War**

From 1956-67 Israel rearmed with powerful tanks from Germany, Britain and the USA and aircraft. With these forces Israeli policy was to strike first and hard in a crisis, and win enemy land to bargain with. Thus when the Straits of Tiran were closed, Israel struck – 5 June.

CAUSES

1956-67 were years of Arab disunity. Nasser hoped that a military victory might bring the Arab states together. Nasser promised support to Syria, which was already fighting Israel, and again Egypt closed the Straits of Tiran. The UN troops were ordered out of Sinai and Egypt and Jordan proposed to invade Israel.

CAUSES

Israeli planes attacked the Egyptians on the gound, destroying 236 for only 19 lost. Syrian and Jordanian aircraft were also destroyed. Tanks captured the Gaza strip and Sinai, and Sharm-al-Sheikh was captured from the sea. Israel struck back at Jordanian troops, clearing Jerusalem and capturing the West Bank. On 9 June Israeli infantry and armoured bulldozers and tanks captured Golan heights from Syria.

ISRAEL

ARAB STATES

EFFECTS

The war was a triumph for Israel, which now had buffer zones in the strategically important Golan heights and in Sinai. Clearance began in the West Bank to integrate the area into Israel.

EFFECTS

This was another humiliating defeat, the Arabs losing 67 000 sq.kms of land. It brought unity to the Arab states, and increased determination. The Palestinians now put their faith guerrilla war.

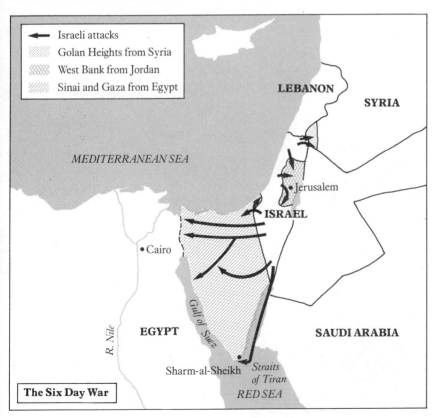

Israeli attacks
Golan Heights from Syria
West Bank from Jordan
Sinai and Gaza from Egypt

LEBANON

SYRIA

MEDITERRANEAN SEA

• Jerusalem

ISRAEL

• Cairo

EGYPT

Gulf of Suez

R. Nile

SAUDI ARABIA

Sharm-al-Sheikh *Straits
of Tiran*
RED SEA

The Six Day War

1973
YOM KIPPUR, or The October War

Israel was confident that the Egyptians were too weak to launch a major attack. Arab manoeuvres has been spotted, but were thought to be exercises. When the attack came on 6 October, the Jewish holiday of Yom Kippur, Israel was taken by surprise.

The years after 1967 saw continued guerilla attacks against Israel, but little was achieved. Egypt now planned a full-scale war to win back Sinai. To keep the plans secret, officers were given leave to go on pilgrimages and troop movements were concealed. At the same time arms and equipment were prepared to enable a rapid crossing of the Suez Canal and a swift advance into Sinai. The attack began on 6 October.

The attack began with missile bombardment, and tanks advanced into Sinai followed by infantry. At the same time Syrian forces attacked the Golan heights. In Sinai Israel struck back. Both sides brought in reinforcements and on 14 October over 1000 tanks fought for supremacy. Superior Israeli tactics won the day and on 15 October Israeli forces crossed Suez. Early Syrian advances also ground to a halt, and another attack by Israeli tanks saw new gains in Syria.

ISRAEL

ARAB STATES

International pressure brought a ceasefire on 24 October. After pressure from the USA Israel agreed to withdraw 30kms from Suez, and back to pre-war lines in Syria. Although victorious, 3000 Israelis were dead or missing. The need for continued arms spending, and for a diplomatic solution was underlined.

Despite defeat, Arab armies had shown greater power in this war. Also, much was gained by negotiation, including key passes in Sinai and oil fields. President Sadat may have been influenced by this war to look for a peaceful solution – he was later to attend the Camp David peace talks.

The Israeli army advances into Sinai, 1956

Land held by Israel beyond Suez at ceasefire

Land held by Israel in Syria at ceasefire

LEBANON

SYRIA

MEDITERREAN SEA

West Bank. Israeli since 1967

Syrian attack on Golan Heights

Golan Israeli-occupied since 1967

Jerusalem

Egyptian attack into Sinai

ISRAEL

JORDAN

Israeli counter-attack Sinai (Israeli-occupied since 1967)

EGYPT

SAUDI ARABIA

RED SEA

Yom Kippur War

The war of 1967. The Israeli army moves onto the Syrian plateau to silence the artillery there

The war of 1973. Israeli guns batter Syrian positions

Summary

1 Use the diagrams and maps to show:
   (a) Who started each war.
   (b) Why the Israelis have achieved victory in the wars.
   (c) What the effects of the war have been on (i) Israel (ii) Arab
   states.
2 These diagrams are all concerned with causes, events, and effects,
   from the point of view of both sides. To help you remember which
   war was which, you might construct diagrams of different shape
   (and colour) for each war.

Since the 1973 war, the Camp David peace talks (see page 282) have brought recognition of Israel from Egypt. The conflict has not ended, and Israel became involved in the Lebanon in 1982, when her troops moved in to root out Palestinian guerillas (see page 271). Israel is still far from secure, though free from an immediate threat of foreign invasion.

Internal problems facing Israel since 1948

Making a Jewish state

The number of Arabs in Israel fell by 540 000 to only 160 000 when the Jewish state was established. They were replaced by 700 000 Jews between 1948 and 1951, and immigration has continued since. Even so, it has been a problem to provide the state with an identity as some of these Jews are Middle Eastern in origin (Sephardim) and others Western (Ashkenazim).

To bring these separate groups together Israel has pursued the following policies:

1 Hebrew as a common language.
2 Emphasis on Jewish culture in the education system.
3 High status of the rabbis in the leadership of the people.
4 Compulsory service for Jews in the Israeli armed forces.
5 Free election of representatives to the Knesset, or parliament, where different views could be exchanged.
6 Development of land by communal effort in the kibbutzim.
7 Settlement of border areas in new communities, such as the West Bank and, for a time, Sinai.

Kibbutz – a collective farm with many families working together and providing for all needs on a communal basis.

Communal work on the kibbutz

Israel's two greatest problems are closely related. Over one third of the income of Israel is spent on arms. This is a terrible strain on the economy, and Israel has only survived by borrowing heavily from the USA. Despite an increasingly efficient system of agriculture and the development of light industry, Israel has been unable to provide for itself and inflation has been as high as 130 per cent per year.

On the other hand, the system of government has weathered these crises. From 1948 to 1953 and 1955 to 1963 David Ben Gurion was prime minister, and leader of the Mapai, or Labour party. His successors included Mrs Golda Meir, and General Yitzhak Rabin. Meir stepped down after a critical report on the Yom Kippur war of 1973. Rabin lost support because of his emphasis on a peaceful solution to Isreal's problems, and because of continued high inflation, as well as corruption, and emphasis on Western ways.

In 1977 the opposition Likud party was elected. Two main policies can be identified with the new prime minister, Menachem Begin. First, he was pledged to help the poorer Sephardim. Secondly, he would do whatever circumstances required to defend Israel. He saw the opportunity of security through peace in his Camp David agreement with Egypt. On the other hand he would make no agreement on the West Bank, and pursued an aggressive policy in the Lebanon. This policy has been continued by his successor, Yitzhak Shamir, who ordered the bombing of the PLO headquarters in Tunisia in 1985.

Israel's position remains insecure. Many people admire the courage of Israel fighting for its permanent place in the modern world. Others are more doubtful, even within Israel itself, and large numbers of Jews have emigrated to the West in recent years. The story continues.

Oriental, orthodox, and western Jews mix on the Sabbath in Jerusalem

17 The fate of the Palestinians

Palestinian refugees flee from their homes in 1948

Despite Irgun terrorism, the climate of international opinion after the Second World War was far more sympathetic to the Jews than to the Arabs. President Truman was one who spoke for the Jews, 'who have been so cruelly uprooted by ruthless Nazi persecutors. Israel represents . . . their only hope of survival.'

This helps to explain why people ignored the plight of the Arabs. In 1948 the Arabs still held the bulk of the land, at least by law, but many had been driven from their homes. A UN resolution read:

The refugees wishing to return to their homes and live at peace with their neighbours should be permitted to do so at the earliest possible date . . . and compensation should be paid for the property of those choosing not to return.

This order was ignored by the Israeli government, which continued its tactics designed to drive out the Arabs, justifying them by arguing that they should resettle in other Middle Eastern countries governed by Arab peoples. Various tactics have been used.

1 Terrorism

The barrel bomb has been one of the most common urban incendiary devices:

It consisted of a barrel cask, or metal drum filled with a mixture of explosives and petrol and filled with two old rubber tyres containing the detonating fuse. It was rolled down the sharply sloping alleys and stepped lanes of Arab urban markets where it crashed into walls and doorways making an inferno of raging flames and endless explosions.

2 Psychological warfare

Attacks on Arab quarters were generally accompanied by loudspeaker announcements: 'get out of this bloodbath . . . if you stay, you invite disaster.'

3 Torture

A number of detainees have undergone torture during interrogation by the Military Police. According to the evidence the torture took the following forms:

1 Suspension of the detainee by the hands.
2 Burns with cigarette stubs.
3 Blows by rods on the genitals.
4 Tying up and blindfolding for days.
5 Bites by dogs.
6 Electric shocks at the temples, the mouth, the chest and testicles.

UN Special Committee report, 1972

Torture is systematic. It appears to be sanctioned at some level as deliberate policy. Torturing is done for three purposes: to obtain information; to induce people to make confessions . . .; and to deter the Palestinians in the occupied territories from resistance activities.

Sunday Times, 1977

4 Clearance of Arab settlements

An Israeli soldier remembers the clearance of Beit Nuba:

The commander of my platoon said that it had been decided to blow up the three villages in the sector . . . for reasons of strategy, tactics, security.

We were told it was our job to search the village houses; that if we found any armed men there, they should be taken prisoner. Unarmed persons should be given time to pack their belongings and then told to get moving.

The houses in Beit Nuba are beautiful stone houses. . . . At noon the first bulldozer arrived . . . ten or more minutes passed and the house with its meagre furnishings and belongings, had become a mass of rubble.

The soldiers grumbled. At night we stayed on to guard the bulldozers, but the entire batallion was seething with anger. . . . No one could understand how the Jews could do such a thing. The fields were turned to desolation before our eyes, and the children who dragged themselves along the road that day will be the *fedayeen* of nineteen years hence.

Search during a raid on Karamah, Jordan . . . the fedayeen of tomorrow?

Fedayeen – guerilla fighters, or literally 'those who sacrifice their lives'.

Over 1000 refugees transferred from their village of Fureidis to Arab territory . . . the fedayeen of tomorrow?

265

Arab refugees at Ramallat . . . the fedayeen of tomorrow?

A Palestinian refugee camp near Beirut airport

The Palestinians have been forced to go into refugee camps in neighbouring countries. A commissioner-general of the United Nations Relief Organisation has described the condition of the refugees:

A large part of the refugee community is still living in dire poverty, often under pathetic and in some cases appalling conditions . . . there are families who still live in dwellings unfit for human habitation: some in dark cellars, others in crumbling tenements, others in grossly overcrowded barracks, and shacks. . . . Nearly all the UNWRA camps are extremely overcrowded with five or more persons living in one small room. They lack adequate roads and pathways and many camps are deep in mud in winter and dust in summer. There are rarely any sewers . . . water supplies are communal and often inadequate, particularly during the hot summer months. Yet the refugees living in the camps . . . are, on the whole, probably better housed and better cared for than many of the three-fifths living outside the camps.

United Nations and Works Relief Agency. This organisation was set up to provide refugee camps. These were in Egypt, Syria, Lebanon and Jordan.

The refugees have also become a political problem for the states where they have settled – at first for Jordan, and since 1970, for the Lebanon.

Question

Why might the children of Beit Nuba, 'the *fedayeen* of nineteen years hence' feel intensely bitter about the early years of their life? Use the documents to explain their attitude as fully as possible.

The Palestine Liberation Organisation

Some Arabs hit back hard at the new Israel, the most well-known Arab group being the Palestine Liberation Organisation. The PLO burst into the headlines of the world press in the early 1970s after a series of terrorist attacks, intended to publicise their case. However, the organisation had been formed in 1964 by a union of Palestinian resistance groups. These included Yasser Arafat's Al Fatah (Victory) and the more extreme Popular Front for the Liberation of Palestine (PFLP) and later, Black September.

Arafat was born in Jerusalem, was a guerilla fighter when only in his teens, and formed Al-Fatah in 1958. Since that time he has been the best-known representative of the PLO. British Overseas Airways Corporation, later absorbed into British Airways.

The first time they hit the headlines, they did so with spectacular effect. In September 1970 five planes belonging to TWA, Swissair, PanAm, El Al, and BOAC were simultaneously hijacked. One of the hijacks failed, and a Palestinian, Leila Khaled, was arrested. The PanAm aircraft was blown up at Cairo. The other three, with 425 people, were all landed at an old RAF strip, Dawson's Field, in Jordan. The PLO demanded the release of Khaled and other named prisoners in Germany, Switzerland and Israel. Britain, Germany and Switzerland agreed to the demands, and most of the prisoners were set free. As a spectacular last gesture of defiance, the three airliners were blown up.

Up to this time the PLO had been based in Jordan. The Dawson's Field affair was the last straw for King Hussein, who set his army

Spectacular terrorism at Dawson's Field, 1970

against the PLO and drove them out. The only state still sympathetic to the PLO was Lebanon. However, the campaign of international terrorism did not stop. As George Habash, the PFLP leader, said,

In today's world no one is innocent, no one a neutral. A man is either with the oppressed or he is with the oppressors. He who takes no interest in politics gives his blessing to the ruling classes and exploiting forces.

We intend to attack imperialist and Zionist interests, wherever we find them in the world.

Acting on this philosophy, a series of international terrorist campaigns was launched. In 1970 the PFLP met with other terrorists organisations including the IRA, the Baader-Meinhof, and the Red Army. In May 1972 the Red Army struck on behalf of the PFLP:

Irish Republican Army; German Baader-Meinhof; Japanese Red Army.

Three young Japanese who had arrived at Lod airport [Israel] on Air France flight 132 from Paris and Rome collected their suitcases in the lounge, took off their jackets and bent down to open their cases. When they straightened up they were holding Czech-made VZT-58 automatic rifles . . . and half a dozen powerful shrapnel grenades. They gave no warning but started to fire into the people grouped around the conveyor belt. Then they threw their grenades. Within a minute destroyed bodies littered the hall. Blood, baggage and fragments of flesh covered the floors as 24 people died and 78 fell wounded. Two of the attackers were also dead, one of them cut down accidentally by bullets from one of his wildly firing companions and the other decapitated by one of his own grenades.

Needless to say this attracted worldwide interest. Soon even a more dramatic stand was taken. In 1972 the Black September movement reconnoitred the Olympic village at Munich, and in a co-ordinated attack eight terrorists burst into the Israeli section. A weightlifter and a wrestling coach were killed. Nine sportsmen and officials were held as hostage for the release of Palestinians, and other terrorists. The Arabs were promised a flight out of Germany, but were ambushed at the airport. They shot their victims and blew up a helicopter in which they had been brought to the airport.

Such action shocked the world. The presence of the PLO in the Lebanon also disturbed the delicate political balance there.

Questions

1 How does George Habash justify international terrorism?
2 What reasons might terrorists give for the incidents detailed above?
3 What is the likely effect of such terrorism on world opinion regarding the Palestinians?

Palestinians in the Lebanon

The Middle East has witnessed many tragedies in recent years, and often the reasons behind them are hard to understand. Perhaps the most tragic, and the least comprehensible, is the situation in the Lebanon.

Since the creation of the Lebanon there has been a delicate balance between the various groups of people who lived there. When the French controlled the area of Greater Syria they decided to make the vital coastal strip into a separate, Christian-dominated state which was dependent on France. Thus, in 1920 the Lebanon was born, and by 1941 it had achieved total independence.

The problem of the Lebanon was that it was made up of three different cultures: The Maronites, or Christians; the Shi'ite Muslims; and the Sunnite Muslims. The Christians looked to the Western world, *Beirut before . . .*

and shared the great wealth of the service industries such as banking which grew up in the Lebanon during the good years. The Sunnites too, were privileged and wealthy. The Shi'ites were poor.

Government of the Lebanon was shared between the three groups: the president was always a Maronite, the prime minister a Sunnite and the president of the assembly a Shi'ite. Seats in the assembly were divided according to the proportion of the population. The Maronites held the majority. For a few years, the system worked. However, the great difference in wealth was always a threat to security, not much was needed to topple Lebanon into civil war. The trigger to this conflict was the arrival of the Palestinians.

After their eviction from Jordan the Palestinians moved into the Lebanon, a sympathetic state bordering Israel. By 1975 the number of Palestinians in Lebanon had risen to one fifth of the total population, many of them living in the refugee camps of Beirut. Amongst them lived the PLO, which used the Lebanon as a base to strike at Israel to the south.

Three-way conflict took place during the early 1970s. The Palestinians raided into Israel, and the Israelis struck back across the border. Furthermore, the Lebanese army, backed by the extreme Christian Phalangists, attacked the Palestinian guerillas. These conflicts split the Lebanon into two: those who were against the Palestinians (the Christians, and right-wing groups under Pierre Gemayal); and those who supported them (Muslims and left-wing groups led by Kamal Jumblatt).

Phalangists – Close-knit, right-wing militia, bitterly opposed to the Palestinians.

At first conflicts took the form of skirmishes. In 1975 this gave way to full-scale and very bitter civil war. The Palestine Liberation Organisation, which was now firmly based in Lebanon, and had taken over complete control of refugee camps, had become entwined with this war.

Civil war in the Lebanon

During the early stages of the war the PLO; with the help of the Shi'ites and Syria, took the upper hand in the fight against the Christians. It was at this time that the dreadful massacre of Damour took place.

A Maronite priest, Father Mansour Labaky remembered:

Apocalypse in this use of the word means doomsday.

The attack took place from the mountain behind. It was an apocalypse. They were coming, thousands and thousands, shouting 'Allahu Akbar! God is great. Let us attack them for the Arabs, let us offer the holocaust to Mohammed!' And they were slaughtering every one in their path, men, women, and children.

I remember something which still frightens me. An entire family had been killed, the Can'an family, four children all dead, and the mother, the father and the grandfather. The mother was still hugging one of the children. And she was pregnant. The eyes of the children were gone and their limbs cut off.

Towards the end of 1975 a victory for the PLO was in sight. It was at this moment that President Assad of Syria changed sides. Instead of helping the PLO he gave support to the right-wing Christian forces.

. . . and Beirut afterwards. Father and son express relief at their survival

Possibly he thought that they would be easier to influence than the leaders of the PLO.

Syrian support quickly enabled the Christians to gain the advantage. They attacked the Palestinian refugee camps in Beirut. In January 1976 an attack began on the camp at Tal-el-Zataar. For months the camp was pounded until, on 12 August, it fell. On that day alone 2000 Palestinians died. Of those who were taken prisoner, some were tortured. A Christian commander justified this:

It was not our policy, but if a PLO man fell into the hands of a man whose family had been killed, or whose sister had been raped, or whose home had been destroyed by them, he would take his revenge. We tried to stop those who wanted to do it, but we didn't always succeed. We admit that some prisoners were tortured. None of us had forgotten Damour.

By 1978 the sides had started to divide within themselves. Christians fought Syrians. The government had lost control and the Lebanon was divided into small, independent warring areas.

Throughout this time the PLO had continued to use the Lebanon as a base for striking at Israel, and in 1978 Israel struck back. Troops numbering 20 000 moved into the Lebanon, and the Israeli air force used cluster bombs to attack specific tartgets. The United Nations sent a force to act as a peacemaker between the two sides.

A follower of Yasser Arafat, a PLO soldier armed for combat with Syria. Soon after this photo was taken, the PLO were exiled from Lebanon

The UN try to keep the peace, the Israelis search for hostile Shi'ites in south Lebanon

Despite this, raids continued, and in 1982 Israel struck again. This time their invasion, code named 'Operation Peace for Galilee', was intended to get rid of the PLO once and for all. The Israeli force, with the help of the Christian Phalangists, pushed forward to Beirut. Palestinian areas of Beirut were pounded by artillery and aircraft.

Under international pressure, and through the negotiations of President Reagan's special envoy Philip Habib, a settlement was reached. The armed units of the PLO would leave the Lebanon, and the Israeli army would withdraw.

These terms were carried out, but any thoughts that the Lebanon would find peace were dashed in September 1982 with the assassination of the newly elected Christian president, Bashir Gemayal. The Christian Phalangists turned in fury on the Palestinian camps of Sabra and Chatila, and terrible butchery followed.

Since 1982 the situation has become even more confused. By May 1985 the Israeli army had pulled back, leaving advisers to help the southern Lebanese Christian army as a barrier between the Jewish and Islamic people. In Beirut fighting between rival militia continued. The Shi'ite Amal militia tried to drive out all Palestinians who they blame for the Israeli invasions. One feature of this campaign was the massacre at Bourj-al Barajneh in May 1985. No mercy was given. At one hospital:

According to a Lebanese witness, Shi'ite militiamen shot dead at least 46 people, many of them patients, in cold blood. A second Palestinian source put the figure at 70, including two orderlies whose throats, he said, were cut.

Guardian, 31 May 1985

The only escape for Palestinians was to flee into sympathetic Druze-dominated areas and fight back with the same ferocity. This militia warfare baffled the world. Imagine a parliament, where there are many representatives, all with different ideas, some agreeing over some things, some over others, and constantly changing alliances from one debate to the next. Now substitute for that a war between armed factions who constantly turn one upon the other. Even the Lebanese find it hard to understand.

A militiaman, Ziyad, aged twenty, was asked by a reporter why he was fighting:

'Against the fascist isolationist collaboraters with Israel.'
'And what does fascist mean?'
'It means Nazism.'
'And what does Nazism mean?'
'I don't know.'

Guardian, 31 May 1985

In 1985 there were possibly 150 rival factions in the Lebanon. On 7 September 33 men women and children were killed in yet another assault on the last Palestinian camp at Bourj-Ai-Barajneh. On the same day 20 were killed and 100 wounded in a battle between Shi'ite and Druze militia over the ownership of an office. The Palestinian problem remains to be solved. Where can they go now?

Druze – the left-wing organisation led by Kamal Jumblatt.

Questions

1 Why was there tension in the Lebanon before the arrival of the PLO?
2 Why was the war in Lebanon so bitter?
3 What have the following groups in the Lebanon been hoping to achieve?
   (a) Syrians (b) Shi'ites (c) Israelis (d) Christian Phalangists (e) Palestinians
   (f) UN forces
4 Why had the situation become so confused in the mid-1980s?

18 The development of Egypt

The Wafd, which originally set out to ask for independence, became an important organisation in government.

The struggle for independence

The Suez canal, dominating the route from West to East, made Egypt of particular importance to Britain, and in 1914 it was declared a British protectorate. During the First World War, when the British army in Egypt was strengthened, anti-British feeling increased. An Arab nationalist movement grew up, and at the end of the war the Wafd ('delegation') demanded independence. The leader of the Wafd, Saad Zaglol, was deported, but by 1922 popular support for independence was so great that the British government decided to compromise. Egypt was declared independent, but Britain kept control of Suez, defence and foreign affairs, and the Sudan. The pro-British Sultan Fuad was named King Fuad I, and he was given sufficient power under the constitution of 1923 to hold down the strong nationalist feelings expressed by the Wafd in parliament. Also, Fuad's power finally depended on British support and arms.

Between 1923 and 1930 Fuad used parliament only when it suited him, and he did not call it all between 1930 and 1935. Britain became worried by the hostility of the Wafd and the people both to the king and to Britain, especially in the light of the Italian invasion of Abyssinia and the rise of Nazi Germany. Therefore in 1936 a further step was made towards real independence – Egypt was given more control of its defence and foreign policy, became a member of the League of Nations, and the British troops were confined to the Suez area alone. In addition, more power was given to parliament, and to the Wafd, against the wishes of the king.

In 1937 the new king, Farouk, turned against both the Wafd and the British. In particular Britain was worried by Farouk's friendship towards the Nazis. When, in 1942, Rommel was advancing towards Egypt and riots were taking place in the capital, the British army stepped in. On 4 February the palace was surrounded by tanks and Farouk was forced to give power back to the Wafd. Even though the Wafd was anti-British, they would govern effectively and stand against Germany.

At the end of the war, the cry for independence was loud, but so too was the cry against ineffective government; Egyptians wanted to be rid of the British, and rid of the king too. Defeat by Israel in 1948 added to the outcry (see page 257). The British adopted a low profile, withdrawing to the canal zone. There was rioting in Cairo, and on 26 January 1952 much of the city was set on fire. The king was the main target. An eye-witness who spent time in the Egyptian court described him as follows:

Even in Farouk's immediate circle princes and diplomats criticised everything he did . . . Farouk's once amusing escapades now only gave rise to disgust. His trip to Europe where he spent most of his time in one casino after another and where he became a favorite target for mockery of the press, now exasperated the Egyptians. In the palace a seedy clique . . . organised the King's

Farouk with his future wife, Irma Minutolo

entertainment, brought down governments, and made Army appointments which were bought at huge prices . . . the King taking his share. There was no longer a man in Cairo who, if he had a handsome wife, was not afraid to take her anywhere she might meet Farouk . . . who seemed to thrive on scandals, trying to kill himself with excesses.

J. and S. Lacouture, *Egypt in Transition*, 1956

On 26 January he received an ultimatum from General Neguib, the leader of a group of army officers:

In view of your misrule . . . your contempt for the will of the nation . . . and because under your protection traitors and swindlers are allowed to amass scandalous fortunes by wasting public monies while the people are dying of hunger . . . The army . . . has ordered me to demand that Your Majesty abdicate . . . . and that he quit the country on the same day before six o' clock

Questions

1 Draw up a timeline to show the main features of British involvement in Egyptian affairs.
2 Examine Neguib's charges against Farouk. Which of them can be substantiated from Lacouture's account?

Nasser and the Suez crisis

Neguib, who had forced the abdication of Farouk, was soon displaced by Gamal Nasser, who, by 1956, had established strong personal government. Nasser's rule in Egypt was to make him one of the most controversial figures in twentieth century history. Outsiders labelled him a new Hitler, while Egyptians regarded him as a great hero figure.

Nasser had three main aims: to complete the policies of driving out

Colonel Gamal Abdul Nasser, leader of the free officers who overthrew the king, and later Egyptian president (1954–70).

The Baghdad Pact was made to stop Soviet expansion in the Middle East. Nasser saw it as another example of Western domination.

Twenty-nine states were represented at the conference at Bandung, Indonesia. They were against all forms of imperialism, Western or Soviet.

foreign influence; to make a union of Arab states centred on Cairo, and to raise the standard of living of the Egyptian people. Having seized power, confirmed by popular support in the referendum of 1956, Nasser confronted his first problem: the British. From the start he made it clear that he wanted an independent Egypt. In 1955, a number of states – Iran, Iraq, Pakistan and Turkey – had joined Britain in the Baghdad Pact. Nasser shunned this alliance, and instead attended the Bandung conference of non-aligned states. He also showed new independence in purchasing of weapons. Farouk had brought weapons from the West, mainly for controlling disorder. Nasser wanted offensive weapons, and when he couldn't get them from the West, he bought them from Czechoslovakia. Britain, who had agreed to a withdrawal of British troops from Egypt, feared that their influence would be replaced by that of the communists: Nasser had no such plans – he never concealed his dislike of communism and was simply buying in available markets.

The greatest crisis of Anglo-Egyptian relations occurred over Suez. The immediate cause of the crisis was the need for money to complete Nasser's greatest domestic project, the Aswan High Dam. A loan of one

Part of the Aswan Dam project, which was eventually financed by the Soviet Union

billion dollars been promised by Britain and America, but there was disagreement over the terms and the loan was withdrawn.

Nasser responded with the following announcement:

We are going to take back the profits which the Imperialist (Suez) Company, the state within a state, deprived us of while we were dying of hunger.

I announce to you that at this very moment our national newspaper is publishing a law nationalising the company, and, as I speak to you, government agents are taking possession of the company!

Nasser, shortly after announcing the nationalisation of Suez

A witness reported:

Everything exploded around us and below us. Gamal was suddenly shaken by an irrepressible laugh: the thrill was enormous.

He shouted in defiance. The canal will pay for the dam . . . today I seize the canal in the name of the people. . . . This night our canal shall be Egyptian, controlled by the Egyptians.

The response from Britain and France was of horror – Nasser was described as 'the new Hitler', 'the insolent plunderer' and 'the barking dictator'. In fact, the terms of the nationalisation were not unreasonable. Compensation was to be paid, and the canal was to be kept open for international traffic. Thus Britain and France had no real cause to use force – interference would be hard to justify. An excuse was needed and it was provided by Israel.

There had been fairly constant raiding between Israel and Egypt since 1953. Israel was worried by the growth of Arab nationalism, the arms deal with Czechoslovakia, and finally in 1955 by the closing of the Straits of Tiran to Israeli shipping (see map, page 258). Israel wanted to strike out, Britain and France secretly added their encouragement: an Arab-Israeli war in the Sinai desert would provide the excuse to send in troops as peacemakers.

The Israeli general, Moshe Dayan, had no doubts as to the importance of the secret agreement:

Well, I should say the entire military plan was based on that . . . it was terribly important.

Neither did he have any doubts about Britain's motives in issuing the ultimatum to the two sides, ordering them to separate:

This ultimatum does not worry Israel. We are not within ten miles of the canal and have neither interest not plan to come closer to it. It is clear that the whole purpose of the ultimatum is to give the British and French governments a pretext to capture the canal.

Anthony Eden, the British prime minister, disagreed. He wrote in his autobiography:

It has frequently been suggested that there was something artificial about our declared intention to separate the combatants and stop the spread of hostilities. Our fear of damage to the canal if there was fighting over the crossing places was genuine and well founded.

Compare this with a letter explaining British motives to President Eisenhower:

I do not think that we disagree about our primary objective . . . to undo what Nasser has done and set up an international regime for the canal. . . . But this is not all. Nasser has embarked on a course which is unpleasantly familiar . . . I have never thought Nasser a Hitler, but the parallel with Mussolini is close. . . . The removal of Nasser, and the installation in Egypt of a regime less hostile to the West, must also rank amongst our objectives.

The plan was duly carried out. When the Israeli invasion began, the ultimatum was sent by Britain and France ordering the two sides to clear the canal area. The order was ignored, perhaps in part because the bulk of the fighting was over a hundred miles away. On 31 October 'Operation Musketeer' began. Egyptian airfields were bombed, and in November paratroops and a seaborne force attacked the canal zone. The invasion force consisted of 90 000 men, 500 aircraft and 130 ships.

International response was swift. Russia threatened direct action if the assault continued, and the USA urged an immediate ceasefire. There was world-wide condemnation of the assault, even without knowledge of the secret deal which lay behind it.

British tank and observer, Port Said, 1956

The Suez crisis had two main effects. Firstly, it underlined the end of the British influence in that part of the Arab world. As Nasser said:

To bring the Israelis into an adventure against the Arabs was very foolish. We were used to hating British policy but then we began to despise British policy.

Secondly the Suez crisis had a dramatic effect on the popularity of Nasser. He could blame defeat in the second Israeli war on Britain and France. In any case, losing the war was insignificant in comparison with the prestige of standing up against the two European countries. Nasser now stood as the driving force behind the causes of Arab nationalism and unity.

United Nations emergency force moves into Gaza, 1956

Questions

1 Why was Britain so sensitive about the policies of Nasser?
2 In what sense can it be said that the Western powers provoked the nationalism of Suez?
3 (a) What are Eden's motives in the Suez crisis according to the letter to Eisenhower, the autobiography, and General Dayan?
   (b) Explain which of these you consider to be the genuine motive, and why the other motives might have been suggested.
4 What was the outcome of the crisis for the powers involved?

Nasser's Egypt

Egyptian control of the Suez canal had been the first of Nasser's objectives. During the next few years he was able to continue this economic nationalisation, bringing other foreign businesses under Egyptian control. However, he was never able to free Egypt from the need for foreign loans, and this was due to the failure of the home economy.

In 1950 the economy of Egypt was in poor shape. Only 15 per cent of national output was industrial, and the great mass of the people who worked in agriculture were in debt, had no security, and on average lived only to 35 years of age. Nasser wanted to change all this. Firstly in 1952 he passed an Agrarian Reform Law. This confiscated large estates and redistributed them to half a million peasant families, who were organised into co-operatives for production and marketing. Many people benefited from this, and from other major schemes such as irrigation, but the mass of landless peasants remained badly off.

Nasser saw industry as the answer. From 1961 he adopted a scheme of economic planning. However, he tried to develop heavy advanced industries which did not make the most of Egypt's large labour force. Heavy borrowing from abroad made the economic situation worse.

Nasser also tried to provide adequate education and welfare services, including school building, urban house-building and the provision of

Nasser, Khrushchev, President Aref of Iraq, and President Sallal of Yemen prepare to open the Aswan High Dam

health clinics. However, there were simply not enough people wealthy enough to pay the taxes to provide comprehensive services and none of the schemes solved the basic problems of Egyptian society.

Nasser was a great Arab nationalist, and during the years 1954–70 he was at the centre of Middle East controversy. He had shown his independence even before the Suez crisis, and in later years pursued a policy of Arab unity. In 1958 Egypt and Syria joined together to form the United Arab Republic. However, there was opposition to Nasser's policies within Syria and in 1961 the union was ended. Later attempts at union with Syria and Iraq also foundered.

Nasser was also a prominent force in the founding of the Palestinian Liberation Organisation. However, by 1966 it was Syria that took over as the leading supporter of the PLO and Nasser remained on the sidelines until 1970, when he negotiated a ceasefire between the PLO and King Hussein of Jordan. Nasser's vision of Arab unity appears to have been a mirage. Far from taking a lead, Nasser was at times attacked for not doing enough for the Arab cause. This criticism may explain the action which Nasser took in 1967 which led to the outbreak of the Six Day War (see page 259).

In this area, too, Nasser's achievement was patchy. Certainly he broke contacts with Europe and the superpowers, and was deeply suspected by them. Even Arab nations, especially the wealthier and more conservative ones, did not trust him.

Yet undoubtedly, at his death in 1970, he was thought of as a national hero. Perhaps it was his promises rather than his achievement which won the hearts of his people:

He overwhelmed us with his magic . . . and the hopes, dreams and promises . . . which he repeatedly announced to us . . . with their pipes, drums, anthems songs and films which made us see ourselves as a great industrial state, leaders of the developing world . . . and the strongest military power in the Middle East.

P. J. Vatikiotis, Nasser and his Generation, 1978

Question

Write an obituary of Nasser as it might have appeared in
(a) A British newspaper, (b) An Egyptian newspaper.

Egypt since 1970

After Nasser's death, Egypt was ruled by Anwar-al-Sadat. He had been closely involved in the overthrow of Farouk, and had remained as vice-president in Nasser's government, though not known for strong views of his own. Yet he was to cause a turn-around in Egyptian policy. In contrast to Nasser, he saw the USA as having an important role to play in a Middle Eastern settlement. Secondly, he saw that Egypt could not afford war, and he was willing to negotiate with Israel. His early attempts at negotiation, in 1971, failed. Frustrated by the lack of progress and the continuing and exhausting border raids, he went to war in October 1973 (see page 260). Henry Kissinger, then US secretary of state, played a significant part in halting the war. Sadat now looked for a more permanent means of security. Egypt could not afford any more wars, and the strain on the economy at home was beginning to tell. Sadat's attempts to gain loans by his 'Open Door' policy had little success. The government was forced to cut spending, and there were riots and demonstrations as the price of basic commodities started to rise.

The 'Open Door' policy meant that the USA and other wealthy states were encouraged to invest in Egypt.

In November 1977 Sadat sought a new way out of the crisis by doing the unthinkable. He travelled to Israel and addressed the Knesset there. Sadat's speech was intended to be an appeal for peace, trying to

exhaust every means in a bid to save my Arab people and the entire Arab nation the horrors of new shocking and terrible wars, the dimensions of which only God himself can forsee. . . . Any life lost in the war is human life, be it that of an Arab or an Israeli. . . . Innocent children deprived of the care and compassion of their parents are ours. For the sake of them all, for a smile on the face of every child born in our land, for all that, I have taken my decision to come to you.

Further talks between the two sides followed, but for some time it seemed that Sadat's gamble had failed. For one thing, he had divided Egypt from the rest of the Arab world. The Beirut newspaper *Al-Safir* summed up the feelings of many Arabs.

All of these people were associated with the founding or development of Israel. Herzl was the founder of the Zionist movement.

Sadat has entered history. As of today his name will be remembered along with those of Herzl, Balfour, Weizman, Ben Gurion, Golda Meir and Moshe Dayan as one of the founders of the state of Israel, the consolidators of its existence, the champions of its imperial dreams. Sadat has entered history – but he will enter it again. The decision rests with the Arab people of Egypt, the Egyptian army, or indeed with any Arab. For he is now the enemy of them all, and it is right of anyone to pass judgement and carry it out.

As well as stirring up this anger, the initiative itself seemed to have failed. Then, during 1978, US President Jimmy Carter became involved and further talks were held at the president's country retreat at Camp David. Even so, agreement could only be reached by further concessions from Sadat. He had fought for some form of self-governing Palestinian state, but had to give way on this in order to make any progress. Finally, in March 1979, a treaty was signed ending the state of war, returning Sinai to Egypt, and recognising the boundaries of Israel. Sadat had achieved what he thought was best for Egypt. However, he had given far more concessions than Israel. He was isolated within the Arab world. Furthermore he had become isolated at home. His policies had moved away from Nasser's socialism towards investment supported by links with the West. Arabs annoyed by recognition of Israel were further angered by this 'westernisation'; which in any case did little to help the poorest.

On 6 October 1981 President Sadat was assassinated by an extreme Muslim faction while celebrating a victory parade. He had paid the price of his foreign policy. Nevertheless, despite the bitter reactions it had caused, Sadat's Middle East initiative did survive him: his successor, Hosni Mubarak, has accepted the Camp David agreement, while attempting to improve Egypt's relations with other Arab states.

Questions

1 Explain why Sadat made the decision to speak to Israel's Knesset.
2 What did *Al-Safir* mean when it said 'he will enter it again' and how was this borne out?

The power of words – Carter, Sadat and Begin at Camp David, 9 June, 1978

Asia

19

The communist victory in China

The Chinese Revolution of 1911

China was ruled by the Manchu dynasty from 1644 until 1911. At its height, Manchu China was a marvellous civilisation. By 1900 it had fallen into decay. The last of the Manchus, the Empress Tzu-Hsi and the boy Emperor P'u Yi, headed a corrupt government which misruled a backward, poverty-stricken country. What little wealth that remained was drained away by the several foreign powers which had interests there.

In the years before 1911 there was much talk of revolution amongst certain groups of Chinese people. Several plots against the Manchus had failed. Then, in 1911, disturbances which began in the city of Hankow quickly spread to other provinces. The government, too weak

The Emperor Pu Yi (standing), with his father, Prince Chun, and his brother

to defend itself, collapsed. The Emperor P'u Yi abdicated in 1912 in favour of a republic.

Two men claimed to be at the head of this republic. One of them was General Yuan Shih-k'ai. Yuan had been the commander of the government forces but then he changed sides. The other was Sun Yat-sen. Sun was a revolutionary who had founded the Kuomintang, or 'Sworn Chinese Brotherhood'. The Kuomintang was the most powerful force behind the overthrow of the Manchus. It was founded in 1905 to fight for three principles for the future of China:

1 Nationalism: a united China, with no foreign interference.
2 Democracy: a freely elected parliament, and a constitution.
3 The people's livelihood: Food, shelter, and a share of the nation's wealth for all.

Sun had travelled abroad seeking help and ideas. Indeed, when the revolution broke out he was in the USA, but he rapidly returned to set up his republic at Nanking. Sun realised that, if he was to control all of China, he would have to fight Yuan. Rather than drag China into civil war, Sun resigned, leaving Yuan to continue the work of the revolution. Yuan quickly betrayed Sun's hopes. He retained all the trappings of the Manchus, and attempted to make himself emperor. For support he relied on the warlords, who controlled their own armies and their own territories, and who ruled as they pleased. Yuan died in 1916. The republic was restored under Sun Yat-sen's in the area around Canton. Elsewhere, however, the warlords remained independent.

There is little doubt that Yuan, a Manchu general, hoped to establish himself as emperor at the head of a new dynasty.

Sun Yat-sen was a thinker, a politician, and not a soldier. This may explain why he was overshadowed by Yuan Shih-k'ai.

Using the evidence: warlord rule

Conditions under warlord rule can be seen from these documents.

A From 1916 to 1928 over 140 wars were fought between the warlords with massive casualties:

A feature of life in Szechuan for many years has been the commandeering of labour for the civil war; almost every day . . . gangs of men may be seen roped together with cords round their wrists being carried off by soldiers to act as transport coolies . . . often they are snatched away in the streets and forced to accompany troops to distant places at a moment's notice, from which journey they may not return for weeks, if at all.

Dispatch from British consul, Chungking, to British legation, August 1924

B A warlord, Chan Fa-K'uei remembered:

Whenever we ran out of food, we would raid a little village to get a few chickens, etc. My men would surround a village before dawn and fire several shots to intimidate the people. Sometimes we killed and carried away little pigs. We took corn, rice, potatoes. Did we take money? No. There was no money to be had anyway.

We had moral principles. We never indulged in . . . rape. We only robbed because we had nothing to eat.

C A European observed Yochow under warlord Chang Chiang-yao's rule:

Every shop, every house in this beautiful and prosperous city had been stripped . . . the place is furnished only by troops, who lie disconsolate, dirty, hungry and demoralised on the floors and counters of the shops. Most of the population has fled.

D Some parts of China were completely taken over by Japan. The British consul observed:

Already Japanese influence is encountered in every department of life. Much of the currency consists of Japanese gold and silver yen notes. Not only is the South Manchurian Railway Japanese, but the Newchwang Electric Light and Waterworks. So is the only . . . modern hospital. Most of the shipping, most of the goods on sale, all the soft coal, and most of the beer is Japanese. Whisky, on sale everywhere under various Scotch labels, is really Japanese, as is the Worcester sauce.

The revolution of 1911 had sought the three principles of Sun Yat-sen:
(a) nationalism (b) democracy (c) the people's livelihood
Use the documents to show how successful the revolution was in each of its aims.

Kuomintang and communists

When Sun Yat-sen died, the Kuomintang was divided between left and right. Chiang Kai-shek favoured the right, but saw that he needed the support of the left for the time being.

During the warlord era revolutionary pressures began to build up again. Broadly, this opposition to warlord rule can be divided into two groups – the Kuomintang, led by Sun Yat-sen, and from 1925 by Chiang Kai-shek; and the newer communist movement, inspired by the revolution in Russia, and led by Mao Tse-tung.

At first the Kuomintang and the communists worked together against the common enemy. Chiang built his strength in the army. The communists were strongest amongst the people. By the summer of 1926 they felt ready to strike at the warlords, and with 100 000 men they launched the first northern expedition.

There was hard fighting against some of the warlords, but one by one they were defeated, Other warlords threw in their lot with the Kuomintang. But the main reason for the victory of 1926 has been pinpointed by an historian:

The masses of ordinary people rose in a veritable wave that swept the expeditionary armies to the banks of the Yangtze.
The spontaneous rising of the people gave the Kuomintang armies little more to do, often, than occupy territory already secured for them.
J. E. Sheridan, *China in Disintegration*, 1975

By 1928 Chiang had control of most of China including Beijing. He declared the foundation of the Republic of China, with its capital at Nanking, and himself as its leader. He had also taken the first steps towards exterminating the communists.

Originally, the Kuomintang and the communists had very similar aims. Both wanted to stop exploitation of China by foreigners; both wanted some sort of democracy; both wanted to improve the standard of living of the people. Sun Yat-sen welcomed the alliance of communists and Kuomintang in 1924, yet within three years the communists were almost wiped out by their recent allies.

The reason for this turnabout lies with Chiang Kai-shek. Personally, he was very ambitious – the opinion of a Russian observer was that he had great

desire for glory and power, and an insatiable urge to become China's hero. His actual understanding of the problems of the revolution, however, is quite another story. . . . He acts according to his personal views only, without the support of the masses.

Chiang claimed to want democracy, but his view of democracy changed. At first he may have wanted democracy in the Western sense, with government elected by the people.
By 1924 he was talking of a

'democracy' in which the populace would turn over power to intellectually superior individuals whom they could control through rights of suffrage, recall, referendum.

Sun Yat-sen (right) and Chiang Kai-shek, 1924

By 1933 his views had moved even further, and could not be called democratic at all – he had become a fascist:

The most important point of fascism is absolute trust in a sagely able leader. The leader has the final decision in all matters. . . . I believe that unless everyone has absolute trust in one man, we cannot reconstruct the nation, and we cannot complete the revolution.
'Fascism in Kuomintang China', Chinese Quarterly No 49

Searching for communists – any evidence would bring the death penalty

This was not a democratic system, but a police state. For example, to make sure that people had 'absolute trust' in him, Chiang controlled the 'Blue Shirt Society' – a political police force which eliminated any opposition.

As well as shifting his ground on the principle of democracy, Chiang shifted on nationalism. The policy of nationalism was against foreign exploitation. Yet concessions were still given to foreigners.

In the Shanghai settlement are the tallest buildings in Asia, the most spacious cinema palaces, and more motor cars than in all other Chinese cities combined. Here are the great Chinese department stores, the powerful foreign houses like the Hong Kong and Shanghai Banking Corporation, the Chartered Bank of India, Australia and China, the Chase banks of New York. In the settlement are head offices of the vast American and British tobacco concerns. . . . There are the 'blue blood' British firms like Arnolds, Jardine and Matheson's, Sassoons. And here are the newer, more aggressive American firms, and they represent hundreds of American factories with everything for sale, from rivets to machine guns and bombing planes.
L. Wheeler, *Edgar Snow's China*, 1981

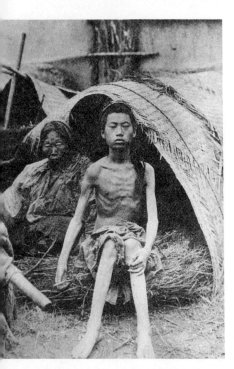

Mother and child, stricken by famine, Hunan province

Addiction to opium was high, especially amongst the wealthier classes. As with all drugs, this gave criminals plenty of opportunity to make their fortune.

The revolution was intended to improve the living standards of the people, but these were terrible years for the Chinese peasantry. In 1929 an observer recorded this sight:

I saw a naked twig-armed child, his belly a balloon from a diet of leaves and sawdust. He was trying to shake back to life his naked father, who had just died on the road.

For many blocks the streets were bordered with men and women and children in the last reaches of starvation.

But these were not the most shocking things, after all. The shocking thing was that in many of those towns there were still rich men, rice hoarders, money lenders and landlords with armed guards to defend them. The shocking thing was that in the cities there were thousands of tons of wheat and millet which could not be shipped to the starving, because Kuomintang generals would release none of the rolling stock because they feared it would be seized by their rivals.

L. Wheeler, *Edgar Snow's China*

Exploitation of the poorer classes continued:

An apprentice system provided small producers and shopkeepers with an inexhaustable supply of child labour working daily up to eighteen and twenty hours in return for a bowl of rice and a board to sleep on.

Over a large area of China, the rural population suffers horribly through insecurity of life and property. It is taxed by one ruffian, who calls himself a general, by another, by a third, and when it has bought them off still owes taxes to the government; in some places actually more than twenty years taxation has been paid in advance. It is squeezed by dishonest officials. It must cut its crops at the point of a bayonet, and hand them over without payment to the local garrison, though it will starve without them. It is forced to grow opium in defiance of the law, because its military tyrants can squeeze heavier taxation from opium than rice or wheat, and make money in addition out of the dens where it is smoked. It pays blackmail to the professional bandits in its neighbourhood, or it resists, and sees its villages burned to the ground.

R. H. Tawney, *Land and Labour in China*, 1932

The Kuomintang government was notoriously corrupt:

Tu Yueh-sheng was the Al Capone of the French concession. Old Tu got his start 'squeezing' the opium merchants while on the police force in French town. In ten years he managed to achieve high place in the Ching and Hung gangs, Chinese gangs which control the illicit opium traffic. Tu is a gentleman now, wears silk gowns, rides in expensive limousines and calls the Nanking officials by their first names.

In 1927 Chiang used Tu's gangsters to help wipe out the communist party in Shanghai.

J. Sheridan, *China in Disintegration*, 1975

The reason for the split between Kuomintang and the communists is clear to see: Chiang's republic had shifted far away from the three principles. His views had become opposed to the views of the communists which, on the whole, had remained the same, and those of the left of the Kuomintang who sympathised with them. The communists

Wealthy Chinese in an opium den

were therefore a threat to Chiang, and even before he had defeated the warlords he wanted to be rid of his old allies.

In 1928, first in Kiangsi, then in Shanghai, Chiang's men went to work. Any communist, any striker, anyone reading anti-government literature, was dealt with on the spot:

After the heads of the victims were severed by the swordsman they were displayed on the tops of poles or placed on platters and carried through the streets. The sight had the effect of creating a reign of terror because the victims were denied the semblance of a trial. The executioners, bearing broadswords and accompanied by a squad of soldiers, marched their victims to a prominent corner where they were forced to bend over while their heads were cut off.

H. Isaacs, *The Tragedy of the Chinese Revolution*, 1983

The execution patrol. Decapitation was found to be a good way of discouraging strikes and communists

Questions

1 How do you explain the defeat of the warlords?
2 Why would Sun Yat-sen have been disappointed by Kuomintang China?
3 Kuomintang and communists had once stood for much the same principles. So why did Chiang try to wipe out communism? Explain your answer carefully.

The survival of communism in China

We have seen that, at first, the communists had much in common with the Kuomintang. Indeed, in 1923, the communists had joined the Kuomintang, and in 1925 the head of the Kuomintang propaganda department in Canton was a young communist, Mao Tse-tung.

Mao – born in Hunan Province, 1893, son of a well-to-do peasant. During his schooling, his teacher-training, and as a librarian, he adopted communist ideas.

The slaughter of 1927 drove the communists out of the Kuomintang, and forced them to attempt to seize power for themselves. When this failed with heavy losses, they were forced to retreat to the remote area of Kiangsi where Mao Tse-tung rose to the leadership of the movement.

I met Mao soon after my arrival [1936]: a gaunt figure, above average height for a Chinese, somewhat stooped, with a head of thick black hair grown very long, and with large searching eyes. . . .

He had the simplicity and naturalness of the Chinese peasant, with a lively sense of humour and a love of rustic laughter.

. . . He is plain-speaking and plain-living, and some people might think him rather coarse and vulgar . . . And yet Mao is an accomplished scholar, an omnivorous reader, a deep student of philosophy and history, a good speaker, a man with an unusual memory and extraordinary powers of concentration, an able writer, careless in his personal habits but astonishingly meticulous about details of duty, a man of tireless energy, and a military and political strategist of considerable genius.

Edgar Snow, *Red Star over China*, 1937

Mao saw two essentials if communism was to be victorious: the support of the peasantry, and the creation of a people's army. From his base in Kiangsi he set out to achieve both of these things. The method was to form soviets on Russian lines, with government in the hands of the peasants. He saw that this would involve the overthrow of the traditional landowners:

A revolution is not a dinner party, or writing an essay, or painting a picture, or doing embroidery. . . . A revolution is an insurrection by which one class overthrows another. A rural revolution is a revolution by which the peasantry overthrows the feudal power of the landlord class . . . to put it bluntly, it is necessary to create terror for a while in every rural area, or otherwise it would be impossible to suppress the activities of the counter-revolutionaries or overthrow the gentry.

Having gained the support of the peasants, he needed their help as soldiers or as citizen helpers in the struggle against Chiang Kai-shek.

Chiang was determined that the communists should be stamped out once and for all. As soon as the war against the last of the warlords lulled in 1930, Chiang ordered annihilation campaigns. Three times in 1930 and 1931 his armies tried and failed to capture Kiangsi. In 1932, the fourth siege campaign began, using one million men and aircraft in support. Gradually, Chiang's army cut into communist territory, drawing the noose tighter. By October 1934 Mao realised that defeat was inevitable unless the communists left the plateau of Kiangsi for the north, where Chiang's rule was weaker.

Using the evidence: The Long March

The story of this great escape, the Long March, is one of the most remarkable in history. Secretly, Mao built up his resources in the south and west of the communist-held area. Then, while guerillas kept the Kuomintang army occupied, the bulk of the communists broke through the enemy line. Approximately 120 000 men, women and children left Kiangsi carrying all their possessions with them. During the next 368 days the communists marched 6000 miles, an average of 16 miles per day. Add to that daily skirmishes with the Kuomintang, 15 days spent in major battles, the crossing of 18 mountain ranges, 24 rivers, 12 provinces and the occupation of 62 cities. No wonder only 5000 people completed the whole march. Such a story as this is bound

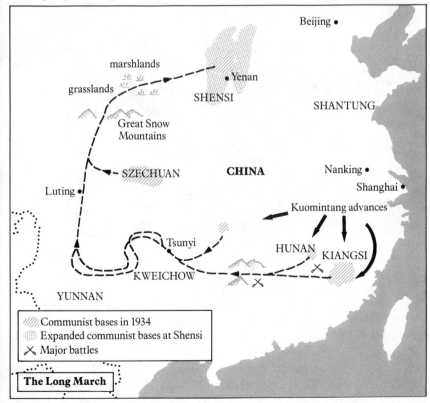

to be the subject of exaggeration. Dick Wilson, who has interviewed many marchers, acknowledges,

Much weight has therefore to be put on the memory of the men involved, and this is only too human.

Even so, a few of these memories can help us to picture the Long March:

A Crossing the Luting bridge:
The Luting bridge was located in a dangerous setting indeed. Below the reddish waters, cascading down from the mountain gorges, pounded against the ugly boulders rising from the river bed. Fording or crossing in boats was out of the question. The bridge was the only way to get to the other side.

We examined it. It was made of iron chains – thirteen in number, each big link as thick as a rice bowl. Two chains on each side served as railings; nine formed the surface walk. Originally planks had been laid across the nine chains and the whole bridge suspended between two cliffs, swayed like a cradle. Now the planks were gone, having been taken by the enemy. All that remained were the black hanging chains.

The Luting bridge

We began our attack at four in the afternoon. All the buglers of the regiment blew the charge call in unison, and we opened up with every weapon we had. Carrying tommy-guns, big knives strapped across their backs, twelve grenades apiece tucked into their belts, twenty-two heroes, led by Commander Liao, climbed across the swaying bridge chains, in the teeth of enemy fire. Behind them came the men of 3rd Company, each carrying a plank in addition to full battle gear.

Just as the assualt squad reached the opposite side, huge flames sprang into the sky. The whole outcome of the attack hung by a hair. Emboldened by our cries, the twenty-two men plunged into the flames. The hair and eyebrows of the men were singed, but, streaming smoke and flame, they continued charging behind Liao, smashing their way into the city.

Yang Cheng-wu

B Crossing the Great Snow Mountain:
We started out at early dawn. There was no path at all, but peasants said that tribesmen came over the mountains on raids, and we could cross if they could. So we started straight up the mountain, heading for a pass near the summit. Heavy fog swirled about us, there was a high wind, and half-way up it began to rain. As we climbed higher and higher we were caught in a terrible hailstorm and the air became so thin we could hardly breathe at all. Speech was completely impossible and the cold so dreadful that our breath froze and our hands and lips turned blue. Men and animals staggered and fell into chasms and disappeared for ever. Those who sat down to rest or to relieve themselves froze to death on the spot.

By nightfall we had crossed, at an altitude of 16000 feet. To avoid enemy bombers we arose at midnight and began climbing the next peak.

Tung Pi-wu

The Long March. Climbing the Great Snow Mountain

C Crossing the grasslands:
From Kangmaoszu, the marshes stretched like a great sea, vague, gloomy, and endless. Treacherous bogs were everywhere which sucked a man down once he stepped off the firmer parts, and more quickly if he tried to extricate himself. We could advance only with minute care, stepping on grass clumps. Even so, one could not help feeling nervous, for the grass mounds sank with the pressure and black water would rise and submerge the foot. It was really like crossing a treacherous quicksand. Fortunately the advance unit had left a coarse hair rope which led meanderingly. We advanced along the rope.

We tried out almost all kinds of wild plants along our way. We discovered a sort of prickly, stumpy tree denuded of leaves but with tiny red berries like cherries. On the sixth day someone dug out a plant the size of a green turnip which tasted sweet and crisp. It proved poisonous. Those who ate it vomited after half an hour. Several died on the spot.

Once I was going forward when the grass mound underfoot jerked, and before I had time to draw away my foot, I was in the deadly ooze. I attempted to clamber to solid ground. Beads of sweat stood on my forehead. But the harder I struggled, the deeper I sank.

More soldiers came up and they pulled like a tug-of-war team; then with a powerful jerk, they pulled me right out of the mud.

Major Tan Chianglin

You are a survivor from the Long March. Astonishingly, along the way you found a few precious minutes to write your diary.
Produce extracts from that diary to show:
(a) Your impression of Mao Tse-tung.
(b) Your feelings on leaving Kiangsi.
(c) The crossing of the Luting Bridge.
(d) The crossing of the Great Snow Mountain.
(e) Your experiences in the grassslands
(f) Your feelings on finishing the Long March – a summary of your achievement.

The defeat of the Kuomintang

The Long March was in itself a triumph for the communists. However, they were still weak, and in 1936 a new Kuomintang army led by General Chang Hseuh-liang was sent against them.

At the same time China was faced by a new and greater threat – the Japanese. Mao made it clear to General Chang that he wished for an alliance on the understanding that, while foreigners threaten, 'Chinese do not fight against Chinese'. General Chang agreed with him, and in November 1936 the two armies made a truce, with the intention of uniting against the Japanese. Chiang Kai-shek was furious when he heard this, and flew to Sian where his northern army was based. Far from disciplining General Chang and his supporters, Chiang Kai-shek found himself arrested until he agreed to abandon the civil war and fight with the communists against the invaders. A month later he was released. He called off the war against the communists, and led the Chinese 'United Front' against Japan.

Japan had an aggressive foreign policy in the 1930s, starting in 1931 with the occupation of Manchuria, but threatening the whole of China.

Japanese machine-gun unit positioned for the attack

There were early setbacks in the struggle. In July 1937 the Japanese used a flimsy excuse to launch an attack on Peking. They also held most of northern China, and were preparing to attack Shanghai and the Yangtze valley. The United Front defended Shanghai fiercely, but on 3 December 1937 it fell, and the Japanese advanced on Chiang's capital, Nanking, which fell on 12 December.

From 1938 until 1941 the two sides fought bitterly, but in December

1941 China gained a new ally. The USA, which entered the war after the Japanese attack on Pearl Harbour, sent supplies and advisers. The Americans mistrusted Mao, and favoured Chiang. Even so, they realised that his army was weak, and admired the tactics of the communists who were steadily winning control of Japanese-held territory.

Nonetheless, with the defeat of Japan in 1945, Chiang began to reassert himself over China. He insisted that Japanese troops should only surrender their weapons to Kuomintang soldiers. He took hold of principal cities and lines of communication. He rejected requests from Mao for a coalition government to rebuild China, and in June 1946 he relaunched his campaign to exterminate communism.

Yet by October 1949 the Kuomintang was defeated, and Mao Tse-tung was able to announce the Chinese People's Republic.

Mao Tse-tung addresses the guerillas' 8th route army, fighting the Japanese in 1944.

Using the evidence: the communist victory

Few people would have said that the communists had any chance at all. Study the following documents, which reveal some of the reasons why the communists triumphed. As you do so, answer the following question:

Make a direct comparison between the Kuomintang and communists under the following headings:
(a) Leadership
(b) Strategy
(c) Treatment of peasants
(d) Supply of weapons
(e) Morale of troops
(f) Effect of government/programme for government
Your comparison should make it quite clear why the communists had defeated the Kuomintang by 1949.

A Communist leadership was excellent from top to bottom. Mao developed a clear, practicable, long-range strategy that put into effect a fast, mobile war aimed at the destruction of the Kuomintang armies rather than a seizure of territory.

Chiang evidently did have a strategy, but it was a bad one; it envisaged the seizure and retention of cities, even when communist control of the surrounding countryside left his troops dependent on airlifted supplies.

Communist field commanders were selected on merit, and given wide latitude to use their own judgement. They generally waged bold, aggressive, sometimes brilliant campaigns. Kuomintang generals, on the contrary, were commonly chosen on grounds of political loyalty, and many demonstrated mediocrity or outright incompetence.

J. Sheridan, *China in Disintegration*, 1975

An 8th Army guerilla unit in the North Shensi hills

Chu Teh was Mao's partner in the creation of the Red Army.

B Communist military strategy:
When the enemy advances, we retreat.
When the enemy halts and encamps, we harass them.
When the enemy seeks to avoid battle, we attack.
When the enemy retreats, we pursue.

Chu Teh

C Instruction to troops regarding contact with peasants:
1 Replace doors when you leave a house.
2 Return and roll up straw matting.
3 Be courteous and polite to the people and help them.
4 Return all borrowed articles.
5 Replace all damaged articles.
6 Be honest in all transactions with the peasants.
7 Pay for all articles purchased.
8 Be sanitary: establish latrines at a safe distance from people's houses.

D The communist soldiers looked fierce enough with their big fur caps and ear flaps, uniforms draped with cartridge bandoliers and hung with dangerous looking home-made grenades. All were well armed, with Japanese rifles or American automatic weapons. In every group of half a dozen or so there would be one with a scrap of paper in his hand. These bore the addresses of the private houses on which the squads were to be billeted. Several times I saw a soldier approaching a knot of bystanders, profferring his paper with a polite bow and a wide smile, ask for directions. On the civilians, at first astounded, and in the end mighty pleased, the effect was enormous.

As the weeks passed standards of politeness, modesty, honesty, and high discipline saw no signs of falling off.

O. B. van der Sprenkel, *New China, Three Views*, 1951.

E The Reds had a very limited output of armaments; their enemy was really their main source of supply. For years the Reds had called the Kuomintang troops their 'ammunition carriers' as they claimed to capture more than 80 per cent of their guns and 70 per cent of their ammunition from enemy troops.

J. Sheridan, *China in Disintegration*, 1975

F Seasonal conscription for the Kuomintang army occurs in spring and autumn. Private dealers in conscripts have organised a trade. They are buying able-bodied men from starved families who need rice more urgently than sons.

J. Sheridan, *China in Disintegration*, 1975

G Having been herded together, the conscripts are driven to the training camps. Over endless roads they walk. . . . Many of those who run away run off during the first few days. Later they are too weak to run away. Those who are caught are cruelly beaten. They will be carried along with broken limbs and with wounds in maimed flesh in which infection turns quickly into blood poisoning.

As they march along they turn into skeletons. Scabies and ulcers turn their skin into a shabby cover of an emaciated body which has no other value than to turn rice into dung and to register the sharp pains of existence as a conscript in the Chinese army.

General Albert Wedemeyer, commanding officer, US forces in China

G Kuomintang China is characterised by 'greed, corruption, favouritism, more taxes, a ruined currency, terrible waste of life, callous disregard of the rights of men.'

T. H. White, *General Stillwell, the Stillwell Papers*, 1949

H Inflation in China (% per annum):

1937–39	50
1939–42	160
1942–45	300

In 1943 civil servants earned 10 per cent of their real income of 1937.

I Mao's plan for national salvation:
Improve people's living conditions.
Raise the pay of workers and soldiers.
Take good care of the families of soldiers.
Abolish taxes.
Reduce rent and interest.
Relieve the unemployed.
Regulate food supply.
Give aid to victims of natural calamities.

J Communist party membership:

1936	40 000
1945	1.2 million

Size of communist army:

1937	between 45 000 and 90 000
1945	between 500 000 and 900 000

Victims of the Kuomintang embargo on supplies to communist held areas

20

China since 1949

The economic revolution

The victory of communism over the Kuomintang was, as Mao Tse-tung acknowledged, only a beginning:

The Chinese people, one quarter of humanity, have stood up. From now on no one will insult us again. To win country-wide victory is only the first step in a long march. Even if this step is worthy of pride, it is comparatively tiny; what will be more worthy of pride is yet to come.

1 Agriculture

The most urgent need was to feed the people, and a programme of land reform began immediately. By the terms of the Agarian Reform Law of 1950, land was taken from rich landlords and given to peasants. Those landlords who were regarded as tyrants were tried by people's courts and condemned to death. No accurate figure exists to show how many died. Certainly many landlords were spared and allowed to keep a small plot, but even so executions ran into hundreds of thousands.

For the time being, the class of rich peasants was protected. Mao justified 'preserving the rich peasant economy in order to further the early restoration of production in rural areas.'

The effect of Mao's policy on landholding can be seen from these statistics:

	% of households	Share of crop area in 1949	Share of crop area in 1952	Average crop area in 1949	Average crop area in 1952
Landlords	2.6	28.7	2.1	116.10 *mou*	11.98 *mou*
Rich peasants	3.6	17.7	6.4	37.75	26.30
Middle peasants	35.8	30.2	44.8	15.81	18.53
Poor peasants	58.0	23.5	46.8	6.25	12.14

Mou – one sixth of an acre (approximately).

Further reform took place in stages. These stages are seen here through the words of a Chinese peasant, Feng Chang-yeh:

I worked on my own land for two years. In 1950 I was able to buy an ox. Things were easier then. In 1952 we organised a *labour group for mutual help*. In 1953 we had got most of the farmers in the village to join the group. There were proper discussions, and divided opinions about doing this. Good workers complained 'if we exchange labour with a bad worker, we shall only lose by doing so.' We explained that in the labour group each worker had a point rating, so that no one would suffer by exchanging labour, nor would anyone gain by being lazy or having a poor physique.

Between 1953 and 1954 we discussed becoming an agricultural *co-operative*. In general one can say that those whose land was not good were for the idea, and those who had good land down in the valley and a lot of manpower, were against it. My neighbour Chao Teh-pa, for example, said 'I don't want to go up the hill and toil on the hill fields. I have good, fertile land down here in the valley.' Well, we reckoned how many days work he would get in an agricultural

The trial and execution of Huang Chin-Chi, in Kwantung: such was the fate of farmer landlords whose crime was exploitation

co-operative. We proved to him that large-scale farming and joint effort was more rational, and that in actual fact he would gain by joining the agricultural co-operative. 'I'll hire people', he replied. We told him that would become rather difficult. There would be no day labourers. We had a serious talk with him. 'You want to hire people to work for you. That's exploitation. Why do you want to become rich on other people's work? Why should only you become rich? You are not to get anyone to exploit. Choose how you want things to be. Do you want to be rich alone or do you want us to be well-off together? Do you want to be a decent person or not?' He thought about it and joined.

In 1954 we had all got more corn than before. We had used our labour more rationally and manured better. We detailed two men every day to go to Yenen to fetch a load of human excrement. We got the shit in return for emptying the latrines. This was fair exchange.

Thought study in the commune, Kwangtung

The next winter we discussed transforming ourselves into a *collective*. Again, those who had better land and those with animals were afraid of losing by it. They did not want their animals to become collective property. After discussion they agreed and we became the East Shines Red Higher Agricultural Co-operative, comprising four villages. We had more manpower and were able to do more.

We went into the Liu Ling People's *Commune* in 1958. The discussion about forming a commune was short. Some people thought it unnecessary. Lo Wen-ming said 'Why should we change everything again now? Things are going well as they are.' But we discussed and made propaganda. The central committee of the Party, of course, said that we ought to form people's communes. They were supposed to be more effective and to give greater possibilities for capital investment. With one we should be maintaining the principle of everyone being paid according to the work he did and be able to help others. After this propaganda work we joined the commune.

The organisation of the commune also involved social care. We give grants to those who are incapable, who are ill, and to families who have got into difficulties for one reason or another. The commune decides what proportion of the harvest should go on this. Illness, death, and accident are no longer catastrophes. Citizens now have security.

Reform of agriculture brought with it significant improvements in the national crop yield, as seen in this table:

	Production (million metric tons)
1949	111
1952	161
1957	191
1958	206

Questions

1 What do the statistics on page 298 reveal about trends in the communist programme of land reform?
2 Feng Chang-yeh's account shows how one community dealt with its problems:
   (a) The problem of inefficiency of small-scale peasant labour.
   (b) Poor peasants had been given land, but often it was poorer land and they could not farm it properly for lack of tools and livestock.
   (c) Agriculture was still based on private property and rich peasants still gained the greatest share of the profits.
   (d) Major projects such as irrigation systems and dams were too big to undertake. The community still had no welfare programme.
   In each case, show how the community dealt with these problems, and with what effect.
3 How much opposition was there to these changes, and how was it overcome?

2 Industry

There was little industry in China in 1949. The owners of industry, the capitalist or bourgeois class, was therefore quite small in number. Even so, they were influential and had given their support to the Kuomintang. One of Mao's priorities was to destroy this class and bring industry under communist control.

Kuomintang property was seized and key industries such as steel, coal, electricity, railways and banking were nationalised. For those who were willing to support the revolution, some compensation was given. However, it was assumed that the capitalist class would oppose the communists, and steps were taken eliminate it. In 1951 there was a 'reign of terror' in which 800 000 people were shot, jailed, or sent to labour camps. Two campaigns, the San Fan and the Wu Fan, sought to uproot corruption within the party and 'cheating' by capitalists. By 1953, 450 000 capitalist enterprises had been investigated by popular courts, and 340 000 of them were forced to confess and repent.

San Fan and Wu Fan mean, literally, 'three-anti' and 'five-anti'.

To develop industry Mao launched a five-year plan in 1952. The plan involved agriculture too, but the main emphasis was steel, chemicals and cement. By 1957 there had been considerable improvement, but industry was still backward in comparison with Western powers. Mao's answer was the second five-year plan, known as the 'Great Leap Forward'.

At the Supreme State Conference Mao launched his programme:

Now our enthusiasm has been aroused. Our nation is like an atom. When this atom's nucleus is smashed the thermal energy released will have really tremendous power. We shall be able to do things we could not do before. When our nation has this great energy we shall catch up with Britain in fifteen years; we shall produce forty million tons of steel annually – now we produce only five million tons; we shall have a generating capacity of 450 000 million kwh of electricity – at present we can only generate 40 000 kwh.

It is possible to catch up with Britain in fifteen years. We must summon our strength and swim vigorously upstream.

Foundry co-operative in Yunan

These were the particular objectives of the Great Leap Forward:
1 To consolidate and further develop socialist ownership.
2 To carry out a technical revolution.
3 To develop industry and agriculture together, but giving priority to heavy industry.
4 To develop the industrial cities.
5 To improve the transport and communications network.
6 To wipe out illiteracy.
7 To promote culture, education, and health.

As far as the ordinary people were concerned the Great Leap Forward meant higher targets for whatever they produced. Industry as a whole was expected to increase its output by 30 per cent each year. Steel was expected to double its output each year.

Albert Belhomme, an American who had defected to China during the Korean war, remembered the effects of these targets on the paper mill where he worked.

We worked day and night for a week in our shop to build seven 64 kilowatt generators. But our generators needed more power than the city could provide, so they got hold of a Polish-made 300 hp diesel engine to run seven generators. Well, the engine ate up too much oil under the strain, and the bearings wore out.

When the big production push started, the party cadres said we could increase output by speeding up the conveyor belt. They cranked up the machine to 120 per minute. No vibrations. 150. No noise. Why not try 200? Up it went. Then the machine started rattling and shaking – even the building was rocking – that was it. We had to stop the machine to order a new belt every week. The machine was idle while we waited and production dropped.

The greatest emphasis was placed on steel production. Belhomme recalls the effect of this campaign:

We were told at a meeting in our factory in September 1958 that a country without steel was like a man without bones. So, to become strong, we must produce more steel. With that, we were ordered to build small ovens in which we could make iron that could be sent to bigger plants to be refined into steel.

This not only meant that we had to cut back on paper at our mill, but as far as I could see, it put a strain on the whole economy. Trains, trucks, and even hand-drawn carts were diverted to transporting bricks, coal, and iron ore for the campaign. My wife and other women were given the task of cracking coal and ore with a cast iron hammer, working twelve hours a day. About five hundred peasants were brought into our factory to help handle the furnaces. Many burned themselves badly. Besides, they should have been repairing dykes and irrigation ditches out in the country.

There are two different views of the Great Leap Forward. One view sees it as a disastrous failure. Some of the reasons for that have already been seen in Belhomme's account. On a broader scale of criticism, it is true that much of the steel produced in backyard furnaces was useless. Critics have also said that Chinese industry was not ready for this pace of industrialisation – it did not have the necessary infrastructure.

Building an airport, Chinese style

The other view sees the long-term benefits of the Great Leap Forward. China was not suited to Western-style industrialisation with an emphasis on machines and large-scale factory production. China's great strength lay in its large population, so it was better to industrialise in small-scale units, through the workshop rather than the factory. Another benefit was the massive projects of irrigation and conservation which involved 100 million peasants. This was to have important effects on agriculture. The scheme to irrigate Hunan province was so vast that collectives joined together to form the type of commune described by Feng Chang-yeh (see pages 298–300).

Mao was impressed by this type of organisation and he encouraged communes in other areas. Communes were not only agricultural units. They were also concerned with industry, welfare projects such as hospitals and education, and eventually community living. Private property and family life had given way to shared society where people ate in communal dining rooms, and lived in communal dormitories. In the Western world the commune was at first greeted with horror, but some China-watchers now accept that many communes have worked well to serve China's particular needs.

For Mao, the commune was also an ideal which aimed to

abolish exploitation of man by man, and to build a classless society in which the difference between city and countryside, between mental and manual work, will disappear, and the idea of 'from each according to his ability, to each according to his needs', will become the order of the day.

Questions

1 (a) Explain developments in industry from 1949–57.
(b) Why did Mao launch the Great Leap Forward, and to what extent did it succeed?

2 Study the following statistics:

Output of pig iron, crude steel, and finished steel in China, 1949–65
(Million tons)

Year	pig iron	crude steel	finished steel
1949	0.252	0.158	0.123
1952	1.929	1.349	1.110
1957	5.936	5.350	4.290
1960	27.50	18.67	11.30
1962	8.80	8.0	6.0
1965	13.80	12.5	9.4

What do the statistics show about the development of the iron and steel industry in China? In what ways are these figures misleading?

Which brand of communism?

The purges of 1949–51 (see page 298) were intended to get rid of opposition groups such as Kuomintang supporters, landlords, and industrialists. After these purges a programme of 'thought reform' was followed to win people to Mao's brand of communism.

Mao believed in an ideal form of communism, and saw that this could only come about if he used his power in the same way that Stalin had done in the USSR (see page 142). Some communists criticised him because they thought that he was going too far too fast, or because they resented his great personal power. These criticisms came from home, and from abroad.

1 The quarrel with the USSR

At first relations between communist China and the USSR were very close. When Stalin died in 1953 Mao paid tribute to him:

The reason why the friendship between the great peoples of China and the Soviet Union is unbreakable is that our friendship is built on the great principles of internationalism of Marx, Engels, Lenin and Stalin.

Mao would have hoped that this friendship, and with it technical and financial aid from the USSR, could continue. However, Mao was shocked when Stalin's successor, Khrushchev, attacked Stalin's purges in his 'secret speech' (see page 193). Mao rose to Stalin's defence by attacking Khrushchev:

In what position does Khrushchev, who participated in the leadership of the party and the state during the Stalinist period, place himself when he beats his breast, pounds the table, and shouts abuse at Stalin at the top of his voice? In the position of an accomplice to a 'murderer' or a 'bandit'? Or in the same position as a 'fool' or an 'idiot'?

From this moment relationships steadily worsened as the USSR moved towards a more moderate brand of communism. In 1959 this was to have damaging effects on the development of China. An historian has commented on the reason for the split:

Khrushchev was on the warpath. In December 1959 he decried the arrogance of certain Chinese leaders, the 'Trotskyism' of the communes 'due to one man's influence.'

At a meeting of Warsaw Pact nations in February Khrushchev announced that nuclear know-how from the USSR would 'not be put in the hands of madmen'.

In July the Soviet Party served notice that within one month the 1390 experts in China would withdraw, and suspend 343 contracts, and 257 projects. At the same time the USSR refused, for the next eighteen months, to supply any spare parts for equipment. There was also a demand for payment of debts for military equipment supplied during the Korean war.

Han Suyin, *The Wind in the Tower*, 1976

Hostility between the two countries increased as a result of border disputes, and rivalry over spheres of influence. In south-east Asia for example, the USSR supported Vietnam whereas China supported Cambodia. The communist world was deeply divided, and has remained so since 1960.

Communism can vary in degree. At one extreme it might be world communism with everything shared equally. At the other it might be limited to one state and allow some personal wealth.

The frontier between the USSR and China has been the cause of disputes such as the clash between the troops of both sides in 1969.

When Kampuchea (formerly Cambodia) was invaded by Vietnamese in 1978, China led a counter-attack, suffering 20 000 casualties.

According to the Anglo–Chinese Education Institute – 'Chinese frontier guards reason with the Soviet revisionist frontier troops who intrude into China's Chenpao Island area. Having a guilty conscience and an unjust cause, the Soviets put their armoured cars in reverse. However, a little big shot keeps arguing.'

2 The ideological struggle inside China

The struggle over ideology has been a constant feature of life in China since the revolution of 1949. In the early years Mao was carried along by the success of his campaign against the Kuomintang. By 1956 he had realised that many people were unhappy with his policies for the development of China. Mao's answer was to launch a campaign under the slogan 'Let a hundred flowers blossom, and let a hundred schools of thought contend'. The idea was to encourage discussion, win arguments, and by so doing bring the Chinese people loyally behind him. At the same time the campaign was supposed to stop a build-up of bad feeling of the sort that led to the 1956 rising in Hungary. Mao must have been shocked by the extent of bitterness of the criticism that arose. Immediately he clamped down again, and purged the party of anyone who had criticised him.

The Great Leap Forward was another attempt to prove his policies. When, by the end of 1958, that too was seen to fail, Mao was forced to resign as head of state. He remained as chairman of the Communist Party. However his reputation was damaged by low industrial growth, poor harvests and famine, the dispute with the USSR, and growing discontent within the party.

Mao was replaced by 'revisionists' such as Chou En-lai, who began a change of course. Communes were broken up, incentives were given for higher production, and the new emphasis was on light industry and more consumer goods.

Revisionists are those who want a more moderate form of communism. Maoists use the term as an insult.

The Cultural Revolution

In 1965 Mao struck back. His campaign began with an article written by his wife Chiang Ching which criticised an anti-Maoist play. The main newspapers were controlled by the revisionists, but Lin Pao, Marshal of the People's Liberation Army, published the article in the army newspaper. This created an upsurge of support for Mao. On 16 July 1966 he gave a signal that he was ready for a comeback. At 73 years of age, he took a nine-mile swim in the Yangtze river. Having shown his fitness and stamina, he called on the youth of China to help him restore true communism.

Mao had already began to recruit support amongst the young. Having won the People's Liberation Army to his side, he had urged army units to send cadres into the schools and colleges to appeal to the students. As soon as Mao's call came, they formed themselves into units of the Red Guard – the first was at Tsinghua, but within weeks millions of young people in every city had joined.

This was the start of the Cultural Revolution, Mao's campaign to purge China of revisionists. His instructions to the Red Guard were:

STRUGGLE against party authorities!
CRITICISE reactionary ideas!
TRANSFORM China's culture!
It is justified to rebel against reactionaries. I offer you my warm support. While supporting you, at the same time we ask you to pay attention to uniting with all persons that can be united with. As for those who have made serious mistakes, after their mistakes have been pointed out, they too should be given work and a way out for correcting their mistakes and becoming new men.

There were several types of 'mistakes'. Those who had criticised Mao were forced to confess in front of jeering crowds. Anyone who showed signs of 'westernisation' (e.g. lipstick), or 'bourgeois ways' (e.g. ownership of personal possessions) was treated in the same way. Confessions of reactionaries, and pure thoughts of Maoists, appeared on giant posters (*tatzepao*) which littered every wall. In every school and

factory workers struggled, criticised, and transformed, forcing China to change from below. The party had little choice but to follow and issued the Sixteen Articles in support of the campaign.

The Cultural Revolution met with some fierce oppostion. One example of this was the Wuhan mutiny. Wuhan is a province of 2.5 million people. There the Red Guard was opposed by an organisation called 'The Million Heroes' backed by the army. Fierce fighting took place from April to June before a truce was negotiated. China-watchers in Hong Kong, unable to find out what was going on, saw some clues to the extent of resistance to the Red Guard:

A number of bodies were washed up on the beaches. They were bound hand and foot in what is known as the great binding of five flowers, that is by means of a rope tying the feet, the wrists and the neck successively, and indicating that they were not victims of random violence, but had been methodically put to death in mass execution.

S.Leys, *The Chairman's New Clothes*, 1981

In 1966 and 1967 the Cultural Revolution was at its height. It appeared at this time that Mao could do no wrong, and people (especially the young) flocked to see him. Mao was raised almost to the status of a god, and his 'Little Red Book' was the Chinese people's bible. A popular song was entitled 'Last Night I dreamed of Chairman Mao'. Newspapers carried this sort of article:

China's victory in the World Table Tennis Championship was the result of holding high the great red banner of Mao Tse-tung's thought. The players have set an excellent example of how to study and creatively apply Mao's thought in all fields of activity.

Peking People's Daily

All those things which conform to the thought of Mao Tse-tung are correct, and we must believe in them and support and approve of them. All those things which do not conform with the thoughts of Mao Tse-tung are wrong, and despite anything that anybody, be he a so called 'master' or 'authority', may say or do, we must not believe them but must expose, criticise and oppose them.

China Youth Daily

How many died? It is impossible to say, and any statement such as the *Guinness Book of Records'* greatest massacre – which quotes a Soviet estimate of 26.3 million for 1949–65 – must be treated with great caution.

Mao wall poster

Here is a description by some young Chinese people of an audience given to them by Chairman Mao:

Oceans will dry up, rocks will turn to liquid before our red heart, loyal to Chairman Mao, will ever change. The earth may tremble, the mountains may move, but our will will never shake. The love of our father and our mother is not as deep as the love for Chairman Mao!

The happiest moment we will never forget for the rest of our lives has arrived! The east is red, the sun comes out! Our great teacher, great leader, great commander-in-chief, great helmsman Chairman Mao, his face rosy and radiant, his body sturdy, comes forward with resolute step and takes his place on the platform. At this moment enthusiastic shouts form like a tidal wave, thousands and tens of thousands of red hearts turn towards the red sun.

O supremely beloved Chairman Mao, ten thousand songs of praise would not be enough to sing of the boundless love which revolutionary fighting men feel for you. Ten thousand red pens could never finish describing the boundless trust which these revolutionary combatants put in you . . .

By 1968 Mao judged that the Cultural Revolution had gone far enough. The Red Guard was demoted, and in 1969 the work of the Cultural Revolution was embodied in a new constitution: to make sure that the revolution would never again go stale, the party was made subject to the views of the masses. Mao ordered further small-scale purges in 1969 and 1970, and in 1971 survived an attempted coup led by Lin Pao. Lin was killed in a plane crash while escaping to Russia. With all this behind him, Mao and his brand of communism seemed secure – an unrivalled leader at the head of what had now become a superpower.

In fact the picture was not that simple: the Cultural Revolution had wrecked the economy; China was regarded with hostility by both the USA and the USSR; and Mao was both old and exhausted – party members were no longer fighting Mao, but they were fighting to decide who should follow him.

In the light of these failings it is easier to understand the turnabout in China's policies since the 1960s. Even before Mao's death, moderates such as Chou En-lai were taking control. This brought about an improvement of relations with the USA. After years of mutual hostility, a trading agreement was made in 1969. In 1971 a US table tennis team and secretary of state Henry Kissinger visited China. This was followed in 1972 by the visit of President Nixon. Admission to the UN in 1971, and contact with other Western countries including Britain gave China international recognition. China's domestic policies also changed. Having restored order after the Cultural Revolution, Chou En-lai and Hua Kuo-feng introduced a major new campaign. This included the 'four modernisations' in agriculture, defence, science and technology. Trade with the West was vital to the success of this programme, but it also depended on boosting production by returning to the incentives and consumer goods so despised by Mao.

When Chou died in January 1976, and Mao died in the following September, the battle for the succession became more intense. Hua

Kuo-feng and Deng Hsiao-ping (discredited for his moderate policies under Mao) took command. Their main opponents, led by Mao's wife Chiang Ching, were publicly tried and expelled from the party.

Deng has continued the programme of modernisation into the 1980s. The communes are being broken up, and foreign trade and the availability of consumer goods continue to rise. Mao's memory is treated with respect, but he is no longer worshipped.

Yet it must be remembered that Mao used the youth of China to fight for an extreme brand of communism. There were many pro-Mao demonstrations at his death, and there are signs that his influence is still strong amongst young Chinese. In November 1985 students were taking to the streets again in protest at the growing influence of Japan inside China. The story continues.

Questions

1 Explain how Mao's brand of communism differed from that of the revisionists.
2 Why, and with what consequences, did relations between China and the USSR deteriorate?
3 Why, and with what success, did Mao launch the following campaigns:
   (a) 'Let a hundred flowers blossom'?
   (b) The 'Cultural Revolution'?
3 How far has China moved away from Mao's brand of communism since his death?

Left: Signs of development in China

Far from the backyard furnaces – the control room of the Shanghai steel plant

21 India: the independence struggle and beyond

The British in India

In the early part of the nineteenth century India was controlled by the British East India Company. From 1857 rule passed directly into the hands of the British government at Westminster. There was a minister responsible for India in the Cabinet. Orders were sent to the viceroy in India, who carried them out with the help of the Indian civil service and the army. Almost all the civil servants were British. All army officers were British.

The situation was explained by Lord Kitchener in these terms:

It is the consciousness of the inherent superiority of the European which has won for us India. However well educated and clever a native may be, and however brave he may have proved himself, I believe that no rank we can bestow on him would cause him to be considered the equal of a British Officer.

This idea of racial superiority and the 'prestige' of the white man in India was widespread:

The average British official in India is always thinking of his 'prestige'. His 'prestige' must be maintained whatever else happens. His idea of prestige is that he must lord it over the people, treat them as 'inferiors', never descend to their level.

One cannot but wish that all officials of this kind, for their own good, could know what people think of their habits, their liquor drinking, their exclusive gymkhanas and clubs, their eagerness for hunting, 'pig-sticking' and killing of animals for the brutal fun of killing, their cynical disregard for the feelings of the people, their haughty and arrogant spirit manifested in everything. One wonders why they cannot see that these things, instead of giving them prestige, are all the while operating to destroy their prestige and to make the Indian people hate everything British.

(From an Indian weekly newspaper, March 1924)

The palanquin – a traditional form of transport, adopted by British colonials in India

Such feelings as these about the British added to the growing Indian nationalism which was common at the start of this century. In the first part of the nineteenth century India was seen in Britain as a most valued imperial prossession. A hundred years later, Indian nationalists may well have asked, why are the British still here now? Here is one of the answers which they might have received:

As long as we rule India we are the greatest power in the world. If we lose it, we shall drop straight away to a third rate power.

Lord Curzon, Viceroy of India, 1898–1905

We did not conquer England for the benefit of the Indians. I know it is said at missionary meetings that we conquered India to raise the level of the Indians. That is cant. We conquered India as an outlet for the goods of Great Britain. We conquered India by the sword, and by the sword we hold it.

Sir William Joynson-Hicks, Home Secretary, 1928

Other reasons may have been offered, but increasingly the motives and methods of British rule were under criticism:

British justice is asserted as the strongest justification for British rule in India. But this claim of justice receives repeated shocks from the numerous instances of assaults and murders of Indians and violations of Indian women, which either receive no punishment at all or else punishment so light as to be hardly better than a farce.

Mr A. C. Mozumdar, *Indian World*, 1909

We went into India to exploit her wealth. We succeeded to the extent of impoverishing her – making her starved, unhappy, uneducated. We have sucked the blood from her veins and scored the flesh from her bones. The state of India is a crime . . . how long are we going allow this crime to remain on the conscience of Great Britain?

New Statesman, 7 November 1919   *British get-together, Lahore, 1913*

It is certain that the condition of the peasantry, the backbone of India, is year by year weakening. Not only are the government land revenue demands exacting and oppressive, but the proportion of land owned by landlords and moneylenders tends steadily to increase.

Sir Bernard Haughton MP, 1927

There are numerable instances in which pedestrians have been abused and struck because they have not lowered their umbrellas at the sight of an Englishman on the highway. It is a common outrage to assault respectable residents of the country because when passing on a road they have not dismounted from their horses as a token of inferiority. There are few Indian gentlemen, even of the highest rank, who have not had experiences of gross insult when travelling by railway because Englishmen refuse to sit in the same carriage as a native.

Sir Henry Cotton, *New Indian*

For those who said the Britain had brought commerce, industry, railway, telegraph and other aspects of modernisation, it could be argued that they were brought to India by and for the British, and the only Indians that benefited were the rich town dwellers. The Indian leader Mahatma Gandhi commented:

Mohandâs Gandhi, 1869–1948. Born in India, educated in Law in London, campaigned for civil rights for Indians, first in South Africa and then in India.

Little do they know how the semi-starved masses of India are slowly sinking to lifelessness. . . . Little do they realise that the government established by law in British India is carried on for this exploitation of the masses. . . . No jugglery in figures can explain away the evidence that the skeletons in many villages present to the naked eye. I have no doubt whatsoever that both the English and the town dweller of India will have to answer, if there is a God above, for this crime against humanity which is perhaps unequalled in history.

A further justification of British rule was that many countries had been raised from backwardness to a stage where they were given independence under democratic governments. One example was the Dominion of Canada. Indian politicians looked on these countries with admiration.

Nowhere in the world can be found governments that are more free or better serve their people's many-sided interests and wants than those of the self-ruling colonies or 'dominions' of Great Britain.'

Jabez and Sunderland, *India in Bondage*, 1932

However, India was not considered ready for dominion status, and remained a subject nation.

Questions

1 How did the British maintain a grip on the government of India?
2 What arguments can be found in the documents to justify the British hold on India?
3 What aspects of British rule were particularly resented by the Indian people?

Indian get-together, grinding corn, Mount Abu

Indian nationalism

Despite all that has been said in criticism of British rule in India, early demands of the Indian nationalists were surprisingly modest – for example, a representative system of government, free competition for recruitment to the Indian civil service, and lower taxation. None of this was revolutionary. Furthermore, when the First World War began, India proved a loyal ally, and an unprecedented number of Indian troops went to fight abroad for the empire.

There were two main nationalist camps with fundamentally different demands.

1 The Indian Congress Movement

This movement represented the majority Hindu view on the future of India and made a statement of demands:

Congress was originally a Hindu organisation set up to campaign for a legislative assembly for India.

First: the fusion into one national whole of all the different elements that constitute the population of India.
Second: the gradual regeneration along all lines, mental, moral, social and political, of the nation.
Third: The consolidation of the union between England and India by securing the modification of such of its conditions as may be unjust or injurious to the latter country.

2 The Muslim League

This group represented the minority view. Here their spokesman is Sir Syed Ahmed Khan:

I do not understand what the words 'National Congress' mean. Is it supposed that the different castes and creeds living in India belong to one nation, and their aims and aspirations be one and the same? I think it is quite impossible, and when it is impossible there can be no such thing as a national congress.

I object to every congress which regards India as one nation.

In December 1916 Congress and the Muslim League met at the same time in Lucknow. They put aside their differences and signed the Lucknow Pact which called for dominion status and an elected government. Muslim fears were calmed by the promise of a satisfactory minimum number of seats.

1919: Nationalist demands and the British response

India may well have expected some reward for her war service in the peace treaty of 1919. The growing nationalism of Asian countries and the spirit of Wilson's Fourteen Points (see page 34) added to the feeling that India was ready for the freedom of dominion status within the British Empire.

The answer given to Congress and the Muslim League in 1919 was hardly satisfactory. Here, it is summed up by Sir Verney Lovett:

Mahatma Gandhi, seen here at Number 10, November 1931

Britain is pledged to establish a democratic system of government in India. The great majority of the Indian people are extremely ignorant and unused to any form of political ambition. Britain does not mean to restore British India to the descendants of chiefs and kings whom she succeeded. She does not propose to set up parliaments which merely represent limited classes. Such parliaments would crumble as they ceased to receive constant British support. Her aim is to hand over eventually the direction of domestic affairs to parliaments representative of all classes. If this goal be eventually reached, a great service will have been rendered to humanity. But many and great difficulties lie in the way.

Sir Verney Lovett, *A History of the Indian Nationalist Movement*, 1920

The rejection of the Indian nationalists' demands, and the limited promises which were received instead, may well have been sufficient to provoke disorder. However, they were combined with demobilisation problems, an influenza epidemic, and food shortages. To help maintain control in this disturbed atmosphere, the Rowlatt Acts were passed giving the British new powers of arrest and imprisonment. These also caused great discontent.

The form of opposition followed the remarkable policy of the leader of the nationalist movement, Mahatma Gandhi.

Here is British foreign secretary Lord Reading's view of the unusual leader:

He is a religious enthusiast who believes he can regenerate human nature. . . . He preaches – and I verily believe with all sincerity – non-violence as the most powerful weapon in the hands of man against those who, like government, exert force and violence. To give you as illustration, he was protesting against the cost of our Indian army and the taxation wrung from the people to support it. I referred to a possible invasion of Afghanistan, and I asked him how he would meet it without an army. He answered that he would go to meet them and conquer them by love. I suggested that while he was embracing them, they would strangle him, to which he replied that even if he knew that would happen he would still take the same course and that the effect upon both Indians and Afghans would be to make his views prevail in the end.

Gandhi's method of protest was the *satyagraha*, or 'firmness of truth'. The *satyagraha* was a form of non-violent protest such as strike, boycott, or other forms of non-co-opereration. This is Gandhi's own description:

Satyagraha is not physical force, does not inflict pain on an adversary; does not seek his destruction; never resorts to firearms. Satyagraha is pure soulforce. Truth is the very substance of the soul. In it burns the flame of love. Ruled by love the world goes on. In English there is a saying 'might is right'. Then there is a doctrine of survival of the fittest. Both these ideas are contradictory to Satyagraha. Deluded by modern Western civilisation, we have forgotten our ancient civilisation and worship the might of arms.

In line with the principle of *satyagraha* Gandhi called for a *hartal*, or strike on 30 March and 6 April 1919. He told his followers:

We are now in a position to be arrested at any moment. If anyone is arrested he should, without causing any difficulty, allow himself to be arrested and appear before a court. . . . No defence should be offered. If a fine is imposed with alternative of imprisonment, imprisonment should be accepted.

However, as Gandhi later acknowledged, he made a 'Himalayan miscalculation'. He failed to anticipate that non-violent protest could easily develop into violent protest, and he failed to anticipate the response of government and armed forces. True, in many areas the *hartal* was peaceful. Elsewhere there was rioting and violence, and in Ahmedabad buildings were burned and the railway lines were torn up.

The Amritsar massacre

At Amritsar the *hartal* had been peaceful, but there were further marches and demonstrations. Some protesters were shot and in retaliation buildings were set on fire, five Englishmen were murdered, and a woman assaulted. Fearing that the problem would get worse, on 13 April Brigadier-General Dyer issued a proclamation banning any public meeting. On that same day, a religious festival, a large crowd assembled in Jallianwala Bagh at Amritsar. Dyer entered the Bagh with troops, and proceeded to fire on the meeting, using 1600 rounds of ammunition. Four hundred people lay dead and another thousand were wounded. Dyer was charged, found guilty by a special commission, and relieved of his command. Here are some views of the tragedy, and its aftermath:

A FRANKENSTEIN OF THE EAST.
GANDHI. "REMEMBER—NO VIOLENCE; JUST DISOBEDIENCE."
GENIE. "AND WHAT IF I DISOBEY *YOU*?"

Explain the Punch cartoonist's idea

Gandhi on his release from one of several prison sentences imposed by the British

General Dyer, the hero of the affair, who actually claimed praise for the deed on the grounds that by it he had 'saved' India, attempted to justify what he had done by the plea that he had forbidden the gathering. It turned out that his proclamation had not been circulated and that large numbers of those present were from the country, having come for a religious festival.

The gathering had passed practically unanimous resolutions condemning the riots and destruction of property. That the object of Dyer in ordering the shooting was not to disperse the crowd, but to vent this anger and 'to teach a lesson that he would never forget' was proven by the facts:

1 That on entering the enclosure he did not order the crowd to disperse, but began shooting at once.
2 That he did not stop firing when the crowd tried to get away.
3 That he did all he could to prevent the people escaping by directing the heaviest fire at the only places of exit until those places were piled high and blocked with dead and dying.

General Dyer confessed that he could doubtless have dispersed the crowd without firing at all; but he said, they 'probably would have come back and laughed at him.'

Jabez and Sunderland, India in Bondage, 1932

Edwin Montagu, Secretary of State for India, had observed that 'Amritsar was a disaster'. But the House of Lords thought otherwise and approved of Dyer's conduct – a sword of honour was presented to him by a group of his admirers and he was presented with a purse of £30 000 raised by public subscription, in response to an appeal by the *Morning Post*.

C. Kumar and M. Puri, Mahatma Gandhi, 1982

Gandhi gave his view in a letter to the viceroy, dated 1 August 1920:

No doubt the mob excesses were unpardonable. Incendiarism, the murder of five innocent Englishmen, and the dastardly assault on Miss Sherwood were most deplorable and uncalled for, but the measures taken by General Dyer and other officers were out of all proportion to the crime of the people and amounted to wanton cruelty and inhumanity almost unparalleled in modern times.

Your excellency's light-hearted treatment of the official crime, the shameful ignorance of events and the callous disregard of the feelings of the Indians betrayed by the House of Lords, have filled me with the gravest misgivings regarding future of the Empire.

When a government takes up arms against its unarmed subjects, then it has forfeited its right to govern.

For eight days after the massacre, all the people living in the street where Miss Sherwood was assaulted, and all those having occasion to pass through the street, were compelled to crawl – and not on their hands and feet, but actually on their bellies, and if they attempted, as some did, to go 'on all fours' they were struck on their backs with the butts of soldiers' guns and compelled to crawl flat on the earth like worms.

Jabez and Sunderland, India in Bondage, 1932

At all stages Indian feelings seemed to be ignored, and Gandhi moved to a policy of non-violent civil disobedience, which was adopted by

Congress. The movement had many strands, including the boycott of foreign cloth, relinquishing of titles, withdrawal of children from government schools, and a *hartal* on the day of the Prince of Wales' arrival in India. Again non-violence turned to violence. In one incident at Chauri Chaura 22 policemen were burned to death in their police station. Gandhi suspended civil disobedience, but was arrested on 10 March 1922 and charged with sedition. He pleaded guilty and was sentenced to six years imprisonment. He was, in fact, freed in February 1924.

By the end of 1922 there was relative calm. Lord Reading wrote to Lloyd George:

Fortunately there is a fine harvest as the result of a good monsoon and this will have its effect. If only we were fortunate enough to get another good monsoon this year, we should have gone a long way towards peace and tranquility in India, for the root of the trouble is undoubtedly in the poverty and misery of huge sections of the population. Then, as you know, the vast majority of people are ignorant and illiterate and easily swayed by sentiment and emotion. And yet, it always seems to be wonderful that in spite of troubles and disturbances British rule has lasted and continues notwithstanding that in a total population of 320 million in India there are less than 200 000 British, including all the military. It is a grand tribute to the British capacity for administration admist alien races and creeds.

Questions

1 In your own words, describe the differing hopes of Hindus and Muslims for independence in 1916.
2 What justification does Sir Verney Lovett give for delaying reform?
3 Why were the feelings of Indian nationalists especially bitter in 1919?
4 Sum up the philosophy of Gandhi using the description by Lord Reading and Gandhi's decsription of *satyagraha*.
5 Using the documents on the Amritsar massacre:
   (a) Devise a list of charges against Brigadier General Dyer.
   (b) How do you explain the various attitudes of people at the time towards Dyer and the massacre?
   (c) What is the attitude of Jabez and Sunderland? Should historians present their evidence in this way?
   (d) What is Lord Reading's attitude towards the continued presence of the British in India in 1922?

The 'Quit India' campaign

With Gandhi and other political leaders in prison, the British tried to win over moderate opinion by ending the Rowlatt Acts and promising reform. It was announced in 1927 that the Simon Commission would investigate the system of government in India and make recommenda-

Sir John Simon was a highly respected Liberal lawyer.

tions. Congress announced a boycott. Some of the radical members went further:

We believe that it is the inalienable right of the Indian people to have freedom and to enjoy the fruits of their toil . . . we believe also that if any government deprives a people of these rights and oppresses them, the people have a further right to alter it or abolish it. The British government in India has not only deprived the Indian people of its freedom but has founded itself on the exploitation of the masses, and has ruined India . . . We believe therefore, that India must sever the British connection and attain Purna Swaraj or Complete Independence.

J. Nehru, *An Autobiography*, 1962

Gandhi persuaded Congress to compromise: the British were given two years in which to grant dominion status to India. Failing this, in December 1929, the campaign of civil disobedience would begin again and Congress would demand complete independence.

The viceroy was willing to promise dominion status, but he would give no time scale. Therefore in 1929 civil disobedience began again – but in a unique form which captured the imagination of world. One of the grudges against the British was the state monopoly of salt manufacture. All salt was taxed. Gandhi decided that this would be his token protest in defiance of the law: he marched 241 miles to the coast, and picked up some natural sea salt. A trivial enough issue in itself, he was breaking the law, and gave himself up for arrest. One hundred thousand others followed his example and were imprisoned. There was some violence, but the majority carried out the idea of non-violent protest, so winning the sympathy of world opinion.

Under increasing pressure, the British government announced a series of round table conferences with nationalist groups. The first took place in London in November 1930, but could do little without Congress representatives. Gandhi was released and attended the second conference in 1931. All other non-violent protesters were freed, and

Civil disobedience in action – the salt burners

concessions were made on salt taxes, but there the talks broke down. The reason was Congress' demand for a united India, whereas the British wanted safeguards for Muslims and other minority groups. Non-violent non-co-operation followed, and once more Gandhi was jailed.

In 1935 Britain passed the Government of India Act. This gave the provinces of India self-government, but failed to satisfy Congress in other ways. In particular, such matters as defence remained in Britain's hands, and the minority problem was dealt with by giving Muslims a disproportionately high number of seats. Nationalist feeling increased further when, in September 1939 the viceroy declared war on Germany. Nehru expressed the view of many Indians:

Jawaharlal Nehru, educated at Cambridge, leader of the Indian Congress, nine times imprisoned, and head of state from the time of India's independence until his death in 1964.

The idea of a great country like India being treated as a chattel and her people utterly and contemptuously ignored was bitterly resented . . . one man, the Viceroy, and he a foreigner, could plunge 400 millions of human beings into a war without the slightest reference to them. There was something fundamentally wrong and rotten in a system under which the fate of millions could be decided in this way.

Congress representatives resigned in protest. Civil disobedience began again. Some Indians, led by Subhash Chandra Bose, formed the Indian Nationalist Army and fought on the side of the Japanese, who were now approaching India's border. There was violence at home too – in 1942 over 1000 deaths occurred and 100 000 were imprisoned. The British were now faced with a major new and hostile campaign – Quit India!

Many Indians were loyal to Britain in the war, and fought against the Axis powers and Japanese. However, there was some irony in the fact that they were being asked to fight for democracy by a British prime minister (Churchill) who said:

We ought to make it perfectly clear that we intend to remain rulers of India for a very long and indefinite period, and though we welcome co-operation from loyal Indians, we will have no truck with lawlessness.

The painful birth of India and Pakistan

The collapse of Japan in 1944–45 and the election of a Labour government in Britain brought the prospects for independence closer. In India, Hindu and Muslim politicians fought for power with words, while in the provinces fighting broke out between rival groups seeking control in their areas. The problem remained: Hindus wanted a united India while

The Labour prime minister, Clement Attlee, had been a member of the Simon Commission. Attlee came to power in 1945 with a promise to give India independence.

The Muslims of India will not rest content with anything less than the immediate establishment of an independent and fully sovereign state of Pakistan.

B. N. Pandey, *Select Documents*, 1979

It became increasingly obvious that the only answer was partition, but how could it be done? Lord Ismay, chief-of-staff to Lord Mountbatten, last viceroy of India, remembers the last stages of negotiation:

A new version of the plan was drafted almost daily, and at long last it took final shape. The Indian peninsula was to be partitioned into two independent sovereign states, one predominantly Hindu, to be called India, the other predominantly Muslim, to be called Pakistan. The provinces of Punjab and Bengal were also to be partitioned. Eastern Bengal and Western Punjab were to go to Pakistan, and Western Bengal and Eastern Punjab were go to India.

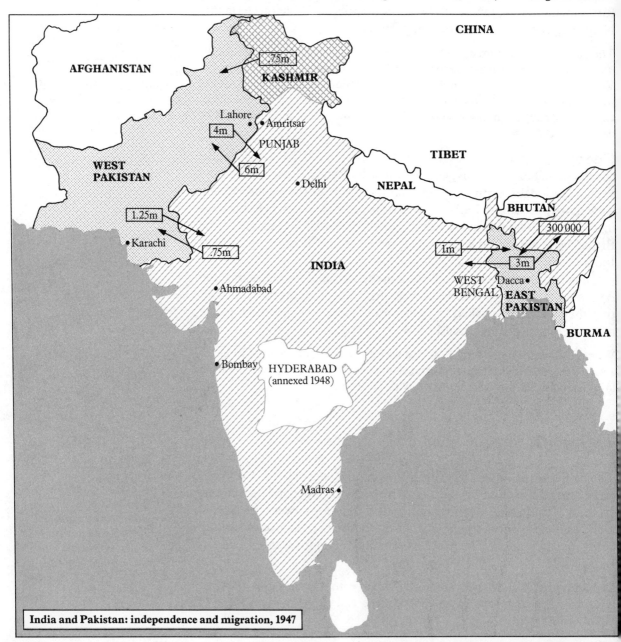

India and Pakistan: independence and migration, 1947

In explaining the principal features of the plan to the Cabinet I emphasised that it was a case of Hobson's choice. No one in India thought it was perfect. Yet nearly everyone agreed it was the only solution which had a chance of being accepted by all political parties. It was not a gamble. There was no other way.

On 15 August the new government of India took power. Jawaharlal Nehru spoke to the people of India:

Long years ago we made a tryst with destiny, and now the time comes when we shall redeem our pledge, not wholly or in full measure, but very substantially. At the stroke of the midnight hour, when the world sleeps, India will awake to life and freedom.

In Pakistan too, there was official rejoicing at the declaration of the new state.

However, rejoicing on both sides was quickly stifled by the events that followed. Thousands of Muslims and Hindus found themselves as minority groups on the wrong side of the border. Violence, which had begun before the declaration of independence, grew worse as Hindu and Sikh on one side and Muslim on the other, fought for survival.

The Sikhs belong to a Hindu warrior community founded in the sixteenth century.

The Sikhs are clearing East Punjab of Muslims, butchering hundreds daily, forcing thousands to flee westward, burning Muslim villages and homesteads.

The Sikh Jathas, armed mobs from 50 to 100 strong, assemble usually in their places of worship before making a series of raids. The Muslims are usually armed only with staves. When threatened they assemble on their roofs and beat gongs and drums to summon help from neighbouring communities, and prepare to throw stones at their attackers. The Sikhs attack scientifically.

Chelmsford Road, New Delhi. Muslim refugees hurry past the bodies of the dead and dying. September 1947

A first wave armed with firearms fires to bring the Muslims off their roofs. A second wave lobs grenades over the walls. In the ensuing confusion a third wave goes in with kirpans – the Sikh sabres, which are also religious emblems – and spears, and the serious killing begins.

Times correspondent, Ian Morrison, 24 August 1947

Janet Lane, travelling in Kashmir, remembered:

The bus from Srinagar to Rawalpindi was very empty, and until we passed Kohala the journey was normal. After Kohala we were held up several times with sticks, axes and ocasionally a gun. All passengers were made to get out, and the boys searched under the seats and among the luggage for Hindus.

The bus reached Rawalpindi station just as the train came in from Kohat. It had been shot up; many passengers had been killed. The journey as far as Lahore was uneventful, although we saw many burning villages and processions of fugitives with their cattle and goods walking along the fields.

Lahore was in chaos; as we got out of the train a man close to me was stabbed and fell.

We were put into a first class carriage and locked in. The station was even more crowded than before. Whole families of refugees with their goods and cattle were camped out on the platform. At about 9 a. m. we set off very slowly. We often passed groups of dead bodies which seemed just to have been left lying. At one place the train stopped, and the door of the next carriage opened, and an elderly Sikh was thrown out, having been stabbed, and was kicked down the embankment.

Hindu and Sikh refugees at Lahore Station, August 1947. The barbed wire is to protect them from the local Muslim community

Two-way traffic. Muslims head towards the shelter of the fort of Purana Quilla, September, 1947

In total, five million Hindus and five million Muslims crossed the borders into their 'home' state. Along the way 1.5 million were slaughtered. Perhaps the most prominent victim was Mahatma Gandhi, assassinated by a fellow Hindu who thought that he had been too kind to the Muslims.

Questions

1 Why do you think the demands of the nationalists changed from dominion status to complete independence?
2 Why did Indians fight on both sides in the Second World War?
3 What problems were created by the rivalry between Hindu and Muslim
   (a) before independence?
   (b) immediately after independence?

India and Pakistan after 1947

The partition of India did not solve the border problem. Some princely states which remained independent in 1947, such as Junagadh and Hyderabad, were only later absorbed by India. However, Kashmir remained an independent state which contained both Hindu and Muslim peoples and which was claimed by both sides. This was bound to cause conflict.

India was by far the stronger of the two countries, but Pakistan was determined to increase its armed force at all costs.

Mohammed Ali Jinnah, speaking at a rally of the All India Muslim League

TOTAL REVENUE AND DEFENCE EXPENDITURE OF PAKISTAN

Year	Revenue (million rupees)	Defence expenditure (million rupees)
1947/8	198.9	154.1
1948/9	667.6	577.6
1949/50	885.4	752.2
1950/1	1273.2	703.0
1951/2	1448.4	907.9
1952/3	1334.3	994.6
1953/4	1110.5	802.3

In 1949 Pakistan gave support to the Muslim hill people of Kashmir, while India gave support to the Hindu Maharajah. By the time later in 1949 that the United Nations arranged a ceasefire, one third of Kashmir was in Pakistan's hands, and this became the new border. However, the threat of war continued.

Liquat Ali Khan, Pakistan's prime minister, reported:

A heavy concentration (Indian armed forces is taking place in East Punjab and Kashmir. As a resul ne bulk of the Indian army is now concentrated against Pakistan's borders.

The Indian prime minister, Nehru, when asked to withdraw his forces, replied:

India's policy continues to be to preserve and ensure peace and avoid war. It is true that certain troop movements have been ordered by us for defence purposes.

Liquat responded:

The strength of India's armed forces at the time of the partition was double that of Pakistan. You have since persistently tried to increase that disparity. Pakistan has therefore, been forced to spend considerable sums on the purchase of equipment.

Tension continued, and clashes occured in 1965 in both Gujarat and Kashmir. Both the UN and the USSR were involved in mediation before the two sides returned to the original border.

In 1971 there were further border clashes, this time in East Pakistan. These clashes led to full-scale war and the defeat of Pakistan. This time there was a significant outcome: India had supported the Awami League, an independence movement in East Pakistan. Victory in the war saw the creation of a new state – East Pakistan became Free Bengal, or Bangladesh. Pakistan was now confined to a single western state.

Residents of Dacca search the ruins for survivors of fighting in the India–Pakistan war, 1971

Tension between India and Pakistan has continued into the 1980s. India, though a non-aligned state, has the backing of the USSR. Pakistan has the backing of the USA. Both are near-nuclear powers, and are continuing with their own arms race.

The economies of India and Pakistan

India, Pakistan, and Bangladesh are still countries of great poverty. Each has pursued its own course to achieve prosperity, but problems of over-population, lack of education, lack of developed industry, agricultural backwardness, and natural disaster have led to an unimpressive outcome.

India pursued a socialist road to improvement – state planning, large-scale industrialisation, and encouragement of labour-intensive industry. In agriculture the 'Green Revolution' was an attempt to make India self-sufficient in food. However, this tended to help the richer peasant at the expense of the poor.

India has made strides forward. It is now an important steel producer, and many large-scale projects have been completed, such as the damming of the River Indus. But the poverty remains.

Men and women working to create a powerhouse

Pakistan has similar problems:

After 30 years of high economic growth, only 29 per cent of the population has access to safe drinking water. The adult literacy rate is 21 per cent. Only 50 per cent of the population aged seven to nine is enrolled in primary education, only 17 per cent attend secondary school. Less than 30 per cent of the population have access to adequate health services or shelter. About 33 per cent of the population live below the poverty line, i.e. have a level of personal expenditure that fails to satisfy even their minimum needs.

Dr Rashid Amjad, 1982

Democracy and dictatorship in India and Pakistan

India boasts the largest democracy in the world. During the office of Prime Minister Nehru (1947–64) the Congress Party dominated the Indian parliament. He was succeeded by Lal Shastri, who in turn was succeeded by Nehru's daughter Indira Gandhi. Her rule saw a division in the Congress Party. Whereas the party bosses, 'the syndicate', had thought that they could control her policies, Mrs Gandhi pursued an independent socialist line. The syndicate turned against her, and in 1975 tried to bring her down with charges of corruption. The high court found her guilty and disqualified her from office for six years. Mrs Gandhi appealed against the ruling, but in the meantime, rather than surrender her power, she declared a state of emergency. Thousands of her opponents were imprisoned, and when her appeal was successful she retained her emergency powers.

In February 1977 Mrs Gandhi called for fresh elections. She was shocked to find herself defeated by the opposition Janata party. Worse was to follow, for she was then imprisoned for corruption. Nevertheless she won the election of 1979 at the head of a new Indian Congress Party. Since her assassination in 1983, India has been ruled by her son, Sanjay Gandhi. Despite the difficulties of the period of emergency, democracy in India seems to have survived.

Indira Gandhi

Dictatorship in Pakistan

Whereas India began its life under the long and stable rule of Nehru, Pakistan's early years were unsettled. Its first prime minister, Jinnah, died in 1948, and his successor Liquat Ali Khan was assassinated in 1951. Furthermore Pakistan proved to be difficult to govern. People in East Pakistan were discontented, and claimed to be under-represented. Pakistan had no common language, no trained civil service, and politicians were thought of as corrupt. In addition, there was a basic division of opinion about the nature of government. Some people wanted Pakistan to be governed by Islamic law, while others wanted the state and religion to be kept apart.

In these circumstances it proved difficult to agree to a constitution which would be acceptable to all. The first constitution was not confirmed until 1956 (and this was changed in 1962, 1969 and 1973).

In 1957 the army commander, Ayub Khan, seized power. Effectively his rule was a dictatorship. Khan justified this by saying that he would rule until Pakistan was ready for democracy. In the meantime he introduced 'basic democracy'. People voted for local councillors, who voted for district, then regional, then provincial, then national councillors. Other important officials were appointed, and Ayub Khan was able to control the decisions of the Cabinet made up from these councillors and appointed officials. At first opposition parties were banned. However, elections were allowed in 1965 and Ayub Khan was victorious.

Several problems faced the newly government: continued economic weakness; opposition from the Awami League in East Pakistan; and continued corruption in government. Unable to tackle these problems, Ayub Khan was forced to resign. His successor, Yahya Khan, resigned after Pakistan's defeat in the war with India. In 1971 Zulfikar Ali Bhutto was elected president. He undermined democracy in Pakistan by use of a federal security force which suppressed critics and opposition parties. Elections were held in 1977 but there was widespread opinion that the results, a landslide victory for Bhutto, were faked. Soon afterwards, Bhutto was overthrown by an army coup led by General Muhammed Zia. Bhutto was charged with several offences, including conspiracy to murder, was found guilty, and hanged in April 1979.

Since that time elections have been suspended, although it has been promised that democracy will return once Pakistan has achieved a sound political and economic position.

Bangladesh also moved from democracy to dictatorship. Awami League leader, Sheikh Mujibur Rahman, won the election of 1973 but in an atmosphere of lawlessness he declared a state of emergency, and became dictator – all other political parties were banned.

The Sheikh and his family were assassinated in 1975 in the first of a series of coups. Stability was achieved, and elections restored, by General Zia ul-Rahman in 1978.

Despair in flood-ridden Bangladesh, 1974

US policy in Asia

The victory of communism in China was a blow to the USA. Despite aid worth $2 billion, the nationalist forces of Chiang Kai-shek had been driven from the mainland to their last refuge, the island of Formosa (Taiwan).

The US government state its new policy in the China White Paper of 1950. This recognised that Taiwan too was likely to fall to the communists, and that nothing more should be done to protect Chiang. An American presence would be maintained in Asia, but in Japan and the Philippines, and not China. For the time being, the USA would give Taiwan diplomatic support, but it was anticipated that in due course communist China must be given official recognition.

The White Paper proposals did not come to pass. At this crucial moment the plan was upset by the unexpected invasion of South Korea by its northern neighbours.

North and South Korea

During the Second World War Korea had been occupied by Japan. At the end of the war Korea was divided into two sectors – the North controlled by Russia, and the South by America. The plan for Korea was that both powers should leave their areas of influence, and that the United Nations should organise elections for the government of a united Korea. However, the plan broke down. In the north the Russians had supported a communist government led by Kim Il Sung. In the south the Americans had supported the setting up of a right-wing republic under Dr Syngman Rhee. Both sides wanted to control all of Korea, but neither side would trust an election. Therefore, from the time when the Russians left in 1948 until June 1950, there were two hostile Koreas.

Then, on 22 June 1950, a full-scale invasion was launched by North Korea. American Secretary of State John Foster Dulles, summed up the US attitude:

> It is possible that the South Koreans may themselves contain and repulse attack, and if so this is the best way. If, however, it appears they cannot do so, then we believe that US forces should be used even though this risks Russian counter-moves. To sit by while Korea is overrun by unprovoked armed attack would start a disastrous chain of events probably leading to world war.

With the North Koreans rapidly overrunning South Korea, President Truman saw the need for immediate action. He ordered the US Seventh Fleet into Formosa Strait, he ordered General MacArthur to land a force to help South Korea, and he appealed to the United Nations to support his action. Reactions to these moves were divided. On the one hand the Chinese condemned the USA for 'aggression against the territory of China' and a further act of intervention by American

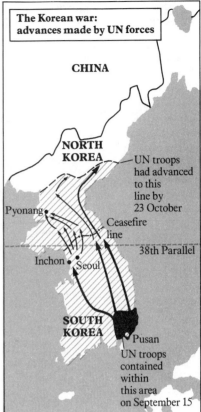

imperialism in the affairs of Asia. On the other hand, the United Nations Security Council urged all members to support the USA. This may seem surprising, but remember that communist China was not a member of the UN, and the USSR was boycotting UN meetings until China was admitted.

The force which landed in South Korea to aid Syngman Rhee was therefore a UN force in name, but in fact it was mainly American, and was commanded by US General MacArthur.

By the time that UN forces arrived, the South Koreans had been driven back to the 'Pusan box' in south-east Korea. However, the North Korean supply lines were stretched and by mounting a daring operation MacArthur was able to cut right through them. He used sea and air forces to land troops at Inchon, far behind the enemy lines. From there his forces were able to advance rapidly, and he 'rolled the iron curtain back' to the 38th Parallel.

MacArthur now used the excuse that there was not yet a united Korea, and in November 1950 advanced into North Korea itself. The UN agreed, but ordered him not to cross the borders of either China or Russia. If the UN wished to avoid further confrontation, they failed. China was not willing to allow the invasion of its ally, and after giving MacArthur two warnings, they struck: 300 000 Chinese troops crossed into North Korea and began to push the US troops back. What had

Left: Outpost 13. US troops guard the 38th Parallel

The Middlesex Regiment goes into action, Korea, 1951

US soldiers guarding strategic points, Korea, 1951

started as a dispute within a divided country was now becoming close to a third world war. Worse still, for the first time since Nagasaki it seemed possible that an atom bomb would be used. This was revealed in a confused press conference given by President Truman on 30 November 1950. The first question was whether it would require a United Nations decision to order an attack on China:

Truman: Yes entirely.

Press: In other words, if the UN resolution should authorise General MacArthur to go further than he has, he will . . .

Truman: (interrupting) We will take whatever steps are necessary to met the military situation.

Press: Will that include the atomic bomb?

Truman: That includes every weapon we have.

Press: Does that mean there is an active consideration of the use of the atomic bomb?

Truman: There has always been consideration of its use. I don't want to see it used. It is a terrible weapon, and it should not be used on innocent men, women and children.

Press: Mr President, you said this would depend on UN action. Does that mean that we wouldn't use the bomb except on UN authorisation?

Truman: No, it doesn't mean that at all. The action against communist China depends on the action of the UN. The military commander in the field will have charge of the use of weapons, as he always has.

This statement caused a world-wide outcry. For example Clement Attlee, the prime minister of Great Britain, strongly argued against the use of the atomic bomb. His worry must have come in part from concern about General MacArthur, who had always pushed for stronger action that the American president desired. Truman, wakened by the outcry, decided to back down and avoid any confrontation over Korea. Instead he decided on a policy of 'containment' and to use

MacArthur gets a tickertape welcome from 7.5 million people, New York, April 1951

economic sanctions. However, at a time when Truman was making offers of settlement, MacArthur issued an ultimatum to China, threatening operations which would 'doom Red China to the risk of imminent military collapse'.

Truman could not tolerate this undermining of his authority, and MacArthur was recalled and removed from his post. Truman appeared on television to justify his action:

In simplest terms what we are doing in Korea is this. We are trying to prevent a third world war. . . . I believe we must try to limit the war to Korea. . . . General MacArthur did not agree with that policy.

The Americans received this with little enthusiasm. When Truman appeared at a baseball match he was booed, and Senator McCarthy stated that 'the son of a bitch should be impeached'. MacArthur, on the other hand, was given a hero's welcome.

Meanwhile the war in Korea dragged on. A Chinese offensive in 1951 was beaten back with heavy losses, and talks began to make peace. Even so, the atomic bomb question was not quite finished. When arguments about Chinese and North Korean prisoners delayed peace, the new US president, Eisenhower, threatened the use of the atomic bomb. The Chinese then agreed that prisoners who did not wish to return need not do so, and an armistice was signed.

Some post-war issues were made clear by the Korean war: that the United Nations, albeit Western-dominated, had teeth; that China was now a power to be reckoned with; that the US would fight against further communist expansion; that the bomb now added a new dimension to international relations. One implication of the war which may have been misleading was that the Americans could win a war in south-east Asia. Such a belief was soon to be smothered in the jungle of Vietnam.

Questions

1 Why did the US decide to become involved in the Korean war?
2 Draw a chart to show how the war escalated, giving the date of increased involvement, the country or countries concerned, and the reason for escalation.
3 Read Truman's press conference statement. According to Truman:
   (a) Whose decision was needed to authorise the invasion of China?
   (b) Whose decision would be needed to authorise the use of the atomic bomb?
   (c) From this conversation, who appears to wield the most power in the Korean war?
4 Why, and with what consequences, was MacArthur sacked?
5 Why did the Korean war become an international crisis, and what does it reveal about US foreign policy in the 1950s?

Vietnam

Although the Korean war was of great significance in modern world history, it has been largely eclipsed by events which took place in Vietnam.

Vietnam had been one part of French Indo-China. Since 1930 there had been communist opposition to the French, and in 1940 the League for Vietnamese Independence, or Vietminh, was founded.

At the end of the Second World War control of Vietnam was returned to France, which found itself fighting a guerilla war against the Vietminh. As in the case of Korea, other powers became involved. After 1949 the communist Chinese gave aid to the Vietminh, and the USA gave aid to the value of $3 billion to the French. Like Korea, this had become a war of ideology.

By 1954 the French realised that this war could not be won. Their key military position was at Dien Bien Phu which had been captured from the Vietminh in a determined paratroop attack. However, it was in the middle of enemy territory, and by May it was obvious that the French would soon be defeated. France decided that they should withdraw under the best possible terms.

At this time there was an international conference at Geneva to decide on the fate of Korea. A decision was made that, for the time being, Vietnam should be divided at the 17th Parallel. This would allow the two sides to disengage, and after two years elections would be held to decide on a leader for a reunited Vietnam. In the meantime the north was governed by the Vietminh leader, Ho Chi Minh, and the south by Bao Dai, and from 1955, Ngo Dinh Diem.

By 1956 it had become obvious that there would be no national election. The USA had refused to sign the Geneva settlement, and was content to support Diem's government. The only election which did take place was a referendum to decide between Diem and the ex-Emperor Bao Dai, who had served under the French. The voting was unusual. Ballot papers were printed in different colours: red (lucky) for Diem and green (unlucky) for Bao Dai. A voter remembered:

[the officials] told us to put the red ballot into the envelopes and threw the green ones into the wastebasket. A few people disobeyed. As soon as they left the agents rounded them up. They poured pepper sauce down their nostrils and forced water down their throats. They beat one of my relatives to pulp. 98.2 per cent of voters supported Diem!

Such tactics may make Diem seem less than an ideal leader – and certainly unsuitable for the role of the standard bearer of democracy. Worse still, he was very wealthy in a poor country, a catholic in a mainly Buddhist country, and he had very little time for the Vietnamese people.

Buddhism is a religion founded in India in the fifth century.

The Vietminh, which had been so successful against the French, and which had won so many friends amongst the peasantry, now continued the fight against the Diem government. They were now labelled the

Above: A lone Vietnamese ranger amongst the bodies of fallen comrades after an action against Vietcong guerillas, December 1964

Right: GIs with helicopter gunships in support

SEATO – the South-East Asia Treaty Organisation, firmly led by the USA as an anti-communist alliance.

Vietcong, and from 1960 they were allied with other groups such as the Buddhists, in the National Liberation Front. The NLF called for democracy, reform and a united Vietnam.

Despite Diem's failings, the Americans felt that they needed to support him against the communists. President Eisenhower believed that the loss of Indo-China would cause the fall of the rest of south-east Asia 'like a row of dominoes'. South Vietnam was brought into SEATO and massive aid, including a body of CIA advisers, was sent to Diem.

When, in 1960, President Kennedy was elected, he had to make a decision – should he intensify American support against the guerillas, or do as the French president, Charles de Gaulle advised – back down, and avoid being trapped in a 'bottomless military and political swamp'? Kennedy's inaugural address made his position clear:

Let every nation know, whether it wished us well or ill, that we shall pay any price, bear any burden, meet any hardship, support any friend, oppose any foe to assure the survival and the success of liberty.

In his belief that Vietnam was 'the proving ground' for democracy in Asia, Kennedy stepped up his 'advisers' to 16 000. He also introduced the 'strategic hamlets' programme: an estimated 40 per cent of the Vietnamese population was resettled within barbed wire compounds where they could be separated from the Vietcong enemy – or so it was thought.

Despite the increased commitment, by 1963 it was evident that the war was not being won. Diem was blamed, and with US encouragement he was overthrown by his generals. Three weeks later, Kennedy was assassinated. President Johnson now had the choice of what to do in Vietnam.

Johnson's views on the problem may be seen in these quotations:

If I left that war and let the communists take over south Vietnam, then I would be seen as a coward and my nation seen as an appeaser. And . . . there would follow . . . a destructive debate that would shatter my presidency, kill my administration, and damage our democracy.

I have seen the glory of art in architecture, I have seen the sun rising over Mont Blanc . . . but the most beautiful vision that the eyes ever beheld was the flag of my country in a foreign land.
(Referring to US intervention in the Dominican Republic)

Most of the communist nations of Asia cannot, by themselves and alone resist the growing might and grasping ambition of Asian communism. Our power, therefore, is a vital shield. And an Asia so threatened by communist domination would imperil the security of the US itself. Moreover, we are in Vietnam to fulfil one of the most solemn pledges of the American nation. Three Presidents over eleven years have promised to help defend this small and valiant nation. We cannot now dishonour our word.

In conversation with a *Washington Post* reporter Johnson produced three letters from the mothers of soldiers in Vietnam which said, things were going better than the stories said, that the US should stick it out and could win, that the US had better draw the line here or it wouldn't stick anywhere. After reading one emotional letter Johnson said to the critical reporter, 'Now doesn't that make you feel like a shit-ass!'

Johnson wanted to win quickly, and was ready to step up the war. He was also encouraged to go further because of two events of 1964: the Tonkin incident, when North Vietnamese torpedo boats attacked US destroyers; and the explosion of the atomic bomb by China, which seemed to call for an American show of strength. The US congress passed 'the Tonkin resolution' which gave Johnson a free hand to increase American involvement.

Early in 1965 the first two battalions of US marines arrived in Vietnam. This was to grow to a force of half a million. Johnson also ordered operation 'Rolling Thunder', the mass bombing of North Vietnam. By 1969 the US had dropped 70 tons of bombs per square mile of North Vietnam. Neither the troops nor the bombing brought Johnson his quick victory. Indeed, in 1968 the Vietcong launched their Tet offensive, a co-ordinated assault on many south Vietnamese towns and cities. Even the capital, Saigon, was captured for a few hours.

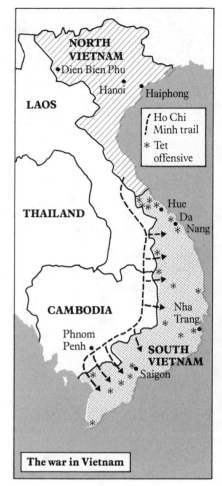

The war in Vietnam

GIs on patrol in hostile territory, 1966

Trends in support for the war in Vietnam

WAR HITS SAIGON, screamed the front page of Washington's *The News*. But newspapers paled beside television coverage, which that evening projected the episode in all its confusion, into the living rooms of 50 million Americans. There, on colour screens, dead bodies lay amid the rubble and rattle of automatic gunfire as dazed American soldiers and civilians ran back and forth trying to flush out the assailants. Audiences heard the staccato voice of a correspondent on the spot, doing his best to explain the chaotic images.

These were images which had a striking effect on popular opinion, and which would remain forever imprinted on the minds of those closely involved. For many Americans this was the last straw, and a ground-swell of opinion called for an end to the war. The death toll of US

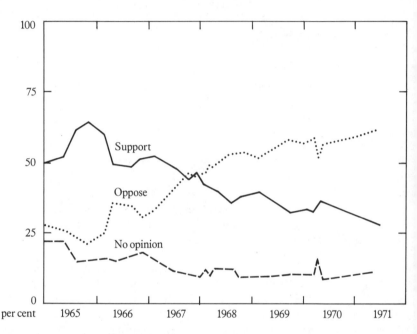

soldiers, many of them young conscripts called up at eighteen for national service, had mounted steadily:

Year	Deaths on active service
1965	1369
1966	5008
1968	14592

Criticism was widespread: 'Hey! Hey! LBJ! How many kids did you kill today!' Mass demonstrations and the lessons of the Tet offensive seemed to have demoralised Johnson, and he began to scale down the bombing and call for peace talks. Even so, his administration was broken by the problem of Vietnam, (see page 216). His successor President Nixon, paid lip-service to the idea of peace talks, but at the same time continued to step up the war. Nixon said that he would get American boys out, and 'Vietnamise' – train the south Vietnamese to defend themselves. However this was a slow (if not impossible) process, and the death toll amongst Americans remained high.

Escaping from napalm, Trang Bang 1972

Meanwhile the bombing continued, both against North Vietnam and on Vietcong supply lines in Cambodia and Laos. Christmas 1972 marked the biggest bombing raid on one place in history – the Americans dropped 100 000 bombs on Haiphong in an attempt to 'bomb them back into the stone age'.

The fall of Nixon and mistrust of the presidency arising from the Watergate affair, as well as growing anti-Vietnam war feeling, led congress to reject President Ford's request for further support. Finally, in 1975 the Americans evacuated Saigon – leaving so quickly that names and photographs of US agents were left behind.

Help! 1.5 miles from HQ is a long way

The war was over. Two million Vietnamese were dead, and four million wounded, against 58 000 and 300 000 Americans respectively. On the one hand, America was shattered by defeat. On the other, many Americans were delighted that the war was over.

Questions

1 What similarities were there between the situation in Korea and in Vietnam at the end of the Second World War?
2 Why do you think that the US became involved as the French withdrew from Vietnam?
3 How do you explain the increased commitment of the US during the years of the war?
4 Look at the sources of evidence relating to President Johnson. What are the different motives he gives for intervention on a greater scale?

The nature of the war in Vietnam

When the USA became committed in Vietnam, not only did the Americans dredge harbours, create islands as supply sanctuaries, build runways and roads, but they equipped their troops for modern war:

An American infantryman could rely on the latest hardware. He was transported to the battle scene by helicopter, and if wounded, flown out . . . His target had usually been 'softened' beforehand by air strikes and artillery bombardment. Tanks and other armoured vehicles often flanked him, and his unit carried the most up-to-date arms – mortars, machine guns, grenade and rocket launchers, and the M16, a fully automatic rifle.

Vietnam also served as a laboratory for technology so sophisticated, it made James Bond's dazzling gadgets seem obsolete – an array of ultra-sensitive devices to detect the enemy . . . and electronic instruments that could smell guerillas . . . defoliants and herbicides to destroy jungles and wipe out crops . . . and air-to-surface missile that enabled a pilot to adjust its course by scanning a screen in his cockpit . . . bombs of nearly every size, shape and explosive intensity, from blockbusters to phosphorus and napalm bombs that roasted their victims alive, cluster bombs whose hundreds of pellets burst out at high velocity to rip deep into the body of anyone within range.

Stanley Karnow, *Vietnam*, 1983

No wonder then that Philip Caputo, a young marine lieutenant, remembers his arrival and his early confidence:

When we marched into the rice paddies on that damp March afternoon we carried, along with our packs and rifles, the implicit conviction that the Vietcong would be quickly beaten.

Yet Caputo continues by saying, 'We kept the packs and rifles, the convictions we lost.'

Using the evidence: why did the USA lose the Vietnam war?

Read the documentary evidence first, then answer the following questions:

1 Explain Karnow's observation that US technology in the Vietnam war made 'James Bond's dazzling gadgets seem obsolete'.
2 Use A and B to explain Hodge's conclusion in C.
3 Use D and E and F to explain why many ordinary Vietnamese supported the Vietcong.
4 Use G, H and I to describe the conditions of war faced by an American soldier in Vietnam.
5 What do J,K,L, and M reveal about the sources of supply for each side, and how effectively those supplies were used?
6 What evidence from the sources above would you use to explain Thanh Quang's actions in N?
7 Use the documents together to summarise: Why did the USA lose the war in Vietnam?

A Diem brought to the presidency a determination quite as ruthless as that of Ho Chi Minh. Non-Diemist forces were suppressed and eliminated, their leaders imprisoned, assassinated, exiled or terrorised into silence. Land reform measures introduced by the Vietminh were reversed, village democracy was overridden, and the hopes of nationalists cruelly destroyed.

A Hassler, *Saigon, USA*, 1970

B General Huyn Han Cao, the south Vietnamese commander of the fourth corps, was a Diem loyalist who had earned promotion over more competent colleagues. He rarely saw action, preferring instead to intrigue in Saigon. Diem constantly played his subordinates off against each other, believing that he could thus prevent conspiracies against him.

Saigon, USA

C There is no possibility, in my view, that the war can be won under a Diem administration.

Henry Hodge, US ambassador to Vietnam 1963

D I myself watched an interrogation in a Mekong Delta town in the late 1950s. Soldiers had brought in a lean youth in black cotton pyjamas who looked like any peasant. The soldiers wired his fingers to a field telephone, then cranked it as an officer spoke with surprising gentleness to the youth, trying to extract either information or a confession. The youth gritted his teeth, his facial muscles taut as the electricity coursed through his body, and he finally blurted out a few words.

Ultimately though, Diem's severity probably created more enemies than it crushed. The indiscriminate offensive against former members of the Vietminh drove many back into the underground who would have preferred to live in peace.

S. Karnow, *Vietnam*, 1983

E [of US troops in action in the village of My Lai] Within My Lai the killings became more sadistic. Several old men were stabbed with bayonets, one was thrown down a well to be followed by a hand grenade. Some women and children playing outside of the local temple were killed by shooting them in the back of the head. The young were slaughtered with the same impartiality as the old. Children barely able to walk were picked off at point-blank range.

Lieutenant-Colonel George Walton, *The Tarnished Shield*, 1973

F In some areas I discovered peasants welcomed Vietcong agents and referred to them as liberators. The Vietcong benefited from the image of the Vietminh, who had distributed land to the poor and helped peasants at their labours. 'If they win' an affluent miller told me, 'I would probably be left alone. They're against the government, not the people. We have nothing to fear.'

Vietcong terrorism was usually selective, as a bus driver from Long Khanh province recounted:

'Five or six Vietcong guys stopped my bus one morning to check the identity cards of the passengers. They dragged two men off the bus and their chief said to them "We've been waiting for you. We warned you many times to leave your jobs, but you haven't obeyed, so now we must carry out the sentence."

'They forced the two men to kneel by the roadside and one of the Vietcong guys chopped off their heads with a machete. They then pinned verdicts to their shirts saying the murdered men were policemen.

Afterwards the Vietcong guys gave the passengers their ID cards saying "you'll get into trouble with the authorities without these".'

S. Karnow, *Vietnam*, 1983

G You never knew who was the enemy and who was the friend. They all looked alike. They all dressed alike. They were all Vietnamese. Some of them were Vietcong. Here's a woman of twenty-two or twenty-three. She is pregnant and she tells her interrogator that her husband works in Danang and isn't a Vietcong. But she watches your men walk down a trail and get killed or wounded by a booby-trap. She knows the booby-trap is there but she doesn't warn them. Maybe she planted it herself. The enemy was all around you.

Marine Captain E. J. Banks

Hue, once a beautiful city, destroyed in the battle for control of South Vietnam

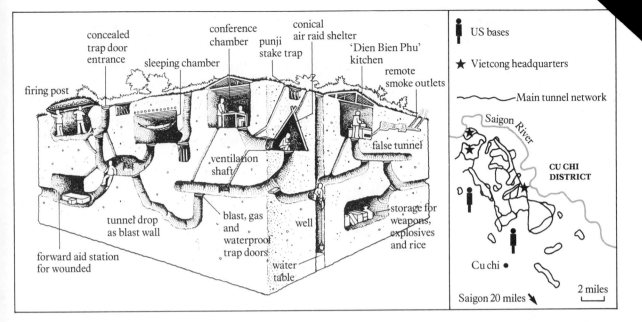

Left: a typical Vietcong tunnel system in Cu Chi showing the various layers of tunnels and the connecting trap doors. The trap doors sealed off each layer so that explosives, gas or water could not permeate. Above: the tunnels, and the positions of Americans and Vietcong troops, in 1968, as recorded by the People's Army of Vietnam.

H We stayed in the bush for three days and three nights simply because we were lost.

US soldier

I The company camped and sent patrols. There was a great explosion. I put out a radio call but there was no answer – and the Captain was joking saying it was probably just a stray artillery round. Half an hour later one of the survivors hobbled back and said 'They're gone, all gone'. We raced out there and only two men were living out of a patrol of eight or so. Just a mess. It was like stew, full of meat and flesh and red tissue and white bones.

US soldier

J On the Ho Chi Minh trail the rainy season had just started, and the route was muddy. Occasionally flash floods forced us to cling to trees and shrubs to keep from being washed away. The jungles were infested with leeches and other insects that swarmed all over us. We crossed deep rivers and streams, and there were the mountains, some so high that it was as if we were walking above the clouds.

The Americans had denuded the jungle with their bombs. Each time they flew overhead our commander ordered us to disperse and dig foxholes. My heart would throb and my whole body tremble inside as bombs exploded.

Tran Thi Truyen, a communist veteran

K The North Vietnamese needed no more than fifteen tons of supplies a day from the north in order to sustain their effort in the south. And since the Soviet Union and China were furnishing North Vietnam with nearly six thousand tons of aid daily, only a tiny fraction had to trickle down the Ho Chi Minh trail for the communists to wage war.

S. Karnow, *Vietnam*, 1983

L At times the Ho Chi Minh trail was so busy it was like the Long Island expressway during the rush hour.

An eye-witness

M To the US Ambassador

Phnom Penh, Cambodia

Dear Sir,

This year, in a matter of a few short weeks, I identified 1269 small-time dealers in stolen C rations and beer. The same people offered me 4000 sets of brand new poplin jungle fatigues, boots, whatever I wanted including guns . . .

Yours sincerely,

Cornelius Hawkridge.

N A Buddhist nun in her mid-fifties, Thanh Quang, had entered the temple compound at dawn, accompanied by a few friends. She assumed the lotus position as one friend doused her with gasoline. Then she lighted a match, immediately exploding into flame as another friend fed peppermint oil on the fire to suppress the stench of scorched flesh.

Soon Tri Quang appeared to distribute to the foreign correspondents copies of a letter that the nun had addressed to President Johnson condemning America's irresponsible support for the Saigon regime.

S. Karnow, *Vietnam*, 1983

The invasion of Afghanistan

In December 1979, for the first time, large numbers of Soviet troops invaded a country outside the Warsaw Pact. President Carter of the USA described the event as a

quantum jump in the nature of Soviet behaviour. And if they get away with relative political and economic impunity it will have serious consequences for the world in years to come.

There had been close relationships between the USSR and Afghanistan since the late 1940s. However, after Muhammad Daoud came to power by a coup in 1973, Afghanistan became friendly with Iran (then ruled by the Shah), and the pro-Soviet Left was suppressed. In 1978, Daoud was in turn removed by a communist coup led by Hafizullah Amin and Babrak Karmal. Amin seized power, sending Karmal abroad. He then pursued hard-line communist policies which aroused great opposition amongst the Islamic and tribal communities of Afghanistan. By early 1979 Amin was faced by rebellion, and only the presence of 5000 Soviet advisers saved him from early defeat. The rebellion grew in scale during 1979. At the end of the year, after repeated requests for help from Amin, the Soviet forces moved in. Amin himself was overthrown, and it was said that he had been tried and executed. Karmal formed a new government which fought with Russia against the rebels.

Neither the immediate reasons for the decision to invade, nor the long-term motives, are clear.

A The Afghan leadership repeatedly asked the Soviet Union for assistance.

Leonid Brezhnev

Soviet helicopters versus Afghan guerillas in Afghanistan. What do the photos suggest about the military nature of this war?

B The Soviet Union was forced to make a choice: we had either to bring in troops or let the Afghan revolution be defeated. We knew that the decision to bring in troops would not be popular in the modern world, even if it was absolutely legal. But we also knew that we would have ceased to be a great power if we refrained from taking unpopular but necessary decisions.

Alex Bovin, political writer, *Izvestia*

C Moscow's primary purpose was to tighten its control of that rebellious country. The tide of Islamic fervour, which had already shaken Iran, was now threatening Afghanistan. Unless it were checked, might it not also spread across the border into the Soviet Central Asian Republics and stir unrest among their substantial Islamic populations?

Time magazine, January 1980

D The Soviets have a vested interest in getting an influence in Iran. It would put them in the position to turn off the oil tap for Western consumers almost at will when the oil shortage really starts to bite later in the 1980s.

A senior British official

E The Russians were trying to stop the collapse of a Marxist–Leninist regime in a neighbouring country. They were afraid of the consequences of its fall, believing that whatever successor regime came to power would be at best uncontrollable and at worst anti-Soviet.

What of the argument that the Soviet move was motivated by expansionism, bringing the Soviet Union a step nearer to both the Persian Gulf and the Indian subcontinent? It requires only a look at the map to see the absurdity of these claims.

J. Steele, *The Limits of Soviet Power*, 1983

Questions

1 Identify the reason given for the invasion in each of these sources.
2 'It is impossible to make historical judgements on recent events. The evidence is contradictory and the sources untrustworthy'. Consider this statement in the light of sources A-E. How far do you agree?
3 In your judgement, why did the USSR invade Afghanistan?

The invasion caused an immediate national outcry, and the USA boycotted the 1980 Moscow Olympics, as well as cancelling delivery of much needed grain. Neither did the invasion succeed in putting down the rebels.

A *Sunday Times* report of September 1985 reveals the problems faced by Soviet troops:

Russian troops, spearheaded by crack Spetsnaz special forces, are battering guerrilla strongholds close to the Pakistan border in an attempt to break the siege of an Afghan army base. The battle is shaping up to be one of the biggest of the war. The Russians are using Spetsnaz units, the Russian equivalent of the SAS, and helicopter commandoes. At first the guerrillas fell back after bombing by jets, assaults by helicopter gunships, and use of ground-to-ground missiles and tanks. But the guerillas have now fought back and both sides have taken heavy casualties.

Failure to subdue rebel forces, desertions from the Afghan army to the rebels, and continued international pressure have prompted comparisons with the plight of the USA in Vietnam. Early in 1986 the new Soviet leader, Mikhail Gorbachev, made statements which were seen as a sign the the Soviet Union was ready for talks to resolve the crisis. Time will tell.

The United Nations

23 The UN: principles and realities

The League of Nations

When President Wilson proposed a League of Nations he had hoped to create an organisation which could maintain peace and resolve disputes by discussion. But it had some notable failings of the League in the next two decades, among them Japanese invasion of Manchuria (see page 294), the Italian invasion of Abyssinia, and the Second World War.

The League of Nations was an experiment in international co-operation which failed for a number of important reasons:

1 It was associated with the victors of the first World War. In many ways the League seemed like a club for the victorious allies. The four permanent seats on the council were held in Britain, France, Italy and Japan. German democratic governments were willing to try and win a place in this 'club' by co-operation. On the other hand, Hitler saw the League as an extension of the Treaty of Versailles, and loathed it.

2 The list of permanent members had startling omissions. The League was President Wilson's idea, but the US congress failed to support him, and the USA was never a member. The USSR did not join until 1934. Other states such as Germany and Japan left the League when it suited them.

3 Nationalism came before internationalism. Not surprisingly, in any crisis each nation put its own interest first. The four permanent members can be taken as examples. Japan and Italy have already been mentioned for their invasions of Manchuria and Abyssinia. Britain and France did not offend in this way, but were unwilling to take a stand against offenders unless directly affected. For example, Britain did not favour strong measures against Italy until the invasion threatened British interests in Sudan and Egypt.

4 The League had no teeth. There was no provision for an army, and no agreement on how such a force could be used if it existed.

Churchill, Roosevelt and Stalin at the Yalta Conference, 1945

The charter and organisation of the United Nations

The wartime conferences between the Allied leaders looked to the future, and the meeting at Yalta in February 1945 saw agreement on the charter of a United Nations Organisation to replace the League. The charter said,

We, the peoples of the United Nations, are determined to save succeeding generations from the scourge of war, which twice in our lifetime has brought untold sorrow to mankind, and to reaffirm faith in fundamental human rights, in the dignity and worth of the human person, in the equal rights of men and women and of nations large and small, and to establish respect for treaties and international law, and to promote social progress and better standards of life in larger freedom.

In order to achieve peace the United Nations agreed to take effective action for the prevention and removal of threats to peace; to suppress acts of aggression, and to settle international disputes by international law. These were great ambitions, and required an organisation that avoided the failings of the League.

On 24 October 1945 the United Nations came into existence with the following organisations:

1 The General Assembly: a place where representatives of all member nations can discuss important issues and pass resolutions. Each member nation has a vote. Normally a simple majority is sufficient to pass a resolution, but in some circumstances such as emergency debates a two-thirds majority is required. The assembly is principally a place for airing views, and is unable to force a country to comply with its resolutions.

2 The Security Council: made up of five permanent members: USA, USSR, UK, France, and nationalist China to 1971, communist China since 1971. There are also ten non-permanent members. The council meets continuously and has the job of preventing and resolving international crises. 'Preventing' includes the responsibility for disarmament.

   The council's teeth lies with the military staff committee, which can raise an armed force to intervene in a conflict.

3 The general assembly elects the secretary-general of the United Nations. The secretary-general and his staff at the UN headquarters in New York form the secretariat, they are international politicians and civil servants. Their chief role is to act as the peacemakers, and to ensure the efficient running of all the UN organisations.

4 The International Court of Justice: This court meets to resolve disputes between nations. Its rulings can only be enforced voluntarily.

5 The Economic and Social Council: This council is responsible for such things as culture, education and health. It supervises specialised agencies such as Food and Agriculture Organisation and the United Nations Educational, Social and Cultural Organisation.

The failings of the United Nations

The first 40 years of UN activity have seen some successes, but the general picture is one of a struggle against overwhelming difficulties. Perhaps the greatest of them is that the UN has reflected, and not resolved, the East-West conflict. For example, in order to take effective action there must be unanimous agreement in the security council. If any of the five members uses its veto, no action can be taken. In fact the veto has been used a great deal, and while that ensures that the UN can never become the puppet of East or West, it also means that the UN will do little more than debate issues.

One exception to this was in 1950, when UN intervention in Korea was without doubt pro-West and anti-communist (see page 328). At that time China was represented by the US-backed nationalist Chinese (Taiwan) and the USSR was boycotting the UN in protest at its failure to recognise communist China.

This was a rare occasion. In normal circumstances a veto would be used, and all the UN can then do is vote for an emergency debate and send observers from the UN Observation Commission. This happened when the USSR vetoed any action in Hungary in 1956 (see page 197), and when Britain and France vetoed any action in Suez (see page 276).

However, there have been occasions when UN troops have been sent to resolve conflicts, often where permanent members have no direct interest or do not wish to be directly involved. Examples are Kashmir (see page 323) and the Middle East. UN involvement in the Middle East has met with little success. The force stationed in Egypt after the war of 1956 was removed at Nasser's request just before the renewal of war.

A UN soldier at Suez

UNIFIL, the force stationed in Lebanon, was seen by the Palestinians as pro-Israeli, and was the target of PLO action.

Successful intervention by the UN seems to depend on the goodwill of the parties engaged in the conflict. More often than not, problems such as borders, race and religion are far greater than the abilities of the UN to solve them. Trouble spots like the Middle East continue to defy solution.

Questions

1 Draw a block diagram to show the organisation of the United Nations.
2 What failings of the League of Nations were recognised and improved upon in the Charter and organisation of the United Nations?
3 Why, even so, has the UN often failed to resolve conflict?

The UN and South Africa

One of the purposes of the UN is to defend human rights. In December 1948 the general assembly of the United Nations passed a resolution that

recognition of the inherent dignity and of the equal and inalienable rights of all members of the human family is the foundation of freedom, justice and peace in the world. . . .

All human beings are born free and equal in dignity and rights . . . without distinction of race, colour, sex, language religion, political or other opinion, national or social origin, property, birth or other status.

Many countries including the USSR, Chile and Brazil have offended this principle, but possibly the most notorious has been South Africa with its apartheid system.

When South Africa became a dominion in 1919, the prime minister, Jan Smuts, favoured racial toleration. However, his successor, James Hertzog, allowed the whites to obtain many privileges. In 1937, a particularly powerful group of whites, the Broederbond, went a step further by creating the policy of separate development. This was to become the official policy of South Africa.

Total segregation should not only be the ideal, but the immediate practical policy of the state. The purchase and separation of suitable and adequate areas for habitation by natives' families should take place at any cost.

Here the native can fulfil himself and develop in the political, economic, cultural, religious, educational, and other spheres.

A native will be allowed to go temporarily to white areas to work but he will not be allowed to take his family.

Natives should be encouraged to move to these native areas. Those who cannot do so must be housed in separate locations where they will enjoy political rights and own property.

After the Second World War a series of acts put this policy of apartheid into practice.

1950	Group Areas Act – put different races in different areas.
1950	Immorality Amendment Act – no sex between races.
1952	Passbook Act – all blacks to carry identification.
1953	Reservation of Separate Amenities Act – transport, restaurants, parks etc. to be reserved for one race.
1954	Resettlement of Natives Act – compulsorily moved 100 000 blacks.

The outcome of these Acts – the total separation of races – was justified by Prime Minister Verwoerd in 1963 when he said 'It is only by creating separate nations that discrimination will in fact disappear in the long run'.

Discrimination against blacks takes place at all levels. In its simplest form, blacks are humiliated in their daily contact with whites, being called 'boy' or 'kaffir', and not considered as individual human beings. Schools are segregated. In transport there are four classes of carriage. For many years there were only there, for whites (first) coloureds

Crossroads squatter camp near Cape Town. Terrible squalor on the doorstep of great wealth

Friendly?

1955 protest – the Congress of People for the Freedom Charter

(second) and blacks (third). Since recent reforms there has been added a mixed class for those who do not wish to use segregated carriages.

Discrimination also hits workers through their wage packets. With the exception of policemen, blacks do not receive the same wages for the same job as whites. With 25 per cent unemployment amongst blacks in 1985, they have to take what work they can get. Wages, educational provision, and mortality rates can be compared on the following table:

	African	Coloured	Asian	White
Population in 1966 (million)	12.47	1.8	0.5	3.48
Annual income per head (rand)	87	109	147	952
Average salary: mining	152	458	458	2562
manufacturing	422	660	660	2058
Infant mortality under 1 year per 1000 live births	no figures	136.1	56.1	29.2
Incidence of kwashiorkor per 100 000	980	410	40	negligible
Unit cost of education (rand)	12.11	62.14	62.14	146.65

Kwashiorkor – an illness resulting from protein deficiency, the cause of many deaths in third world countries, especially amongst children.

Welcome Valley – foreground, blacks; background, whites

Figures compiled by UNESCO

At the extreme, apartheid means total separation of black and white into different areas of South Africa. Blacks are allowed to travel to work in white areas, but cannot take their families and have no political rights there. When their work is terminated they have to return to their own 'homeland'.

One such black township which feeds white areas with labour is the city of Soweto. Here are two views of Soweto:

The population is officially 600 000, but is probably closer to one million owing to the number of illegal residents. Soweto, which was originally an arid area in the veldt, is now becoming much more attractive with tarmac roads and street lighting. The township itself contains 140 schools, 167 churches, 5 swimming pools, 102 sports grounds, 39 childrens' playgrounds and 42 tennis courts.

Patrick Wall MP,
Chairman of the Anglo–South African Parliamentary Group

Theoretically, Soweto, a vast dormitory town for Johannesburg black workers, housed 600 000 people in its 100 000 'housing units'. In fact the real number of inhabitants was probably about 1.5 million, with hundreds of thousands of desperate job-seekers crowding anything from six to twenty-five into its little three- or four-bedroom boxes of houses. Some 86 per cent of the houses have no electricity, 97 per cent have no running water. There is one hospital for what is one of the largest cities in Africa. Over half the population is under twenty and the majority of children suffer from malnutrition. The township was continuously racked by a hideous crime rate.

R. W. Johnson, *How Long Will South Africa Survive?* 1982

Protest within South Africa has grown steadily, and has been marked by increasing violence. One notorious incident was the result of protest against the pass laws of 1952. Pass books had to be carried at all times.

It contains such personal details as his identity card with photographs and fingerprints, name, group and tribe. It contains employment details and *Soweto*

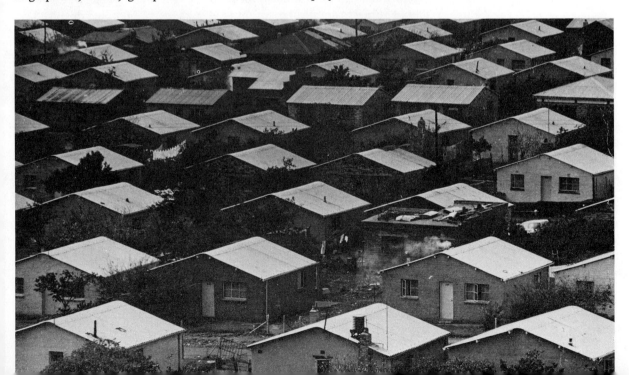

evidence of payment of taxes; and finally it contains influx endorsements by an official of the government concerning his *right to remain* in an urban area, the *time* he may be there, or the *reason* for which he may remain there.

South African Foundation

Demonstrations against these pass laws ended in the 'Sharpeville massacre'. Here an historian has attempted to piece together what happened:

Eye-witness accounts of the 'Sharpeville massacre' vary considerably in their assessment of the mood of the crowd that surrounded the police station on 21 March. Witnesses sympathetic towards the demonstrators testified that the crowd was unarmed, amiable, well-mannered and unaggressive. They estimated that the size of the crowd at the time the shooting occurred was between 3000 and 10 000. Police witnesses testified that the number of people was much larger (official reports placed it at 20 000) that many were armed with sticks and other weapons, and that the crowd's mood was hostile, aggressive and volatile.

Tear gas had failed to halt the demonstrators marching through the town earlier in the day. The size of the crowd, the insults and threats shouted, combined with the anxiety of white men surrounded and outnumbered by people whom they regarded as the 'enemy', brought police nerves after several hours to snapping point. No order was given to shoot, and no warning shots were fired. In a moment of panic, a line of white policemen opened fire on the crowd and continued to fire (from ten to thirty seconds) as the demonstrators fled. Sixty-seven Africans were shot dead, the great majority hit in the back as they ran. One hundred and eighty-six others were wounded including 40 women and 8 children. White press reporters on the scene recorded the carnage in a series of grisly photos that were to appear all over the world in the days that followed.

Karis, Carter and Gerhart, Documents of African Politics 1882–1964

In 1976 another notorious incident took place. As one part of a programme of educational reform, the government ruled that certain school subjects should be taught in Afrikaans, a language despised by the black communities. Black students and schoolchildren protested. World newsreels showed savage attacks by the police on young people. One black leader, Steve Biko, died mysteriously while in police custody. A boycott of classes by students at Elsie's River produced this incident:

A police van suddenly stopped and policemen, both uniformed and in camouflage gear, jumped out and baton-charged the people on the pavements. One youth was caught, brought to the ground, and beaten by at least four policemen with batons. A group again gathered at 2.30 p. m. According to Mrs Enid November, who lives opposite, a blue kombi drove past and was stoned by the group. A man lying in the back of the kombi passed a shotgun to the driver, who opened fire on the crowd. The men in the kombi were not wearing full camouflage gear, but the kombi is registered with the South African police.

D. Pinnock, The Brotherhoods, 1984

In 1985 there were further protests and considerable loss of life. One particular focus of protest has been the continued imprisonment of

Nelson Mandela, leader of the African National Congress. The South African government refuses to release him while he continues to advocate violence as a form of protest. While he is in prison his followers continue to use violence, including, on 22 December 1985, bombing of white shopping areas in Durban.

At the same time the black community has organised peaceful protest in the form of a boycott of white shops, with a telling effect on the economy. However, the death toll remains high and restrictions on foreign reporters introduced in 1985 suggest that conflict will continue.

Nelson Mandela

United Nations action on South Africa

Since 1945 South African policy has been the subject of many debates in the United Nations. Firstly, the UN has sought to put pressure on South Africa to abandon apartheid. Secondly the UN has tried to remove South African control of South West Africa, or Nambia.

The campaign against apartheid began in 1946 when Dr Xuima, president of the African National Congress, took the South African case to the United Nations. Since that time, the attack, usually led by the representatives of other African or Asian countries, has continued. As well as debates there have been other methods of protest – for example, a walk-out when the South African representative has risen to speak.

Border encounter, South West Africa/Angola. Nambian troops under attack from SWAPO

The United Nations has formally condemned apartheid on a number of occasions. In 1960 the Security Council passed a resolution which state that 'South Africa's policies led to international friction, and if continued, might endanger international peace and security.' A resolution of 1972, and another of 1973, which agreed with the international convention on the suppression and punishment of the crime of apartheid, reinforced the UN position. Other resolutions have been passed condemning specific aspects of apartheid, such as the establishment of the Bantu homelands in 1976.

Action of various types has been taken in attempt to enforce these resolutions. In 1960 a resolution requested

All states to consider taking such separate and collective action as is open to them in accordance with the Charter of the United Nations to bring about the abandonment of apartheid policies.

Two years later the pressure was stepped up with a resolution requesting members to close ports and airports to South African ships and aircraft. Further motions against arms sales to South Africa were passed in 1967 and 1977.

Attempts to tighten sanctions further, and even to expel South Africa from the United Nations, have failed. One such motion was the programme of action against apartheid of 1976, which would have imposed a mandatory oil and arms boycott, ended nuclear co-operation, and stopped any loans to South Africa. The failure of this resolution underlined the ineffectiveness of UN action. The following documents reveal some of the reasons for that failure.

1 South Africa on the attack

In recent years a development has taken place at the United Nations which was not foreseen – the addition of a large number of new states, particularly in Africa but also in Asia. They created a block of countries which were completely inexperienced. Both the western bloc and the communist bloc seek the support of the Afro-Asian bloc. South Africa is landed in a position where both sides attack her because in this way the friendship of the Afro-Asian states can be sought.

Prime Minister Verwoerd, House of Assembly debate, 1961

It may be regrettable that the United Nations no longer embodies the hopes of mankind. Everyone must face the fact that since young, duck-tailed nations practically took charge, the UN commands little respect. It is a platform for their display of juvenile aggressiveness and their inferiority complexes.

Prime Minister Verwoerd

Under the rule of President Amin (1970–79), Uganda suffered terrible atrocities, and constant infringements of human rights.

Gulag Archipelago is one of the notorious labour camps in the Soviet Union.

The motion to expel South Africa from the UN was proposed by Uganda's foreign minister, representing a country which has become synonymous with oppression and indiscriminate execution of dissidents. When the motion went to the Security Council it was supported by ten votes. Nearly all of them are themselves guilty of violating the principles of the UN declaration. Russia and China, operators of their own vast Gulag Archipelago, voted to expel South Africa.

Eric Sevareid, CBS newscaster, USA

In the general assembly in 1962 the Soviet foreign minister drew applause when he described South Africa as 'the private domain of the slave owner'. Mr Gromyko, speaking from a home base littered with prisons and labour camps with an enslaved population exceeding eleven million at one time....

L. De Villiers, *South Africa. A Skunk among Nations*, 1975

The action continues

The most oppressed negro in South Africa has more to eat than millions of Africans in 'liberated countries'. The most rabid white extremist will not treat negroes in the way negroes treated whites in the Congo, Uganda, and other African states.

Yosef Lapide, Israeli reporter

Israel's support for South Africa has resulted in its loss of economic and diplomatic relations with most African countries.

The British journalist Adam Raphael of the *Guardian* and his friends tackled the dust on the furniture in South Africa while ignoring the grime on the floor elsewhere where Britain has business interests. On sugar plantations South African black workers were earning five times the wages paid to tea leaf pickers in Sri Lanka.

L. De Villiers, *South Africa. A Skunk among Nations*

Raphael was identified as an opponent of the regime in South Africa because of his scathing articles in the liberal newspaper, the *Guardian*.

It is perplexing to ponder the almost total lack of criticism in the world press on atrocities in Burundi, Nigeria, and the Central African Republic. Apparently it is simply that black racists are less offensive to liberals that white racists are.

Dennis Duggan, *Newsday* magazine

2 South Africa's importance to the Western powers

Attention will be drawn particularly to South Africa's undoubted mineral wealth which the West cannot afford to lose. There will be mention of the likelihood of a world uranium shortage and that South Africa has large supplies. The importance of the Cape Sea route will be stressed. For these and other reasons the West will be urged to take a stronger protective role.

R. W. Johnson, *How Long Will South Africa Survive?*, 1982

Possibly these reasons explain why Britain and France have consistently voted against sanctions. They were joined by the USA in voting against the proposals of 1976.

3 UN resolutions ignored by member states

UN member countries were under orders not to supply arms of any kind to South Africa. Neverthless, through roundabout routes revolvers, automatics, rifles and shotguns continued to filter through. Ironically, iron curtain countries had a big finger in that pie. In 1976 the Russians and Czechs were active in selling firearms to South Africans. Among other countries were France, Italy, Spain and Brazil.

B. Hitchcock, *Flashpoint South Africa*, 1977

4 UN action defied by South Africa

Possibly the best example of this defiance is the case of South West Africa, or Namibia. Namibia had been a German territory, and was mandated to South Africa in 1919. The mandate allowed South Africa to rule Namibia as its own territory, but to keep it as a separate state and to be answerable to the League of Nations for its good rule there.

By 1945 South Africa had already adopted policies towards Namibia which were disliked by the new United Nations. The UN demanded that the mandate be given up, but South Africa refused. The South African government argued that the end of the League marked the end of the mandate, and that Namibia had now become a South African possession.

From 1960 to 1966 the case of Namibia went before the International Court of Justice. In the meantime South Africa even refused to allow UN officials into Namibia as observers. The international court was slow and indecisive in its judgement, at first finding for South Africa on a technicality, then finding that South Africa's occupation of Namibia was illegal. In 1967, backed by the court, the UN established a council for Namibia. South Africa ignored the council and took steps to integrate Namibia fully into South Africa. In 1973 the general assembly recognised the South West Africa Peoples' Organisation (SWAPO) as the true representatives of Namibia. In 1978 this was strengthened by UN approval of a programme for Namibian independence. SWAPO, a communist-backed organisation, continues to fight for Namibia, using sympathetic neighbours as a base. Neither UN disapproval nor SWAPO action has had any marked effect on the policies and attitudes of South Africa.

The struggle over South Africa continues. It could be argued that the world of sport, where boycotts have been more effectively imposed, has stolen more headlines that the international politicians. 1985 was a year of crisis for south Africa, with increasing violence and poor economic performance. In April 1986 President P. W. Botha announced reform of the pass laws but violence and protest continued. If further reforms do come, the United Nations may applaud, but will deserve little of the credit.

Questions

1 How does South Africa offend the UN resolution of 1948?
2 Why do you think that non-white groups in South Africa have had so little success in reforming apartheid from within? What developments are taking place within South Africa today?
3 Chart attempts by the UN to reform South Africa from the outside.
4 What charges have South Africans made against other states? How far does this help their case?
5 Why have Western countries ignored UN resolutions?
6 Explain the failure of the UN to repossess Namibia.

Index

Acknowledgements

The author and publishers wish to acknowledge, with thanks, the following photographic sources:

Anglo-Chinese Educational Institute pp. 292, 293, 305, 307, 309 right;

Associated Newspaper Group pp. 43 top, 188;

Associated Press p. 155;

Barnaby's Picture Library pp. 60, 72 centre, 116 bottom, 235, 269, 308;

BBC Hulton Picture Library pp. 18 top, 31 bottom left, 31 bottom right, 32;

Bridgeman Art Library, Museum of Modern Art, New York p. 61;

Camera Press pp. 2, 21 bottom, 24 (photographs Imperial War Museum), 108, 343 top, 245, 248, 351 centre, 351 bottom, 352, 353, 355 top, 355 bottom, 357;

Detroit News p. 164;

Imperial War Museum pp. 2, 9, 12 bottom, 13 top, 13 bottom, 14, 15, 16, 18 bottom, 19 right, 21 top, 30 top, 30 bottom, 31 top, 101 top left, 104 bottom, 150, 153, cover;

International Aid and Defence Fund p. 351 top;

Peter Newark Western Americana pp. 158, 159 bottom, 162 top, 162 centre, 162 bottom, 165 left, 166, 168 top right, 168 bottom, 173, 177, 181 top left, 209, 215 bottom, 219 right, 334 right;

Novosti pp. 19 left, 116 top, 118 centre, 118 bottom, 122, 135 bottom, 144, 146 top, 146 bottom, 147 top, 195, 201 bottom;

Photo Source pp. 47 top; 47 bottom, 49, 55, 67, 68, 74, 89 top, 91 top, 117, 121, 125 top, 186, 236 bottom, 242, 243 bottom, 244 left, 253 bottom, 260, 261 top, 262, 271, 272 top, 272 bottom, 275, 276, 278, 280, 284, 294, 295, 296, 297, 299 bottom, 301, 309 left, 315 bottom, 324, 325, 327, 343 bottom;

Popperfoto pp. 2, 26 bottom, 41, 51 top, 53, 59 top, 59 bottom left, 64, 70, 71, 72 top right, 83, 93, 94, 95, 97, 99 top, 99 bottom, 100 top, 103 top, 103 bottom, 104 top, 124, 129, 131, 132, 136, 145, 157, 159 top, 161 left, 161 right, 178 left, 190, 192, 197, 198, 201 top, 208, 212, 219 left, 223, 231, 232, 233, 236 top, 239, 241 top, 241 bottom, 245, 246, 247, 255 left, 255 right, 261 bottom, 265 bottom, 266 bottom, 268, 282, 287 top, 287 bottom, 288, 289 bottom, 299 top left, 299 top right, 311, 313, 318, 321, 322 bottom right, 326, 327, 330 top, 331, 336, 337, 340;

Press Association p. 77;

Punch pp. 11, 12 top, 37, 39, 43 bottom, 88, 91 bottom, 189, 196, 315 top;

Standard Newspapers pp. 81, 89 bottom;

Suddeutscher Verlag pp. 63 bottom, 72 top left, 73, 204, 205;

Topham Picture Library pp. 2, 26 top left, 26 top right, 44, 45 top, 45 bottom, 48, 51 bottom, 56, 58, 59 bottom right, 63 top, 82, 85, 92, 96 left, 96 right, 100 bottom, 101 top right, 101 bottom, 105, 106, 111, 113, 114, 118 top, 119 top, 119 bottom, 125 bottom, 133 top, 137, 143, 147 bottom, 165 right, 168 top left, 169, 174, 175, 176, 178 right, 181 top right, 181 bottom, 183, 203 left, 203 right, 210, 211, 215 top, 220, 222, 225, 230, 243 top, 244 right, 246, 253 top, 256, 263, 264, 265 top, 266 top, 277, 279, 289 top, 303, 310, 314, 322 top, 322 bottom left, 323, 329, 330 bottom, 334 left, 338, cover photo.

The publishers have made every effort to trace the copyright holders, but if they have inadvertently overlooked any, they will be pleased to make the necessary arrangements at the first opportunity.

The author and publishers wish to thank the following who have kindly given permission for the use of copyright material:

The Free Press, a Division of Macmillan Inc., for extracts from *China in Disintegration* 1912–1949 by J. E. Sheridan, 1975;

The *Guardian* for extracts from the 17.9.78 and 31.5.85 editions;

Monthly Review Foundation for an extract from *The Peoples Republic of China* by Mark Selden. Copyright © 1979, Mark Selden;

Oxford University Press for extracts from *Germany 1866–1945* by G. Craig, 1978;

A. D. Peters on behalf of J. Noakes and G. Pridham for extracts from *Documents on Nazism*, Jonathan Cape Ltd, 1974;

Norstedts Forlag AB for an extract from *Report From a Chinese Village* by J. Myrdal;

St. Louis Post-Dispatch for an extract from the 3.9.40 edition;

Martin Secker and Warburg Ltd for extracts from *The Reichstag Fire* by F. Tobias;

Steimatzky Ltd for extracts from *The Revolt* by Menachem Begin;

Times Newspapers Ltd for extracts from the 1.9.39, 2.9.39, 5.9.39 and 14.10.81 editions of *The Times*.